ACCLAIM FOR *You Fascinate Me So*

"*You Fascinate Me So* is an insightful and informative biography of Cy Coleman's life and career. I was a close friend of Cy Coleman's for many years and worked with him on the Broadway musical *Seesaw*. Andy Propst's honest reporting is extraordinary. He has captured the essence of the Broadway musical and the composer, Cy Coleman, who defined it! I highly recommend this book."

— LAINIE KAZAN, actress

"Composer Cy Coleman was as fascinating as the dazzling string of hit songs and Broadway shows he created. Andy Propst's compelling biography captures both this multifaceted man and the creative journey he took—from eight-year-old child prodigy performing at Carnegie Hall to a night-clubbing jazz pianist to one of Broadway's greatest."

—DAVID ZIPPEL, Tony-Award-winning lyricist

"The chapter on *City of Angels* made me smile from ear to ear! Thank you, Andy, for letting me in on all the stuff I didn't know and for writing this long overdue book about our Cy with such love."

—RANDY GRAFF, Tony Award–winning actress

"Cy Coleman, genius composer, friend, and human, deserves this thoughtful and caring homage. Thanks to Andy Propst for sharing things about Cy I didn't know, always wondered about, or relish remembering!"

—DEE HOTY, actress

"I never met a musician who didn't love playing a Cy Coleman tune. Those of us who were fortunate enough to know him and play with him will never forget his chops, humor, sassiness, hipness, and the love he had for his fellow musicians. As far as deep cats go, Cy was one of the deepest. For those of you who never knew him, Andy's book is damn close to feeling like you're playing 'Witchcraft' with Cy himself."

—JOHN MILLER, bass player/musical coordinator

YOU FASCINATE ME SO

YOU
FASCINATE
ME SO

The Life and Times of
CY COLEMAN

Andy Propst

With a foreword by Shelby Coleman

AN IMPRINT OF HAL LEONARD CORPORATION

Published in 2015 by Applause Theatre & Cinema Books
An Imprint of Hal Leonard Corporation
7777 West Bluemound Road
Milwaukee, WI 53213

Trade Book Division Editorial Offices
33 Plymouth St., Montclair, NJ 07042

Printed in the United States of America

Book design by Michael Kellner

Library of Congress Cataloging-in-Publication Data

Propst, Andy.
You fascinate me so : the life and times of Cy Coleman / Andy Propst ; with a foreword by Shelby Coleman.
    pages cm
 Includes bibliographical references and index.
 ISBN 978-1-4803-5590-3 (hardcover)
1. Coleman, Cy. 2. Jazz musicians–United States–Biography. 3. Composers-
-United States–Biography. 4. Pianists–United States–Biography. I. Title.
 ML410.C739P76 2015
 780.92–dc23
 [B]
                          2014046378

www.applausebooks.com

For Daddy, Mother, and John . . . and Susan, who started it all . . .

CONTENTS

FOREWORD

I am delighted that Andy Propst has written this account of Cy Coleman's life. And he has done it just in time. He was able to interview Cy's contemporaries, collaborators, family members, friends, and me—his wife. Cy Coleman was the love of my life. So I am not the one to write an unbiased biography. Andy is. Out of the mountains of scrapbooks, demo tapes, interviews of Cy throughout his career, photos, playbills, and news clippings, Andy has created an entertaining and cohesive biographical work.

Everybody knows Cy Coleman's music, but now, thanks to Andy, readers can get to know the man. Cy had a shelf full of Tonys and Grammys and received just about every accolade an artist can receive, but he never became a household name. Why? His theory was that he wasn't easily categorized and that critics couldn't figure out who he was. That's because he wanted to experiment in every genre, including classical, jazz, pop, and musical theater. He said, "I want to use all the colors in my palette."

Cy's life was never boring. As his wife, I had a front-row seat to that life, and I want to mention a few things that aren't in the book.

Cy was the King of New York. Presidents and movie stars, as well as waiters, ushers, and the mounted cop who policed Broadway, called him Cy. His easy smile for everyone was real.

He had a razor-sharp wit and was never at a loss for a quick retort. Once, while practicing scales in his rented apartment on Fifty-seventh and Third, an upstairs neighbor called and said, "If you don't stop that piano playing instantly, I am going to jump out the window!" Cy replied, "My, you are a good sport."

People would ask him, "How do you write a song? Inspired by nature or emotion?" He would say, "No, it's not like the cliché of a composer sitting in front of the piano, pencil in hand, plinking out notes." He'd point to his temple and tap it as he said, "It's all right here, Opus 1, 2, 3. It's already in my head." Cy was great at avoiding the "secretarial work" of putting the notes on paper. Pruning his trees at the beach house or helping me rearrange bookshelves was a good enough excuse.

He told me he had at least three hundred songs in his head that he hadn't written down yet, just waiting for the right place. "A few of them are pretty good," he said.

When working on a show or preparing to play in public, he became completely absorbed in the task and wasn't easy to live with. The people around him became invisible; his temper and his patience ran short. He always felt bad about it and made amends—*after* the show.

Cy worked and played hard. Sports cars, gambling, and playing jazz late into the night eventually gave way to beach vacations, travel, and reading big books by the pool. He could relax and forget about work better than anyone I ever knew.

I don't believe there was any separation between Cy's everyday life and music. Upon landing in Paris, Cy told me to be very quiet and listen to the beat of the city. "It's very different than New York. Do you feel it?" He heard music and rhythms everywhere. No one could get the drop on Cy. He swore that he could hear the criminal intent in someone's footsteps. Very useful in New York City.

Cy's workday started in bed; he never scheduled anything before noon if he could help it. He read all three daily papers, in bed with his coffee and me, and later our baby, Lily Cye. From there he worked the phones, lingering as long as possible. His call list was long, and he made sure to touch on at least three projects every day. "You have to keep a lot of balls in the air; you never know what is going to pop first," he said. I learned everything I know about show business from listening to his morning calls.

Among other things I learned:

Never say "never," especially in show business. You are bound to work with the same people again, like it or not.

Always call the losers after an awards show. No one else does.

Return every phone call right away, no matter how much you don't want to.

People always like their own ideas best.

Don't worry so much about what people think about you, because so few people do.

Cy knew exactly what he wanted to do from the age of four. He honed his craft with laserlike ferocity and created a life built on one thing: music. Cy told me shortly before his sudden death that he couldn't have married any earlier than he did: "Wouldn't have been fair to the woman. Music was my mistress." I am glad that he felt he had finally achieved enough in music to settle down and enjoy a family life. He brought the same engaged, focused, and brilliant mind to being a husband and father.

Having a baby really tickled Cy. He welcomed her in the office and the theater and showed her off at every opportunity. The last day of Cy's life found him sitting in a miniature chair, built for kindergartners, boasting lovingly about his four-year-old daughter to her teachers.

I was lucky enough to know Cy pretty well. Now Andy Propst has written a book that will give you a window into the world of a great and good man.

—Shelby Coleman

PREFACE

"Why Cy Coleman?" It's a question that I've been asked hundreds of times while I have worked on this book.

My answer always began with something like "Well, the first musical I ever saw was *Sweet Charity*. . . ." And it's the truth. When I was just in third grade—making me nine, I guess—I was taken to see a production of the first show Cy wrote with Dorothy Fields.

The tale of the dance-hall hostess with a heart of gold may not have been exactly kiddie fare, but it captured my imagination, and my ears. I still have the program that Colleen Dodson (who played Charity and went on to appear in shows like *Nine* on Broadway) and her castmates signed and plastered with big red lipstick kisses. It even became my show-and-tell that week, which, unsurprisingly, resulted in some pretty brutal kidding from my classmates.

Soon the original cast recording was getting repeated plays on the small portable turntable in my bedroom, and I was dancing—a bit maniacally and not at all Bob Fosse–like—to "Rich Man's Frug" and singing along with songs like "Baby, Dream Your Dream" and "There's Got to Be Something Better Than This."

That's the basic answer to "Why?"

I've come to realize, however, that the impetus behind the book stems from something much deeper. The reason I, as a young person, gravitated toward *Charity*, and later Cy's other shows, like *I Love My Wife*, *On the Twentieth Century*, and *Barnum*, was that they managed to be theatrical while also sounding like "real music"—you know, the things I heard on the radio or songs my folks liked.

My dad might have been trying to instill in me a love of Gilbert and Sullivan and Scott Joplin (this was, after all, the era of *The Sting*), but I was turning to these shows because Cy's operetta for *Century* and his rags for *Barnum* didn't feel like antiques. They had (and have) a modern vibrancy to them. With *I Love My Wife*, I heard contemporary-sounding music, but it also told a story.

This sense of the "why" behind the "Why?" only dawned on me while I was immersed in Cy's music and his life while working on this book. In the 1970s, however, I only knew I responded on a gut level to what I was hearing.

Beyond having always liked Cy's work, there was another reason for my wanting to delve deeper into his life. I was curious about the man whose career could have so many distinct facets.

Cy didn't just write Broadway musicals. He started off in the classical arena before moving to jazz, and before he was twenty-one he was appearing daily in the then-emergent medium of television, even while he was doing radio programs and nightclub appearances. Furthermore, at two points in his life (first in the mid-1960s and later in the 1980s), he scored big-budget Hollywood pictures.

This remarkable elasticity has allowed me to journey into nearly fifty years of theater history while also taking excursions into America's pop-cultural history from mid–last century forward.

It's been a genuine privilege to travel alongside Cy down so many different paths, but there've been hurdles. It probably will come as no surprise that memories of events from seventy or eighty years ago have blurred over time, and so there will be moments when this book may become rather a collagelike representation of actual events. Whenever necessary I will point out contradictions in the historical record or the accounts I've gotten from the people who knew Cy.

Almost a constant in the interview process were people's descriptions of the music that seemed to emanate from him. Terri White, who was in two of his shows, imagined him sleeping: "All you'd see is floating notes everywhere." Lyricist Marilyn Bergman also remembered his flair at the piano: "There was a showman thing about Cy which also made him such a man of the theater, because he understood showmanship and . . . he wasn't hunched over the piano playing discreetly. He was out there." And during conductor Fred Barton's time on *City of Angels*, he asked Cy about his work and what compelled it. Cy said simply, "Fred, I like to entertain." As Barton put it, "In those five words, he summed up Cy Coleman."

It's the predominance of these qualities, as well as Coleman's own guarded approach to his personal life, that have informed the book. Personal anecdotes do appear, but as Shelby says, music was Cy's mistress until late in his life, and so this book primarily concentrates on his career as a composer and performer, with occasional excursions into his private life.

Ultimately, what I hope is that this book will bring Cy Coleman—in all his various incarnations—to life for not only fans like me but also for those who have never experienced his music or known that he was the man who penned the melodies for such songs as "Witchcraft," "The Best Is Yet to Come," and, oh, that number from *Sweet Charity*, the one with that instantly recognizable vamp: "Big Spender."

—Andy Propst

ACKNOWLEDGMENTS

There are so many people who have helped make this book happen, starting with Shelby Coleman, who had the faith in me from the outset to write this chronicle of her husband's life and work.

Furthermore, I must thank Ken Bloom, whose initial support and ongoing encouragement has been invaluable, as well as Damon Booth at Notable Music, who has been on hand to help with my requests for materials and backup from the company's files.

I also need to thank Erik Haagensen, whose keen eye and insight have helped shape what's contained in these pages; and Ted Kociolek, who not only opened his home to me for an interview but welcomed me back time and again to play through unrecorded pieces of music, giving me a deeper sense of Cy's creative process.

To the many friends, old and new, who have been on hand to lend materials, their counsel, and their patience, all of which combined to make this book possible, I also need to say a heartfelt thank you: Danny Abosch, Dan Bacalzo, Brian Belovarac, Chris Byrne, Aaron Cahn, Mark Charney, Michael Croiter, Helene Davis, Joe Dziemianowicz, Josh Ellis, Peter Filichia, Harry Forbes, Dan Fortune, Merle Frimark, James Gavin, Bob Gazzale, Scott Gorenstein, Karen Greco, Simon Greiff, Erik Hartog, Harry Haun, Paulette Haupt, David Hurst, John Issendorf, Judy Jacksina, Chris Johnson, Ken Kantor, Maryann Karinch, Darrel Karl, Penny Landau, Daniel Langan, Brian Scott Lipton, Joseph Marzullo, Alan Mehl, Keith Meritz, Ken Miller, Peter Monks, Bob and Carol Nagle, Charles Nelson, Richard C. Norton, Craig Palanker, Gail Parenteau, Joshua S.

Ritter, Caesar Rodriguez, Bill Rudman, Jim Russek, Frank Scheck, Bob Sixsmith, Stephen Soba, Doug Strassler, Richard Tay, Peter Tear, John Torres, Joseph Weiss, and Andrew Wilkinson, as well as a superlative cadre of friends from P.S. 41 on Staten Island.

Deep appreciation also goes to Cy's collaborators, colleagues, and friends who so generously gave of their time, sharing their memories of him (and sometimes even mementos): Sue Agrest, Ruth Allan, Russell Baker, Fred Barton, Alan and Marilyn Bergman, Pat Birch, Michael Blakemore, Tony Bongiovi, Mark Bramble, Mike Burstyn, Mary-Mitchell Campbell, Carleton Carpenter, Keith Carradine, Barbara Carroll, Emile Charlap, Charles Cochran, Eric Comstock, Chuck Cooper, Jerome Coopersmith, Nick Corley, Avery Corman, Bill Crow, John Cullum, Terrie Curran, Clifford David, Ed Dixon, Harvey Evans, Robert Fletcher, Larry Fuller, Ira Gasman, Yaron Gershovsky, Anita Gillette, Joanna Gleason, Judy Gordon, Ilene Graff, Randy Graff, Leonard Green, Jonathan Hadary, Sheldon Harnick, Valerie Harper, Gordon Lowry Harrell, Sam Harris, Jack Heifner, Jim Henaghan, Dee Hoty, Ken Howard, Houston Huddleston, Nancy Huddleston, Susan Israelson, Craig Jacobs, Bobby Kaufman, Judy Kaye, Lainie Kazan, Bruce Kimmel, Allan Knee, Jess Korman, David Lahm, Paul Lazarus, Michele Lee, Steve Leeds, Mundell Lowe, Ronald Mallory, Alan Marcus, Daniel Marcus, Sally Mayes, Charlie McPherson, Sylvia Miles, John Miller, Liza Minnelli, Jerry Mitchell, Ray Mosca, Lee Musiker, James Naughton, Bebe Neuwirth, Phyllis Newman, Julie Newmar, Christine Ohlman, Thelma Oliver, Michon Peacock, Ezio Petersen, Don Pippin, Hal Prince, Louise Quick, Teri Ralston, Lee Roy Reams, Chita Rivera, Jana Robbins, Bill Rosenfield, Annie Ross, Irv Roth, Susan Schultz, Barbara Sharma, Keith Sherman, June Silver, Eric Stern, Lynn Summerall, Marianne Tatum, Tommy Tune, Ken Urmston, Betsy von Furstenberg, Robin Wagner, Tony Walton, Fred Werner, Lillias White, Terri White, Mark York, David Zippel, and Alan Zweibel.

YOU FASCINATE ME SO

1

"Baby, Dream Your Dream"

t's hard to imagine that a tenement home in the Bronx where Yiddish was the primary language and the music being played was primarily religious or klezmer would prove to be the breeding ground for a career and body of work as broad as Cy Coleman's, but Coleman was born and raised in just such a place. He described it in later life as a "phony religious house. . . . My mother would go with us to a Chinese restaurant and place her order. I'd say, 'Mom[,] that's pork you're ordering. She'd say, 'It's chicken.'"[1]

Coleman came into the world as Seymour Kaufman on Flag Day, June 14, 1929, just a little over four months before the Wall Street crash that began the Great Depression. He was a "surprise" baby, the fifth child for Max and Ida Kaufman, arriving in the twentieth year of their marriage.

The couple's relationship had begun in their native Bessarabia, a region of Eastern Europe that had been ruled by Russia and was later part of Romania before becoming part of Moldavia and ultimately a part of the Republic of Moldova. Their families arranged the marriage even though Ida, according to family lore, had been in love with another man.

Ida's passion for this other person meant the foundations of her marriage were rocky at best. The union was strained further by the fact that she and Max made such an unlikely couple temperamentally. She was outspoken and fierce, while he was a meek, mild-mannered soul.

Also complicating their lives was a disparity in their upbringing. As Coleman's nephew Robert Kaufman recounted, "Max was a late-in-life baby, so late that his brothers had children older than him, and they had dispersed, two of them allegedly to England and one to New York. . . . Then, when Max was six, Great-Grandma and -Grandpa died. Nobody knows how or why. The neighbors gave him a trade, and he became a carpenter and a cabinetmaker, and when he was about twenty he got matched up with grandma, who came from 'the rich' family."[2]

Despite their differences, the two managed to forge a life together. In 1913, three years after they were wed, Max and Ida immigrated to the United States, the same year in which their first child, Adolph, was born. Three other children—Sam, Sylvia, and Yetta—followed over the course of the next twelve years.

Ida was unable even to sign her name, but her business acumen was sharp, and the family thrived. She ultimately came to own several tenements in the Bronx, including the one at 547 Claremont Avenue in which Seymour was raised.

Ida's business affairs meant that tending to Seymour fell to his older sister, Sylvia, who was thirteen when her baby brother was born. She didn't necessarily want to be in charge of looking after an infant, but it was an era in which one did not overtly disobey one's father or mother, particularly a woman as formidable as Ida.

Sylvia's oversight of her younger brother led to one of the first major pieces of lore about Coleman's youth. In the spring of 1932 Sylvia was out playing with her friends while her three-year-old brother sat on the stoop watching. She was unaware that just at that moment a massive manhunt was on for Charles Lindbergh's kidnapped son, a blond boy whom Seymour resembled because of his own fair curls. Furthermore, Sylvia had no idea that the police had been ordered to pick up any child who fit the description of the Lindbergh baby, so she was shocked when she turned away from her friends to check in on her baby brother, only to see him being bundled into a police wagon.

It peeled away and Sylvia sprinted after it, following all the way to the precinct house. The situation was sorted out in short order leaving behind an anecdote about a brush with history that would make the family laugh for years to come.

But it was overshadowed by the events of a year later, after the Lindbergh headlines had faded but papers continued to report on the extreme hardships the country was suffering in the Great Depression. Ida herself had been victim to the period's economic vagaries, seeing tenants come and go depending on their ability to pay rent and leaving her to figure out how to pay the taxes on the properties she owned. One family renting from Ida slipped out in the middle of the night, taking their belongings with them in a hasty departure.

But there was one item that they could not move during their getaway. It was just too bulky, and moving it might have given Ida some idea of what they were up to. And so, when she discovered that they had gone, Ida found an upright piano standing in the otherwise empty apartment. Pragmatic as always, Ida brought the instrument into the Kaufman home, figuring that at least she had gotten something from her former tenants.

The arrival of the piano was an addition, not the introduction, of music into the family's lives. Stories among the Kaufman children and grandchildren include reports of a radio, as well as a phonograph. In addition, Seymour's eldest brother, Adolph, had for a while studied violin, an instrument on which he had shown promise. His son Robert remembered: "According to Grandma, my father was an excellent violinist, and there came a point when some folks said they wanted to take my father to Vienna to learn violin. And all Grandma understood was, 'They are going to take the oldest away,' and her response was, 'Well, no, you're not.' So that sort of ended his career as far as that goes."[3]

One might think that Adolph would have gravitated toward the newly arrived piano, or maybe even Yetta, who was just about grade-school age. But it wasn't. Instead, it was the youngest Kaufman, little Seymour—only four years old—who took to it instantly, showing almost immediately signs of significant musical talent.

Seymour's playing initially consisted of plunking on the keys. But before long he was piecing together music that he had heard on the radio or ditties that his siblings would sing and then ask their little brother to replicate on the keyboard.

"I was obsessed with the piano," Coleman said in adulthood, adding,

"The piano was mine and my obsession. As a matter of fact, it got to a point that my father got so bugged about hearing the piano over and over again, he nailed it shut one day. It wasn't mean; he just couldn't take it. But I pried it open and the battle was won."[4]

This tale, often repeated by Coleman and by those who knew him well, became something of a mythic creation story, and like all legends, it was embellished through the years. Scenic designer Robin Wagner, who designed four of Coleman's shows, recalled that he had heard that Seymour had gone so far as not only to remove the nails that held the piano lid down, but also to dismantle the screws from its hinges, so that the lid could be removed entirely, ensuring unrestricted access to the instrument.

Seymour's playing eventually caught the attention of neighbors, notably the family's milkman, who promptly recognized the child's potential and arranged for his own son's piano teacher, Constance Tallarico, to visit the Kaufman home to hear the young man for herself.

A native New Yorker, Tallarico had established herself as a successful music instructor by the time she met four-year-old Seymour. For evidence of her skill one need look no farther than her own family. In 1928 her fourteen-year-old son Victor had been one of the gold-medal winners of the prestigious citywide New York Music Week competition. Victor would go on to study at Juilliard, enjoy a long career as a pianist, and raise a much-heralded musician himself: Victor's son is (after a name change) none other than Steven Tyler, of the rock band Aerosmith.

On the day she visited her prospective student, Tallarico was accompanied by her husband, conductor Giovanni Tallarico. After hearing Seymour play, both Tallaricos agreed with the deliveryman's assessment: Seymour was talented and would benefit from musical training and guidance.

The issue of payment arose instantly. Coleman described what happened when talking in 1990 with his old friend pianist Marian McPartland on her radio program *Piano Jazz*: "[The Tallaricos] spoke to my mother, who had no idea about music and couldn't care less about it. She was like, 'It's musical and nice, but it's certainly not a serious thing.'" But Ida, the consummate businesswoman, knew how to haggle, and ultimately a deal was struck. The couple agreed to provide two free lessons for each one that the Kaufman family paid for. Coleman remembered that Ida eventually soured on—and often complained bitterly about—the agreement: even though she wasn't paying for two of her son's three weekly lessons, she was still paying for his music books.

So Seymour's education began in earnest in 1933 under Tallarico's guidance. In later years he would remember her sternness, going so far as to compare her to the taskmaster title character played by Shirley MacLaine in the 1988 movie *Madame Sousatzka*. Seymour studied for years with Tallarico in Manhattan and at the music camp she and her husband established on a property they held in Sunabee, New Hampshire. Called the Trow-Rico Farm, the camp was established in 1935, and Coleman, quite tellingly, would hold onto one detail from his trips there well into adulthood.

According to Terrie Curran, who worked for Coleman from the early 1970s until his death, one evening early in their relationship he began telling her about his childhood and in particular his trips to the camp. He wistfully described how all along the road there were banks of tiger lilies, ending the recollection with, "And I loved tiger lilies."[5]

This memory is made all the more poignant when one learns why Tallarico insisted that Seymour be separated from his family during the summer. She was not looking to provide the child with a bucolic getaway from the city, where he might indulge in playtime activities. Instead, she was ensuring that she could keep a careful eye on him and his progress while also ensuring that he constantly practice.

And though Tallarico's demands on Seymour might have seemed to be too much for a little boy, dividends were paid in short order. In 1936 he was entered into the Music Week competition, playing in Steinway Hall. He won a gold medal in his category, and on June 10, just four days shy of his seventh birthday, he was playing Town Hall at the concluding ceremonies for the annual event.

His achievements in the competition that year are especially impressive given that the event had its largest pool of entrants ever, because for the first time young people from the city's parochial schools were eligible.

This added some twelve thousand participants to an already formidable pool of school children.

Seymour continued to play in contests, and just a year and a half after his first win another victory provided him with a scholarship to study with another master pianist, Rudolph Gruen, an interpreter of the classics renowned in New York and nationwide thanks to his radio broadcasts. Gruen, a faculty member at the New York College of Music, continued drilling Seymour, and before he was a teenager he began taking part in recitals at the school.

It was around this time, too, that a proposal came to the Kaufman family—it may have been the doing of Gruen, Tallarico, or both—suggesting that Seymour be sent even farther away than New Hampshire: to Germany. It was there that his mentors believed he could receive the training to become not only a premier pianist, but also perhaps one of the world's great conductors.

Ida refused to send Seymour away, much as she had when it had been proposed that her oldest son travel to Europe for his own musical education. But in Seymour's case, her reasons for keeping him close to home were slightly more ambiguous. On one level, her refusal to send her boy away could have stemmed from her disdain of music as a potential career path, which she had already made quite clear when he first began to study. On another level, however, she might have been inspired by genuine maternal feelings of not wanting to be separated from her youngest—her baby—or by her awareness of the danger inherent in sending her child to Adolf Hitler's Germany.

This foiled opportunity to travel and study troubled Coleman throughout his adult life, as did another event involving his achievements as a child performer. Family members and Coleman's friends agree on how the incident began: after Seymour had won a competition and was presented with his prize. He was beaming with pride. Some say that he had worked particularly hard for this event because he had specifically wanted the reward: a beautiful etching set. Others remember Seymour as simply winning a medal.

And there's further agreement on what happened next: a little boy who had lost to Seymour began to cry and scream uncontrollably. To placate the boy, Seymour was told to relinquish his prize.

Once again, however, accounts vary as to who told him to do so. Some say it was his mother, Ida, while others say it was Tallarico. In either case, Seymour did as he was told, but it was an event that would leave a lingering scar; in adulthood, Coleman would fight vociferously and tenaciously in business to retain what he had earned.

Despite this incident, Seymour continued to study dutifully and avidly through the rest of his grade-school years and into his teens. But as he did, he found himself coping not only with another of his mother's rankling decisions but also with a growing restlessness about the artistic path being laid out for him.

2

"Tall Hope"

Following grade school, Seymour moved on to New York's High School of Music and Art (the institution that eventually became the city's High School of Performing Arts, immortalized in the movie *Fame*). There he was surrounded by fellow artists, some of whom would become his colleagues in adulthood. Lyricist Marilyn Bergman, whom Coleman would work with on the board of ASCAP and who would become one of his collaborators over fifty years later, graduated in the class just ahead of Seymour. Also at the school was Mitch Leigh, who would go on to write *Man of La Mancha*, a musical that would, nearly two decades after their graduation, overshadow Coleman's own musical, *Sweet Charity*.

Seymour proved to be a solid student throughout his time at the school, earning primarily As and Bs in both his academic classes (English, social studies, science, etc.) and his music coursework. Early on, some instructors felt that the boy needed to be more cooperative in class (particularly music theory), but by the time he graduated in 1947, he was considered outstanding in all areas, including "School Citizenship."

As for Seymour's musical education, he was drilled both at school and by his private teachers in all the components of a classical music education, and his work papers demonstrate how meticulous his training was. On some sheets he wrote out, in delicate cursive, the rules he was learning, such as "A perfect interval when chromatically altered becomes either augmented or diminished. Never major or minor" and "An imperfect interval when chromatically altered becomes either augmented, major, minor, or diminished. Never perfect."

In a 1990 *Piano Jazz* interview Coleman recalled his early education and its strictures with fondness, appreciation, and even a modicum of humor: "I studied strict counterpoint for so long; [you] *had* to study counterpoint. . . . But it helped me with composition later so much. . . . And you study that for years and years and years and then after you finish they say, 'Now do what you want.' But I think it's a very good principle learning the rules and then breaking them. But you've got to know them before you can break them."

It was during high school that Seymour's education also began to include composition. Unfortunately, unlike his school papers, which are plentiful, little has survived of his work as a budding writer in the classical vein; luckily, one fragment of a four-part fugue still exists: twenty bars that display Seymour's grasp of the form. He starts with a simple set of notes in the treble clef that he slowly builds upon and varies. At the fourteenth bar he adds in his bass line, and by the twentieth the piece has attained a discernible, even compelling momentum. Sadly, whatever he wrote after that has not survived.

Nevertheless, the fugue fragment provides a glimpse of a young artist who was already beginning to chafe at classical forms. Written in G major, it is not "pretty"; it's a dissonant composition, filled with chromatic tones (sharps and flats not associated with the key), and often the notes collide aggressively.

It's almost as if Seymour was writing this and thinking about one of his new activities: his work as the pianist in the school dance band, led by an older classmate, pianist and drummer Mickey Sheen. Sheen, like Seymour, had begun playing as a child, although his realm had been popular music. When Sheen looked back on his time at the school, what he remembered most was that it was the moment he was introduced to classical music—an irony, since it was through his work with Sheen that Seymour was getting to play something other than the classics.

Marilyn Bergman didn't remember Seymour's work with the dance band, but, she said, "I just know that in a school like that—or any school I guess—star pupils, no matter what the discipline, stand out, and other, lesser people know of them. I remember in the art department [that abstract painter] Wolf Kahn, for example, was well-known, and everybody knew he was going to be a successful painter. And Cy was one of those people that other students knew about."[1]

Concurrent with Seymour's high school years, Ida diligently worked to improve her investments, which included buying a parcel of farmland in Monticello, New York, in the Catskills, a popular destination for Jewish families every summer as an escape from the heat of the city. It was on this spot that the family built the Kaufman Bungalow Colony, just next door to the more opulent Kutscher's Hotel resort. The Kaufman colony consisted of a main house for the Kaufman family along with about fifteen to twenty units that could be rented out. This upstate business was indeed a family affair. Seymour's father built the guest units, and he recruited his sons, including Seymour, to dig the swimming pool. The colony also had a handball court and a recreation room that could be used as a children's playroom or for shows, in which Seymour would sometimes participate.

The serenity of this upstate spot suited Seymour's father, as evidenced by one particularly telling story Coleman recounted: "I remember seeing him once sitting alone under a tree in Monticello [seemingly talking to someone]. I said to Max—I called him Max—'Who are you talking to?' He said, 'To some very intelligent people.'"[2]

Being in the Catskills was something on which both Max and Ida could agree, and her interest and fondness for being on site at the upstate business proved to have a profound consequence for Seymour. While he was still in high school, Ida decided that she and Max would take up full-time residence in Monticello; this meant that if Seymour was to continue his studies, he would have to find some way to live in New York City. Obviously, as a teenager he couldn't live on his own, so eventually it was decided that he would move in—piano and all—with his now-married sister, Sylvia, and her family.

It was a shift that added another level of bitterness to Coleman's memories of his mother; and yet, ultimately, her presence in Monticello and his time there during the summer, as well as his continued residence in the city, would prove to be a boon for his career.

In Manhattan, not only was he finishing up at the School of Music and Art; he was also continuing his studies at New York College of Music, where he was now performing under the guidance of the school's director, Arved Kurtz, and its assistant director, Warner Hawkins. Both of these men had old-guard classical backgrounds similar to those of Seymour's other mentors. Kurtz, who came from a family with an impressive musical pedigree, was not only the head of the school but also an acclaimed performer in his own right. As for Hawkins, a pianist and organist, he too had attracted attention with his work as an arranger and soloist, interpreting not only composers from the past but also those who were deemed the moderns of the period, including Grieg and Debussy.

At the New York College of Music Seymour frequently took part in recitals led by Kurtz and Hawkins, performing such pieces as Ravel's *Jeux d'eau* and the first movement from Beethoven's Piano Concerto no. 3 in C Minor, op. 37. This latter piece was the final offering in one recital, and for it Seymour was joined by "Dr. Pollak at the second piano." Seymour's placement on the bill and the choice of his partner give a clear indication of the esteem in which his teachers held him.

The broad exposure he was getting not only helped Seymour improve his technique and demonstrate his prowess at the keyboard; it also instilled in him a love of certain composers. Throughout his adult life Coleman would take refuge from the rough-and-tumble world of Broadway and the pop-music scene by listening to Beethoven. He also would use classical music to humorous effect. On rainy days, for instance, he would play gloomy pieces by Rachmaninoff, often to the chagrin of friends and loved ones.

Coleman described his training as "very staid, very Germanic. [The college] took its serious music very seriously."[3] And though Seymour knew he was being groomed for a career as a concert pianist, he yearned for something else. It had been awakened in his work with Sheen's dance ensemble, and Seymour quickly found other outlets in which to express himself in a less stolid manner.

In Manhattan he got gigs playing at weddings and other private parties. In addition, Seymour began entertaining the troops during World War II: "When he found that he was too young to be inducted [into the army], he asked permission to play the piano in servicemen's canteens, in their camp shows and similar places, and he got it."[4] For these engagements he began with his classical repertoire, but he soon discovered that the enlisted men and the Army brass were much more receptive if he played songs by the likes of the Gershwins and Rodgers and Hart.

Seymour also found ways to play popular hits in Monticello, sitting in with the dance bands at the larger resorts near his family's bungalow community. At one of these he was playing with a group that also included jazz trombonist Sammy Sherman, whose daughter, jazz singer Daryl Sherman, would count Coleman as one of her musical mentors. Eventually Seymour formed his own band for upstate engagements.

Flipping through his scrapbooks from the period reveals that not only was Seymour beginning to establish himself as a performer of popular music of the day; he was also beginning to cultivate the persona of a roué, which would be integral to his image throughout his adulthood. One picture of a pretty young woman in a bathing suit lounging poolside carries the handwritten caption "Hang up time," while just below it a group shot with the caption "The Band" features Coleman in bathing trunks—cigarette in hand—with six other young men, all of them looking like they are about to have the time of their life.

The scrapbooks also reveal what a sense of humor he had about his varied activities. Under one stately picture of him with his band in formal attire, he wrote, "Weddings, bar mitzvahs, meat market openings and classy affairs that require tux."

In interviews in adulthood about his shift away from the world of classical music and into the world of pop, Coleman would describe his motivations in many ways. There were times when he would say that it was part of a teenager's rebellion. At others he'd wax more philosophical. For instance, in a 2004 interview, Coleman said, "I would say it was probably because I had the need to do something myself. I had the need to express myself in other ways."[5]

Seymour got an exceptional opportunity to experience (and express himself in) a nonclassical vernacular while he was still a high school senior. He got a job as rehearsal pianist for the Broadway musical *If the Shoe*

Fits, a modern reworking of *Cinderella*. The show gave him his first taste of bringing a show to the stage and allowed him to do some writing, as he was on board to provide some vocal arrangements for the musical as well.

If the Shoe Fits came to Broadway under the auspices of producer Leonard Sillman, a man who by the mid-1940s had a remarkable track record in recognizing and fostering young talent through his *New Faces* revues. The first of these, for which Sillman served as book writer and performer, had hit Broadway in 1934 and featured Imogene Coca, a future star of television's *Your Show of Shows*, and future screen legend Henry Fonda.

When a new edition of the revue arrived in 1936, Sillman served as director and producer, and the cast once again included Coca, along with another future screen star, Van Johnson, as well as Ralph Blane, who would go on to distinction not as a performer but as a composer and lyricist for such shows as *Best Foot Forward* and, perhaps most notably, the movie *Meet Me in St. Louis*.

If the Shoe Fits marked Sillman's debut as a producer of something other than a revue. For the show's music, he had turned to David Raksin, the composer of the score for the hit movie *Laura*, which had been released just two years earlier. Raksin had previously orchestrated for Broadway shows, including *New Faces of 1936*, but *If the Shoe Fits* marked his debut as a composer for the stage.

His collaborator on the venture was June Carroll, Sillman's sister, who had established herself as a lyricist with numbers in the *New Faces* revues and other shows. Carroll also wrote the book for *If the Shoe Fits* with performer Robert Duke, in his sole outing as a writer for Broadway.

Not much is known about what Seymour contributed to *Shoe*; the Playbill for the show does not even credit him. It does, however, inform its readers that "the theatre is perfumed with Spring Rain by Charles of the Ritz." The importance of this aspect of the production is emblematic of the lavish attention that was given to its physical look and feel (and scent). *If the Shoe Fits* featured an elaborate, complex set by Edward Gilbert that replicated a pop-up picture book, and the design was the only aspect of the show to receive praise from critics.

Otherwise reviewers savaged the show's book, lyrics, and music. The December 11, 1946 *Variety* review summed up the experience bluntly with the opening line "'If the Shoe Fits' doesn't," while Brooks Atkinson, in his December 6 review for the *New York Times*, described the musical as a "precocious vulgarization of the Cinderella legend." As for the music, Atkinson wrote, "The score consists of one of the most continuous unpleasant sounds of our times."

Atkinson's assessment makes sense, even by standards set by musicals that followed. Listening to portions of Raksin's score as recreated for a mid-1980s radio broadcast reveals an often jagged set of melodic lines. For audiences of the period, accustomed to the lush melodies of Richard Rodgers or the jaunty tunefulness of Irving Berlin, the sounds emanating from the pit at *If the Shoe Fits* certainly would have been disconcerting.

The show folded after twenty-one performances at the New Century Theatre, and in adulthood Coleman never brought it up in interviews. Among the concrete references that survive about his involvement with the production include a mention of it in liner notes from the 1957 album *Cy Coleman*, and Broadway musical director Mary-Mitchell Campbell remembered Coleman casually referencing his work on the musical when they were collaborating on his musical *Grace* in 2000–2001.

Beyond its serving as Coleman's introduction to Broadway, *If the Shoe Fits* offers an interesting chicken-and-egg conundrum, because it represents the first moment he was linked with the singer Adrienne, who played Widow Willow. When Coleman talked about the beginnings of his career in adulthood, the singer's name came up frequently, as did that of her husband, Michael Myerberg, a daring producer of shows ranging from Thornton Wilder's *The Skin of Our Teeth* to Samuel Beckett's *Waiting for Godot*. However, Coleman never mentioned them in the context of the failed musical. Instead, he would recall how he had served as her accompanist to make some money after school.

What's unclear is whether his relationship with the singer had begun before *If the Shoe Fits*, which would explain how he got the job, or if it was a friendship that had started on the show and then continued. But regardless of the order of events, Coleman always mentioned the role that

Adrienne and Myerberg played in the next step in his career. When they would meet to rehearse, Coleman told his old friend Skitch Henderson on the radio show *The Music Makers*, "I would play some of my original compositions for her, and she sent me to Jack Robbins, who was a very feisty music publisher at the time."

This was no small introduction. Robbins was the head of J. J. Robbins & Sons, one of the most influential and successful companies in the industry. In 1946 *Billboard* described J. J. Robbins and Warners' Music Publishers' Holding Corporation as "two of the top publishing groups in the music business."[6] At the time Robbins held the publishing rights to Victor Herbert's extensive catalog of operettas and popular songs from the early twentieth century. It also had the rights to tunes from Broadway shows of the day, including *The Day Before Spring*, an early effort by Alan Jay Lerner and Frederick Loewe, who would go on to write the landmark hit *My Fair Lady*, and *Song of Norway*, which marked the Broadway debuts of Robert Wright and George Forrest, who would later create the musical *Kismet*.

Seymour wasn't daunted by his opportunity with Robbins. He presented himself to the older man, played for him, and described his desire to compose. Robbins immediately saw in the young man a midcentury incarnation of George Gershwin and asked him to write a series of preludes in the style of that composer.

But before the writing commenced, Robbins, according to Coleman, "decided that he had to give me a more commercial-sounding name. He said: 'We're going to change Seymour Kaufman to Cy Coleman.' Nobody wanted the name Seymour—it was so nebbishy—so I was glad to change that to Cy, and he said the change of last name wasn't too extreme: 'It's close, and it's not like you're trying to escape [seeming] Jewish.'"[7]

The decision provoked a pair of amusing incidents. The first occurred immediately after he'd chosen to adopt the new name. When he told his mother about his decision, she replied simply, "You want to change your name, be my guest. Do whatever makes you happy, Seymour."[8] Coleman and his family would also recount an event that came later when Ida was introducing her family to guests. She pointed at her children and introduced Adolph, Sam, Sylvia, and Yetta by name before indicating her youngest and saying, "And this is Cy Coleman."

Irrespective of his mother's reaction, the newly minted Cy Coleman went to work on what Robbins ultimately published as *New York Sketches*, a trio of pieces called "Morning," "Noon," and "Night." Listening to the sole recording of the triptych on the CD *Classical Broadway*—made nearly sixty years after they were written—reveals that Coleman took quite seriously the notion that he was following in Gershwin's footsteps. In fact, reviewer Steve Schwartz wrote: "It's more Gershwinesque than Gershwin—less focused than the real thing," but added, "Coleman's little suite has its attractions. The piano writing is assured and varied. He makes use of the entire keyboard."[9]

Seymour, as he was still known by school administrators, graduated from the High School of Music and Art less than a month after *If the Shoe Fits* folded, and he was at Robbins's office a few months after getting his diploma. For a young man who had not yet reached eighteen, he already had two impressive credits on his résumé, but within the span of just two years (and well before he would hit his twentieth birthday), Cy Coleman's curriculum vitae would become quite a bit longer.

3

"Hey, Look Me Over"

After he graduated from the High School of Music and Art in early 1947, Coleman continued for a while with studies and performances at the New York College of Music, but there came a point when he needed to move on from that institution as well. He learned of the school's decision when he was summoned to the dean's office, where he was told that the administration felt that they had done all they could for him and that it was time for him to study with a master teacher who would help him refine his work. As Coleman recalled, the dean said that they were "sending me to the best."[1]

The best turned out to be Adele Marcus, who since the 1920s had been making a name for herself as both a performer and an educator. At the time Coleman went to her, she was gaining particular acclaim for her influence on another pianist, a man who would become one of Coleman's lifelong friends—Byron Janis.

Coleman admitted to having been, during their first meeting, "a little nervous, but cocky, as you can only be when you are eighteen" and to thinking that he would dazzle his prospective mentor with his performance of the Bach *Chromatic Fantasy and Fugue*. Her response to his performance was, "I am still on the first page,"[2] and Coleman took this to mean that she was somehow jealous of his abilities.

As the meeting progressed, he played several other pieces before she asked him to do a few exercises, culminating with an A major scale in double thirds, which he, by his own description, performed "clumsily." She then took to the piano herself, and Coleman recalled how she "effortlessly glided through the A major thirds. It was as smooth as a fine piece of silk gently falling off of a table."[3]

The audition ended cordially but coldly, and the next day Coleman complained to the school that he had been humiliated by Marcus, convinced that she must have used some sort of trick fingering to maneuver through the exercise that he had fumbled. For weeks afterward, though, he couldn't let her demonstration go, and he finally called her to inquire about a second meeting. She eventually acquiesced after Coleman offered a "feeble apology" and agreed to her terms for the way in which his studies would proceed. Coleman later described his work with her over the following years as being among "the best musical experiences of my life."[4]

Besides continuing his education, Coleman needed to cobble together a living, and in this his talents and tenacity served him well. His work as an accompanist continued to provide some income, and he also played private functions around New York. He also worked for his brothers Adolph and Sam, who had followed in their father's footsteps after their tours of duty in World War II by opening Kaufman Brothers, a furniture company in the Bronx.

For a teenager with Coleman's talent and ambitious drive, having to piece together an existence like this must have made it seem as if a genuine breakthrough might never come, but in the middle of 1948, just after he turned nineteen, his networking, charm, and skills as a pianist combined to give his career arc a decisive upswing.

It all started on July 4, 1948, when Leonard Sillman, who had begun a radio program similar to his *New Faces* revues, put the spotlight on Coleman during a national broadcast. Sillman introduced his guest with lavish praise: "We want you to meet our guest new face of the week—the brilliant young pianist Cy Coleman." Patter from Sillman's cohosts on the program, including June Carroll, followed, and then Coleman played "his own version of 'Yankee Doodle.'" For a man born on Flag Day, receiving such attention on the national holiday seems a more than fitting choice. Sadly, there are no recordings of the program showing how the young Coleman embellished or expanded upon the familiar tune.

A few months later Coleman moved from this national gig to his first important one in New York's club scene, an engagement that he got through his unflagging tenacity. Realizing that he needed representation, he went one day to the offices of Leonard Green, who had opened a small agency on Forty-second Street in 1946 and rapidly established himself as an important force in booking artists in clubs, both in New York and also around the country.

Green handled two sorts of musicians. There were Latin bands, which, just after the war, were among the hottest music attractions in the United States. Among Green's clients were the Lecuona Boys, José Curbelo, and Freddie de Alonso. Green had also taken on a handful of non-Latin groups, such as the Irving Fields Trio and the Claude Hopkins Quartet, as well as pianist Joe Harnell (who would go on to serve as singing legend Peggy Lee's pianist for many years).

According to Green, Coleman simply arrived at his office one day—not unusual for young performers at the time. Green agreed to see him, and when he heard the young man play, he realized that "Cy was, without a doubt, one of the best I ever heard. He was a sensational musician."[5]

The agent believed in Coleman so strongly from the get-go that he got in touch with an old friend, Billy Reed, to see about getting Coleman a job. Reed was a performer who had started in burlesque. He had been a part of the team of Gordon, Reed, and King, which played the Palace during its vaudeville heyday, and then gotten a Broadway credit appearing in Cole Porter's *Fifty Million Frenchmen*. In 1947 Reed opened the Little Club, which boasted as its first headliner a blonde who had just broken off from Les Brown's band: Doris Day.

In fact, Green attended Day's debut, having booked the La Playa Quartet (which later morphed into the renowned La Playa Sextet) into the venue. He remembered the evening and how Reed came over and whispered to him and Bert Lahr (a man most memorably known as the Cowardly Lion in the film *The Wizard of Oz*), "Wait until you hear this girl."[6]

Day's reception in a review in *Variety* on March 5, 1947 was probably not as glowing as Reed might have hoped. The paper's critic praised the singer only modestly but was nonetheless enthusiastic about the potential of the venue: "It has all of the earmarks of becoming a potential hangout because of the generally congenial auspices and the attractive environment. It's one of those long rooms with enough bar space up front for the dropper-inners, and the main interior possesses a tiny dance floor."

After its opening, the Little Club went through some changes, and at one point Reed scaled back the entertainment to a lone piano player. But by mid-1948 the place was hitting its stride, prompting the *New Yorker* to describe it amusingly as "a halfway house to Broadway and Park Avenue" and admiringly as "a throwback to the bustling twenties."[7] Reed agreed to take on Green's client, and Coleman made his debut at the Little Club in September 1948.

Coleman's stint there only lasted two weeks, because, as he remembered, "I was a brash kid and Billy Reed didn't like it. He said I was playing too much and too loud. I think I was playing every note. Everything was fast, and there was a lot of technique. I wanted to show off. I played a few ballads in between, but we had a lot of arguments, and I left after two weeks in a huff."[8]

Coleman was followed by a much more established name at the time: Sonny Kendis, who had been part of New York's entertainment scene for a while and in the early 1940s had been featured with his group on an album that paid tribute to the legendary nightspot the Stork Club. Just a year after his gig following Coleman at the Little Club, Kendis hit the television airwaves with a CBS music program bearing his name. Coleman would need to wait a bit longer than Kendis for a shot at television, but there was little question that as 1948 drew to a close he was making a name for himself as an entertainer and, thanks to Green's representation, establishing a foothold in the Big Apple.

Coleman's most continuous work as a performer in New York's niteries began just three months after his engagement at the Little Club. By the beginning of 1949 he had a gig at the Hotel Park Sheraton's Mermaid Room, serving as one of three pianists in a venue that provided continuous music throughout the evening for its patrons. (Another was Billy Barnes, who became the creator of a series of popular revues and a writer of special material for television's *The Carol Burnett Show* and *Laugh-In*.)

Years later Coleman would wax nostalgic about his five months at this venue: "It was [a] wonderful room to play, and of course you didn't get paid much. When you did get paid, you were lucky to get it from them. It was a wonderful place to work, a really good atmosphere. It was intimate and had good lighting. . . . I miss that kind of room in town."[9]

Despite his fondness for the Mermaid Room, Coleman left in May 1949. This time it wasn't because of disagreements with management; rather, he had gotten a featured slot at Vito Pisa's Le Perroquet on Second Avenue. Pisa, who would ultimately go on to lord over the highly renowned Chez Vito, had opened the club in late 1948 and, given his modest show budget (a mere $400 a week for all of the entertainers), he often had to turn to up-and-comers, like Hugh Shannon, who made some early appearances there and was at one point on a bill alternating with Coleman. In later years Shannon would remember his young colleague as being "very shy."[10]

Coleman's stint at Le Perroquet garnered him recognition in the trade journal *Variety* as a "New Act," and in the May 4, 1949 edition of the paper he received his first full review:

> Cy Coleman looks like a find for intimeries. A pianist with a classical background, this teenster distinguishes himself with fanciful melodic patterns, individualistic interpretation and a mature styling.
>
> Coleman has a fresh approach which takes him off on noncommercial cadenzas with complicated counterpoint best understood by the Carnegie Hall-pewholders. But fortunately these lapses look well on his keyboard and frequently cause the customers to cease conversation and listen.
>
> In alternating between classics and pops he embraces a variety of styles, but once Coleman determines where he wants to go, it's most likely he'll get there.[11]

Coleman's playing also attracted two Manhattan tastemakers: Serge Obolensky, president of the Sherry-Netherland Hotel, and Popsy Whittaker, from the *New Yorker*. Coleman remembered the latter fondly: "[He] was a dear, and it's a sad loss not to have Popsy around."[12] He also recalled how Whittaker had shown him clippings from the magazine's "Goings On About Town" listings in which the writer had used such adjectives as "brilliant" and "dazzling" to describe Coleman's playing.

Coleman was pleased but also brash, as always. He remembered that, after looking at the write-ups, "I said, 'Does anybody read that small print?' But it wasn't really meant to be smart."[13]

Whittaker wasn't fazed by the quip and remained supportive of Coleman's work, as did the magazine's music critic, Douglas Watt, in the years to come. As for Obolensky, he opted to book Coleman into the Sherry-Netherland that summer.

This new job meant that Coleman would experience for the first but hardly the last time what it was to juggle two concurrent professional obligations; he already had another project on his schedule for the summer: the production of his first musical, *You Got a Regatta*, which was slated to premiere in August at the Bellport Summer Theatre on Long Island.

The theater was founded in 1947 by Lesley Savage, who, although raised on the Upper East Side, had spent her childhood summers in the small beach community. The theater was a way of returning to her roots while also affording her the ability to continue the acting career she had begun as an adult.

Savage had garnered only one Broadway credit in her career, appearing opposite future film star Fredric March in *The American Way*, but she had worked extensively in touring productions and summer stock. In addition, during the war years she had appeared in USO shows entertaining troops, and though it's not documented, it seems likely that she and Coleman may have struck up a friendship at one of these events while he was doing his part for the war effort as a teen entertainer.

Bellport Summer Theatre distinguished itself by offering seasons that included some of Broadway's most recent hits with name talents. In 1949, two years after its founding, the theater was continuing that tradition with *The Vinegar Tree*, by Paul Osborn (who is best known today from revivals of his play *Mornings at Seven*), and Noël Coward's *Blithe Spirit*, and it was adding premieres to its lineup—not just *Regatta*, but also what was billed as a pre-Broadway tryout of *The Proud Age*, a comedy by Stanley Richards, who would go on to have a notable career as an editor of theater-related anthologies.

For *You Got a Regatta*, Coleman worked with lyricist Lawrence Steiner and Savage herself, who penned the book. The show centered on a young man and woman who find themselves at odds with one another over a sailing race, much as their folks had done when they were young. As the musical unfolds, the boy's wifeless father and the girl's widowed mother step in to make sure that the young people don't make the same mistake of allowing a competition to squash their budding romance.

According to Ruth Allan, who was a member of the show's ensemble of young people and went on to become executive producer of the Gateway Playhouse, which evolved from the Bellport Summer Theatre, Coleman was present during preproduction. He taught the songs to the company and served as rehearsal pianist, all duties that he could have accomplished before heading to the Sherry-Netherland at night.

When the show did open, Dwight Schoeffler, in his August 18 *Patchogue Advance* review, assessed it as "a frothy musical frill . . . which bounces merrily and unconcernedly through two fast acts producing a rather mellow glow on a happy late-summer crowd." He didn't feel it necessary to mention Coleman by name, but after describing the show's story as being "uninteresting," he did point out that "some pleasant music and rollicking dancing more than compensate for any shortcomings."

The show also attracted an industry review, and the August 31 *Variety* write-up specifically praised the show's songwriters: "Cy Coleman and Larry Steiner, in the music and lyric department, respectively, show promise. Coleman, a nitery pianist and composer, has turned out a listenable score, while Steiner shines in spots with some clever wordage."

Sadly, the script for the show has vanished, and even more distressing is that eleven of the show's twelve numbers have shared a similar fate. The reviews give some titles and even a sense of what Coleman and Steiner wrote. "Daddy Why?" was a comic number in which a young woman asked about the nature of love and sex; there were also a ballad called "Strange How Love Can Last" and a humorous duet titled "I Love to Love."

Allan didn't recall these latter two numbers but remembered how infectious Coleman's tune was for "Daddy Why?," which Steiner filled with double entendres. "My mother used to sing it all the time," she recalled, "but she didn't know exactly what all of the lyrics were implying."[14]

Neither of the reviews—nor Allan—talked about the one number that does still exist from the show, "You've Got to Lose to Win." The song, a bit of advice about how women sometimes have to take a back seat to the men in their lives, was presumably a song for the mother to sing to her daughter. Coleman took an interesting approach to the tune, writing a melody that almost sounds like an old hymn. The musical style ends up giving Steiner's ironic lyric, which contains lines such as "Though we know too well we're superior / There are times, many times, when we've got to lose to win," unexpected gravitas.

You Got a Regatta turned out to be a genuine crowd-pleaser and enjoyed a brief extension through the Labor Day holiday, even as Coleman was moving into his third month at his chic hotel gig. His engagement at the high-toned spot didn't receive any official reviews, but in its listings the *New Yorker* was touting him with superlatives week in and week out. One lauded the "interesting experiments in pianoforte diatonics" that Coleman was offering.[15] Another commended "Cy Coleman's virtuoso fretwork on the piano."[16]

Coleman's work at the Sherry-Netherland also catapulted him into society columns, particularly after Mrs. Cornelius Vanderbilt attended his first performance there. Photographs of the twenty-year-old pianist and the Upper East Side dowager hit the papers. She was so impressed with his work that she invited him to tea at her Fifth Avenue mansion the next day.

In 1977 Coleman recalled the incident in an interview with Sheridan Morley for the *Times* of London: "I got through the door and they wheeled her over to me and she said 'Who are you?' and I reminded her that she'd heard me play the night before and asked me to tea, so that seemed to satisfy her and after another hour or so in the house they wheeled her over to me again and she asked who I was and I said I was Cy Coleman and playing piano at the Sherry Netherland [*sic*] and she said great, she must come and hear me sometime. That was my start in high society."[17]

And while it might seem as though Coleman's sense of humor about his work in the rarified space might only have come in hindsight, it didn't. In a column from the period, Leonard Lyons reported an encounter that Coleman had with his boss: "[Obolensky] visited the room where Cy Coleman, the 20-year-old pianist, entertains. Obolensky was accompanied by Artur Rubinstein. Coleman recognized the distinguished visitor, blinked, and then told his employer, Mr. Obolensky: 'You're sure going to a lot of trouble to tone me down.'"[18]

The story is indicative of Coleman's brashness with his employer, and it might even be considered the precursor to the conversation that brought Coleman's work at the hotel to an end. As Coleman recalled, "I played solo piano at the Sherry-Netherland, and then I decided I wanted a trio. I went to Serge Obolensky, who had a room downstairs called the Carnaval Room, and I said, 'Why don't you put me in there with a jazz trio?' And he said, 'No, I don't want to put you in there. I like what you're doing upstairs.' And I said, 'Why don't you put me downstairs or I quit?' So I quit."[19]

Coleman wasn't out of work for long. Within a month he had moved on to a brief engagement at the Hotel St. Moritz, where he got to work with the trio he had envisioned, and by November he was ensconced in the newly opened Shelburne Lounge in the Murray Hill hotel of the same name, where his performances were carried as live radio broadcasts throughout the country.

A script for the November 10, 1949 broadcast gives an indication not only of the songs he was playing (a quartet of songs from Rodgers and Hammerstein's red-hot hit *South Pacific*, including "Bali Ha'i" and "There Is Nothing Like a Dame") but also the charmingly laid-back public persona he was developing. At the end of this broadcast he told listeners: "We start 'round about ten every night. So . . . here's an invitation. C'mon over . . . we're at 37th Street and Lexington . . . and we set up shop at ten. And now . . . this is Cy Coleman returning you to our studio."

It didn't take long for critics to pick up on Coleman's presence at the Shelburne, and less than a month after he started there his work prompted a rave from Douglas Watt in the *New Yorker*. "Master Coleman whizzes off infernally complex treatments of such numbers as 'Just One of Those Things' and 'I Get a Kick Out of You,' and manages to be interesting about it, too."[20]

Watt went on to complain about the noise in the room and his annoyance with the crowd's potential inability to hear Coleman and his unnamed trio-mates before concluding: "My point is that Coleman is very, very good, and I feel that any pianist who takes the trouble to carefully crack open a nightclub chestnut like 'Just One of Those Things,' break it into a lot of little pieces, and put them all back together again in a more daring shape at least deserves to be heard."[21]

The management at the Shelburne and broadcasting executives both agreed with Watt's assessment. Coleman continued at the Shelburne well into 1950, even as his career branched off into new realms.

4

"Be a Performer"

As the new decade dawned, Coleman remained a fixture at the Hotel Shelburne, even as the performers around him rotated on and off the venue's bill of entertainers, which had started singer-guitarist Josh White and vocalist Patricia Bright. Among the people who entered Coleman's sphere were Juanita Hall (who would come to the club after she had performed in *South Pacific* on Broadway), comedienne and singer Kaye Ballard (who would retain a fondness for Coleman's music throughout her career), folk balladeers Josef Marais and Rosa de Miranda, singer Jane Harvey, flamenco guitarist Carlos Montoya, mentalists Lucille and Eddie Roberts, and the Golden Gate Quartet, the acclaimed African-American spiritual group.

With each change reviewers would return and find new ways to praise Coleman's contributions to the entertainment. When Ballard joined the roster at the Shelburne, a reviewer in *Variety* offered this assessment of the space and Coleman: "The Shelburne Lounge is continuing to purvey an adult brand of entertainment. Policy is apparently paying off as this spot is one of the sleepers around town. Located out of the theatrical district in a room which has tried a multitude of policies, it is getting into the tall coin with moderate priced talent. Show, as well as the Lounge, appears to be on solid ground. . . . Cy Coleman's pianistics give the room no lulls. His work is interesting enough to command attention at all times."[1]

As Coleman's engagement extended further into the year, the critics' compliments became more profuse. The February 22 *Variety* review described Coleman's group as "a versatile combo that gets plenty of music out of an aggregation of piano, guitar and bass. Coleman is a pianoforte virtuoso who specializes in intricate melodic patterns." On March 25 *Billboard*'s Bill Smith delivered this high praise: "The Cy Coleman group (Coleman on piano) is rapidly becoming one of the best show-cutting outfits around. The Boys are all young and work with an infectious enthusiasm."

With the arrival of spring there was still plenty of praise for Coleman and his fellow musicians, but concern among the critical community began to surface about the venue's overall programming philosophy: "The Shelburne is still enjoying lush business on the strength of tasty presentations with standard talent. The Lounge, now a click in after-dark entertainments, has been remiss in one respect. Spot has been loath to take a chance on new talent. Regular patrons at this spot deserve a chance to get in on some discoveries. Under current conditions, the boite is a good exhibition hall, but it's shamefully neglecting any creative flair."[2]

The snipe at the programming choices had no effect on Coleman, who continued to play and broadcast from the venue through the middle of the year, when it shuttered for the summer season. But even if Coleman had been rotated off the bill at the Shelburne, he would have remained a busy performer, because in February 1950 he'd also begun his first stints on television.

It all started when the DuMont Network—a national broadcaster that at the time had the potential to rival CBS, ABC, and NBC—entered the realm of programming daytime television with a show called *Shopper's Matinee*. The two-hour weekday broadcast was divided into fifteen-minute sections featuring a wide range of performers. Coleman's trio occupied the first slot, and the February 22 *Variety* review assessed the inaugural broadcast:

> Trio's TV booking gives combo its third current showcase via three different mediums. Group, besides appearing on video, is also spotted at the Shelburne Lounge, N.Y. from whence WNEW picks it up for three 15-minute airings a week.
>
> A personable lad, Coleman conducts the show with ease in addition to offering some firstrate musicalizing. Composed of

Burt Kent on the electric guitar, Jerry Wolff on the bass and Coleman at the keyboard, trio's handling of the various tunes offered on the show heard Monday (20) was melodic and entertaining. Branching out from straight instrumentalizing, program offers Holly Harris in the vocal department. Gal did okay with "Falling in Love With Love" and "I Don't Want to Be Kissed by Anyone But You." Trio gave solid backing to both numbers and also came through effectively with [a] hep arrangement of 'Adios' and another tune in the samba vein.

Show impresses as being a smart entry since it doesn't necessitate concentrated viewing. Innocuous chatter between Coleman and Harris served as an okay padder on Monday's show. Trio is also set as a permanent fixture for Bill Williams' "Welcome Mat," another segment in the two-hour program series.

For anyone considering this show and the nature of its importance to Coleman's career from the perspective of 24/7 television programming, it's vital to remember that someone turning on a television set in the middle of the day in the first months of 1950 did not necessarily expect to find anything airing.

Just a few weeks after DuMont launched *Shopper's Matinee*, an article in *Variety* described how broadcasters were "gradually spreading out into daytime television."[3] Not only was the network filling previously unused air time; it was providing a new kind of programming, shifting away from public-service segments (such as tips on housekeeping and cooking) to ones that were more entertainment oriented, thanks to its use of artists like Coleman.

Even as DuMont was breaking ground with its programming, NBC was looking toward launching a daytime lineup in May, while CBS had yet to decide whether or not it would air anything. Given all of this, Coleman's inclusion on the show, regardless of critical reception, meant that for a time he was among a select few performers who would be seen by a majority of home viewers during the afternoon hours.

Coleman's seeming omnipresence as a performer on television and radio and at the Shelburne even attracted the attention of the *New York Times*, and on March 19, 1950 Jack Gould, while writing in the newspaper about a resurgence in the popularity of straight jazz as compared to be-bop, assessed Coleman and his work:

> There also is another young practitioner in the field who is decidedly worth a hearing. He is the twenty-year-old pianist named Cy Coleman, who with his trio appears several nights a week on WNEW (10 P.M.) and also is a weekday afternoon feature (2:30) on the local DuMont television station, WABD.
>
> Mr. Coleman gives the symphonic touch to jazz and occasionally his arrangements may be almost too elaborate, but his mastery of counterpoint and contrast on the keyboards is self-evident and his enthusiasm is highly contagious.

The powers-that-were at DuMont certainly recognized Coleman's popularity with critics and audiences alike as they moved to strengthen their position in programming for Sunday evenings. To that end they developed a new two-hour musical revue series, *Starlit Time*, once again giving Coleman a prominent role.

But the show failed to impress the critics. A review in *Variety* on April 12 reported that *Starlit Time* was "a modest-budgeter that stretches its talent too thinly over such a long period." DuMont attempted to revamp the program quickly, cutting it back to a single hour but not removing Coleman from the lineup. According to a *Variety* review on May 3 of the program that aired on April 30, Coleman had offered only an "interesting arrangement of 'Bali H'ai.'"

Ironically, this last review ran just as Coleman had begun working for a different network: NBC, which had launched its daytime programming on May 2 and hired Coleman for a show called *Date in Manhattan*. The variety program was broadcast live at 11:30 a.m. Eastern Time weekdays from Tavern on the Green. The show also featured Ed Herlihy, a familiar voice—if not face—thanks to his narration of countless newsreels, and Lee Sullivan, who had starred in *Brigadoon*.

The debut of the show and NBC's other daytime offerings that began alongside it prompted John Lester, in a May 3 *Long Island Star-Journal* column, to extol a new era in television programming: "This also marks near-round-the-clock telecasting, in which further strides will soon be made, and now, for the first time, viewers can have something on their screens from 3:30 A.M. through midnight, merely by switching stations."

The show's diverse elements (many of which would be used by later network morning programs like *Today* and *Good Morning America*) garnered praise. The May 3 *Variety* review described it as "breezy, lightweight entertainment," and "a candid clambake of music, celeb interviews and aud participation games." Overall, the reviewer said, "this airer manages to maintain a good pace amid a completely informal atmosphere. Hausfraus will find it easy to take without, at the same time, any compulsion for attentive viewing."

Sam Chase, reviewing the hourlong show for *Billboard* ten days later, was less charitable than his *Variety* colleague: "It was so typical an audience participation airer that by catching only the audio portion, one could imagine himself back in radio's heyday. Ed Herlihy is, like the man says, genial. There's lots of hearty laughs, gags with gals in the audience, stunts and contests, Lee Sullivan singing (sometimes to a female from the audience) plus some good music from the Cy Coleman trio."[4]

Assessments from the general press were equally dismissive of *Date in Manhattan*: "Central Park's famed Tavern-on-the-Green locales the 11 to noon hour with a show called 'Date in Manhattan.' The entire morning built fairly well to this point and should have continued but I'm afraid 'Date' will be the weakest link unless quickly re-worked and improved."[5]

The show endured nevertheless, and while it did Coleman and his trio, astonishingly, managed to work mornings while still performing their late-night gigs around New York. Coleman also managed to find other outlets for his work and creativity, essentially developing an around-the-clock work schedule.

Coleman recalled one particularly difficult morning when exhaustion did indeed set in: "I fell asleep during the show. It was New Year's. We were out New Year's Eve, and we said why bother going to sleep. So I was still in my tux. I was out formally, and I leaned my head on the piano. And they kept shooting me all during the thing, saying, 'The day after.'"[6]

For some it might have been the sort of life that would inspire exhaustion and irritability, but Coleman appears to have been energized by it all, and traits that friends and colleagues often remember about him (throughout his life) shone through during this period.

Drummer Charlie Sheen, who had led the dance band Coleman had played in during high school, recalled how loyal Coleman had been when opportunities had started coming his way. In a 1977 interview about his own career, Sheen mentioned getting a call out of the blue from Coleman: "The next week I was at NBC doing 11 television shows a week as a freelance."[7]

A member of Coleman's trio on the show, guitarist Mundell Lowe, remembered both the demanding schedule and an exceptional kindness from Coleman: "When we were working on *Date in Manhattan*, I got married, and Cy went to Bell and Howell, which [was] one of the sponsors on the show, and talked them into giving me a wonderful movie camera as a wedding present. Just on his own. And then he very quietly presented it to me after he got the camera. And I thought, 'What a nice thing to do without being asked.' He was that kind of a guy."[8]

Coleman's loyalty and thoughtfulness remained intact throughout the unforgiving schedule, as did his sense of humor. During his first year on *Date in Manhattan* a producer, believing that people didn't want to sit and watch a guy just play piano, asked him to attempt some tricky keyboard work on a toy piano. Coleman described his reaction: "It was news to me as I'd been playing concert halls for 17 years, with folks paying good money to sit and just watch and listen."[9]

Nevertheless, Coleman agreed to do what the producer asked, and it turned out to be such a hit with audiences that it started to be Coleman's signature on the show and in clubs. There was, however, a downside. Coleman had been working on an album of classics when he started doing the bit on the mini-keyboard. Given the acclaim this bit of gimmickry garnered, the label decided to scrub its original idea and instead asked him to do a novelty recording. As Coleman wryly put it, "that damn toy" was enough to sink the deal.[10]

Coleman did stick with the toy piano, however, and as late as 1957 he was playing it on television on *Art Ford's Greenwich Village Party*, clips of which still circulate online. He even wrote a number specifically for the children's plaything, "Toy Piano Blues," recorded in 1958 by pianist Mitt Mittens.

Despite the setback, Coleman made strides as a recording artist in 1950. He was signed to Decca's Coral Records label, which gave him his first commercially released recording. *Billboard* took notice of the single and, in its weekly roundup of new records on May 6, 1950, labeled him a "brilliant young pianist" who delivered the last of Paganini's Twenty-four Caprices in "a pulsating samba tempo."

Coleman's relationship with Decca deepened over the course of the next year, and by September 1951 the company had signed him to an exclusive contract as it worked to adapt to the recording-buying public's changing tastes. News of Coleman's deal was carried in a front-page story in *Billboard* about how major record labels like Decca—along with RCA Victor, Capitol, and MGM—were all investing huge portions of their resources into developing and promoting younger artists in an attempt to attract the youth market. Sales of records by well-established names like Bing Crosby and the Andrews Sisters had cooled considerably during the first two years of the 1950s, while others, from the likes of newcomers Tony Bennett and Rosemary Clooney, were among the top-selling records for the period.

Coleman's first outing for Decca proper came in November 1951. It featured George and Ira Gershwin's "It Ain't Necessarily So" (from *Porgy and Bess*) on the A side and "Lullaby of the Leaves" (by the long-forgotten team of Bernice Petkere and Joe Young) on the B side. To ensure the record did not sound as if it had come from a staid or old-fashioned performer, the disc's label was emblazoned not with "The Cy Coleman Trio," but with "Cy Coleman His Piano and The Cytones."

Unlike Coleman's previous recording, on which he worked in a strictly instrumental and predominantly classical vein (albeit one souped up with jazz and Latin rhythms), this later release reveals an artist who is beginning to incorporate more pop elements into his work. Not only are there taut harmonies from a group of studio singers on both sides, but also they, along with Coleman, navigate some tricky, jagged syncopations and intricate melodic progressions that give both sides a pretty cool feel. If Decca wanted someone who sounded "fresh," Coleman certainly delivered with the two cuts, particularly the Gershwin, in which a tune that was already over a quarter of a century old began to surge with a new sort of modernity.

Critics, however, gave the disc mixed reviews. Regarding Coleman's take on "It Ain't Necessarily So," Mike Gross, in the November 7, 1951 issue of *Variety*, wrote that it "offers a good sampling of his impressionistic and imaginative keyboard-arranging techniques" but also complained that the rendition "deviates too often from the tune's original rhythmic flow to make it more than just an esoteric interpretation." The *Billboard* assessment on November 17 echoed these sentiments, calling the work "an experiment of some sort which just is too cluttered up in conception to come across."

At this juncture in Coleman's career, though, this kind of negative press had little effect on his forward momentum. He had become a celebrity in his own right through his regular television, radio, and club work. In September 1950 he added movies to his résumé when he got a contract for an RKO short, *Package of Rhythm.*

Released in theaters around the country in early 1951 alongside features ranging from the Victorian-era drama *The Mudlark* to the film adaptation of the Broadway revue *Call Me Mister*, it's the earliest surviving video of Coleman in performance. The film chronicles his audition for a pair of stereotypical agents, playing an arrangement of "La Campanella" that he's done for bass and drums (played by Mundell Lowe). It impresses the guys, and the group is hired. Before the film has ended, Cy and his bandmates have donned tuxes and are backing a female singer (played by Margaret Phelan) in a swanky club.

What shines through in the film is the young pianist's charisma, making it entirely understandable why, in late 1950, there was even a push to turn him into a bandleader in the tradition of Tommy Dorsey or Benny Goodman.

That idea surfaced in a November 25, 1950 *Billboard* article about how the Music Corporation of America (MCA) was looking to reenter the arena of promoting big bands and orchestras: "The agency also is trying to talk keyboardist Cy Coleman into converting into a band leader. Coleman, a lad of some twenty-two years, has developed into a prime cocktail piano fave in the smart supper club set here."

Coleman eventually opted to move away from MCA and the idea of becoming an orchestra leader, preferring instead to traverse the vagaries of being a nightclub entertainer and television personality. In all this he even found some time to write a classical composition, the Sonatine in Seven Flats, for his mentor Adele Marcus, who, even as she instructed artists like Coleman, Stephen Hough, Byron Janis, and Horacio Gutiérrez, had maintained an active life as a piano recitalist.

While Coleman's sonatine has not survived, one photo from Coleman's scrapbooks captures how closely and collegially the two worked on the piece in preparation for its debut. A program for a concert that Marcus gave at Town Hall on January 25, 1952, labeled her performance of Coleman's work its "First New York Performance," but that had actually come a little over a month before, when, according to a listing in the *New York Times* for a recital Marcus gave in Brooklyn on December 16, 1951, she included Coleman's piece on her program.

Coleman most likely would not have been able to attend this latter event because of his own work. During the last part of 1951 he and the trio were appearing at LaDelfa's Hotel in Mount Morris, where they were touted in advertisements as "stars of radio, movies and Decca Recording artists." During Coleman's time in Mount Morris, the RKO short played alongside the celebrity-laden cavalcade *Starlift* for a couple of nights, and the trio even appeared at the movie house alongside the film.

The LaDelfa's gig was just an extension of the group's itinerary during this busy two-year period. From the Shelburne, Coleman's engagements had included a couple of weeks at Bop City, playing sets alongside ones by the Illinois Jacquet Orchestra and Ella Fitzgerald, who, as he recalled years later, gave him sage advice about his performing: "She said, 'Cy, calm down. You're never going to play louder than me and Illinois doing "Flying Home." Why don't you just cool it, do your thing? They'll come to you eventually.'"[11]

Coleman followed this stint with a long stretch at Monte Posner's La Vie en Rose, after which he got a new gig at the Park Sheraton, where he returned as the venue's headliner, and once again his performances were broadcast live several nights a week.

But as 1951 drew to a close, Coleman was performing not in Manhattan but at the Circus Lounge in Brooklyn, where he was the star attraction for New Year's Eve. And when he played "Auld Lang Syne" at the stroke of midnight, he probably could have not have foreseen the directions in which his career would take him in 1952.

5

"It's Not Where You Start . . ."

Some of the new directions in which Coleman found himself moving in 1952 were tied to a short paragraph in a theater column that ran in the *New York Times* in the middle of 1951: "In the works is a musical fantasy by Cy Coleman and Joseph McCarthy Jr., based on the famous novel by James Branch Cabell called 'Jurgen.'"[1] The squib marked the first time Coleman was linked with McCarthy, a lyricist whom publisher Jack Robbins had suggested as a possible collaborator for the composer and a man who would become a significant force in Coleman's early career.

Unlike Coleman's, McCarthy's family life was filled with music and artistry. His father, also a lyricist, had started his Broadway career contributing lyrics to the 1912 tuner *The Wall Street Girl*. And while his efforts for that show have been all but forgotten, his work on subsequent hits, such as *Kid Boots*, *Rio Rita*, and perhaps most notably *Irene*, lives on. Among his best-known songs are "I'm Always Chasing Rainbows" and "You Made Me Love You."

McCarthy Jr. made a name for himself not on Broadway but through his work on pop tunes in the 1940s. He wrote several songs with John Benson Brooks, notably "A Boy from Texas, a Girl from Tennessee," which had been performed by the likes of the King Cole Trio, Vic Damone, and Rosemary Clooney. McCarthy, with Joseph Meyer, had also written a tune called "Meadows of Heaven" that was recorded by Perry Como, Bing Crosby, and Mel Tormé.

Whether or not Coleman and McCarthy ever began work on the adaptation of *Jurgen*—a fantastical tale about a man's journeys through a vaguely medieval world after he's wished himself to be single once again—remains a mystery. There are no records of it in Coleman's files, and the only other mention of it in the press came a few weeks after the initial report of the project, when the *Times* reported that Saul Richman would serve as the show's general manager. After that, however, the possible tuner disappeared from the public eye, even though, in the original story about the show, Coleman had indicated that "a good portion of the necessary backing was on hand."[2]

Nevertheless, Coleman and McCarthy did begin collaborating, and two undated tunes bearing their names could very well represent their initial efforts together. One, "Whippoorwill," sounds as if it might have been taken from the elder McCarthy's trunk: it's a syrupy waltz for a lovelorn soul pining to know whether or not a loved one reciprocates his or her affection. And while its title might make it sound as if it came from the same trunk, there's a fascinating jazz syncopation to the team's "An Old-Fashioned Christmas" that makes a pretty standard holiday ballad sound so new that Helen Reddy recorded it several decades later on a seasonal album.

McCarthy and Coleman would continue to write together for several years, but in the interim Coleman had another new prospect on the horizon: his Broadway debut.

Word of Coleman's arrival on Broadway came in January 1952, when first the *Brooklyn Daily Eagle* and later the *New York Times* announced that he and the trio would be providing music for a new comedy-drama, *Dear Barbarians*, by Lexford Richards. Coleman wouldn't be composing songs; rather, he would be providing incidental music for the production.

The play centers on an aspiring composer whose well-heeled parents disapprove of the young woman he has been dating. To forestall their son's further involvement with his girlfriend, they conspire to have him connect with an up-and-coming chanteuse, the younger sister of another woman he once dated. They select this woman not because she and the son share a love of music, but because she's from the same social echelon as their family.

The show, which at one point was also known by the coyly poetic title *O Perfect Love*, came to Broadway under the auspices of Gant Gaither, who had previously produced several plays, including tepidly received revivals of George Kelly's *Craig's Wife* and St. John Ervine's *The First Mrs. Fraser*, along with two new works—*The Shop at Sly Corner* and *Gayden*—both of which lasted a mere seven performances.

Gaither's lack of success as a producer and the fact that *Dear Barbarians* would be marking his Broadway debut as a director did not stop him from attracting a first-rate cast. For the young man's parents he turned to a pair of highly experienced performers: Violet Hemming and Nicholas Joy. Donald Murphy, who was cast as the young lover, came to the production with a healthy résumé; he would follow *Dear Barbarians* with Arthur Laurents's *The Time of the Cuckoo*.

As the principal woman in the young man's life, Gaither cast Cloris Leachman, who would go on to win an Oscar for *The Last Picture Show* and multiple Emmys for her work on *The Mary Tyler Moore Show* and *Malcolm in the Middle*. At the time of *Dear Barbarians*, Leachman had just made a splash in a play called *A Story for a Sunday Evening*, winning a Theatre World Award (to honor an outstanding bow in a major role), and in a photo feature in the July 1951 issue of *Theatre Arts* she had been described as "one of the most promising Broadway actresses."

The fifth member of the company was Betsy von Furstenberg, who played the young woman brought in to destroy the hero's romance. It's the smallest of the roles, and yet von Furstenberg's was the first casting decision Gaither announced. Anyone with a cynical bent might have considered the choice of von Furstenberg a mere stunt. Of all of the company members, she had the least experience, with only one Broadway credit; but her presence guaranteed press, because even as the show was finalizing casting and scheduling, an offstage drama involving von Furstenberg was brewing that ensured the production would be covered in gossip columns around the country.

During the latter portion of 1951 von Furstenberg was often seen on the arm of Conrad Hilton Jr.—the heir to the hotel fortune, Paris Hilton's great-uncle, and the man who had the distinction of having been, for a grand total of 205 days, Elizabeth Taylor's first husband. There were even reports that von Furstenberg and Hilton had gotten engaged in late September after a whirlwind two-week courtship, but no wedding date was announced. And even before her casting in *Dear Barbarians*, wags were wondering why she wasn't sporting a ring from her supposed fiancé, fueling rumors about a possible reconciliation between Hilton and Taylor.

The gossip mill ground on into early 1952 as rehearsals began, with Dorothy Kilgallen reporting: "Betsy Von Furstenberg's much-publicized engagement to hotel heir Nicky Hilton hasn't depressed the New York swains to the point where they've given up. Current rehearsals of 'Dear Barbarians' at the John Golden Theatre are interrupted most often by the backstage telephone—it rings all day, and the voices on the other end all belong to optimistic young men trying to arrange dates with Betsy."[3]

Kilgallen's fascination with von Furstenberg continued after the show had begun its tryout run in Philadelphia, when she wrote: "Betsy von Furstenberg juggling more beaux than any girl her age in town. Presumably engaged to Nicky Hilton, she's wearing a costly sparkler from Peter Howard, who still takes her places, and another—a white sapphire surrounded by diamonds from John Reynolds, Jr. of the real estate clan. And then, there's pianist Cy Coleman, etc. etc."[4]

Von Furstenberg rebutted reports that she and Coleman might have been more than friends, saying that there never was any sort of affair, although she admitted that "he was irresistible" and continued, "I think both Cloris and I had crushes on him."[5] She found herself working with him during rehearsals, however, because his responsibilities extended beyond simply arriving to provide music in between the acts.

Von Furstenberg said that Coleman was there to "ghost play" for Taylor when his character was demonstrating his compositions and to help her with her singing, principally to train her how to perform a number badly. As she later recalled, "He must have done it well. I got good reviews."[6]

Indeed, von Furstenberg, her fellow performers, and the play all got terrific notices in Philadelphia. Maurice Orodenker, reviewing for *Billboard* on

February 16, 1952, predicted that the play, after some "polishing . . . should have a long and hilarious run when it reaches Broadway." The *Washington Post*'s critic Richard L. Coe, after catching the show in Philadelphia, asserted in his February 21 review that "a pleasant surprise" was on its way to New York. And a critic for *Variety* echoed this sentiment in a February 13 review, saying that the show had "amusing dialog, a sophisticated plot, and an engaging cast," meaning that it could "stand a chance in the Broadway competition."

However, the reception that came in New York following the play's opening on February 21, reportedly attended by both Hilton and Howard, was exactly the opposite of what had come while the show was out of town. In his *New York Times* review the next day, Brooks Atkinson dismissed the piece: "If 'Dear Barbarians' were produced as the senior class play in a dramatic school, the faculty, as well as the fathers and mothers, would beam with pleasure and hope."

Richard Watts Jr.'s review in the *New York Post* took a stronger view, describing it as "a wan and wistful striving after bright and youthful sex comedy that is dismally lacking in the required qualities of charm, humor and dexterity."

Although they disliked the play, critics could all find merit in the performances. The *Times*'s Atkinson noted that Leachman and von Furstenberg "can act with subtlety and charm," while the *Post*'s Watts wrote that von Furstenberg "possesses a fresh, engaging and original approach to light comedy."

Coleman's presence and work were generally received glowingly in both cities. *Billboard*'s Orodenker wrote that Coleman's group inserted a "novel note" as they played, and the *Washington Post*'s Coe cited "Coleman's smart quartet playing tinkly cocktail tunes from a box" as one of the assets of Gaither's "smart" production.

The best sense of what Coleman did during the production came from Robert Coleman's February 22 *Daily Mirror* review, which concluded: "Incidentally, Gaither provided something of a novelty via a gaily caparisoned instrumental quartet, which set the mood for the three cantos. Perched in boxes they proved startling at first, but wore well as the evening progressed." And Coleman's most admiring review came from John McClain, who exclaimed in the *Journal-American*, "But that Cy Coleman and Trio in the box—they're solid!"

Such praise wasn't enough to give *Dear Barbarians* any sort of run, and it folded ignominiously on February 24 after four performances. The company banded together in the face of disaster, as companies often do, and von Furstenberg remembered nights on the town with Coleman and Leachman: "None of us had money, so the three of us—mostly—would end up after the shows someplace on the West Side or in small clubs in the Village, and when the show finally closed the three of us went out on a terrific bender."[7]

On this last spree she quipped, "It was the only show I ever did when all of the flowers I got for opening night were still alive when we closed."[8]

With *Dear Barbarians* shuttered and no evening work at hand (he wasn't able to schedule bookings at clubs while contracted to do a Broadway show), Coleman had to look for other sorts of employment.

The first opportunity presented itself just two weeks after the show's closing, and on March 7 he was performing in Brooklyn—not at a posh supper club or nightspot, but at the opening of a new appliance store, where he played the toy piano as part of the "Kiddie Carnival." Also on the bill for this portion of the event were Robert Penn, who was then starring in Lerner and Loewe's *Paint Your Wagon*, and radio personality Eileen O'Connell, who served as the hostess for the kids' entertainment. It was a blip on Coleman's career path, but a telling one that showed exactly how far he would go to simply perform and keep a roof over his head.

However, he didn't need to wait for things to begin shifting back to normal. That started in April, when Decca released his newest recording, a single with a pair of tunes that turned the clock back to the 1920s: "In a Little Spanish Town ('Twas on a Night Like This)," with music by Mabel Lewis and lyrics by Sam M. Lewis and Joe Young, on the A side, and "South," by Bennie Moten and Thamon Hayes, on the B side.

Coleman, working solo on this disc, sounds as though he's channeling his inner saloon piano player, delivering the two pieces with virtuoso rapid-fire key work that has the tremulous, silvery sound that brings to mind the sort of music heard in old westerns. The recording is at the opposite end of the spectrum from Coleman's previous outing with Decca, and it garnered more praise than its predecessor. *Billboard*, in a review on April 19, carried praise for Coleman's work, particularly the B side, where it was noted that the Moten-Hayes tune was "expertly played" and had a "clever gimmickly [*sic*] sound."

The release would be Coleman's last with Decca. By October he had left the label to join MGM, where he was to begin working immediately on a full album. At the same time he was returning to New York, having played a monthlong gig at Chicago's Towne Room, to start a stint at the prestigious Café Society in Greenwich Village, where he was part of a bill that also included a number of other members of the MGM recording stable, including Virginia O'Brien and Gene Baylos.

During his time at Café Society Coleman got some terrific notices, including one in the November 26 issue of *Variety*: "Coleman is an artistic pianist who should be left more to his own musical resources than confined to an act. He's a terrific 88er when he's on his own or with light background."

And while Coleman was doing nightly stints downtown, he was also starting a new television gig on *The Kate Smith Show*. Singer Smith was finding her career, which had begun in the 1930s, greatly galvanized by her work in the new visual medium, and Coleman got to enjoy some of the rewards of her newfound success. By his account he ultimately appeared on thirty-five (or nearly a full year's worth) of the shows, which were a cross between a variety special and infomercial, most performers being required to plug a certain product during their spot on the program.

Coleman's task, beyond playing, was to offer up a brief pitch for one of the show's sponsors, Libby's Vienna Sausage. He not only had to talk about the product; he had to sample it on camera, and it inspired a lifelong hatred for the miniature frankfurters. He held on to the memory, in his inimitably wry way, by keeping a tin of them in his office until the time of his death in 2004.

But even as Coleman was biting into the sausages, he had to be think-

ing about something else. He and McCarthy had a tune that was beginning to make a big splash. It was a song that would significantly redirect
the course of Coleman's career.

6

"Tin Pan Alley"

Throughout 1952, despite his exhausting, sometimes nearly around-the-clock career, Coleman managed to find time for a social life, particularly with his bandmates and the ever-growing circle of acquaintances he met in the clubs.

Both Mundell Lowe and drummer Ray Mosca, an intimate of Coleman's who would officially join the trio in 1956, remembered their nights out after appearances in the clubs. Sometimes they would head to another place to drink and perform, and sometimes they would just head back to someone's apartment for a night of chatting, drinking, and music making.

At Coleman's side, too, on many of these nights was his songwriting partner, Joseph A. McCarthy Jr., as well as McCarthy's girlfriend and future wife, the former film siren Veronica Lake, who had catapulted to stardom in the early 1940s in films like *Hold Back the Dawn*, *This Gun for Hire*, and *So Proudly We Hail*. Her stunning good looks and the wave of blond hair that cascaded over one eye (a modern visual equivalent would be Jessica Rabbit's crimson 'do in *Who Framed Roger Rabbit?*) made her the apple of every G.I.'s eye, and along with Betty Grable she was one of the choice pinups during World War II.

She had fallen on hard times by the early 1950s, and as Lowe remembered it, "Things had gone bad for her [in California] and she had moved back to New York. I think she was working as a hostess at one of the upscale restaurants or something like that. Anyway, she and Cy and Joe McCarthy were friends, so she came by [the club], and we all had a drink and had a laugh before we departed and went home."[1]

Bassist Bill Crow, who was working with the Don Elliott Quartet at the time and would occasionally sit in with Coleman, also remembered McCarthy's and Lake's presence. "He used to love to hang out at jazz clubs, and for a while he was going with the movie star with the long hair, Veronica Lake. They would come into the Hickory House and wait for us to finish, which was something like 3:30, and then they would take us clubbing."[2]

Crow also recalled that McCarthy's drinking could become problematic: "He liked to go up to Harlem and hang out at the after-hours joints. And he was not a very good drunk. He would get angry. His idea of having fun was to break up the joint. A lot of times—if they saw him coming—the place would suddenly close."[3]

On the nights when barhopping wasn't on the agenda, the musicians might head to Coleman's place off Central Park, or sometimes, as Mosca said, "We'd head down to Joseph McCarthy's house in Greenwich Village, where he was living with Veronica Lake."[4]

It was on one such night downtown that, Lowe remembered, "Joe and Cy started messing around with the tune 'Why Try to Change Me Now?' And that's where it started—about four or five o'clock in the morning."[5] After Coleman and McCarthy refined the song, it found its way to singing legend Frank Sinatra, who was at a crossroads in his life and career.

It's difficult to imagine Sinatra as ever being on hard times, but in 1952 the singer was at a low ebb personally and professionally. He was deeply in debt. His tumultuous marriage to Ava Gardner was considered front-page news. CBS had canceled his television show. And, after the failure of the film *Meet Danny Wilson* at the beginning of 1952, Universal Pictures had opted not to renew his contract for another film.

Sinatra's currency was so low that the *New York Times* review of *Meet Danny Wilson* and its premiere began with a description of the surprisingly subdued reaction that had greeted the actor-singer when he had appeared at the film's opening, commenting, "Perhaps it is the beginning of the end of an era."[6] Perhaps worst for Sinatra was the situation that he faced at Columbia Records, where he and producer Mitch Miller were at loggerheads. Things there were so bad that Sinatra was about to be fired.

As the year progressed and Sinatra saw that his time with Columbia was running out, he recorded a series of tunes that seem to be designed to editorialize on his situation, including "There's Something Missing," "The Birth of the Blues," and "Don't Be Afraid to Go Home." In his final session for the label, on September 17, 1952, he recorded "Why Try to Change Me Now?"

Coleman was present on the day of the recording with Percy Faith and His Orchestra and found that the singer had changed the melody of the opening section of the song somewhat. He didn't say anything and later described listening to the record: "It sounded so natural, the way Frank did it, that I thought to myself, 'He's right!' So I left it that way. So I changed the music! That's the first and only time I've ever done that."[7]

When reviews of the disc started to appear, it was the A side recording of "The Birth of the Blues" that attracted attention, while Coleman and McCarthy's song garnered scant praise. The November 1 *Billboard* review, for instance, said simply that Sinatra had delivered "the pretty ballad with warmth and taste." Nevertheless, by the time January 1953 rolled around, it wasn't "The Birth of the Blues" that appeared in the *Variety* listing of "Songs with Largest Radio Audience," but rather "Why Try To Change Me Now?"

In retrospect, comparisons between the two sides seem unfair, because each has its allure. The A side is a powerhouse of vocals and brass, with an orchestra led by Axel Stordahl, while the B side is quiet, almost silent in contrast, strings delicately wafting around and under Sinatra's wistful tones. This combination of vocals, arrangements, and orchestrations established the songwriting team of Coleman and McCarthy and proved an enduring hit for years to come. The song also paved the way for their Broadway debut as a songwriting team, which would come in a new revue being planned by John Murray Anderson.

Anderson had burst onto New York's theatrical scene in 1919 as the writer, director, and producer of *The Greenwich Village Follies*. The show was heralded by the *New York Times*, which enthused about the production's songs and its visuals, adding, "and where it does not win outright on these points it scores on novelty, burlesque, and comedy."[8]

The show went on to run 232 performances (enough to certify a hit in the days before shows that run for decades) and spawned additional editions through 1924.

After that Anderson went on to larger revues, such as the *Ziegfeld Follies of 1936*, and new musicals, including a little-known Rodgers and Hart trifle set during the Revolutionary War, *Dearest Enemy*, and the team's circus extravaganza, *Jumbo*.

Anderson's eye—which could marry taste with extravagance to sublime effect—attracted the attention of Hollywood as well as the Ringling Brothers Circus. From 1942 to 1951 he was responsible for putting together the glamorous three-ring event that thrilled audiences nationwide, and he even staged the musical and dance numbers for Cecil B. DeMille's 1951 big-top Technicolor epic, *The Greatest Show on Earth*, which boasted a cast that included Charlton Heston, Betty Hutton, Dorothy Lamour, and Jimmy Stewart.

Anderson had anticipated returning to the theater during the 1950–51 season with a revue titled *John Murray Anderson's Almanac*, and there were even reports that he had secured Vernon Duke and Ogden Nash to write the show's songs. But this production never materialized, and instead Anderson directed a new incarnation of Leonard Sillman's *New Faces* franchise in 1952, followed by *Two's Company*, a revue that brought none other than screen legend Bette Davis back to the stage.

The latter show received decidedly mixed notices, limping through three months of performances on Broadway. With *New Faces*, however, both Anderson and Sillman were at the top of their game. The production introduced a host of performers who would become household names, notably Eartha Kitt, Paul Lynde, Carol Lawrence, and Alice Ghostley.

Given the runaway hit status that *New Faces of 1952* was enjoying, Anderson found that he could once again begin putting together his *Almanac* revue, and as late as December 1952 producers were vying to back the project, which according to period reports would cost $200,000 (close to $2 million by modern standards) to produce.

For the show's headliner, Anderson signed Hermione Gingold, giving the noted and quirky British actress her Broadway debut. Across the

Atlantic Gingold had built a solid reputation through her appearances in numerous West End revues, most notably the long-running hit *Sweet and Low*, which opened in 1943 and ended up playing for nearly six years, becoming something of a tourist attraction for American soldiers in London after World War II.

For subsequent generations Gingold's work in such musical bonbons as this and *Almanac* was eclipsed by her memorable performances in other roles, on both stage and screen. She won a Golden Globe Award for her performance in the movie musical *Gigi*, in which she sang "I Remember It Well" with Maurice Chevalier, and she earned a Tony Award nomination for her portrayal of Madame Armfeldt in Stephen Sondheim and Hugh Wheeler's *A Little Night Music*.

In *Almanac* Gingold was paired with Billy De Wolfe, who was also making his Broadway debut. Yet he wasn't an untested commodity, being already quite well-known for his wit as a master of ceremonies in clubs in New York and beyond. In addition, he had just appeared with Ethel Merman in the film version of *Call Me Madam*.

Almanac's comedic elements were bolstered by the addition of Orson Bean, who had been making a name for himself around New York in spots like the Blue Angel, and who would go on to enjoy a several-decades-long career as a funny man on the big and small screen and onstage.

Anderson plucked another artist out of New York's nightclub scene. He cast the velvet-voiced singer Harry Belafonte after catching him at the Village Vanguard. Belafonte recalled Anderson as "an effervescent figure, always just in from Paris and making an entrance with two or three theatrical grand dames." Belafonte remembered getting the call about *Almanac* when the producer announced, "I've selected you to be in my revue. That means you're with the best there is!"[9]

Belafonte was the show's principal male vocalist, while Polly Bergen, who had just begun her ascendancy as both an actress and a singer in film and on television, was the lead female vocalist. As the revue's singing and dancing couple Anderson cast Carleton Carpenter, who had started his career on Broadway and was at that time enjoying a string of film successes (*Summer Stock*, with Judy Garland, and *Take the High Ground!*, which was opening just as *Almanac* began rehearsals), and Elaine Dunn, who would make a name for herself on television variety shows in the 1950s.

The show also featured a host of future luminaries as singers, dancers, and showgirls (or, as the souvenir book labeled them, "Almanac Beauties"). In the last category audiences got an early glimpse of Tina Louise, who had been in Anderson's *Two's Company* and would later appear on Broadway in shows like *Li'l Abner* before taking the role that she would be most identified with: that of glamorous movie star Ginger Grant on the television series *Gilligan's Island*. In the male chorus Anderson cast Larry Kert, who later originated the role of Tony in *West Side Story*. In the female ensemble there was Kay Medford, who would later play two memorable mothers: Mrs. Peterson in *Bye Bye Birdie* and Mrs. Brice in *Funny Girl*.

And while Anderson was in charge of the show's spectacular production numbers, it was British actor-director Cyril Ritchard, just a few years away from his turn as Captain Hook opposite Mary Martin's *Peter Pan*, who staged the non-musical sections of the show, while song-and-dance man Donald Saddler was on hand to choreograph.

Just as he had with the cast, Anderson assembled a first-rate team of writers for *Almanac*. Several sketches came from Jean Kerr (best remembered for penning the essay *Please Don't Eat the Daisies*, the play *Mary, Mary*, and the book for the musical *Goldilocks*, which she wrote with her husband, theater critic Walter Kerr). Other material came from a trio of writers who had provided material for Gingold's work in Great Britain.

The bulk of the show's songs came from a team making its Broadway debut: Richard Adler and Jerry Ross. The men would go on to write two of the most enduring hits from the 1950s: *The Pajama Game* (which opened just five months after *Almanac*) and *Damn Yankees*. But other songwriters also contributed, including Belafonte himself, Sheldon Harnick (future writer of shows like *Fiddler on the Roof* and *She Loves Me*), and the team of Cy Coleman and Joseph A. McCarthy Jr.

For a brief period in preproduction Anderson had toyed with the idea of calling his new show *Harlequinade*, and even though he ultimately reverted to his original *Almanac* conceit, he gave the show the subtitle "A

Musical Harlequinade," perhaps simply so that he could justify the opulent concept he had for the opening, when all of the main company members were introduced as stock commedia dell'arte characters.

From there the revue cascaded into solo sketches for Gingold and De Wolfe, as well as ones that paired them. The other central performers had their own spots. Bean performed monologues, Belafonte was seen in three numbers, Carpenter and Dunn had spots in each act, and Bergen was deployed as a soloist throughout.

Beyond all of this, an Italian comic, Harry Mimmo, who bolted unexpectedly the day after the show's New York opening, was showcased in each act, and then there were production numbers that were generously interspersed throughout. One was a recreation of one of Anderson's earliest successes, a lavish musical tableau based on Oscar Wilde's story "Nightingale, Bring Me a Rose," which had originally been in an edition of *The Greenwich Village Follies.*

Another grandiose number was "Ziegfeldiana," where the themes of love and marriage led to one bit of heartbreak during rehearsals. During the course of this sequence, the showgirls appeared as brides (Louise was "The Winter Bride"), while the female dancers paraded after them en pointe as attendants. During one rehearsal Lee Becker, the show's dance captain and a woman who would go on to become the head of the estimable American Dance Machine, broke down.

According to Ken Urmston, a member of the dance ensemble in the show and a man who would continue his Broadway career for several decades, "She suddenly exclaimed in the middle of the number, 'I trained in ballet all my life to hold the train of a showgirl?' I can't do it! I just can't do it!'"[10] Nerves were calmed and Becker remained with the show, but the tale gives a good indication of the splendor Anderson was lavishing on each number.

He paid similar attention to Coleman and McCarthy's contribution, "Tin Pan Alley," although getting the tune written seems to have been somewhat of a tough assignment for its composer.

On an undated sheet with a draft lyric, publisher Jack Robbins implored: "Cy: For God's sake please write a verse at once for the song."

Later, on Robbins's letterhead, a handwritten note dated October 2, 1953 informed Coleman that Anderson had let him know that "Tin Pan Alley" would be a centerpiece number in the show, and again Robbins asked Coleman to rush the music. Coleman eventually submitted a gently lilting melody that is distinctly and appropriately old-fashioned for McCarthy's lyric, which pays tribute to the legendary birthplace of a bulk of the American Songbook.

Anderson staged the number so that it unfolded in sections. Carpenter was on hand to deliver the song itself, and then the proceedings evolved into musical routines that cast a backward glance toward such genres as "Mammy Songs," "Rhythm Songs," "Torch Songs," and "Patriotic Songs." Each of these was delivered by a different set of performers wearing costumes appropriate to the song style being saluted. Eventually all of the singers and dancers came together to create a tableau tribute "observed" by cartoon cutouts of three songwriting greats: George Gershwin, George M. Cohan, and Irving Berlin.

Urmston, who performed during the first dance section of the number, remembered that it was during rehearsals for it that Anderson's dedication to beauty flared. He watched Urmston and Ralph McWilliams perform Saddler's choreography, which included knee slides. Urmston said that Anderson immediately asked what they would be wearing. "We said, 'White pants,' and Murray just said, 'Well, they can't do a knee slide in white pants.' He didn't care about the physicality of something or trying to make it work. He wanted the beautiful picture."[11]

Anderson's attention to detail extended even to the way in which the curtain was drawn. What he had not looked at was how his compendium of divertissements was totaling up in terms of time. When *Almanac* finally played its first performance at Boston's Shubert Theatre on November 4, it was running three and a half hours, a length that critics made sure to note in their reviews and that prompted *Boston Globe* critic Cyrus Durgin to write, "As the city edition deadline approached, 'Almanac' was going strong, with some seven numbers still to come."[12]

Despite the show's length, the critics found much to praise, from Gingold's and De Wolfe's work in the central sections to Harry Belafonte's numbers to the sequences that featured Mimmo, Bean, Bergen, and the team of Carpenter and Dunn. The main objections were to the songs themselves. The November 11 *Variety* review of the Boston engagement bluntly stated: "The music is relentlessly humdrum throughout."

Nevertheless, the show was a hit in the making. In his November 6 *Boston Globe* review Durgin said, "My hunch is the show will turn out well." The *Variety* review echoed the assessment: "There's enough good stuff in it to insure an extended Broadway run."

Anderson got down to the business of reshaping the show. "Tin Pan Alley" got moved from its prime location at the top of act 2 ("Ziegfeldiana," with brides and twirling ballerinas, took its place) to a spot toward the end of the first act. A thread involving Tina Louise's primary character, Miss Rhinestone of 1953, was removed.

Along with cuts there were additions, notably a bit of theatrical satire, "Don Brown's Body," which imagined what a Mickey Spillane detective story might look like onstage if it were treated to the same sort of theatrics seen in the drama *John Brown's Body*.

During the Boston run, Anderson also attempted to satisfy the critics' desire to hear more from singer-dancer Dunn. Urmston recalled, "They gave her a number—'Going Up'; it was an elevator song. And they put it in in Boston, and it stopped the show cold. And so what was told to me was that Polly Bergen said that is the last time she'd be doing that. 'I'm the singer in the show. She's supposed to sing and dance with Carleton Carpenter.'"[13]

Anderson's work paid dividends even before the show had started its journey back to New York. *Boston Globe* critic Durgin revisited the production and on November 24 wrote: "Anderson has cut, swept, trimmed, shortened, paced, re-arranged, brightened, tightened, and otherwise polished his revue. . . . All told, 'Almanac' now is close to the shape it must be in for its test on Broadway."

In New York the show settled into the Imperial Theatre on Forty-fifth Street and opened officially on December 10, 1953. The critical reaction from the New York press corps was essentially the same as that of the reviewers in Boston. They all felt that the production's exceptional parts never quite added up to an entirely satisfying whole.

Each critic had his own thoughts about what aspects of the production worked best. Most were quite enthusiastic about Jean Kerr's last-minute contribution, "Don Brown's Body," and about Gingold's and De Wolfe's work in "Dinner for One." Belafonte's numbers were also uniformly praised; he earned a Tony for his work in the production.

As for "Tin Pan Alley," the song and number went unmentioned in all but one review. In his December 11 notice in the *New York World-Telegram*, William Hawkins wrote, "Like most new musicals, 'Almanac' seems overloaded. I would never miss 'Tinpan [*sic*] Alley' or 'Hold 'Em Joe.'" (This last was Belafonte's major calypso number.)

But even in this review enthusiasm for the show outweighed any negative reaction. Hawkins went on to say that Gingold's work in a sketch about a cellist and Medford's imitation of Dame Judith Anderson in "Don Brown's Body" were enough to compensate for any of the production's deficits.

The show settled into a comfortable run at the Imperial, but in January its momentum was stalled by Anderson's unexpected death from a heart attack. The production continued under the supervision of producer Harry Rigby.

When *John Murray Anderson's Almanac* concluded its Broadway run on June 25, 1954, it had played a respectable 299 performances, and though Coleman and McCarthy didn't get the sort of reviews that make for a breakthrough debut, *Almanac* was a solid Broadway credit. In addition, the revue provided Coleman with his first trunk song, "The Riviera," which had been intended for the show but never used. It was a tune that proved to be a valuable commodity as he continued his ascent as a songwriter.

7

"I'm Gonna Laugh You Out of My Life"

The unused tune from *John Murray Anderson's Almanac* became useful to Coleman as he bolstered two aspects of his professional life that had been fallow for a few years: those of accompanist and arranger.

The opportunity came about thanks to the long-standing relationship between Joseph A. McCarthy Jr. and the famed chanteuse Mabel Mercer, whose career had begun in her native England in the 1920s when she appeared in touring music-hall productions. She eventually made her way to the West End, appearing in *Lew Leslie's Blackbirds of 1926*. From the theater she had moved on to London's supper clubs and eventually boîtes in Paris. There she most notably played the chic club Bricktop's, where she became a favorite of American expatriates enjoying the heady atmosphere of the City of Light between the wars. After World War II broke out Mercer settled in New York and promptly became a fixture at Tony's West Side, a club on West Fifty-second Street that combined the elegance of the East Side with more bohemian qualities.

Mercer's performance style was simplicity itself. She sat next to the piano with her hands clasped in her lap. While she sang, she rarely moved. There might be a gesture to accent a word of phrase, but that was it. It was a style that caught on with clubgoers, and by 1953 she was performing in the aptly named Show Case, a small space created especially for her above the bustling Byline Room on West Fifty-Second Street, just blocks away from Tony's.

Mercer's devoted following prompted Atlantic Records to celebrate her work in a series of albums. The first installment featured Mercer delivering popular songs by established songwriters. By the time the company issued its second Mercer album in early 1953, she was performing both standards and titles by new talents. One of these was "Over the Weekend," which had a lyric by Coleman's writing partner McCarthy and a melody by Jerome Brooks.

Such selections were indicative of Mercer's passion for interesting untested material, and given that she could "make" a song by performing it, it's little surprise that songwriters aggressively plugged their work to her. One of Mercer's close friends, visual artist Beata Gray, recalled, "She also got the lead sheets of musicals before they were produced, and so she would start singing some of the songs even before they appeared on the Broadway stage. I think people just gave them to her."[1]

This certainly was true of Coleman once he had been introduced to Mercer. Years later he looked back on their friendship and collaboration: "When I first started writing, she was the one who was picking up every song I wrote. And she did so many of my songs . . . even silly little things, and she would make them sound like something."[2]

One such song was "The Riviera," which had been intended for the John Murray Anderson show and then found its way to Atlantic's third *Songs by Mabel Mercer* album, which carried the subtitle "Written Especially for Her." Also on the disc was another Coleman-McCarthy song, "Early Morning Blues," as well as tunes by writers like William Roy and Bart Howard, two other Mercer favorites.

Coleman's involvement with the album extended beyond providing the music for two of its tracks; Mercer also had him serve as the arranger for all eight tunes on the disc and as her accompanist. The songwriting and Coleman's oversight resulted in a compendium of songs that provides a compelling snapshot of progressive music and lyric writing at the time; in many ways it's an early 1950s equivalent to recordings that Audra McDonald made to spotlight new songwriting talent some fifty years later.

"Early Morning Blues" serves as a perfect example. It's a bittersweet monologue about the way in which love dies after a night of passion, and Coleman's melody and accompaniment combine elements of jazz and classical music to heighten the intensity of McCarthy's lyric. On other tracks Coleman, as accompanist-arranger, easily shifts between different styles and moods even as he lends graceful support to Mercer's gentle, perfectly phrased vocals.

Unfortunately, critics were unimpressed. A review in the *New Yorker* complained that the selections were "marred by self-consciousness in the writing."[3] And in the January 23 issue of *Billboard*, Bob Rolontz wrote dismissively, "The set will appeal strongly to that special audience to whom the best songs are sad songs."

Mercer's album was the second to be released during the period that featured Coleman. The first, *Keyboard Kings*, was his sole outing with MGM, which had signed him back in 1952, an eight-song extended-play release that featured Coleman's interpretations of standards by the likes of Cole Porter, Jerome Kern, and Arthur Schwartz.

The pleasant but unremarkable recording went largely unnoticed, and, when combined with the lack of response to "Tin Pan Alley" in *John Murray Anderson's Almanac*, a sense of a career stalling could certainly have begun swelling in Coleman as he approached his twenty-fifth birthday on June 14.

One springtime highlight for him came as he returned to the Mermaid Room at the Park Sheraton, where the management touted his engagements with weekly ads in publications such as the *New Yorker*. One other perk for Coleman (as well as the club's patrons) was reported by syndicated columnist Leonard Lyons: "Martha Raye, who has been *spurning* $15,000-a-week cafe offers, accompanied Cy Coleman in a dozen tunes each night last week at [the] Mermaide [*sic*] Room for free."[4]

But something was troubling the seemingly unstoppable Coleman, and during the summer of 1954 he disappeared from the performance world of Manhattan.

How he spent this time is undocumented, but it would seem that he retreated to Monticello and the Kaufman Bungalows. Irv Roth, in thinking about his vacations there between 1954 and 1957, wrote, "He created a sensation here one week-end when he drove up with a male friend and Veronica Lake."[5] As Coleman's professional activities from 1955 to 1957 would have kept him in Manhattan on weekends, it stands to reason that Roth's memory focuses on the period when Coleman took a hiatus from his career.

That he needed some time off is understandable. He had been performing almost nonstop for nearly twenty years. Also, one suspects that he might have used the time to contemplate whatever had compelled him to start visiting therapist Morton B. Cantor eight times a month during early 1951.

What might have been troubling him? Conversations with friends revealed a number of hypotheses. Some think he might have been struggling with the guilt he felt over disappointing his mentors and parents by pursuing a career in jazz. Others speculate that it might have been to discuss issues surrounding his rapid success in clubs and on television and radio.

Such issues don't easily disappear, and in mid-1954 he obviously needed some time to reflect and maybe even work through what might be considered a quarter-life crisis.

Coleman's resiliency and drive took over just before the end of the year, when he, along with a newly assembled trio, were hired to play at a newly opened club, the Composer, on West Fifty-eighth Street. His "streamlined modernist piano and the quiet fretwork of his trio" were offered six nights a week through the end of the year.[6]

As 1955 dawned, however, work at the club came to an end, and by February Coleman was facing some tough times financially. He described his plight in a letter dated February 16, 1955: "I have not worked steadily since Park Sheraton. . . . Nothing but low money jobs, scale in fact (on some) since then. I have numerous creditors, all of who I am trying to pay off at the rate of ten dollars a month."

Coleman wrote this while playing, presumably, one of those "low money jobs" at L'Aiglon Restaurant in Miami Beach, where he received a letter from Boston clothier Zareh Thomajen, who extolled Coleman's work there. Thomajen also enclosed a copy of an advertisement he and his company placed in the Boston papers about his vacation, which implicitly underscores the distinction of wearing the brand. Describing Coleman's talents, the advertisement says, "[They] do things with piano, bass and drums that will take 20 years off'n your spirit."

After his time in Florida, Coleman's career back in New York started on an upswing. Within the month of his return he was back at the Composer, where he stayed through the spring and summer. Almost concurrently he got a new record deal, and before the Memorial Day holiday. a May 25, 1955 *Variety* review of his new album, *Piano Patterns* (released on the Benida label), praised how Coleman, along with drummer John Cresci and bass player Eddie Furtado, were giving "the eight standards an inventive and rhythmic beat that displays a progressive attack." The word "standard" was a bit of a misnomer, because alongside songs like "Taking a Chance on Love" and "Heat Wave," it also contained one Cy Coleman original, "One-Two-Three," which Coleman reused for the song "By Threes" in *I Love My Wife* in the mid-1970s.

Just as this notice appeared, the trades and general press began revisiting Coleman's work as a club performer, and reviews of his work ran regularly. Perhaps the highest accolades he got came from Douglas Watt in the *New Yorker*, who had praised him so lavishly several years earlier. After taking in Coleman at the Composer, the music critic wrote: "There's never been any doubt in my mind about his dazzling technique; it was just that his work used to sound too calculated. Now there's a lot more warmth and inspiration to it."[7]

The refinements in Coleman's technique caught the attention of the management of the Waldorf Astoria Hotel, and he and the trio were lured away from the Composer in late 1955 with a gig at the hotel's famed Peacock Alley, where they became the first jazz ensemble to play that refined venue. The group's arrival was so notable and well received that rumors began to swirl that an album based on the trio's performances there might be developed.

Given the way 1955 started, Coleman could have taken pleasure in this engagement and the acclaim it received alone, but in November he also found new success as a songwriter.

At some point during this period (perhaps during their getaway to the Catskills), Coleman and McCarthy crafted a new song: "I'm Gonna Laugh

You Out of My Life." While Coleman couldn't recall the date of the song's writing, he clearly remembered its genesis: "[Joe] came in and he said, 'You know, I've got this title, "I'm Going to Laugh You Out of My Life," and it's sort of like "Just One of Those Things."' . . . I was feeling in a very romantic mood, a little bluesy and self-pitying, you know as you do at that age. And I said, 'No, no, I couldn't do that. I've been listening all day to Judy Garland singing "Last Night When We Were Young."' I think I was also listening to 'Tristan and Isolde' before that, and I just couldn't get my head up into the rhythmic clouds of 'Just One of Those Things' that he was thinking about. And he kept saying to me, 'No. You see, it's really like one of those sophisticated, smart fast songs.' And I kept saying, 'No. No. No. Joe. No you understand, it's a ballad.' And actually that's what happened; it became a ballad."[8]

And it was one that perfectly suited Nat "King" Cole. The singer had previously been one of the many artists to record McCarthy's "A Boy from Texas, a Girl from Tennessee," and by the time he opted to record the new song from McCarthy and Coleman, Cole's currency had surged to new heights.

The single, which was released in late 1955 and featured Kal Mann and Bernie Lowe's semi-holiday-themed "Toyland" on the A side, began instantly to attract attention. On December 10 *Billboard* made it one of its "Spotlight" picks for the week, and two weeks later it was included in the week's "Best Buys" for retailers (releases that were "recommended for extra profits"). By January 1956 "I'm Gonna Laugh You Out of My Life" was in the *Billboard* 100. It stayed there for an additional four weeks, peaking at number 57. The song also became, according to *Variety* rankings, one of the "Top 30 Songs on TV."[9]

The recording's allure remains evident. Cole's signature smoothness and a string-filled orchestra led by Nelson Riddle give the already melancholy song a sense of palpable heartbreak that's mitigated by the gentle ironies in McCarthy's lyric.

At the time the recording was peaking Coleman was in Florida, where he was playing a two-month engagement in Harry's American Bar at the Eden Roc Hotel. This spot, located just off the pool deck at the luxury establishment, was a place where on any given night one might glimpse the glitterati of the period, including Jackie Gleason, Joe DiMaggio, Lauren Bacall, and Humphrey Bogart, in a casual setting.

It was during this stint that his ambitions as a songwriter came more fully into focus and—simultaneously—appeared to be becoming a reality. In an interview with syndicated columnist Mel Heimer from mid-February, Coleman said quite simply, "I want to compose now. I was a boy prodigy pianist and I once almost had a sonata of mine played at Carnegie and I used to play at the Shelburne Lounge in New York where the waitresses wore cellophane skirts—so what else is there?"[10]

Apparently Coleman knew the answer to his gently sarcastic and seemingly rhetorical question, because before the end of the column Heimer announced that Coleman and McCarthy would be contributing material to a highly anticipated new version of *The Ziegfeld Follies*, which had been the epitome of theatrical extravagance during the first quarter of the century.

The new show had been making news for nearly a year after word circulated that its headliner might be the inimitable husky-voiced siren Tallulah Bankhead, familiar to audiences from her work in films like *Lifeboat* and *A Royal Scandal* and from early stage successes such as Lillian Hellman's *The Little Foxes*. Bankhead's casting became a reality in November 1955, and the show's neophyte producers, Richard Kollmar and James W. Gardiner, began packing the show with a veritable who's who of stage and screen.

Carol Haney, who had wowed audiences with her dancing in *The Pajama Game* on Broadway, was cast. So were blues singer Mae Barnes and Broadway vet Joan Diener, who had won raves for her work as an original star of *Kismet* and would later become forever associated with the role of Aldonza in *Man of La Mancha*, which she took on ten years later.

The producers also convinced Irving Berlin to let them use the song "A Pretty Girl Is Like a Melody," first performed in the *Ziegfeld Follies of 1919*, for just $1.00. Furthermore, they lured Christopher Hewett away from the cast of the just-opened hit *My Fair Lady* to direct the *Follies* sketches, and for its dance numbers the producers hired red-hot choreographer Jack Cole, who in the years just preceding the show had created the dances for *Kismet* on both stage and screen and choreographed the movie version of the musical *Gentlemen Prefer Blondes*.

The show's company was also studded with an array of future stars, including Larry Kert, who had been in the *Almanac* ensemble; Beatrice Arthur, who would carve a name for herself first on Broadway in shows like *Mame* and later on television in *Maude* and *The Golden Girls*; and Julie Newmar, who left the Cole Porter musical *Silk Stockings* to be in the show and would go on to play Stupefyin' Jones in *Li'l Abner* on stage and screen, but who may be best remembered for her work as Catwoman on the 1960s *Batman* TV series.

The production was to be lavish. Earl Wilson reported that the show's total cost would be $400,000 (twice as much as the reported expense for *Almanac* just three years earlier), and to design it they turned to Raoul Pène Du Bois, who had served in the same capacity for John Murray Anderson and garnered uniformly glowing reviews.

Julie Newmar remembered how audiences were stunned by the show's opulence from the opening moment when "the fountain number was revealed. I remember distinctly when that curtain rose, it went straight up; it didn't part from side to side. . . . And there I was standing in this tall fountain with almost nothing on, but I was weighed down with beads, and I had this very long piece of chiffon draped around me that went from one side of the stage to another."[11]

When the show opened in April in Boston for the first of its two out-of-town tryouts, *Boston Daily Globe* critic Marjory Adams was quick to praise the show's visuals, writing in her April 17 review: "It lives up to all expectations of lavishness, glitter, and glamour." Her praise wasn't limited to the production's look; it also extended to the material and the performers. She concluded the piece by remarking that all that was necessary was for the creators to keep "all of the plums in their pudding and throw out the few prunes."

The trade papers, however, were less generous. The *Variety* review on April 18 reported that the show "failed to impress the anxious-to-enthuse first-night tryout audience." This critic also took pains to note that some theatergoers had failed to stay through to the final curtain. Cameron Dewar, in the May 5 edition of *Billboard*, described the production as having "[a] legion of unutilized talent, so-so dances, songs and sketches that don't quite come off."

The Coleman and McCarthy contribution to the production was a song called "The Lady Is Indisposed." It was a gentle comic tune delivered in the second act by Barnes, playing a jaded society type, from her extravagant bath while attended by her maid (Newmar) as well as several "Gentlemen of the Bath." This number, as well as Barnes's own song "Go Bravely On," were two that *Variety* singled out as being among the show's attractions.

The negative critical response did nothing to dissuade theatergoers in Boston, where the revue played to capacity houses. After completing its engagement, the show traveled to its second tryout city, Philadelphia. There it received "unanimous disapproval,"[12] fueling speculation that the show would close on the road. Indeed, this is what happened, and Sam Zolotow's May 11 theater column in the *New York Times* carried the news that the production would not make it into New York, closing in Philadelphia "a week earlier than expected."

Although he had contributed the one song (other contributors were Floyd Huddleston, Albert Hague, and Jerry Bock), Coleman would not have been present for the show's tryout engagements, as he was continuing his stint at the Waldorf, where he and the trio played through October.

From this gig the group moved on to a new venue, one of which Coleman himself was proprietor: the Playroom, located at 130 West Fifty-eighth Street. The spot opened on November 8, and in addition to the trio the bill included pianist Don Abney and bassist Aaron Bell. As Coleman recalled, he became involved with the Playroom when "the guy who ran the Italian restaurant downstairs gave me a deal. [He said,] 'If you open up in this little club, I'll give you half of it.' So I moved up the block from the Composer. Little did I know I was working for cheaper than at the Composer."[13]

Coleman nevertheless did pack the place with a first-rate group of musicians. In addition to himself, he remembered, "I had a lot of people come in there. I had Randy Weston, Don Elliott, Billy Taylor, and Don Shirley." The bill was enough to prompt the *New Yorker* to call it a "conservatory of futurism" and "the littlest room of them all and devoted mainly to the proposition that the old order is dead."[14]

The clientele at the Playroom ranged from average jazz aficionados to celebrities with an interest in the form. Among the place's patrons were *Follies* star Bankhead, as well as Steve Allen, Arlene Francis, Jackie Gleason, and Martha Raye, who had all become Coleman fans. Another face in the crowd was Hugh Hefner, who, like Coleman, was exploring what the future might look like, in his case with the magazine *Playboy*, which he had launched in 1953. The publisher's exposure to Coleman's work at the Playroom would pay dividends as the 1960s dawned.

As for the music Coleman was playing, Douglas Watt said in his December 8 *New Yorker* "Tables for Two" review that Coleman was offering a "brilliant" series of variations on Cole Porter's songs from *Anything Goes* and a "richly figured interpretation" of DuBose Heyward and George and Ira Gershwin's "Bess, You Is My Woman Now," from *Porgy and Bess.* Watt's review also noted that Coleman had begun singing in addition to playing the piano, meaning that overall he had "developed into a skillful and attractive entertainer."

It's possible to get a sense of what Coleman and company's work at the Playroom might have sounded like by listening to the eponymous LP that SEECO Records released just as the club was opening. The second side of the album recycles tracks from Coleman's previous *Piano Patterns* LP, but the first showcases how the Cy Coleman Trio was making songs like Irving Berlin's "Alexander's Ragtime Band" surprisingly modern, with variations that create conversations with the original melody and then expand on it as well as the song's central emotional core.

But Coleman wasn't just the main attraction onstage at the Playroom. He was also the place's host, and his drummer Ray Mosca described the way Coleman would table-hop between sets: "He had all of these different people he knew, so when we would take a break, he'd go to this corner and then he'd go to the other side. He had this whole entourage."[15]

The space and activity seem to have rejuvenated Coleman, because even as he and the trio were performing there they spent several weeks scurrying to the Versailles, over a mile away on East Fiftieth Street, to play backup for singer Dick Haymes. The inclusion of Coleman's group, which in addition to Mosca at this point also boasted bassist Nabil Totah, helped to give crooner Haymes a new jazz sound.

But even as Coleman was showing this entrepreneurial spirit, he wasn't losing sight of his desire to compose. During the year he wrote "Alley Cats" to pay farewell to Peacock Alley, and he also began to look for possible lyric-writing partners other than McCarthy.

In an interview with Robert Viagas for the book *The Alchemy of Theatre*, Coleman described McCarthy as being "a very slow worker. He would sweat every 'the,' 'and,' and 'but.' In those days, we didn't use tape recorders, which meant I had to sit at the piano and play the melody over and over again while he went through the labor pains of writing the lyric. Complicating the procedure was the fact that Joe developed something of a drinking problem and would sometimes become morose and work became more and more difficult."

One of the first people Coleman hooked up with was Bob Hilliard, who had written the lyrics to Jule Styne's music for the short-lived tuner *Hazel Flagg*. Hilliard had also provided the words for a number of pop hits, including two for Frank Sinatra, "In the Wee Small Hours of the Morning" (music by David Mann) and "The Coffee Song" (music by Dick Miles), and he had recently worked with composer Sammy Fain on songs for the Disney animated feature *Alice in Wonderland*.

The first outing from the team of Coleman and Hilliard was "The Autumn Waltz," which was released in October 1956 as the B side to Tony Bennett's recording of "Just in Time," a song with music by Styne and a lyric by Betty Comden and Adolph Green that was part of the score for the forthcoming Broadway show *Bells Are Ringing*.

Coleman and Hilliard's song, labeled "a fine seasonal ballad" in the October 17 issue of *Variety* and "a leisurely three-quarter time thing of striking beauty" in *Billboard* on October 27, immediately caught on. It hit the *Billboard* Top 100 for the week ending November 14, when Elvis Presley's "Love Me Tender" and "Don't Be Cruel" were sitting, respectively, in the first and fifth positions on the list. "Autumn Waltz" remained on the list, peaking at number 41, until after the beginning of 1957.

This rather traditional waltz ballad, which is set apart by—and feels more modern because of—its striking use of minor shifts in the melody accentuated in the orchestration for Percy Faith and His Orchestra, marked a promising start for the newly formed songwriting team, and they would follow it up with other songs in the year to come.

But during the fall Coleman also turned to another new collaborator, one who would be at his side on and off for nearly twenty-five years. Their work was to swiftly eclipse anything he would write with Hilliard.

8

"Witchcraft"

Bob Hilliard wasn't the only one Coleman turned to during the course of 1956 as a possible substitute or adjunct to his writing partner Joseph McCarthy Jr. The composer also initiated a professional relationship with a woman who was enjoying a wave of success of her own: Carolyn Leigh.

Leigh, born in 1926 in the Bronx, had come to the music business later than Coleman. She had always been interested in writing and had begun penning poetry before she was a teenager. Her interest in being a wordsmith continued through her years at Queens College and New York University, and after graduation she worked in a variety of jobs that utilized her love of language, including one as a copywriter at an ad agency.

In 1950 the Memphis-based Armo Music Corporation, a subsidiary of King Records, took notice of a verse she had written and offered her a one-year contract. During that time she penned several songs with Nacio Porter Brown, the son of songwriter Nacio Herb Brown, known for his collaborations on songs like "Singin' in the Rain" and "You Were Meant for Me." One of Leigh's songs with the younger Brown, "Just Because You're You," was recorded by Jo Stafford, and another, "Our Future Has Only Begun," made a minor splash for singer Denise Lor.

More important was another of Leigh's collaborators during her early years: Henry Bernard Glover, a composer who also happened to be a producer at King Records. Just as she was starting her contract, the two wrote "I'm Waiting Just for You," which, as recorded by bandleader Lucky Millinder, with vocals by Annisteen Allen and John Carol, finished as one of the top R&B songs of 1951, even making a brief crossover onto the pop charts. The tune received a couple of additional recordings, including one by Rosemary Clooney, who was then riding a crest of popularity. Other songs followed, but none gave Leigh a mainstream hit.

Then, in 1953, Leigh and Johnny Richard wrote "Young at Heart." Frank Sinatra recorded it, and it became a hit, going on to inspire a movie of the same title. The song also led to her first Broadway outing.

Another composer with whom Leigh had been working was Mark "Moose" Charlap, and shortly after "Young at Heart" was released the team was hired to write a few numbers for a new version of J. M. Barrie's play *Peter Pan* that was to star Mary Martin. When the producers decided that Martin deserved a full-blown musical rather than just a play with music, they commissioned additional numbers from composer Jule Styne and lyricists Betty Comden and Adolph Green, but much of what Leigh and Charlap had written remained, including the enduring classics "I've Gotta Crow," "I'm Flying," and "I Won't Grow Up."

The success of the musical onstage, and later on television, led to other work for Leigh, including a 1955 television musical based on the children's book *Heidi* that featured melodies by Clay Warnick. But by 1956, despite some other collaborations and gigs, she, like Coleman, was looking for inspiration from a new collaborator.

There are a number of different stories about how Leigh and Coleman came to work together. Sometimes the two would say that an agent-manager, Abe Newborn, brought them together. More often they claimed that their partnership had started with a casual conversation in the Brill Building, in the heart of Tin Pan Alley.

Leigh once said, "I remember that first meeting with Cy. We were walking through a building, which was one of the headquarters for publishing on Tin Pan Alley, and Cy said to me, 'When are we going to write a song together?'"[1]

Coleman remembered it slightly differently. He believed that they struck up a conversation in the Turf, the casual restaurant in the Brill Building, which famously featured lines of telephone booths that aspiring songwriters, unable to afford actual office space, could use for their business calls. He even thought that it might have been Leigh who raised the idea of working together.

Despite the varying reports, there is a consistency to what happened after they first thought of working together. Coleman and Leigh decided to take a stab at it on the spot, and within the next twenty-four hours they had written their first song, one inspired by their hasty decision to collaborate: "A Moment of Madness."

Pleased with their effort, they took the tune to a publisher in the building, former bandleader George Paxton, and played it for him. Coleman recalled what happened next during a 1980 interview with Paul Lazarus on *Anything Goes* on New York's WBAI radio: "[Paxton] said, 'That's a great song! I think Sammy Davis is coming up for a date.' And we said, 'Wonderful!' and signed the song over to him."

A typed copy of the lyric from Leigh's files is notated with the date September 27, 1956, and other notes indicate that Davis received it five days later. Coleman remembered that Davis recorded the song the week he received it, but the result wasn't released until late 1957. When it did hit the market, a November 4 *Billboard* review described it as being "a smart, sultry ballad with fine lyrics."

But "A Moment of Madness" wasn't the first Coleman-Leigh tune to hit record store shelves. That distinction belongs to "In Pursuit of Happiness," which they wrote while still feeling the exhilaration from their first outing together. Heard on the B side of a Louis Armstrong 45, the song hit the shelves just as Coleman and Hilliard's "The Autumn Waltz" was ending its stint on *Billboard*'s Top 100, and even though a January 12 *Billboard* review deemed "Happiness" "pretty," with "more on-the-air interest indicated here," the song didn't have the staying power of "The Autumn Waltz."

As 1956 progressed, other songs and recordings followed. Anthony Roma released a pair of Coleman-Leigh songs in July, "Good Intentions" and "Too Good to Talk About Now," and in September Patti Page recorded their song "My How the Time Goes By," putting it on the B side of "I'll Remember Today."

Both writers were also busy elsewhere as they fulfilled commitments to projects they had agreed to before their September 1956 meeting. Ironically, one of Leigh's tasks was to finish the lyrics for *The Ziegfeld Follies of 1957*, the reconstituted, refinanced version of the show that Coleman had been a part of one year earlier. As for Coleman, he started 1957 not just as a songwriter but also as the proprietor and star attraction at the Playroom. But it was a responsibility that he only held for the first half of the year. The club shuttered in June, though not before Coleman had had the chance to offer a few live radio broadcasts from the home he had created for himself.

According to drummer Ray Mosca, the decision to close the club had to do with Coleman's increasing focus on his collaboration with Leigh. But Coleman never saw the relationship with Leigh as the cause of the club's demise. It was there, he said, "I found out about having somebody from your own family behind the cash register," adding that throughout his time there he "was working for cheaper than at the Composer, because I never saw any of the profits."[2]

Nevertheless, years later Coleman could find humor in his outing as a club owner: "I put on weight at that club. We had a terrific cook there. He used to cook six-course meals, but nobody came in and ate because the tables were too small for the plates."[3]

With the closing of the Playroom Coleman found himself free to concentrate on other projects, chief of which was writing music for *Compulsion*, a much-anticipated Broadway play based on Meyer Levin's book of the same name about the infamous 1920s Leopold and Loeb murder case, in which two University of Chicago students were convicted of the brutal and random killing of a young boy.

The road to getting this play to the boards was a bumpy one. Before rehearsals began, Levin and producer Michael Myerberg (whom Coleman had known since the mid-1940s and the days of *If the Shoe Fits*) wrangled over the script, leading to suits and countersuits. Eventually the play opened with the intriguing credit of "Dramatization by (Producer's Version) Meyer Levin." Further complicating matters before the show's October 24, 1957 opening at the Ambassador Theatre was an illness that forced Frank Conroy, who was playing the character based on attorney

Clarence Darrow, to withdraw from the cast. He was replaced by future screen star Michael Constantine.

Nevertheless, the show did reach its opening night, and for a portion of it Coleman's music was quite literally center stage of a Broadway theater as an onstage band played four 1920s-style pastiches he had written. The music was heard in a scene unfolding in a speakeasy, where the killers spend an evening after they have committed their crime.

Unlike *Dear Barbarians* five years before, when Coleman was part of the evening's entertainment, *Compulsion* did not feature the composer as one of its musicians. Instead, the band comprised four men whom Coleman had personally picked, including two of his frequent collaborators, drummer Mosca and bass player Aaron Bell, as well as trumpet player Harry Goodwin and pianist Warren B. Meyers. Mosca remembered how easy it was to perform in *Compulsion*: "It was big for us, because we only worked on the stage for twenty minutes." In addition, he recalled that the group used to interact with the actors: "I used to do a drum bit with Roddy McDowall [who played one of the killers]."[4]

Music publisher E. H. Morris certainly had high hopes for the jaunty tunes Coleman had written. The four pieces were collected in an eight-page folio that went to print before the show opened, bearing an unadulterated authorship credit for Levin and Conroy's name as one of the show's principals.

Critical reaction to *Compulsion* was respectable. The play enjoyed a four-month run and was turned into a movie, in which Dean Stockwell reprised his acclaimed performance as one of young killers.

Coleman also took on a new recording project during the second half of 1957—an album of jazz covers of Harold Arlen and E. Y. "Yip" Harburg's songs for the musical *Jamaica*, which starred Lena Horne and Ricardo Montalban.

Cover albums like this were becoming all the rage in 1957, thanks to a disc that had been released at the end of 1956. Officially it was called *Shelly Manne and His Friends, Volume II*, but the cover read: "Shelly Manne & His Friends: modern jazz performances of songs from Alan Jay Lerner and Frederick Loewe's *My Fair Lady*," and it stayed in a top position on jazz charts for a year and a half. The disc's success prompted record companies to issue myriad albums filled with jazz versions of songs from musicals, ranging from Meredith Willson's *The Music Man* to Lerner and Loewe's film *Gigi*.

Given that *Jamaica* was a reunion for the men who penned such hits as "Over the Rainbow," expectations for the show, both onstage and as a trove of great songwriting in general, were high. And alongside Coleman's album, released by Jubilee, three other labels—MGM, RCA Victor, and ABC-Paramount—recorded LPs with jazz versions of the *Jamaica* score.

Coleman's recording was made before the show officially opened on October 31 and was in stores almost concurrently with the musical's cast album. The LP contains a combination of piano solos, some instrumental ensembles, and perhaps most interestingly (and delightfully surprising) the first commercially available recordings of Coleman himself singing.

When reviewing not just the original cast recording for the show but also several of the covers in the December 15 *New York Times*, John S. Wilson gave Coleman's piano work high praise, calling it "easy and flowing." Wilson's praise of the album also contained a teliing swipe at the show overall and its star: "Even in [Coleman's] jazz variations, he seems able to find more melodic meat in a tune such as 'Cocoanut Sweet' than Miss Horne does."

This assessment of the cast album versus the recording isn't far off the mark, but it is a little less than generous, simply because of the difference between the worlds of Broadway and jazz. In a full musical production, certain things, such as brash orchestrations and choral work, are expected. Coleman, working in a nontheatrical context, had more of an opportunity to explore the essences of the Arlen-Harburg songs, so his interpretations were better able to spotlight the gentle shifts in Arlen's melodies and the utter whimsy of Harburg's lyrics. It's much easier to sell a song like "I Don't Think I'll End It All Today" when one isn't pushing it as a monstrous production number.

Both *Compulsion* and the *Jamaica* album, coinciding with the closing of the Playroom, point to a career shift for Coleman: he was moving away from the cabaret scene toward a life in the theater. It was a change that publisher Morris, known familiarly as "Buddy," was actively promoting. He wanted Coleman to sign a publishing contract and start writing more music for the theater.

The idea inspired mixed feelings in Coleman; he did not want to completely abandon his work as a performer. After all, it had been providing him with an income and was something that he enjoyed. But Morris persisted, and as Coleman recalled, "Buddy came and took me out on a yacht and he told me, 'You can still play the piano in clubs and you can do this too. So why don't sign up and write?'" Coleman eventually acquiesced, and as he put it, "So Carolyn and I started doing a lot of show scores."[5]

On June 13, 1957 it looked as though Coleman and Leigh had their first assignment when Louis Calta's theater column in the *New York Times* announced that Myerberg had acquired the rights to a musical that had been a hit in Hawaii—*13 Daughters*, about a Chinese merchant who marries a Hawaiian princess and finds that he becomes a father to thirteen girls—and planned to bring the show to Broadway.

When it premiered, the show featured book, music, and lyrics by Eaton Magoon, but for its Main Stem outing Myerberg confirmed to the *New York Times* that *13 Daughters* was to have a score by Coleman and Leigh. A few days later *Billboard* reported that E. H. Morris would be publishing their songs for the show.

The songwriters had, in fact, been working on the project for a while before the paper got wind of their involvement. Leigh had completed work on a lyric for one proposed number, "The Luau Song," by April. By June 7 there was a full song list that accompanied a scene-by-scene breakdown of the show.

The project continued to be something that the songsmiths and the press referred to as being on Coleman and Leigh's plate for another eighteen months or so, but then their association with it ended. Eventually *13 Daughters* made it to Broadway, during the 1960–61 season, with Magoon as the sole creator. It ran for twenty-eight performances.

The last time the show was mentioned as being a Coleman-Leigh property was in November 1958, when *Billboard* ran a story about the success they were having in turning tunes written for aborning musicals into pop hits. The article mentioned several of the tunes the two had penned for *13 Daughters*, including a long-forgotten comic number, "Hibiscus," which had been recorded by Jo Stafford. The story also referenced "You Fascinate Me So," which had been written for *Daughters*. It was then enjoying life in a revue, *Demi-Dozen*, playing at Julius Monk's Upstairs at the Downstairs, and would go on to be one of their most enduring tunes, performed by artists as varied as Mabel Mercer, Peggy Lee, Bobby Short, Liza Minnelli, and Sam Phillips.

The *Billboard* article failed to mention another pop recording Coleman and Leigh had gotten out of the show, "Melancholy Moon," which was released in two versions at the very beginning of 1958. The first, from the Andrews Sisters, was described in a January 20 review as being "a haunting ballad." The second came a few months later when Felicia Sanders recorded the tune, putting a gentle Latin spin on Coleman's melody that evoked the soft sway of waves on the ocean.

Yet the principal reason for the November *Billboard* article was not to tout the songs from *13 Daughters* (that was a happy sidebar) but to put the spotlight on the phenomenal success that the team had had during the year with songs from another musical that they ultimately did not write: *Gypsy*.

The show was to be based on Gypsy Rose Lee's much-discussed and widely popular memoir about her life growing up as a child performer in vaudeville and her eventual fame as a striptease artist. The book was published in May 1957, and before it had reached store shelves producers were eyeing its terrific potential as source material for a musical. Among those interested in the show were David Merrick, who had produced *Jamaica* and was about to emerge as one of Broadway's most influential and controversial figures; Leland Hayward, who had brought shows like Rodgers and Hammerstein's *South Pacific* and Irving Berlin's *Call Me Madam* to the boards; and Herman Levin, who was enjoying a gargantuan Broadway hit with *My Fair Lady*.

By the end of May Merrick succeeded in winning the rights. Speculation arose almost immediately about the two women who would Lee and her domineering mother, and about who would create the book and score for the show.

Popular thought was that Merrick would reunite the team of Styne, Comden, and Green, whose hit *Bells Are Ringing* was still drawing crowds. In a column in the *New York Times* on July 14, Louis Funke confirmed Comden and Green's involvement as the book and lyric writers, and on September 8, 1957, a story from Arthur Gelb in the same paper read: "Jule Styne is a man who likes to keep busy. Being well into the score of Richard Bissell's 'Say Darling,' [he's] already thinking about the music for Gypsy Rose Lee's 'Gypsy.'"

Both Funke's and Gelb's stories, however, proved to be premature. By the end of 1957 Comden and Green had withdrawn from the show because of scheduling conflicts: they were busy writing the screenplay for the movie version of the comedy *Auntie Mame*. After this, Styne's involvement was up in the air. In a *New York Times* column on January 22, 1958, Sam Zolotow wrote, "Merrick lacks an adapter, composer and lyricist [for *Gypsy*]."

During the first few months of 1958 Coleman and Leigh tried their hands at penning material for what has come to be known as the quintessential backstage musical. And while their efforts did not secure them the job, they did get a tune that would prove to be important in further establishing their street cred: "Firefly."

They had written the jaunty 1920s-sounding tune as a number for Baby June, the younger sister of the show's title character. After they had been rejected for *Gypsy*, Coleman and Leigh turned the song over to Tony Bennett, who recorded it in early August 1958 with the Ray Ellis Orchestra and Chorus, for a single with a chipper, twinkly quality.

Bennett's rendition of the song was released as the B side of Hal David and Burt Bacharach's "The Night That Heaven Fell" a few weeks later, and on August 18 it was a *Billboard* "Spotlight Winner": "his best offering in a while." Record buyers agreed, and soon the 45 was climbing the charts, ultimately reaching number 20 on the Top 100 in the paper. While "Firefly" was enjoying its success, Coleman and Leigh did take the opportunity to mail a copy of the recording to Merrick. Before 1958 ended Bennett had rerecorded the song, using a chart created by Count Basie, and while it was the first edition that hit the charts, it's the later, sultrier version that endured.

Among the other numbers that Coleman and Leigh developed for *Gypsy* were two that they later used in the 1962 musical *Little Me*. The fourth was a tune called "Do Unto Others," a playful hymn of sorts—most likely intended for the part of Gypsy's mother—that includes the motto, "So do unto others as though they were your brothers, before they get around to doing you."

"Firefly" was one of two successes from Coleman and Leigh's *Gypsy* score, according to a *Billboard* article that appeared a month later about the team's luck in turning such rejected or unused material into pop gold. The article said that the other (and even more visible) hit from their *Gypsy* work was "Witchcraft," which had become a best seller for Frank Sinatra.

Unfortunately, this appears to be a bit of revisionist history, and while the song might have been proposed as one that could be used in the show, it was not specifically written as part of the team's audition material for Merrick.

Leigh had actually been holding on to the word as a possible title for a song for a while, and the song was completed in early 1957, almost a year before the work on *Gypsy* began. As she once said, "I did have an idea and I was dying to do it with Cy. I told him about it and that it was called 'Witchcraft.' My feeling was that we shouldn't do a typical AABA song because it seemed to me it would take away the excitement and meaning of the word . . . *witchcraft*. I wanted to try a new form, and if you inspect that song, you'll note that it has a totally different construction. It's built almost like a pyramid."[6]

Coleman was game to try Leigh's idea and developed a melody, which he described to Michael Anthony on the WHPC radio show *The Unforgettables* in 2004 as "a very exotic song." Both recognized that what he had written was good, but it wasn't right. And then one day he said, "We were playing around, and I came around with another opening strain, and she said, 'That's "Witchcraft"!' And that's how it was born." The original melody wasn't, however, lost forever. Coleman later included a piece of it in his own rendition of the song on his 2002 CD *It Started with a Dream.*

Coleman and Leigh completed work on "Witchcraft" in April 1957 and sent a demo of it to Frank Sinatra. Frank Military, a music publisher who was an intimate of Sinatra's as well as scores of other performers, remembered the day on which the singer was considering songs for his next sessions: "Voyle Gilmore [a producer at Capitol Records] picked one disc, put it on the turntable, put the needle on, and it was a song called 'Witchcraft.' We all sat and listened. As he played it and it finished, Frank looked at us and we looked at him, and Hank [Sanicola, Sinatra's manager] shook his head no. And Frank said to Voyle, 'Play it again,' so he put it on again, we went through it again, and he looked at us and Hank again. Then he said, 'This is the song I want to record. You guys put whatever songs you like on the rest of the session, but this is the song I like.'"[7]

A telegram went out on May 10 informing Leigh that Sinatra would be recording it the following Thursday, May 16. Just two months later Walter Winchell promised: "'Witchcraft' will be Sinatra's big hit soon. Clever lyrics by Carolyn Leigh, haunting melody by Cy Coleman."[8]

Winchell's use of the word "soon" might have been optimistic. The recording, featuring a lush, appropriately exotic orchestration from Nelson Riddle, didn't come out until January 1958, but when it did it made a splash, and soon it was climbing the Top 100 chart, becoming a fixture on the radio, and making good on the prediction in the December 30 *Billboard* review that it was "in line for loot."

When the very first Grammy Award nominations were announced, "Witchcraft" figured prominently. It received nods for song of the year and record of the year, and Sinatra, in a host of nominations, garnered a nomination for best male performance.

The song attracted more than critical and popular accolades. Other songwriters took note of what Coleman and Leigh had created. Leigh would always remember the thrill she felt when she learned that Richard Rodgers had taken Coleman to lunch and congratulated the younger man on the originality of the song's construction.

"Witchcraft," which ultimately may or may not have been proposed to

Merrick for the *Gypsy* score, set the stage for a very busy two years for the team and for Coleman individually, paving the way for achieving their goal of having a show on Broadway.

"In Pursuit of Happiness"

"Witchcraft" and "Firefly," along with the tunes from *13 Daughters*, were just a few of the songs that Coleman and Leigh had hitting record stores in 1958. Their prolific output seemed to know no bounds. During the first quarter of the year they had an additional three songs released, starting with the long-forgotten "My Last Frontier," which got a recording by a group known as the Upbeats. The tune, a gently rolling western ballad, presupposed some of the work they would do a few years later on their first musical, *Wildcat*, but, as *Variety* succinctly put it on March 5, the song was "just another oatune."

The same could be said of a song that came out a month later, "Small Island," which was delivered by Les Paul and Mary Ford. This Hawaiian-flavored tune, filled with plucked ukuleles and a backing chorus, sounded as if it might have at some point been a thought for *13 Daughters*. Or perhaps, with a line like "Come back to me, small island," Coleman and Leigh might have been signaling their disappointment over the fact that they were no longer associated with the musical.

More impressive was the song that debuted in April on a new Tony Bennett single, "Now I Lay Me Down to Sleep." The song was the A side on a disc that had "Young Warm and Wonderful," by Lou Singer and Hy Zaret, on the B side. A *Billboard* review on April 28 called "Sleep" "a lovely new Cy Coleman and Carolyn Leigh ballad." The write-up in *Variety* two days later was more extravagant, labeling it "a standout class ballad."

Indeed, the song, which evocatively referenced the lullaby that gave the work its title, described a man's quiet jubilation over finding his true love and how her presence in his life allowed him to sleep soundly. Leigh's shrewd lyric, Coleman's slightly melancholy melody, and Bennett's heartfelt vocals all combined to create a gorgeous musical exploration of the fragility of a relationship.

This little gem of a song was complemented by trio of others that came to be ranked among their finest. Interestingly, two of the tunes were paired on singles from two very different singers: Blossom Dearie and Claire Hogan, both of whom had long been part of Coleman's circle from his work in clubs.

Dearie, whose willowy voice had begun attracting devoted fans through the 1950s, was a favorite of Julius Monk, the man who ran Upstairs at the Downstairs, where Coleman and Leigh's "You Fascinate Me So" was being introduced as part of the revue *Demi-Dozen*. Hogan was a former band singer with a full-throated, commanding voice who toured with Jimmy Dorsey and then moved on to a career as a solo performer. She had befriended Coleman during his days at the Composer. As cabaret performer Charles Cochrane remembered it: "They would go to clubs together, and they had very much the same taste in music. Their senses of humor were compatible."[1]

The inspiration for these pieces couldn't be more different. In the case of "It Amazes Me," the impetus for the lyric was quite personal: Leigh hoped to come up with a way in which she could express her gratitude to publisher Buddy Morris for his ongoing support and encouragement of Coleman and her work. And while there was careful intent behind that tune, "A Doodlin' Song" came about quite by accident. Coleman was absentmindedly fiddling with the piano keys, and Leigh started vocalizing to what he was playing.

Dearie's single hit the market in October, and Hogan's followed in December. Reviews for both were enthusiastic, and for those who followed columnist Dorothy Kilgallen, buyers knew in advance there was a special treat to be had on Dearie's version of "A Doodlin' Song." In a late September syndicated "Voice of Broadway" column, Kilgallen wrote: "Watch for Blossom's record with Cy Coleman on which they 'Doop-Doo-De-Doop'— it's a beaut."[2]

Both tunes would go on to enjoy subsequent recordings. Perhaps the most famous for "A Doodlin' Song" was Peggy Lee's 1963 rendition that was on the B side of her "Got That Magic" single. Interestingly, she was inspired to use the song only after encountering it for the first time in the revue *Graham Crackers*, another Monk revue at the club where "You Fascinate Me So" had premiered.

Dearie debuted one other gem of a song during this period, "I Walk a Little Faster," which she included on her album *Give Him the Ooh-La-La*. The tender tune didn't attract much interest at the time, but eventually, thanks to other renditions by Tony Bennett, Rod McKuen, and Bobby Short, it became a something of a standard for connoisseurs. In a 1988 issue of *New York Magazine* dedicated to romance in New York, radio host and music historian Jonathan Schwartz opined that, in the pantheon of songs about the city, Coleman and Leigh's rarely heard tune was "the most romantic of them all."[3]

But the songwriters' success in the world outside of the theater did not stop them from pursuing other musical projects. One that would continue to be in their thoughts for another two decades began to come to life during the second half of 1958: an adaptation of James Thurber's novella for young people *The Wonderful O*.

It's an idea that reflects the pop-cultural zeitgeist of the second half of the 1950s, when some of the most popular programs on television were musicals that had been written for children. Leigh obviously knew of the phenomenon firsthand because of the success of *Peter Pan*, which had originally been aired in March 1955 and then was restaged and rebroadcast in January 1956. The subsequent success of Rodgers and Hammerstein's *Cinderella*, broadcast in March 1957, convinced producers that such fare had the potential to make profits, and so by the middle of that year networks were rushing to arrange for composers and lyricists to create more musical programming aimed at the kiddie set.

Individually, Coleman and Leigh had both been involved in this rush. According to the June 3 issue of *Billboard*, Leigh was working on "several fairy-tale scores," and Coleman was negotiating with CBS to "write a series of scores for a projected puppet-show version of Grimm's Fairy

Tales." The story touted other shows as well, including a production of *Aladdin* to be written by Dorothy Fields, Burton Lane, and S. J. Perlman (Cole Porter eventually wrote the songs for Perlman's book); a *Pinocchio* that would star Mickey Rooney; and a TV version of *Hans Brinker, or the Silver Skates*. Each of these titles was eventually broadcast during the course of 1957 and 1958, charming television viewers and spawning popular and profitable soundtrack LPs.

The Coleman-Leigh adaptation of *The Wonderful O* was to be a continuation of this trend. Thurber's tale centers on two pirates, Black and Littlejack, who, while searching for treasure, land on the island of Ooroo. When they cannot find the riches that they desire, they begin a linguistic reign of terror on the populace, which is based on Black's utter abhorrence of the letter "o." He bans all words and objects containing the letter and demands that the people of the island rework their language.

It's a whimsical tale containing many of the elements that are part of children's fare and musical comedy alike: romance, a sense of good versus evil, and even a cautionary moral, for young and old alike, about the need for freedom. Given this, it's little surprise that Jule Styne was concurrently working to develop a stage version of the book.

Coleman and Leigh, over a period of sixth months, completed, or nearly completed, a dozen numbers. The material was ideally suited to Leigh's fondness for wordplay, and for Coleman it served as a catalyst for experimentation.

For *Gypsy* Coleman tucked surprises into his tunes while still working within the constraints of the musical vernacular of the 1920s, but for *The Wonderful O* his melodies have an almost avant-garde sound. "Nothing Ever Changes," the opening number, is a complex staccato song written for three sets of overlapping voices. With another song, "The New Scale," Coleman and Leigh use a detail from Thurber: Black's edicts remove the notes of *do* and *sol* from the scale because they contain the offending letter. The result is a jagged little melody that could simultaneously prompt a smile and raise an eyebrow.

Coleman and Leigh's score also included several more standard numbers, including two, "A Little What If" and "Bouncing Back for More," that they would later use in a different show, and one, the haunting ballad "There's a Change in Me," that would surface years later on Randy Graff's album dedicated to Coleman's work.

For reasons that remain unclear, after Coleman and Leigh completed what seemed to be a full score for *The Wonderful O*, the project stalled. Yet it continued to be a part of Coleman and Leigh's life even after rehearsals began for their first Broadway show. An article in the August 17, 1960 issue of *Variety* announced that producer Kermit Bloomgarden had picked up an option on their work, and by the end of 1960 the *New York Times* carried a story saying that Bloomgarden had secured Wolf Mankowitz to write the show's book.

After this flurry of press, *The Wonderful O* again went into a kind of theatrical limbo until thirteen years later, when Coleman and Leigh would attempt to secure the rights to the book themselves so that they could attempt to revive the project. The idea was ultimately dropped.

As the 1970s drew to a close and the 1980s began, *The Wonderful O* continued to haunt Coleman. In a 1977 Associated Press feature about Coleman's proclivity for juggling multiple projects, he pointed to projects that he regretted had not come to fruition, notably "[the] wonderful score for James Thurber's 'Wonderful O.'"[4] Four years later Coleman and Leigh, along with Jack Heifner (who had written the Off-Broadway hit *Vanities* and was working with them both on individual projects), once again revisited the property, only to find that the rights were unavailable.

All of this work with Leigh during 1957 and 1958 did not derail Coleman from his career as a performer. During these two busy years of songwriting and knocking on Broadway producers' doors for a crack at a first musical, he ventured into new directions and expanded in some existing ones. Perhaps most notable and visible was his inclusion in the television series *Art Ford's Greenwich Village Party*, which debuted in September 1957. Ford had been making a name for himself throughout the first half of the 1950s as a radio emcee on such shows as *Ford at Four*, *Make-Believe Ballroom*, and the all-night show *Milkman's Matinee*.

Ford's love of jazz and the downtown scene had inspired him to venture into the world of moviemaking, and in 1953 he shot a documentary, *The*

Village at Night, comprised of candid scenes from various clubs, galleries, and even apartments. Ford's excursion into television was an extension of this desire to showcase the culture and nightlife that he experienced during his nocturnal sojourns below Fourteenth Street.

When announcing *Greenwich Village Party*, Ford said the show "will not try to encompass the whole Village, but what it does encompass will be as accurate and real as we can make it, not a stereotyped caricature of Greenwich Village."[5]

The program debuted on Friday, September 13, 1957 and featured Ford in a recreation of a well-appointed apartment (in actuality the show was initially shot on a set at the DuMont network and later on one in New Jersey) where he was hosting a cocktail party. The show didn't have a script; rather, it relied on Ford's ability to improvise chats with the guests, including people like songwriters and performers Betty Comden and Adolph Green. Accompanied by Coleman, they performed "I Get Carried Away," one of their most grandiose numbers from *On the Town*. Others who performed included pianist Eddie Heywood and folk singer Susan Reed.

Not everyone assembled for the show was there to show off his or her talents. Some were just on hand to talk with Ford, such as Broadway producer Max Gordon. Similarly, gallery owner Nancy Miller discussed the art that she had curated for the set: selections from up-and-coming artists.

Coleman, who was joined by his drummer Ray Mosca Jr. and bass player Aaron Bell, wasn't merely an accompanist; he was also part of the entertainment, and on the premiere episode he gracefully delivered his first big hit, "Why Try to Change Me Now?" On a later episode he even took center stage with the famous toy piano.

When *Variety* reviewed the show on September 18, it praised Ford's accomplishments: "[He] got an inspirational hold on the atmosphere of Greenwich Village, a feat not successfully accomplished by far more costly video adventures."

Ford's guests a few weeks later included singers Polly Bergen, Julie Wilson, and Alan Dale, and this episode was greeted with moderate praise by Charles Sinclair in the October 21 issue of *Billboard*: "It is a pleasant, casual show tailored to New York tastes and a showcase for many a show business name." His chief complaint was that each of the guests at the party had some sort of new project to plug.

Coleman remained a mainstay of the show for the next fifteen months, during which time the program's popularity with critics and local audiences alike set off rumors about a record spinoff and a theatrical incarnation.

As *Art Ford's Greenwich Village Party* was leaving the airwaves and Coleman was finishing up work with Leigh on *The Wonderful O*, he traveled to Chicago for his first appearance at London House, George and Oscar Marienthal's club in the heart of the Loop that was rapidly establishing itself as one of the country's preeminent jazz clubs.

Cabaret performer Barbara Carroll, a colleague and close friend of Coleman's who would also go on to perform at this venue, remembered its genesis: "[Oscar Marienthal] decided he wanted to do in Chicago what had been done in New York with the Embers. So he came to New York, tape measure in hand, rulers in hand, and measured the height and width of the stage at the Embers, and he patterned the music at London House after what was going on [in New York]."[6]

Coleman's three-week engagement at London House started on November 26, and expectations among the Chicago press were high. Columnist Herb Lyon touted his arrival in the *Chicago Tribune* on November 21: "This new musical whiz, Cy Coleman (who's only 27), must be quite a fellow. Among the many expected here for his Chicago debut . . . are TV's Jackie Gleason and Actor [*sic*] Bill Holden, both ravin' fans. And this is a fact, not the usual press agent hokum." Coleman charmed Chicagoans thoroughly. He would return to London House year after year until the mid-1960s, always garnering critical accolades and enjoying—or perhaps enduring, as in New York—columnists' coverage and scrutiny of his social life.

During this period writers such as Dorothy Kilgallen, Walter Winchell, and Earl Wilson began increasing the attention they paid to Coleman's life, particularly the women he was dating. There had always been oblique references to Coleman's romantic life or speculation about it. In the early

1950s some wondered whether he was dating Betsy von Furstenberg during *Dear Barbarians*, and there was a period when writers inferred something more than friendship in Coleman's relationship with singer Claire Hogan, but as the decade proceeded their columns carried more spirited—and prurient—notices. Just before Coleman departed for Chicago, for instance, Kilgallen wrote: "Cy Coleman's idyll with Madeleine Carr appears to have faded," and a few months later Winchell leered, "Cy Coleman, the Roundtable piano star, reserves his dates for stunning Lorna Kennedy, 22, a Southampton socialite."[7]

The mention of the Roundtable in Winchell's column refers to an additional club that Coleman had added to the growing roster of venues he could call home. Another was Arpeggio, where he enjoyed an extended engagement and for a while was on the same bill as Carroll and her trio.

Carroll remembered this room with genuine delight: "Arpeggio was a small club with a sort of circular bar in the middle, and at one end of the room was a little stage and that's where you performed. Arpeggio's claim to fame was, believe it or not, that Joey Gallo used to hang out there. He was a gangster who was killed at Umberto's Clam House. They did him in. But he liked music and he used to hang out at the bar there. We didn't know how famous he was or who he was. . . . It's not important. Those rooms had a lot of color (so to speak). They were fun."[8]

A trio of albums from the Westminster label was also part of Coleman's agenda as 1958 turned into 1959. The company, which had specialized strictly in classical recordings, was taking its first steps into new musical arenas and turned to Coleman for its initial jazz release, *Cool Coleman*, which hit stores in November 1959.

Both the cover art and the song list for this LP reflected the new heights that Coleman by now had reached. On the front of the album he was perched rather imperially on two giant blocks of ice, as if to proclaim not just his coolness but also his supremacy in the field. As for the selections, it was the first album on which he and the trio (in this instance bass player Bell and drummer Charlie Smith) were playing almost an equal number of Coleman's own works alongside standards.

In fact, two of the songs were world-premiere recordings of Coleman's work. The A side opened with "Jazz Mambo," one of the first jazz tunes that Coleman had written and one that he described in the liner notes as being "intended as a jazz satire [that] pits the Latin feeling and the jazz against each other." On the B side the opener was "Alley Cats," the hep tribute that he had written as he finished his gig at the Waldorf Astoria's Peacock Alley.

These two tracks, combined with "Witchcraft" and "You Fascinate Me So" (delivered as almost a delicate music-box melody), make the recording one of the best snapshots from the period of Coleman's versatility as both writer and performer.

In addition, his work on "Fascinate" on this album—he highlights the vaguely Asian influences for the song, which was supposed to be sung in *13 Daughters* by a young Hawaiian woman—set the stage beautifully for his next record on the Westminster label: a jazz interpretation of Rodgers and Hammerstein's *Flower Drum Song*. For this album Coleman brought in a new drummer, G. T. Hogan, and according to the liner notes "surrounded him" with a host of instruments beyond his usual percussion set, such as antique cymbals and two gongs. The additional pieces helped to produce some highly exotic sounds on the disc, ones that deftly underscored and enhanced Coleman's arrangements, built on the Asian influences in Rodgers's music as refracted through a jazz prism.

In a rather sarcastic review of three albums inspired by the songs from *Flower Drum Song* in the *Washington Post* on February 15, 1959, Tony Gieske wrote, "Jazzmen have resuscitated some pretty terrible stuff. . . . Only the Cy Coleman Trio (Westminster 6106) achieves anything resembling music from this awful pap, at the cost of Heaven knows how bad an aesthetic hernia."

Coleman's third Westminster release, *Why Try to Change Me Now?*, came out just a month later, offering up standards like "Smile" and "This Time the Dream's on Me" alongside Coleman's title track. The effort of putting out three LPs over the course of about six months shows on this one. Coleman's work is still fine, but the overall experience pales in comparison to his two previous outings for the label. Nonetheless, the editors at *Vogue* remembered it by year's end, putting it on their list of recommended "30 Records for Christmas" and calling it "a fine entertainment concocted of unhackneyed tunes, virtuoso piano by Coleman, and a steady, contagious beat provided by his associates Aaron Bell on bass and Edmond Thigpen on drums."[9]

Coleman told publisher Buddy Morris to expect this level of activity away from songwriting when he signed his contract. Leigh was also aware that this was part of the agreement that the two had made, and yet Coleman's work as a performer fueled notes of discord between them. In 2002, Coleman recalled, "I warned them. I said, 'Listen, I'm doing this, but I have a very good career that's supporting me nicely, and I like it. And I'm not giving it up. So if that deal is not good for you, let's not do anything.' But he took the deal, and Carolyn took the deal too, but she didn't want to honor it. And so we had a lot, a lot of fights about that."[10]

Squabbles notwithstanding, Coleman and Leigh's work auditioning for *Gypsy* and drafting scores for *13 Daughters* and *The Wonderful O* had established them as a promising new team for musical theater, and Morris was simultaneously working to promote them to Broadway producers. Their collective efforts seemed to pay off in August 1959, when producers Cy Feuer and Ernest Martin announced they would be using Coleman and Leigh for an original musical called *Skyscraper.*

Becoming part of the Feuer-Martin "family" of artists at this time was quite the coup for the composer and lyricist, because the producing team had an almost perfect record of generating hits. Their success dated back to 1948, when they introduced composer-lyricist Frank Loesser to Broadway with *Where's Charley?* They followed this show with Loesser's *Guys and Dolls*, which would run twelve hundred performances and become a staple of the American musical theater canon, and then Cole Porter's *Can-Can*, which put future star Gwen Verdon into a featured role. Feuer and Martin produced a second Porter show in 1955, *Silk Stockings.*

In between these two musicals they also gave Sandy Wilson's frolicsome valentine to 1920s musicals, *The Boy Friend*, its American premiere, and with it Feuer and Martin had a hand in bringing to the United States a performer who would become one of America's most beloved screen icons. When *The Boy Friend* debuted at the Royale Theatre on September

30, 1954, it starred Julie Andrews, who would catapult to international attention a scant eighteen months later with her portrayal of Eliza Doolittle in Lerner and Loewe's *My Fair Lady*.

The producers stumbled with their sixth venture, *Whoop-Up*, which ran only fifty-six performances, but their reputation for taste and excellence remained undamaged.

In the *New York Times* announcement on August 28, 1959 about the plans for *Skyscraper*, Feuer and Martin were quoted as being "very excited" about having Coleman and Leigh do the score for this show about a woman who refuses to sell her brownstone to developers wanting to demolish it to make way for a high-rise. It was to have originally been written by none other than Rodgers and Hammerstein, but because the songwriting greats had been working on two others shows, *Flower Drum Song* and *The Sound of Music*, they had stepped away from the project and allowed Feuer and Martin to search for a new writing team.

Ultimately, *Skyscraper*, which was to have opened during the winter of the 1959–60 season, quietly faded into the background after Feuer and Martin announced another venture: a musical version of Elmer Rice's 1945 play *Dream Girl*, which would have a book by the Pulitzer Prize–winning dramatist himself and music and lyrics by Coleman and Leigh, who had been shifted away from their previous assignment. In addition, the producers announced that this new musical would star Carol Channing, who had captured audiences' and critics' attention with her performance as Lorelei Lee in *Gentlemen Prefer Blondes* some ten years earlier.

Dream Girl centers on Georgina, an aspiring novelist who escapes the realities of her life in daydreams. Ultimately, however, she learns that in order to achieve real happiness, she has to stop fantasizing about what could be and embrace the truth of the world around her. Rice, who in the 1920s had written *The Adding Machine*, a seminal drama about the dehumanization of workers in a quickly modernizing workplace, experimented with form again in *Dream Girl*, which, as either play or musical, was meant to be a fluid experience for audiences, with naturalistic scenes giving way to heightened imaginary ones within the space of a line or two.

Coleman and Leigh, seemingly inspired by the wealth of possibilities provided by Rice's plot, developed a range of song ideas. They outlined "Gemutlichkeit" for a Tyrolean fantasy. They also started work on two songs for the heroine, "Spare Me Your Kindness, Sir" and "In My Inimitable Way." For the book critic who disdains Georgina's worldview and also becomes the man to whom Georgina finds herself begrudgingly drawn, Leigh drafted two sets of lyrics: one for a song to be called "Reading the Blurb" and another for a tune that would explain his methodology for writing a review.

Sadly, little of what Coleman might have contemplated for these songs exists either as drafts in his files or in demo recordings. One explanation might be that Coleman was suffering from an apparently crippling writer's block during the first few months of 1960, even as Leigh was working on her lyrics.

In a letter to Bud Morris dated March 7, Leigh wrote: "He told me several times that he hadn't the 'heart' right now to sit down and right [*sic*] 'just' songs—although he wasn't sure he'd always feel that way." Leigh doesn't mention *Dream Girl* in the three-page letter, but she does write about a conversation she'd had with the singer Andy Williams: "I mentioned when he asked what other pop stuff I had, that I was set on writing 'The Rules of the Road'—and he leaped immediately at the idea . . . [he] wants to see it the moment it's even half done. Now if only Cy would try some more. . . . He's given it a little time, but I know that what he said is true. . . . His heart isn't in it."[11]

Leigh offers some speculations about what might have been troubling Cy. She wonders about his ongoing analysis: "I know from what people tell me it's a difficult thing to go through." Furthermore, she considers the frustrations that he might have been having with the meetings regarding Broadway projects: "He's as anxious to have a hit song as anyone—but he labels working at it futile."[12]

Coleman confirmed the feeling in public just a few weeks before Leigh's letter. In one of his regularly syndicated "My New York" columns, Mel Heimer reported on a conversation he'd had with the songwriter: "'I've been attending more darned meetings,' Cy said as we sat back and listened amiably to Clyde McCoy's chiseled corn, 'and have had my head filled with more darned suggestions. Gee, the other day, I finally got so weary that I just said—kind of pathetically, I suppose—'Hey, fellows, can I just go home and write some music now?'"[13]

There's no record of how or exactly when Coleman pulled himself back to the piano to write, but news in the *New York Times* on April 12, 1960—just five weeks after Leigh's letter to Morris—must have had a hand in his return to work and helped, at least in part, to dispel some of the futility he had been feeling.

10

Wildcat

C oleman's sense of futility about endless meetings and no time for
songwriting came to an end in early 1960, when he and Carolyn
Leigh found themselves on a fast track to a Broadway opening
for a musical that would star Lucille Ball.

For years Ball had been the toast of television in the iconic series *I Love
Lucy*, playing the lovably antic Lucy Ricardo opposite real-life husband
Desi Arnaz's Ricky Ricardo. Before this she had made a host of films but
had done little work onstage. Coincidentally, one of her primary theater
credits was a production of Elmer Rice's *Dream Girl* that had toured the
summer stock circuit in the late 1940s.

Reports of Ball's desire to appear on Broadway had circulated before
1960. At one point it seemed that a stage version of Dorothy Parker's
short story *Big Blonde* would be the vehicle that would help the star realize her goal. This drama, however, turned out not to be the show that
would bring America's most beloved redhead to the Great White Way,
and in an early March column Hedda Hopper delivered the news about
the show that would. "Lucille Ball's new play will be a musical titled *Wildcat*, which Richard Nash has written. Jimmy Van Heusen and Sammy
Cahn are doing the music, and Michael Kidd will direct."[1]

Hopper's announcement came just one week after another major story
about the actress broke: on March 3 Ball filed for divorce from Arnaz.
This was news that made the front pages of papers around the country
and also ensured that any show Ball chose would be heavily reported on.

By the end of March, Ball was throwing herself fully into a life that would not involve her husband, business partner, and costar, and she traveled to New York to begin discussions about *Wildcat* and start the preparations for her relocation from California. During an interview on this trip with columnist John Crosby, she mused about the new directions she was taking with the show: "I've clowned a couple [of songs]. I've satirized a song. Now I've got to sing. I'm working on—what do you call it?—projection. I've got a two octave range."[2] Crosby's article also mentioned that Kermit Bloomgarden (who had been responsible for bringing such dramas as Arthur Miller's *Death of a Salesman* to Broadway) would be producing the new musical.

Within two weeks of the story, however, the team for *Wildcat* had changed dramatically. First, an April 6 *Variety* article—with the banner headline "New Writers Duet in Legit"—announced that Coleman and Leigh had become the songwriters for *Wildcat* and that their projects for Feuer and Martin, *Dream Girl* and *Skyscraper*, had been "put in abeyance." Shortly after this, director-choreographer Kidd and book writer Nash took over as producers, although the show's financing—almost its complete $400,000 capitalization—was ultimately provided by Desilu, the company co-owned by Ball and Arnaz.

Kidd, new to producing, was anything but a neophyte when it came to staging musicals. At the time he was represented on Broadway by *Destry Rides Again*, starring Andy Griffith, who would shortly become a television star in his own right, and Kidd had staged and choreographed the musical *Li'l Abner*. In addition, he had provided the dances for shows ranging from *Finian's Rainbow* to *Guys and Dolls* and *Can-Can*.

Nash, on the other hand, came to the show with no direct experience. He had never served as a producer before, and while he had written the screenplay for the film adaptation of *Porgy and Bess*, starring Sidney Poitier and Dorothy Dandridge in the title roles, he had never written a musical. His biggest hit to date had been *The Rainmaker*, which enjoyed a respectable run of 125 performances during the 1954–55 season and went on to become a film starring Burt Lancaster and Katharine Hepburn.

Beyond *Rainmaker*, which would ultimately serve as the source material for the musical *110 in the Shade*, with a score by Tom Jones and

Harvey Schmidt, Nash's track record on Broadway was spotty. He had had another five plays produced, but three of them closed within days of their openings. The others limped to runs of about two months, including *Girls of Summer*, which starred Shelley Winters and George Peppard and featured a title song by none other than Stephen Sondheim.

Nash had been contemplating the story of *Wildcat* for nearly three years. He originally thought it would be a play but realized during his development of the script that "the hoped-for vigor and color and American excitement of this material could be best captured in a musical."[3]

Nash's book, which evolved under Kidd's guidance, centers on Wildcat "Wildy" Jackson, a woman traveling through the southwest in 1912 looking to strike it rich in the oil business. At her side is her younger sister, Janie, who has a clear-sightedness that her sibling lacks. Wildcat pins all of her hopes for finding a gusher on one man, Joe Dynamite, an itinerant derrick foreman whom she has never met. Ball described what happens after the two meet: "We fight all through the thing. . . . Do I have to tell you what happens with [Joe] and me at the end?"[4]

Beyond Wildy's search for oil and her relationship with Joe, there is a second-tier romance between Janie and Joe's bosom buddy, Hank, and a subplot involving an erstwhile countess. Other characters include Sookie, the colorful old coot who owns the land that Wildy decides to drill on, and a corrupt sheriff, who is out to get his own portion of the riches the oil boon promises.

Once Ball committed to the tuner and preproduction began on all fronts, she decided to take on another project in an effort to distract herself from her divorce. She accepted a summertime movie, *The Facts of Life*, a gentle comedy about two old friends, both married to other people, who find themselves falling in love with one another.

Filming was supposed to take only a few weeks in June and July, but midway through production there was a mishap on the set. Ball, after taking a break, returned to a boat that was moored in a water tank for a new shot. As she started to get aboard, she slipped and struck her head against the edge of the craft. The impact was enough to knock her unconscious, resulting in a concussion. In addition, she suffered a long gash on her left leg.

After a brief hospitalization and recuperation, Ball resumed filming a couple of weeks later but then needed additional treatment for her leg injury after an infection developed due to a piece of nylon stocking that had not been removed from the cut. In short, she would soon be rehearsing a musical in which she would be dancing with a just-healed leg—not a promising prospect.

Despite her injuries and alongside her filming and plans for relocating herself, her children, and her household staff to Manhattan, Ball continued to be integrally involved in the preproduction process of *Wildcat*. Part of her work involved revisions to the script. Bill Brader reported on a meeting he had with Ball in June to discuss *The Facts of Life*: "There apparently are still some rough spots in the 'Wildcat' script, however. The interview was interrupted by a phone call during which Miss Ball had some pungent points to make about enlivening the play."[5]

Ball was also involved in casting. During the course of the summer, Kidd and Nash flew to California to hold auditions while Ball was recuperating. Some impressive names were bandied about in gossip columns regarding likely casting choices. Anthony Quinn, Stephen Forrest, and Stephen Boyd were all mentioned as possibilities for Ball's leading man, while performers like Julius La Rosa and Phyllis Newman were touted as being candidates for the roles of Hank and Janie, respectively.

Eventually, it was Keith Andes, then the lead on the television police drama *This Man Dawson*, who won the role of Joe Dynamite. Unlike his costar, Andes was no stranger to the stage. He had starred in the short-lived musical *Maggie*, and after touring the country in Cole Porter's *Kiss Me, Kate*, he succeeded the show's original star, the legendary Alfred Drake, on Broadway.

Other principals in the cast included Paula Stewart—who had attracted notice when she starred in a revival of Frank Loesser's *The Most Happy Fella* in early 1959—as Wildcat's sister. Clifford David, an actor who would go on to appear in shows like *On a Clear Day You Can See Forever* and *1776*, got his first Broadway musical role as Hank. Character actor Don Tomkins, who had been in the original casts of two long-running 1920s musicals, *Good News* and *Follow Thru*, came out of retirement to play

Sookie, and Edith King, an actress with significant work on Broadway in both new plays and the classics, was cast as the Countess.

Coleman and Leigh busily worked on their score during casting. They had signed their contracts in early May, and a few days later December 15 was set for *Wildcat*'s opening night. This timeline suggests that the team had about four months to complete their songs, provided that rehearsals began sometime in September.

In actuality, however, they had even less time, because Kidd opted to have a series of prerehearsals with the principals starting in late July and early August. The songwriters had to have Ball's numbers completed for this, and foremost on their minds was what they would write for their star—the first notes that the one and only Lucille Ball would sing on Broadway.

For a while they avoided tackling the task, writing other numbers instead. They also went through their existing songs to see if anything might fit into the fabric of the show, and in the process they dusted off a pair of tunes they had developed for *The Wonderful O*: "A Little What If" and "Bouncing Back for More" (although both songs again went unused).

Some of this work they did in the Catskills, not at the Kaufman Bungalows in Monticello but at the upscale Grossinger's in nearby Liberty, New York. Coleman's choice may have been intended as a rebuke to his mother, who throughout the 1950s questioned the validity of his profession. This changed with the news of *Wildcat*, as he told an interviewer in 1987: "When my mother read about 'Wildcat' in the *Daily Forward*, that's when she knew I wasn't wasting my life."[6] Coleman also mentioned in later years that his mother ultimately had been more interested in getting tickets to see Ball film her television show than she had been in seeing the musical he had written for the star.

As troublesome as all of this must have been for him, Coleman simply pushed forward with Leigh, and over the course of the summer they were able to complete nearly all of the required numbers. Their drafts and early ideas even went so far as to bring the presence of the southwest's Mexican culture into the score. For a scene in the second act centering on a fiesta they developed "Es Muy Simpatico," writing it in English, Spanish, and Spanglish. The song was ultimately not used (it was succeeded by the less linguistically challenging "El Sombrero"), but it did plant the seed for another Coleman creation that would reach the stage over a decade later.

But even with the bulk of the score under their belts, there still was the question of what the opening number for Ball would be. As Coleman put it: "Here was a problem: how to write for a woman who had five good notes. And not just any woman, but the biggest star in the world at the time. What is she going to sing when she steps out on that stage for the first time? She had to land big or else we were all dead."[7]

Finally, Coleman remembered, "Carolyn could see I was stuck and because she knew me so well, she figured out a way to take the pressure off. She said, 'Cy, let's get the specter of this big star out of our eyes. What if it wasn't Lucille Ball? What if you had to write the opening song for somebody who had just an ordinary amount of talent?'"[8]

Coleman immediately plunked out a line of music that he thought might be effective. It was straightforward, but nothing that seemed like anything the songwriters would want to put their names on. Then, as Coleman related, "One morning she called and said, 'You know that funny little melody you left with me. I have a really funny lyric. You are going to break up.'"[9] It was then that she sang the first words to "Hey, Look Me Over."

Coleman and Leigh continued with the melody and lyric, still not fully believing in what they had written. Their minds were changed, however, when they took this song, along with others, to their publisher, Buddy Morris. He adored what they had written and assured them that they had a hit song.

Eventually it came time for them to share what they had crafted for Ball. It was a memory that Coleman never forgot: "We finally met her in the publisher's office. What impressed me was that she was more frightened than I was."[10] He played through the score, leaving "Hey, Look Me Over" for last. After he played it, she was delighted with what she heard, and a major hurdle for both star and composer was cleared.

Kidd's prerehearsals took place in Los Angeles "at the Masonic Temple on Hollywood Boulevard. We started the beginning of rehearsals in Los Angeles, because Lucy lived there and it was easy, and she and her mother, DeDe, lived out near me in the Brentwood area," Clifford David recalled. He also distinctly remembered his first encounter with Coleman: "This very kind and just really all-around good guy came up to me and said, 'I'm so glad that you're going to be doing some of my songs.' . . . It was that kind of largesse that exuded from Cy."[11]

Once rehearsals shifted to New York, another member of the company met the composer: future television star Valerie Harper, who remembered him as being "a cute guy. He kind of looked like the guys I went to high school with. He was funny and wisecracking and warm . . . a Jewish guy. And he was so unassuming and [there was] nothing pretentious about him at all. I always remember him as being fun."[12]

Throughout rehearsals Ball reshaped the material, particularly the book. Intimations that Wildcat had been running scams were eliminated. Bits of comic business that had been centered on other characters were altered so that the laughs would belong to Ball.

Coleman and Leigh's score, however, remained largely intact. Ball's numbers included not only the brash march "Hey, Look Me Over," but also the wistful ballad "That's What I Want for Janie," the raucously comedic "What Takes My Fancy," and an antiromance duet for Wildy and Joe, "You're a Liar." In addition, Ball was featured prominently in four production numbers.

For someone who was admittedly neither a singer nor a dancer, it was a heavy load. And yet her much-lauded workaholic personality and dedication to perfection took over. She might have joked with reporters about her singing, "If you can take it, or if I can, I'll be singing 10 songs. . . . However I sing they'll hear me, darling, they'll hear me."[13] But she also had turned to Carlo Menotti, whose pupils included Judy Garland and Tony Bennett, for voice lessons.

Her work with the instructor did seem to pay off, at least when she was presenting herself to the press. A few weeks later she was sounding more sure of herself: "I'm not going to do any of that talking-off-a-song stuff the way some non-singers do." She did admit, however, to being relieved that "I'll have mostly funny or action type songs. That means I'll be doing a lot of cavorting around while I'm singing, and maybe that will keep people from paying too much attention to the quality of the voice."[14]

Coleman, however, was frustrated with the star's vocal abilities. This was, after all, the woman who would be delivering his first Broadway score. So for his own sake, her sake, and that of the production, he worked with Ball closely all through the rehearsal period. During this time she would sometimes ask him about what key a particular tune was in. "Knowing she wouldn't know the difference, I would say anything."[15]

Yet despite uncertainty about her ability to deliver the songs and the fact that she was still feeling the effects of her summertime leg injury, she persevered and must have been feeling relatively confident in her progress with the show. Before *Wildcat* had even begun its tryout at Philadelphia's Erlanger Theatre, she agreed to do a semibiographical television special, *Lucy Goes to Broadway*, which would also feature many of the regulars from her famous series.

When *Wildcat* had its out-of-town opening, Arnaz—Ball's soon-to-be ex-husband but still her business partner, close friend, and *Wildcat* "angel"—was in attendance, and regardless of what they thought of the production, theatergoers were thrilled to see him toss an orchid across the footlights as she took her first curtain call in the show.

The reviews, however, were nothing to cheer about. Ball herself called them "mild" but noted that the show played to "packed houses for the duration."[16] But the songs elicited praise, notably in the city's most prominent paper, the *Philadelphia Inquirer*, where Henry T. Murdock wrote in his review on October 31: "[The] melodies are far from stately; they have an occasional barrel-house growl. . . . 'Far Away from Home' and 'Tall Hope' should keep the balladeers busy." The November 2 *Variety* review also pointed to these two numbers as among the show's best and stated unequivocally, "The Cy Coleman tunes and Carolyn Leigh lyrics are an important asset [to the production]."

What the critics had trouble with was the book. Many noted that the show was running too long, but more problematic than that was its overall quality. Ball was "frantically trying to contend with a conventional, cliché ridden musical," as Ernie Schier wrote in the *Philadelphia Daily News*.

The process of rewriting began, and for Coleman and Leigh it meant losing two numbers and writing a new song to replace one of the excised tunes. In addition, they had to cope with the stumbling block of whether or not the show would have a title song before the production journeyed back to Manhattan.

The new song would replace a duet shared by Andes and David, the praised "Far Away from Home," in which Coleman's bittersweet melody is beautifully matched by Leigh's melancholy lyric about what a person must have in order to feel that he or she belongs somewhere. The song exemplifies the qualities that catapulted the team to fame, being simultaneously smart, slightly sophisticated, and a model of simplicity. In contrast, its replacement, "You've Come Home," is pleasant and certainly in keeping with the necessary sentiment, but it possesses a directness and bluntness that approach the saccharine.

It was in Philadelphia, too, that Coleman and Leigh wrote the musical's title song. In an early draft of the script, there seemed to be an ideal place for an exuberant number for Wildcat, just after she had realizes that she has done enough to get Joe Dynamite to consider working for her (and maybe even like her a little). For this moment the team had drafted "I Got My Man," and it was this number that morphed into "Wildcat," in which Wildy, still excited about potentially getting Joe's interest, sings about how terrific she is, with a full chorus of oohs and aahs behind her.

Along with changes to the music came alterations to the book, and as David remembered: "She was smart enough as a businesswoman to understand why people were coming. . . . They ripped that show apart to make it what people wanted, which was *I Love Lucy* discovers oil."[17]

David's admiration for this process could be considered surprising, given that it meant that he'd lost a number; but Ball's dedication to the show and her compassion for her co-workers won not only his respect but also that of the entire company. In her memoir, *I, Rhoda*, Harper recalled: "Lucy looked after all of us. The first time she visited us in our chorus dressing room, she was shocked by how grim it was. She came from Hollywood, the land of clean, well-lit dressing rooms, so she was unaccustomed to the lack of glamour backstage in the old Broadway theaters. When she saw the rough, dirty cinder-block walls, she exclaimed[,] 'I don't want you living like this. We've got to paint the room.'" Ball's "we" meant herself as well, but once the management learned that she was behind the movement, they stepped in to make the alterations. Harper wrote: "It was clear that she used her stardom to help us."[18]

As the show was gearing up for its run in Philadelphia—and before the repainting of the Alvin's dressing rooms—Coleman and Leigh's publisher was doing his utmost to make sure the public knew what they had written. There were no restrictions placed on the songs in the *Wildcat* score, meaning that any artist could record or perform them.

Thus, a single from the Scandinavian jazz trio the Swe-danes featuring "Hey, Look Me Over" was in stores just as the show started its run in Philadelphia. In addition, Rosemary Clooney released a single with that tune and "What Takes My Fancy" in late November, and a host of others were on the way, including several of the cut "Far Away from Home."

Morris's general professional manager, Sidney Kornheiser, summed up the effort of attracting artists to the material, saying, "If the show's a big hit, you haven't lost anything, and if it's not, you may have a hit record going for you at the very time the show can use a lot of action."[19]

In the case of *Wildcat*, Ball's presence was probably the only push the show needed once it finally opened on December 16—one day later than announced because of a snowstorm that had blanketed the Northeast, stranding three of the eight trucks carrying scenery, costumes, and props on the roads between Philadelphia and New York.

It was a night of nervousness for Coleman, who showed up at the Alvin Theatre in his tuxedo and mismatched shoes—one black, one brown. For Arnaz, it was a night to celebrate, and after the curtain had fallen he hosted a fete for Ball and the company at 21. Ball recalled the evening: "We sat waiting for the reviews to appear. . . . Finally I went over to Cleo [her cousin] and whispered[,] 'Let's leave. . . . I know they're keeping the reviews from me.' On the way back to the apartment, we stopped to pick up four or five papers. They were full of 'Welcome, Lucy' stuff but were tepid about the show."[20]

Indeed, the notices on December 17 were grim, particularly for Nash's book and the production overall. Walter Kerr, writing for the *New York Herald Tribune*, condemned Nash for having taken "the characters and the atmosphere and even the whimsy of his attractive play, 'The Rainmaker,' and transformed them lock, stock, and ranch-hands to musical comedy territory. . . . These aren't very comfortable in the broader, bolder humors of the song-and-dance stage." Robert Cole, in the *New York Mirror*, called the book "pedestrian," but like many of his colleagues he cheered Ball's arrival on Broadway: "'Wildcat' has its faults, but it also has the one-and-only Lucille Ball to cover them with her terrific showmanship."

The most cutting assessment of the show came not from a daily critic but from columnist Dorothy Kilgallen, who slammed it in her syndicated "Voice of Broadway" column the week after it opened: "[Ball] has absolutely nothing to work with; the book by N. Richard Nash is inexcusable." She went on to say that Kidd's staging was "appallingly old-fashioned" and condemned what she believed to be the caricature of an Irishman that Andes was being asked to portray: "If Mr. Andes played a Negro, with the same lines and direction, the NAACP would be down on 'Wildcat' like a ton of bricks."

Coleman and Leigh, at least, could take some satisfaction in the notices their work received. The reviewers' opinions might have varied, but at least there was a general level of praise.

The most lukewarm was in the *New York Times*, from Howard Taubman, who wrote that "only several of the songs by Cy Coleman and Carolyn Leigh rose above routine," and in the *Journal-American* John McClain delivered the assessment that "the music by Cy Coleman, with lyrics by Carolyn Leigh, has a certain brash and rowdy quality in keeping with the locale but again it falls short of eminence."

Frank Aston, writing for the *New York Herald-Telegram*, was more enthusiastic about the team's work: "Tunes and words are just plain healthy and happy, free of that theater pestilence marked by neuroses, syndromes and other signals of gloom." Richard Watts Jr., writing in the *New York Post*, came down on both sides of the score: "It is fortunate that there are Mr. Coleman's songs to fall back on," he wrote, but added that he thought Leigh had provided "less-than-brilliant" lyrics.

Ball's work with (or in spite of) the material was admired, and there was one other aspect of the show that received universal acclaim: designer

Peter Larkin's colorful, cartoonlike set, which included an oil rig that was constructed onstage each night and, at the climactic moment, gushed petroleum on cue.

In the wake of these notices, and to give the *Lucy* fans what they wanted when they arrived at the Alvin, new changes were made to the show. One of the first was the excision of "That's What I Want for Janie," the delicate, warm number in which Wildy lets her guard down about her dreams for her sister. It disappeared from the production within weeks of the opening. Perhaps the song made the brash Wildy too sentimental. Perhaps it simply was too much for Ball, who was almost constantly onstage and beginning to suffer from a variety of new injuries as she acted, sang, and danced her way through the show.

Swen Swenson, a dancer who played one of Joe Dynamite's workers, recalled: "She was forever hurting her legs, spraining her ankles. . . . Then, I noticed her feet were not strong. They were almost rounded on the bottom. So I started giving her exercises. Before she'd go on, I'd warm her up—bring her out on stage and give her very simple ballet to strengthen her feet and the legs to get the blood flowing."[21]

But Ball's injuries had nothing to do with the fact that she was not getting the gales of laughter that she had gotten used to while shooting *I Love Lucy*. She had discovered that by improvising and referencing the TV show, she could get the reaction she wanted. One night, when a character appeared in nightshirt and tasseled nightcap, like the outfit William Frawley sometimes wore on the series as a sight gag, Ball famously quipped, "Hey, do you know Fred Mertz?"

Given the success Ball had with such ad libs, Arnaz asked for Nash's permission to bring in Bob Carroll and Madelyn Pugh, the writers for the series, to see if they could remedy the situation. They wrote a host of jokes for Ball's first scene, all of which were greeted with silence. Nash remembered going to her afterward and saying, "It's a different medium, Lucy. It's early in the show, they can hardly hear you, they haven't accustomed themselves to the acoustics of the theater, to your voice coming over the orchestra." The writer continued, "She took out the lines instantly. That was a bad shock for her. In television, those lines had worked."[22]

What Nash didn't mention is that the person audiences were meeting at the top of *Wildcat* was unlike anyone they had previously encountered. Of course, most people had seen zany housewife Lucy Ricardo in some unusual getups, but only after they had been with her for a while in her generally immaculate dresses and suits. At the start of *Wildcat*, Ball, dressed in shirt and dungarees, emerged from underneath a dilapidated jalopy smothered in grime. And instead of her perfect hair, a mane of red locks cascaded down the actress's back.

Once Ball knew that scripted gagging wouldn't pay off, she relied on improvised clowning. During a panel discussion for the Drama Desk in January, she even "disclosed that she felt there were not enough laughs or funny lines."[23]

Another change also crept officially into the show's score. Eventually a brief reprise of "Hey, Look Me Over" replaced the title song that had bedeviled Coleman and Leigh, and neither it nor "That's What I Want for Janie" made it to the official final edition of the script. Both tunes were preserved, however, for the original cast album made for RCA Victor just two days after opening.

The recording session took place at Webster Hall, and, as was the norm, it was a daylong process, starting early in the morning and lasting until well into the night. A quip from Ball that day, now part of legend, gives a glimpse into her mental and physical state: "She walked into the studio in her mink coat and slumped against the wall grumbling[,] 'I have all the money in the goddamn world and I have to get up at eight a.m. to make an album.'"[24]

Then, in early February, Ball contracted a viral infection. She traveled to Miami to recover, and during that time the show went on hiatus rather than running with an understudy in the lead role. "Lucy is the one who made the show what it is,"[25] was the statement from a production spokesperson. Her condition became front-page news. The press also monitored Ball's recuperative period, including her active social life in Florida. Kilgallen wrote just a week after the temporary closure of the show, "Lucille Ball continues to do the Miami spots with comedian Gary Morton [who became her second husband], the chap who met her plane when she landed."[26]

Of course, not all illnesses require continual bed rest, and given that Ball came back to the show on schedule and made an appearance on *The Ed Sullivan Show* performing "Hey, Look Me Over" with Paula Stewart, her time away from the rigors of the production, regardless of how it was spent, appeared to be all that had been needed.

It was as if she had never left. Box-office revenues returned to the level they had been at before her illness, and as soon as it was released the *Wildcat* cast recording began climbing *Billboard*'s list of "Retail Album Best Sellers." It debuted at number 36 on February 15, 1961, and stayed on the ranking for twenty-eight weeks, peaking at number 10 and spending most of the summer in the Top 20.

By early April audiences probably didn't know that anything was wrong with the actress, at least based on the way she was behaving at the end of the performances: "[Ball] is now giving audiences a little bonus solo act at the curtain calls. She makes an informal thank-you speech, does a few bumps to comedy sound effects by the drummer, dances a little and then calls for another chorus of the show's top tune, 'Hey, Look Me Over.' The customers lap it up."[27]

On April 22, however, Ball didn't make it to the final curtain of *Wildcat*. She fainted during "Dancing on My Tippy Tippy Toes," the opening number of the second act. Shelah Hackett, who was a dancer in the show and also Kidd's assistant, finished the performance, and Ball did appear by her side at the curtain call that evening.

Performances continued as usual after this event, but just a little over a month later, during a Wednesday matinee performance, Ball collapsed again. By this point an understudy, Betty Jane Watson, was prepared and went on for Ball for the remainder of the show and for the evening performance, ending up finishing out the week.

Six days after the second fainting spell news came that the show was going on hiatus, effective immediately, for a full two months. It would reopen at the end of the summer. Ball was suffering from "a serious respiratory infection complicated by exhaustion."[28] The following day *Variety* reported that the idea of doing the television special that would have highlighted the show had been abandoned. Then, nine days later, Kidd and

Nash announced that *Wildcat* would not reopen on August 7 as planned. They blamed the closing on the musicians' union, which was demanding full salary for the twenty-six-piece orchestra for the nine-week hiatus.

Coleman pleaded with the union to reconsider its stance, to no avail. During a 2002 documentary on BBC Radio 2, he recalled the production's demise sadly: "So the show closed—a hit show—full audiences, 100,000 albums sold in the first six months, and that was a lot in those days."

Nevertheless, he and Leigh had achieved their goal of getting a production on Broadway. It had enjoyed a run of 171 performances and spawned a hit song that would itself be newsworthy for years to come. And though it might have been tempting for either writer to wallow in self-pity about the premature death of *Wildcat*, too much had been happening or was in development for them to allow themselves that luxury.

11

"The Best Is Yet to Come"

Coleman and Leigh's ambition and drive meant that they never allowed themselves to become so immersed in any one project that they neglected to pursue other writing possibilities. And so, even as they tackled writing on spec for some projects or began preparations, rehearsals, and production for *Wildcat*, their schedules were filled and their output was significant.

One of their biggest career hits, in fact, had its roots from the time when they were writing material for *13 Daughters* and *Gypsy*, but it didn't hit store shelves (or the charts) until the middle of the *Wildcat* run.

The melody started out simply as an instrumental that Coleman had written for his club engagements, where Leigh was frequently on hand as an interested audience member. Coleman's drummer Ray Mosca recalled, "She'd be sitting in a booth, right next to the trio. And she'd always be taking notes, I guess of tunes we were playing."[1]

Indeed, she was listening for potential material. Coleman joked about her propensity for looking for new songs in his work: "The fact is that [she] was such a voracious lyric-writer that I used to say, 'I have to hide my arpeggios from her, she'd put words on 'em.'"[2]

Coleman said that the tune Leigh had latched onto in 1959 was one that "was very fast and it went all over the place. And Carolyn came to me and said, 'I want to write a lyric to that.' I said, 'Carolyn, you're crazy. Who's going to do this?' She said, 'I can do it.' And I said, 'Nobody will ever sing it.' And so, we slowed it down and it became 'Out of the tree of life I just picked me a plum.'"[3]

That lyric, of course, became the beginning of the song "The Best Is Yet to Come." Once it was finished, toward the middle of 1959, Coleman made a demo of it, and he and Leigh sent a record off to Frank Sinatra (after all, they had done well by him as a team with "Witchcraft" and with other partners on "Young at Heart" and "Why Try to Change Me Now?").

Sinatra liked what he heard, but with one caveat: he felt that the song needed to be longer. So Coleman and Leigh developed an extension for the tune. Coleman recalled that he did something unusual for this: "I'd started off in the key of A-flat, and I ended up in the key of A. But it seemed natural and I thought, 'This is very unusual. How are we going to do the key signature on this? Is it going to be A-flat or A?' And I said, 'Oh, we'll let everybody else worry about it.'"[4]

Sinatra didn't mind the shift and agreed to record the song. But then there was silence.

About a year later, Tony Bennett asked Coleman and Leigh if they had a song that might prove to be as big a hit for him as "Witchcraft" had been for Sinatra, and they suggested "The Best Is Yet to Come." Sinatra didn't balk when they asked about Bennett recording the tune, so they sent it off to Bennett, who was immediately enthusiastic about what he heard.

He decided to record it as soon as possible, but, as he later recalled, "I couldn't get any of my usual top-drawer arrangers on such short notice, though I did find a writer who was able to turn it around overnight. The next day he dropped by the studio and unceremoniously dumped the chart on me about an hour before the session and then split. We didn't have a conductor, but Cy was there and when we started going over the orchestrations, we realized it wasn't what we wanted, so Cy rewrote it. When it was finally finished we knew we had a winner."[5]

It was a moment when all of Coleman's talent and training coalesced into an ideal whole, and his classical-music background provided the necessary tools for both artists to realize their vision for what the song could and should be.

The recording session for "The Best Is Yet to Come" took place at the end of July 1960. The resulting Columbia single—with another Coleman-Leigh tune, "Marry Young," on the B side—hit the market in early 1961, just as Lucille Ball was about to face her first bout of illness during *Wildcat*.

Critics gravitated toward the record from the outset. The *Billboard* review on February 27 said that the A side would be "on deejay turntables from coast to coast for many months." And a few weeks later *Variety* described "The Best Is Yet to Come" as an "excellent ballad delivered at the top of this singer's form."

Pretty soon other singers started to perform and record the tune. Peggy Lee had it in her act by the end of the year, and both she and Sarah Vaughan had released their own recordings of it within a year. Eventually Sinatra made a recording of it in 1964, including it on his LP *It Might as Well Be Swing*.

Bennett's rendition of the song, however, did not constitute its first major public performance. That distinction belonged to Coleman himself, who offered it up on the premiere episode of *Playboy* magazine founder Hugh Hefner's syndicated television show *Playboy's Penthouse*.

Hefner and Coleman had become friends during the songwriter's days playing in New York at places like the Playroom, and once he started his gigs at London House in Chicago, where Hefner and his growing magazine empire were based, their relationship deepened. It was during Coleman's second gig at this club that Hefner approached him about writing a theme song for a new television venture.

The show Hefner created had basically the same format as that of *Art Ford's Greenwich Village Party*, on which Coleman had been a fixture. Each week on *Penthouse* Hefner welcomed some of America's pre-eminent artists into his apartment (actually an elaborately realistic set on a soundstage that had cost the then-astronomical sum of $15,000, about $125,000 in 2014 dollars) for an unscripted, unrehearsed party. As Hefner said on the show's debut episode, it was "a sophisticated weekly get-together of the people that we dig and who dig us."

To set the tone for this weekly televised event, Coleman wrote "Playboy's Theme," a suavely swinging number that played during the show's opening moments. As with the set, Hefner spared no expense in recording the melody for the program. He brought together a forty-piece orchestra featuring members of the Chicago Symphony for the number.

The show was an astute extension of Hefner's ongoing efforts to establish the *Playboy* brand as a tastemaker for the era. Guests on the debut episode included singing legends Nat "King" Cole and Ella Fitzgerald; writer Rona Jaffe, who was enjoying the limelight as the movie version of her novel *The Best of Everything* opened; and comedian Lenny Bruce, who got to offer up his brand of "sick" humor without the meddling of producers and sponsors.

Hefner's efforts to ensure that the show had a spontaneous feel were largely successful. When Fitzgerald performed she paid no attention to the camera, giving the impression that she was just vocalizing among a group of friends. Bruce's conversation with Hefner sparked, albeit tamely in hindsight, and Jaffe found herself defending some aspects of her writing. It all was persuasive enough for a *Variety* reviewer, who wrote, "It convinced . . . that this was an actual taffypull, happening spontaneously."[6]

As for Coleman, he didn't just provide background on and perform "The Best Is Yet to Come." He also offered up some history on "Witchcraft" and delivered "You Fascinate Me So," while one of the many gorgeous Playmates who populated the show sat by his side on the piano bench ogling him.

During this broadcast Hefner said that he had started to think that he would release the show's theme song on a record, and by the end of the year a single was being test marketed in Chicago. By the beginning of 1961, Playboy Records' PB-1001 was released nationally. The disc's B side featured Coleman as pianist-vocalist, along with full orchestra, delivering a sparkling version of "You Fascinate Me So."

The success of this 45 led to an LP, *Playboy's Penthouse*, released by Everest Records just as *Wildcat* was beginning its full rehearsal period and as Hefner's show was going into its second year of syndication, reaching a dozen markets nationally. The ten-song album, featuring Cy Coleman and His Orchestra, offered up a brassier incarnation of the Playboy theme, along with covers of such tunes as Irving Berlin's "Top Hat, White Tie, and Tails," Thelonious Monk's jazz standard "'Round Midnight," and

"Just in Time," the Jule Styne–Betty Comden–Adolph Green hit from *Bells Are Ringing*.

Perhaps most notably, the album, described by *Billboard* as "nice jockey wax for hip spinners,"[7] also featured two other Coleman originals. There was "Dorothy's Dilemma," which began as a sort of mournful film noir–like number before transforming into a more mod, Latin-infused piece, the two styles cleverly illustrating the conundrum of the title. In "Tennis Bum Blues" Coleman created a dapper, swinging mood with piano and brass that managed to evoke the sense of crisp whites glistening under the sun as a match was being played.

Coleman's appearance and affiliation with *Penthouse* helped to define him not just as an urbane man about town but also as a man who was part of a social set that embraced the daring and new. After all, this program, like Art Ford's show, depicted parties where whites and blacks mingled. In an era before the civil rights movement, this was a profound occurrence, and Hefner said, "The appearance of black performers on 'Playboy's Penthouse' in a social setting in what appeared to be my apartment assured me no syndication in the still-segregated South, but it made me a hero on the South Side."[8]

It's a facet of Coleman that Mrs. Vanderbilt and the other guests at the Sherry-Netherland would not have expected when he started his career there in the late 1940s, although manager Serge Obolensky might certainly have seen Coleman's desire to branch out into such directions. He had, after all, told Coleman that he wouldn't allow jazz at the hotel, prompting Coleman to quit and find employment at the Shelburne Lounge, where the waitresses were clad in cellophane skirts.

In the intervening decade, however, Coleman had learned to shift fluidly between "uptown" and "downtown," starting with the late-night sojourns with Joseph A. McCarthy Jr., Veronica Lake, and appearances in the early 1950s at Cafe Society, whose motto was "The wrong place for the right people."

Coleman's sometimes immersion in the world below Fourteenth Street deepened as 1960 dawned, thanks to the new woman in his life, actress Sylvia Miles. When the two met she was appearing at the original

Circle in the Square Theatre in one of the hottest and most controversial shows running: the New York premiere of Jean Genet's *The Balcony*, which paints a scathing portrait of society as a string of dignified men, all representing different aspects of the upper crust, visit a brothel while a revolution unfurls in their unnamed country.

Miles, who would receive Academy Award nominations for both the 1969 film *Midnight Cowboy* and the 1975 picture *Farewell, My Lovely*, had been working steadily as a stage actress since the early 1950s. Among her other credits was Jose Quintero's staging of Eugene O'Neill's *The Iceman Cometh*, which starred Jason Robards and also ran at Circle in the Square.

The couple met, as Miles remembered, from Coleman being "around." She thought that Mickey Sheen, a drummer who also worked with the trio, might have introduced them. It was an era in which the seeds for the tumultuous decade that followed were being planted, as Miles put it: "The flower children and all were in the '60s, but what precipitated it was the '50s."[9] Among the people in their social circle were comedian Bruce, composer Burt Bacharach, and James Lipton, who at that time was playing Dr. Dick Grant on the CBS soap opera *The Guiding Light*.

After Miles and Coleman became an item, he often had to play the stage-door Johnny, and on some evenings he would wait for her at Alfredo Viazzi's restaurant Portofino, on Bleecker Street. It was there that he came to know Elaine Kaufman, who would go on to establish her own eponymous restaurant on the Upper East Side, a place that would serve as a watering hole for Coleman and many of his friends and colleagues.

"I've always felt that I deserve a special place on the long list of Elaine-philes since I was one of the very first to know her and banter with her about the world at large and the state of practically everything," Coleman once recalled about his time with her downtown. She could "make you feel comfortable when you're alone at a bar waiting for the curtain to come down around the corner, which I did, night after night."[10]

Portofino wasn't just a restaurant. Like many of the tiny eateries in the Village at the time, it was also a hub for the Off-Broadway crowd. On Monday nights there would be readings of new plays there, much like the ones that avid theatergoers could also find at places like the famed Caffe

Cino, where playwrights such as John Guare and Lanford Wilson had their earliest works done.

It was in places like this, and in the galleries and bars the couple frequented, that Miles remembered Coleman not only meeting future collaborator Lipton but also writer A. E. Hotchner. In addition, the fare seen at these venues—along with work at places like Julius Monk's club—was providing Coleman with a broad education in theatrical forms and styles.

The Miles-Coleman pairing attracted the eyes of gossip columnists, who chronicled some of their comings and goings at clubs around town. What they couldn't know was the playfulness that the couple enjoyed. Coleman would often recount how, in the apartment at the Parker Meridian that he shared with pianist Byron Janis, Miles would lounge nude on the floor, doing crossword puzzles.

Miles herself related one story to a reporter ten years later during an interview about her role in *Midnight Cowboy*. "What do you think of my chest?" she asked Coleman one night at her apartment. "Wonderful! Let's play," he said, meaning "Let's play chess."[11] (One of the centerpieces in her Central Park South apartment was a faux-antique chess set that she had made herself out of "linoleum, plywood and discarded dime store chessmen.")[12] Coleman's quip disarmed her: "And that's the first time I ever lost to anybody who didn't play well—I was that distracted."[13]

Eventually, however, the time came for both to move on. They had survived his rehearsal time with *Wildcat* and that show's opening. They had also coped with a particularly busy period in her career, when she was commuting by motor scooter between two downtown shows every night. She would do the first act of *The Balcony* (the only part of the play in which she appeared) in the West Village, and then perform in a revival of Tennessee Williams's *Camino Real*, which was playing in the East Village and featured her only in the second act.

Columnists did try to make the end of the affair stormy, but it wasn't. The two remained friends for years.

The printed "bust-up" notices—according to columnist Lee Mortimer, Coleman sent Miles a dozen red roses with the note "Say it ain't so"[14]—

roughly coincided with Lucille Ball's first illness in *Wildcat* and Bennett's release of "The Best Is Yet to Come" and "Marry Young."

These songs weren't the only pop tunes that Coleman and Leigh had coming out during this period, though. In late 1960, for instance, Fran Jeffries released the LP *Fran Can Really Hang You Up the Most*, which had a gentle Coleman-Leigh ballad, "April Song," on it; and Margaret Whiting came out with a tune they wrote in the spring of 1961, "On Second Thought," at the end of the year.

At the opposite end of the spectrum from these varied love songs is one other tune from the period: a jingle they developed for Newport cigarettes. It was a not-so-well-hidden secret that some of Broadway's best had been writing for Madison Avenue for quite some time. Coleman and Leigh joined the ranks of writers like Richard Adler, Frank Loesser, and Harold Rome with the tune, which, in a series of three different spots, proved remarkably versatile. It could be sort of rock 'n' roll for a younger audience and decidedly staid for an older demographic.

With all of this writing, it could have been easy for Coleman to put his performance activities to one side, but he didn't. His stints at London House continued in the spring of 1961, and while traveling to the Windy City might have been seen as an excuse to escape some of the *Wildcat* drama, he also did his own jazz cover album for the show's tunes that spring. The LP, *Cy Coleman Plays His Own Compositions from "Wildcat,"* hit stores just about the time that the show should have resumed performances after Ball's scheduled July vacation. As it was, however, the album came out just as the show was sliding into the history books, and Coleman and Leigh were moving on to other Broadway ventures.

For a while during mid-1961, it looked as if the next Coleman-Leigh score would be for a musical version of the gently satiric novel *The King from Ashtabula*, by Vern Schneider (the man who penned the hugely successful *The Teahouse of the August Moon*). Gore Vidal, who'd recently had back-to-back Broadway hits in *The Best Man* and *A Visit to a Small Planet*, was slated to write the adaptation. Morton Da Costa, who staged *The Music Man* and who was busy with the movie version of the Meredith Willson show, was announced as the director for *Ashtabula*.

But almost as quickly as the show hit the news it faded. In its wake came word of another tuner, one that would reunite Coleman and Leigh with Feuer and Martin, the producers who had planned on giving them their first Main Stem outing. It would also introduce the duo to a book writer who, like themselves, had just one Broadway credit to his name—Neil Simon—while bringing Coleman and Leigh face to face with another of America's most beloved comedians, Sid Caesar.

12

Little Me

For a good part of the late 1950s one of the most famous little boys in the world was Patrick Dennis, a child who had found himself in the care of his flamboyant aunt after his father unexpectedly passed away. Patrick and his new guardian had experienced the Roaring Twenties, the Depression, and the dawning days of the Cold War together with decided and often hilarious panache, and their tale was immortalized in *Auntie Mame*, which was published in 1955. The phenomenal success of the book inspired an equally successful stage adaptation, starring Rosalind Russell in the title role. She also went on to reprise her performance in the equally popular film version of the play. Yet Patrick Dennis, both the character and author, was the invention of Edward Everett Tanner, as was the author's "memoir."

In early 1961 Broadway producers Cy Feuer and Ernest Martin, smelling another hit, acquired the stage rights to Dennis's next novel nearly a full year before its publication. Like *Auntie Mame*, this new work of fiction would be comedic, taking a shot at the "as told to" biographies of celebrities that were all the rage at the time. Dennis imagined a star of stage, screen, and television, Belle Poitrine (which, translated from French, means "beautiful breasts" or "shapely bosom"), who would reveal her life to him, and as the book flap promised, she would be "pulling no punches, sparing no trivial detail." Belle's odyssey, much like that of Mame Dennis, involved numerous quixotic turns of fate and countless men, many of whom became her husbands.

After acquiring the rights to the book at the start of the year, preproduction began while the publication was moving forward, and on March 29 the *New York Times* reported that Feuer and Martin were considering Dennis himself as the possible book writer for the show. According to the paper, he would be writing an outline for the musical, and "should this prove satisfactory to Messers. Feuer and Martin . . . Mr. Dennis will tackle the stage transition." The paper also announced that the show would "probably" have a score by Coleman and Leigh.

Feuer and Martin actually had offered the show to the team, but they were not that interested in working with the producers, because, as Coleman recalled: "We were furious with producers Feuer and Martin. They tried to screw us up on *Wildcat*. So we turned *Little Me* down."[1]

For a brief while it even looked as if they had made the right decision, because not long afterward Robert Fryer and Lawrence Carr (who, ironically, had brought *Auntie Mame* to the stage) offered them the gig on *Ashtabula*. The official word of the project and a firm creative team came at the end of April, and by mid-May potential investors were being solicited and advised that "a possible pre-production picture deal may be set with Columbia Pictures."[2]

By June Feuer and Martin were able to announce two key components of the *Little Me* team: Neil Simon would write the book, and the show would star Sid Caesar.

In hindsight it might seem that choosing Simon was a simple decision, but it was actually something of a gamble, since he was still a relative unknown in the theater world. He had written only one play, *Come Blow Your Horn*, and though it had proven to be a hit, such seminal comedies as *The Odd Couple* and *The Sunshine Boys* and the films *The Goodbye Girl* and *The Heartbreak Kid* were still in his future.

But at the time he was announced for *Little Me*, Simon had significant experience writing for television. He'd been a staff writer for *Your Show of Shows*, which featured not only Caesar as a regular but also Imogene Coca and Carl Reiner. In addition, he had experience in his television career that prepared him for writing a musical: "After *Your Show of Shows* went off the air, I'd stayed with Max Liebman, the producer, who was doing a series of specials—two a month. The first would be a revue, with people like Maurice Chevalier and Marcel Marceau, international stars. The other part of the month we would adapt a Broadway book show: *Best Foot Forward, A Connecticut Yankee, Dearest Enemy*—all Rodgers and Hart shows. Some Gershwin shows. The books were dated, so we got permission from the estates of those properties to update them. It was another learning experience for theater: I learned to write books for musicals."[3]

The casting of Sid Caesar, on the other hand, was a major coup that on its face would be certain to draw audiences. *Little Me* was a triumphant return to Broadway for Caesar. He had been one of the performers in the 1948 revue *Make Mine Manhattan* but soon afterward took his comedic talents, honed in New York clubs and in the Catskills' Borscht Belt, to television. There he scored tremendous success, not just on *Your Show of Shows* but also with his own series.

Caesar initially didn't want to do *Little Me*; only Simon's insistence and vision for the musical convinced him. Even though Dennis's book focused on Belle, Simon was in the process of turning the men in her life into the show's centerpiece by having them played by one actor. It meant that Caesar would have the potential for creating a comedic tour de force.

In his autobiography *Where Have I Been?*, Caesar recounted how Simon convinced him: "You're the only one I know who has the physical strength to do it. . . . Besides, it's not much tougher than what you did on 'Your Show of Shows.' I used to watch you play four or five characters a night, with those quick costume changes just offstage between skits. Amazing. That's basically the same as what you'll be doing in this play for me."

Caesar agreed, and Feuer and Martin were able to announce the deal in mid-June 1961. They couldn't, however, commit to naming the songwriting team for the production. But before the month ended they were able to announce that Coleman and Leigh would indeed write the songs for the show.

It was an unexpected turnaround, and Coleman later recalled how *The King from Ashtabula* had fallen apart and the way in which he and Leigh came back to *Little Me*: "Vidal decided afterward he didn't like the musical theatre and the people who write in it, so he dismissed the project. We had to go hat in hand to Feuer and Martin and say we wanted to do *Little Me*. We did it and lost a part of the percentage for that little maneuver."[4]

Despite the to-do that accompanied their arrival on the project, Coleman and Leigh quickly started on the writing process. Feuer and Martin had announced that the production would tentatively open in the spring of 1962, meaning that rehearsals would begin sometime in late 1961. Thus, they had about five months to write the songs for *Little Me*, as compared with the three or four they had had for *Wildcat*.

As they had a year earlier, Coleman and Leigh retreated from Manhattan for their writing; but instead of heading to the mountains, they went to the beach. During an interview on Skitch Henderson's *Music Makers* radio show on WDBF Radio in the early 1980s, Coleman recalled, "We both had houses in East Hampton; it was on the Three Mile Harbor and her house was about twenty yards from mine. That was my daily swim. And I'd swim over to her house, and she'd come down to the dock and meet me with a towel, and we'd write, and then I'd swim home."

The assignment was on many levels a heftier one than they had ever had before. Belle's tale spanned some fifty years and involved a panoply of characters beyond the men who became her husbands. In addition, the show had the potential to make use of her work as a performer, meaning that Coleman and Leigh might have to write material for shows within the show. Beyond that, they had a leading man who had been painfully explicit about what he would and wouldn't do in the show. Feuer remembered, "'I am not a dancer,' Caesar declared, and 'I do not intend to become one.' He also was not a singer, which was apparent, and he declared that he would not sing more than three songs. 'I have an aversion to lyrics.'"[5]

Rather than daunting the team, however, these challenges seem to have inspired them. They ultimately would develop nearly three dozen songs for *Little Me*. Melodically, Coleman tinkered in a host of styles. A pair of tunes, "Big Man on Campus" and "Frankie Polo," gave him the chance to experiment with collegiate fight songs, the likes of which reached their stage apogee in *Best Foot Forward* with "Buckle Down Winsocki." Another tune, "Bluebirds," found Coleman humorously evoking the kind of dramatic romanticism associated with Max Steiner's scores for movies of the 1930s. Coleman also drafted a song at the opposite end of the musical spectrum, "Sophisticated Twist," a complex and jagged riff on the song that inspired the 1950s dance craze.

The songwriters didn't want to simply borrow from the styles of the periods the show covered, nor did they want to appear as if their work was judging Belle: "If you do not feel compassion, pity even, for Little Me, the show has failed. . . . The songs, several of them, seem mockery, seem satirical—but the spirit of understanding and warmth and compassion is beneath."[6]

Interestingly, Coleman and Leigh realized that they had two comic, period-sounding songs on hand, each from their days waiting for a Broadway break, that suited *Little Me*: "Be a Performer" and "Dem Doggone Dimples," from their work for *Gypsy*. After some tweaks to both, they added these numbers to the mix of songs for the show.

Both of these tunes ultimately became part of the final score, while others developed specifically for the project only found life after the show had opened. In one instance, a song that Coleman and Leigh began drafting over the summer, "When in Rome (I Do as the Romans Do)," became one of their final hits as a songwriting team, thanks to recordings by Barbra Streisand and Peggy Lee. In the other, Coleman simply cached a melody. The tune that he began as "Hollywood Hills Hotel" would later transform into a full number in *Barnum*, a show that would reach Broadway nearly twenty years later.

Over the summer, as Coleman and Leigh worked on the songs and Simon continued his adaptation of the still unpublished novel, Feuer and Martin were equally busy. Not only were they in the last stages of bringing *How to Succeed in Business Without Really Trying* to Broadway; they were also finalizing preproduction arrangements for *Little Me*. Perhaps their most important task was choosing the director and choreographer.

For the latter position, they turned to Bob Fosse, who was in the process of creating the dances for *How to Succeed*. Fosse was rapidly becoming one of Broadway's most sought-after choreographers, thanks to the distinctively sharp-edged yet remarkably fluid routines he created for shows like *Damn*

Yankees and *Pajama Game*, in which "Whatever Lola Wants" and "Steam Heat," respectively, were song-and-dance showstoppers. Beyond his work on these shows, he had also been a performer himself on *Your Show of Shows* dancing with Mary-Ann Niles, meaning that he would come to *Little Me* familiar with the production's star.

Fosse had, however, begun to crave more creative control in his work, looking to become a director-choreographer in the mold of Jerome Robbins. Unfortunately, his previous outing in this dual capacity—on the musical *The Conquering Hero*—had ended badly. He was replaced during the show's tryout. In his memoir *I Got the Show Right Here*, Feuer recalled in very simple terms the decision to give Fosse the double credit: "He wanted to become a director, so I gave him a credit as codirector."

In actuality, there was a bit more to getting Fosse involved. Feuer and Martin had announced that Fosse would do musical staging for *Little Me* a full two months before *How to Succeed* formally opened; but before accepting the assignment, Fosse held out for something bigger, and it wasn't just a directing credit. Feuer and Martin had to agree to—and ultimately did—sign a letter officially recognizing the newly formed Society of Stage Directors and Choreographers as a condition of his working on the show.

By October, and just a few days before the novel *Little Me* hit stores, Dorothy Kilgallen reported that Simon had finished the book for the show. Then, within weeks of the book's release, the musical was postponed. Rather than opening in February 1962, the show would reach Broadway during the 1962–63 season.

Earl Wilson and Leonard Lyons delivered the news of the delay in the show's arrival almost in tandem in early December, but neither columnist offered any explanation for the reason behind it. In an article in *Back Stage* on December 8, 1961, the postponement of *Little Me* (along with two other shows that had planned spring debuts) was attributed to the health of the 1961–62 theater season. The article went on to speculate that other shows would also be rescheduled owing to a shortage of available houses. In one instance, the premiere of Richard Rodgers's musical *No Strings* was believed to be dependent on the closing of *My Fair Lady*.

Both Caesar and Coleman took advantage of the new timeline for the production to take on other projects. Caesar agreed to appear in the film *It's a Mad, Mad, Mad, Mad World* and accepted an offer to do a series of television specials. For Coleman, the news meant that he could pursue several opportunities as a performer. In January 1962 he flew to Chicago to record the album *Broadway Pianorama*, and while he was there he also spent a night accompanying his friend Claire Hogan as she opened a stint at Mister Kelly's, a club owned by the men who also ran London House, the venue where he had become a regular.

For Feuer and Martin, shifting *Little Me* meant they were no longer facing the possibility of having a second show opening that could potentially compete for audiences and awards with their gargantuan hit *How to Succeed*. Shrewd businessmen that they were, they most likely also counted on being able to take full advantage of the publicity that the book itself was generating as it climbed the *New York Times* best-seller list alongside works like Harper Lee's *To Kill a Mockingbird* and J. D. Salinger's *Franny and Zooey*.

Publicity for the gestating musical could also be had from the search for the show's leading lady—or, as it turned out, leading ladies. Because expectations were that the heroine of the book would become a plum role by the time *Little Me* hit the stage, politicking and auditioning for the part began even before the novel was published. Caesar reportedly wanted Patricia Barry, with whom he had worked on *GE Theater*, to play the woman his characters would marry or almost marry.

By the end of 1961 Earl Wilson reported that Feuer had "tested 150 gals for 'Belle Poitrine' in 'Little Me,'"[7] including risqué singer Belle Barth. But he still he hadn't found the right actress. In short order columnists, along with performers themselves, began their own campaigns for the role. In a Christmas wish list in *Back Stage*, Michael Sean O'Shea asked the producers to cast Tony winner Dolores Gray, who had most recently starred in *Destry Rides Again* opposite Andy Griffith. Early in 1962 Wilson informed his readers that "Julie Wilson, in a blonde wig, auditioned for 'Little Me.'"[8] A few days later Dorothy Kilgallen chimed in on the casting process, writing, "Patrick Dennis wants Annie Ross (the delectable girl interest in the Lambert-Hendricks-Ross trio) to audition for the role of Bell [*sic*] Poitrine in the Broadway musical version of 'Little Me.'"⁹

Neither Wilson nor Ross was mentioned again in the columns, and as spring rolled around, two other actresses—Edie Adams and Dorothy Provine—were reportedly being considered for the role. Adams seemed to be a natural choice. She had started on Broadway in shows like *Wonderful Town* and *Li'l Abner* before finding wider fame in movies and on television, where she appeared most notably with her husband, Ernie Kovacs. As for Provine, she would have been making her Broadway debut in the role, but in a relatively short period of time in the 1950s she had earned a substantial string of television and film credits.

Adams, recently widowed after Kovacs's death in a car accident, eventually pulled out of the running for the role, opting instead for a more lucrative engagement in Las Vegas. By the end of the year Provine would tell reporters that she had turned the producers down because of the role that she had accepted in the movie Caesar—and Adams—had made over the summer, *It's a Mad, Mad, Mad, Mad World*.

Other actresses whose names were mentioned during the spring and summer as being candidates for the role included Barbara Harris (still a few years away from her starring roles in *On a Clear Day You Can See Forever* and *The Apple Tree* but soon to costar with Caesar on his series of specials); singer Jane Morgan; Angie Dickinson, who had already begun her several-decades-long career as a television performer; and even Florence Henderson, who was then touring in the national company of *The Sound of Music*. According to *Chicago Tribune* columnist Herb Lyon, Henderson had even received a full week of coaching from Coleman.

The role ultimately went to Virginia Martin, who had delivered a breakout performance as the shrewdly vapid Hedy La Rue in *How to Succeed*. In his *New York Times* review of the show, Howard Taubman described Martin in this role as "looking like come-hither alabaster poured into garments that cling and caress."¹⁰ In other words, she was a visual ideal for the curvaceous Belle Poitrine.

As the summer of 1962 drew to a close, the producers gave a steady rollout of names for the other principals in the show. Nancy Andrews, who was Ethel Merman's standby and eventual replacement in *Call Me Madam* and who created roles in the short-lived musicals *Plain and Fancy* and *Juno*, was cast as the older incarnation of Belle. Mickey Deems, who had been playing the role of Moon in an Off-Broadway revival of *Anything Goes*, came on board for a heavy-duty assignment: not only would he play a host of secondary characters—he would also serve as Caesar's understudy. As for the other important man in Belle's life, her childhood friend George Musgrove, the role went to dancer Swen Swenson, who was in Coleman and Leigh's *Wildcat*.

Rounding out the cast were Broadway vets Joey Faye (*High Button Shoes* and *Top Banana*) and Mort Marshall (*Gypsy*'s original Mr. Goldstone), who played the Buchsbaum Brothers, a couple of producers who catapult Belle into vaudeville; and Claiborne Cary and Mitzi McCall, who played Polly and Penny Potter, a pair of sisters with their own act. Cary, Cloris Leachman's younger sister, had been in a previous Fosse show, *New Girl in Town*, and would go on to a healthy career in television and cabaret. McCall, who was just starting out, eventually settled into a career that included stints on *Laugh-In* and *The Twilight Zone*, among others.

The *Little Me* ensemble also included a number of future boldface names. Gretchen Cryer, who went on to a career as a performer-songwriter and is perhaps best known for her musical *I'm Getting My Act Together and Taking It on the Road*; Barbara Sharma, who would move on to a featured dancer spot in another Fosse-Coleman collaboration, *Sweet Charity*, before making a name for herself on television; and Michael Smuin, who would eventually found an influential dance company bearing his name.

Beyond the cast, the production boasted scenic and lighting design by Robert Randolph and costume design by Robert Fletcher, both of whom designed *How to Succeed*. Many expected that show's orchestrator, Robert Ginzler, to provide his services as well, but instead the job of creating the total sound for *Little Me* went to Ralph Burns, who began his career in the world of big-band jazz before he gradually shifted to musicals. Burns had had a few gigs orchestrating musicals before taking on Richard Rodgers's *No Strings*, which immediately preceded *Little Me*, but it was only with this score, so informed by Coleman's own jazz sensibilities, that the vernacular of jazz began to take full root in the Broadway pit.

It can be difficult to hear the innovative sound at work in *Little Me* more than half a century after its debut, because so much of what was new has become part of the aural experience of a musical. But there is one still-startling moment in Burns's work, and it comes in the entr'acte, when "On the Other Side of the Tracks" is played with a bossa nova beat.

Rehearsals for the show commenced in September, and Simon recalled the period as having "endless day-to-day rewrites."[11] It wasn't just the book that was being revised. Dancer Sharma recalled, "You'd come in every day and there would be changes and, of course, with Fosse you might do a very new show in the evening."[12] One number that proved particularly troubling for Coleman was "The Truth," which opened the show. According to copyist Emile Charlap, it "went through twenty-five revisions" before the musical bowed officially.

The process of revising *Little Me* was complicated even further by the need to craft certain aspects of the show to meet Caesar's demands. Fosse had to find ways of staging numbers that did not make him get up and dance; so in one, Caesar lay in bed and the production number unfolded around him. In another, Caesar's character was confined to a wheelchair, which the ensemble pushed as they danced.

And then there were Caesar's rage issues and the politic ways in which he had to be approached regarding notes. For his part, Simon "always followed the dictum, 'Let sleeping large angry comedians lie.'"[13] Another hurdle was the comedian's problem with addiction, which he referenced subsequently in both his autobiography and in interviews.

Eventually, it came time for the company to move to Philadelphia for the tryout at the Erlanger Theatre (where Coleman and Leigh had also been with *Wildcat*), and *Little Me* opened to the press on October 8. In the *Philadelphia Inquirer* the following day, Henry T. Murdock offered the most effusive of the write-ups the production received, proclaiming it was "the one we've been waiting for, that elusive, big one designed to restore the faltering pulse and make us screaming addicts of show business again." In a follow-up piece about the production on October 14, Murdock wrote that Feuer and Martin had offered theatergoers a show that "displayed more opening night potential than even their 'How to Succeed in Business Without Really Trying.'"

Other reviews were more muted, and the October 10 *Variety* assessment of the show initially deemed Coleman and Leigh's score merely "suitable"; but before the piece concluded, the reviewer added, "The songs seem to be spotted more for continuity values than their hit potential"—high praise indeed, since it meant that the team had written a integrated score for the picaresque tale of Belle's life.

Murdock's second story alluded to the fact that producers were concerned about shoring up the second act, and his information was correct. Over the next five weeks *Little Me* would boast a variety of numbers at the top of act 2, including "Smart People," performed by the Buchsbaum Brothers and the Potter Sisters. It was a clever comedy song for two couples about the fights they have had, but it was cut, as were the women's roles, before early November.

Then the creators tried "Don't Let It Getcha," a tune also performed by the Buchsbaums, along with Otto Schnitzler, one of Caesar's most gleefully crafted characters: a tyrannical German film director making a comeback on a feature film starring Belle. When this number went into the show, Caesar was well over the limit of three songs that he had agreed to perform when he first met with Feuer, Martin, and Simon. Eventually it was pulled and replaced with a pungent solo for Martin, "Poor Little Hollywood Star."

Coleman and Leigh weren't the only ones having to recraft their work now that it was in front of an audience. Simon, too, was making revisions, some big and some small. Two examples of the latter involve single lines that had to be changed. At one point, a character came onstage and announced, "War has been declared." Unfortunately, just after the tryout began, so did the Cuban Missile Crisis. Everyone feared that such a blunt proclamation could cause a panic, so the line was changed to "World War I has been declared."

Another tweak was to a line that worked too well. When Prince Cherney thanked the prosperous Belle for the money that had saved his country from bankruptcy, he did so by saying, as copyist Charlap recalled, "'I crown you Queen Nafka.' The audience broke up. 'Nafka' is 'a whore' in Yiddish. You know what happened after that? They didn't have one joke that got a laugh. And they had to take it out of the show. The biggest laugh they had, they had to take it out."[14] Simon ultimately replaced the title with the still funny but less disruptive "Countess Zoftic" (a play on the word *zaftig*, which describes a curvy, full-figured woman).

Such concerns, however, were minor compared to a bigger challenge the entire creative team faced. The show's act 1 finale, "Lafayette, We Are Here," wasn't getting the response they had hoped for. In this number Belle, along with the female chorus, arrived on the front lines of France during World War I to entertain American troops. According to Feuer, "It was a very nice song, everyone liked it, but like so many of these things that defy explanation, we just couldn't get it to work."[15]

Dance arranger Fred Werner recalled the number in a less flattering light: "'Lafayette' was just a disaster and nightmare, and Carolyn kept rewriting lyrics for it."[16]

Despite Leigh's ministrations and Fosse's own attempts at restaging it, the number simply did not enthuse or entertain. Soon word circulated through the company that the difficult number would be cut, but what the replacement might be was unknown. Sharma said, "It was a number with very heavy, skirted costumes, and it was a can-can number that you killed yourself in . . . and then nothing much happened at the end of it. And you knew it was going to be cut, and you had to keep doing it until it was."[17]

Indeed, the decision had been made. Feuer delivered the news that the song would be cut when "I called a meeting onstage after the show. Fosse, Doc [Simon's nickname], Cy Coleman, Carolyn, and myself. I said, 'I'm making the decision to cut the number.'"[18]

It was a declaration that exacerbated what had already become a very tense situation for the team. Coleman once bluntly recalled: "Caesar was going through a bad time in terms of his health and his habits. Director Bob Fosse and he were not getting along, and book writer Neil Simon and Fosse were barely getting along. Carolyn Leigh did not get along with any of them. It was one big fight all the time."[19]

From most accounts, Leigh heard Feuer's announcement and promptly made one of her own. She would not allow the number to be cut, insisting that her Dramatists Guild contract ensured that changes could be made to her material only with her consent. She and Feuer argued, and finally she stormed out of the theater.

Leigh returned in short order with a police officer—some say a traffic cop—and demanded that he arrest Feuer, Simon, and Fosse for their complicity in violating her contractual rights. The situation was eventually defused. Feuer remembered the cop as saying "Lady, I don't know what you're talking about" before leaving.[20] Others remember him asking for a couple of passes to come see the show. Further variations on the tale extend to its timing. Some remember Leigh getting the policeman after arriving at the theater and learning some lyrics had been changed. Others remember it happening while the show was in performance and culminating with the officer asking if he might be able to stay to see the second act of the show.

There is one consistent detail in the accounts of Leigh's attempts to find justice as *Little Me* evolved. She never demanded that Coleman be arrested.

Regardless of when this fracas occurred, there was still one question after Feuer's announcement about "Lafayette," namely, what song or number would replace it?

As the show moved closer to the point of being "frozen"—the moment when no more changes could be made so that the performers could settle into the show before the New York critics would see it—no answer was in sight. It was at this point that dance arranger Werner decided to pursue an idea he had been harboring for a while: replacing the boisterous can-can "Lafayette, We Are Here" with a gentle wisp of a waltz, "Real Live Girl."

"I went to Gwen [Verdon, Fosse's wife] and I said, 'How about "Real Live Girl?" And she got very entranced about the idea, and she said, 'I'll talk to Bob.' . . . She twisted Bob's arm. He said, 'Okay, I'll give you one day, and we'll put it in Monday night. And if it works, we'll keep it.'"[21]

The day Fosse had given Werner and Verdon was the company's day off, and the two of them spent it with the dancers. "She and I put the routine together and taught it to everybody, and it was a simple enough number so that the dancers could learn it very quickly. There were the finger snaps and all of that stuff—that was all Gwen. Bob had nothing to do with it. He didn't see the number before it went in."[22]

That evening, Fosse and Verdon waited in the lobby of the Erlanger to see what the audience's reaction to the change would be. Copyist Charlap was also there and recalled that after the male ensemble finished singing the number "the audience went into applause that you just wouldn't believe. Bob Fosse's there and he's listening and then . . . would you believe he did cartwheels out in the lobby of the Erlanger Theatre!?!"[23]

After this last revision, the show finished its run in Philadelphia and moved back to New York, where it settled into the Lunt-Fontanne Theatre on Forty-sixth Street.

For everyone involved, the opening night of *Little Me* on October 17 was fraught with tension, and not simply because nerves had been stretched to the breaking point during rehearsals and the tryout. They also had concerns about the audience that evening. A vast portion of the house had been filled with a theater party, which meant that some theatergoers would be late and, worse still, some might have overimbibed at the dinner preceding the show.

Simon described the scenario: "The house was half-filled as the overture started, two-thirds filled as the curtain went up, and the final three hundred stragglers filed in feeling for their seats in the half-darkened theater all during the first scenes." It wasn't long before one tuxedoed theatergoer roused himself and began to stagger up the aisle in search of a men's room, and as he passed Coleman, Simon, and Fosse at the back of the theater, "He screamed at the top of his voice, 'This is the worst piece of crap I've seen since *My Fair Lady*.'"[24]

The creators' worries were compounded by what was happening on the stage. Caesar was delivering an erratic performance, mangling laugh lines by changing words and coughing while speaking. Meanwhile, Simon recalled, Fosse was at the rear of the darkened theater physicalizing the death their work was suffering: "[He] very simply put his arms down at his sides, closed his eyes, and fell backward, every part of his body hitting the floor simultaneously."[25]

Because the opening for *Little Me* was held on a Saturday night, the creators, cast, and crew had to wait until Monday, November 19, until the papers ran reviews. When the critics' assessments finally appeared, they didn't mention theatergoers' behavior or Caesar's idiosyncrasies. In fact, most reviewers agreed that Caesar had made a triumphant return to the stage in the musical. "All Hail to Caesar!" proclaimed the headline of the review in the *Journal American*. "I Come to Praise Caesar" was George Oppenheimer's headline for his assessment of the show that ran in *Newsday* on November 21. In it he wrote, "[Caesar] has never been in righter form than in the various and hilarious roles that he plays here."

Similar sentiments were to be found in *Time* when the magazine's review ran on November 30. It began: "Caesar vanquishes Broadway in a one-man comic population explosion." The article continued: "It is more wonderful than getting a genie out of a bottle to have that full-grown master of comedy, Sid Caesar, released, at last, from that little 21-in. glass box."

Fosse's dances also earned accolades from many writers, particularly "Rich Kids Rag," which Norman Nadel described as "the choreographic coup of the season so far" in his *New York World-Telegram* review. Fosse's work on "I've Got Your Number," the solo dance for Swenson, also got high marks. John Chapman said it was "the highlight of the show" in his *Daily News* review: "As a performer, [Swenson] has the style and class of a male Gwen Verdon."

But even as critics admired the dancing and attempted to single out which of the seven roles Caesar was playing was their favorite (his turn as the German director was often the choice), their assessments of other aspects of the show weren't as glowing. Simon's book took some particularly hard shots. Melvin Maddocks, in his November 24 *Christian Science Monitor* review, described it as "cheerfully slapdash. Occasionally, it pretends to satire. But it has no more bite than a month-old baby." And in the all-important *New York Times* review, Howard Taubman wrote that the plot "plods as much as it romps."

Coleman and Leigh's work got kinder (but still decidedly mixed) no-tices. Walter Kerr said in the *New York Herald Tribune* that "controlled slyness slips in and out of Carol [*sic*] Leigh's lyrics and Cy Coleman's melodies without begging for favors or pushing the beat." And in the *New York Post*, Richard Watts Jr. described Coleman's music as "bright and attractive."

At the same time, however, their work was being labeled merely "stur-dy" by Associated Press writer William Glover, and in the December 1 issue of the *New Yorker*, John McCarten wrote, "The score, by Cy Cole-man, isn't more than serviceable, and the lyrics, by Carolyn Leigh, aren't long on originality."

The critics' reactions overall were best summed up by the UPI's Jack Gaver, who concluded his review by saying that it was one of those shows where "if you don't like the star, don't go. Caesar is the works," and by Maddocks, who wrote: "The aura of a hit has been so skillfully imitated that, in a business where hits, after all, are only an impression in the pub-lic mind, the imitation has almost the same effect as the real thing."

Theatergoers must have been eager for a chance to catch Caesar and to believe that *Little Me* was a hit, because from the moment it opened it did capacity business, even in the wake of a newspaper strike, which began only a few weeks after the opening and continued into March of the following year. Through February 1963, in fact, it was sometimes as difficult to get a ticket to *Little Me* as it was to get one for one of the other blockbuster hits—such as *How to Succeed* and Lionel Bart's Dickens ad-aptation, *Oliver!*.

But with the arrival of March the numbers at the Lunt-Fontanne box of-fice started to slide rapidly. Feuer and Martin hadn't committed to any dis-play advertising to promote the raves that the show had received, but with the newspaper strike grinding forward, it's uncertain whether keeping the show in front of ticket buyers in that manner would have been worthwhile.

They did, however, institute a first on Broadway. In a column in early March, Earl Wilson announced: "For the first time, a Broadway show is going to take telephone orders for tickets. ('Little Me' due to the newspaper strike.)"[26] Dorothy Kilgallen also announced the unprecedented step in her column that week, adding that "[Caesar] has promised to accept some of the calls himself between the matinee and evening performances."[27] The innovation worked for a brief period, but by the time the newspaper strike ended, the show's grosses had been cut by a third, and when all Broadway shows suffered during the Easter holiday season, the grosses were down by almost 50 percent.

There were some positives in what otherwise might have been a steady free fall. Just after the company of *Little Me* appeared on *The Ed Sullivan Show*, performing "Deep Down Inside," Coleman and Leigh's faux hoedown number with Fosse's exuberant choreography, the show got a substantial boost in ticket sales.

Similarly, the announcement of the Tony Award nominations for the 1962–63 season also helped boost the box office. *Little Me* scored a total of ten nominations, tying with *Oliver!* Coleman and Leigh's score got a nod, the first in what would become an almost unbroken string of nominations for the composer. With the exception of *Welcome to the Club* in 1989, Coleman was nominated for each of his subsequent Broadway shows.

Other nominations went to Caesar, Swenson, and Martin in performance categories. In addition, Simon was recognized with a nomination for his book, while Feuer and Fosse were nominated for their work as co-directors. Fosse received an additional nomination for his choreography.

When the awards were finally handed out at the end of April, *Little Me* walked away with only one: Fosse earned the fourth in a long string of Tonys for his dances. Caesar lost his bid for an award to Zero Mostel, another funnyman, who had made a mark that year in the rollicking *A Funny Thing Happened on the Way to the Forum*, and while it might be easy to assume that Stephen Sondheim's score for this show had trounced *Little Me*, it was Lionel Bart who took home the prize that year for *Oliver!* In fact, Sondheim's work was ignored in favor of the now mostly forgotten *Bravo Giovanni*.

A Funny Thing Happened, which had gotten nine nominations, actually ended up winning the majority of awards that season, including one for Larry Gelbart (Coleman's future collaborator), who, with Burt Shevelove, won for his book for the show.

Immediately after the Tonys *Little Me*'s slide at the box office accelerated perilously. When they looked back on the events of spring 1963, Coleman and his cocreators often mused about what the reasons. Some pointed to the fact that Caesar was not only doing a television show, which meant his fans could still catch him for free once a month, but also that he was doing one that wasn't terribly popular. When the monthly series of specials began airing on ABC after *Little Me* opened, the *Variety* critic gave the backhanded compliment that with the show "Caesar furnished an insight into human behavior, but generally failed in the entertainment sector."[28] And Rick Du Brow, in his UPI review of the debut episode, announced that the special "never reigned but it bored."[29]

But while potential ticket buyers might have wondered about the quality of the performance they might catch at the theater, they walked in knowing a good deal of Coleman and Leigh's score. As he had done with *Wildcat*, publisher Morris made a push to get the music out to the public early. George Chakiris (who starred as the Sharks' leader, Bernardo, in the film of *West Side Story*) recorded a version of "I've Got Your Number" infused with a seductive Latin sound, and both crooner Jerry Vale and the felinesque thrush Kitty Kallen did "Here's to Us." These records and others preceded the original cast album, which was attracting attention in the trade papers before the show hit its one-month anniversary, and just after the first of the year the album (in both its stereo and mono versions) was charting in *Billboard*.

Regardless of how the music was being received when separated from the production, Feuer and Martin had to figure out a way to keep the production alive. They attempted to shore up their receipts and gain some word of mouth on the show by offering twofers in late May, but in less than a month, and in a scenario all too familiar to Coleman from *Wildcat*, Caesar fainted onstage.

In this instance, however, it wasn't exhaustion that caused the star's collapse. Throughout the run, despite the rave reviews he received, he was plagued by his own "paranoia and lack of self-esteem." It got so bad that he began to believe he was contributing nothing to the show: "Even though I was getting applause through the performance, I'd listen to [Swenson's] applause [for "I've Got Your Number"] and say to myself: 'The people aren't coming to see me. They're coming to see Swenson.'"[30]

Caesar further admitted, "One night, in *Little Me*, the pressure finally did catch up with me. Someone gave me a new, strong tranquilizer. 'This will really give you a zoom,' he said. It gave me more than a zoom. I collapsed on the stage and had to be rushed, unconscious, to Roosevelt hospital."[31]

Understudy Deems finished the performance, and Caesar was back in the show the next night. But at this point the producers decided to post a closing notice, announcing that *Little Me* would embark on a national tour with the star, who, despite his personal problems, had committed a full two years to the musical.

The show ended its Broadway run on June 29, 1963, having played a disappointing 257 performances. For Coleman, the musical would remain one for which he had an ongoing fondness, and it would come back into his life frequently through the next thirty-plus years.

The musical was also one that ultimately provided him with two of his most enduring hits and one song that would become part of pop-cultural history. "Here's to Us" became a favorite of Judy Garland's, and she performed it for the final episode of her television series, *The Judy Garland Show* (although the segment was never aired). When Garland died in 1969, the song was so much a part of her life that, according to the *New York Times*, "Jack French, Miss Garland's musical accompanist, began the funeral with an organ rendition of one of Miss Garland's favorite songs, 'Here's to Us,' from the Broadway production 'Little Me.'"[32]

But as the curtain fell on *Little Me* on Broadway, such recognition could not have been imagined. Besides, Coleman was facing other issues and prospects, both personally and professionally.

13

"Poor Little Hollywood Star"

The events surrounding the rehearsal and production of *Little Me* took a toll not only on Sid Caesar; they also dealt a blow to the songwriting team of Cy Coleman and Carolyn Leigh. Under the strain of writing and then furiously rewriting and crafting new material, their already fractious relationship buckled. A feature interview with syndicated columnist Whitney Bolton that ran just before *Little Me*'s tryout gave them a chance to openly discuss their partnership.

During the conversation, Leigh admitted that arguing was "the best way for us." She went on to describe what might happen if she didn't like a melody that Coleman thought they should work on. She'd bluntly tell him, "'Cy, no. I won't write words for that.'" And when Coleman described their summertime of writing together in the Hamptons, he told Bolton that their proximity to one another was important, because "snarling on a telephone is empty compared to insults face to face. Besides[,] on a phone the other collaborator can always just hang up."[1]

It's the sort of humor that signals storm clouds in a relationship, and, indeed, within a month of *Little Me*'s opening, word of a split was in the papers. In early December Earl Wilson reported, "Composer Cy Coleman and lyricist Carolyn Leigh (who wrote the 'Little Me' score) had a most unhappy bustup of their writing partnership."[2]

Just after New Year's Coleman confirmed to Wilson the dissolution of his working relationship with Leigh, saying, "It had been coming on for a long time."[3] In later years, Coleman would describe the five years of their working together as being a "stormy relationship."[4]

As for the reasons behind what he once called "legendary battles,"[5] Coleman commented that it had to do with "my working with the trio. . . . Carolyn was very jealous of that fact. She wanted me all to herself. Carolyn was very possessive and she was tough."[6]

Leigh would also remember that their fights could stem from a variety of issues, both personal and professional. After much reflection she acknowledged, "We were growing up. . . . There were a couple of very sensitive egos involved."[7] As proof of this, one only need look at the alternating billing that they had written into their contracts for *Little Me*. In some instances, Leigh's name appeared first; in others, it was Coleman's.

Eventually, the two chose to forget what exactly had caused them to part ways. During a 1982 interview in *Newsday*, Leigh remembered the process of mounting the show as having been "stressful—to me, and I think to Cy too." And then she added, "I don't know what happened, but I know we came away from that not speaking to one another and with a music publisher [Buddy Morris] in tears. He built an office for us and the day he wanted to show us the office, we had split up."[8]

For Coleman, the dissolution of the relationship was so painful that he flew off to London immediately after *Little Me* opened and stayed there for a month, simply trying to sort out what his next steps would be. Before he left, he took another important step, filing papers to legally change his name from Seymour Kaufman to Cy Coleman. In 1982 he recalled this period during a WBAI radio interview with Paul Lazarus, "When you break up a collaboration, it's very difficult. You wonder what you're going to do. And then, you're not anxious to become involved in another."

The indefatigable Leigh, on the other hand, took little time finding another collaborator, and by the end of February Dorothy Kilgallen reported that Leigh and E. J. Kahn would be working on a new show together, *The Big Drink*. During the course of the year two other projects would surface. One was a musical version of *Roman Holiday* with Richard Adler. The other was a show called *How Now Dow Jones*, based on an idea of Leigh's, which she began with writer Howard Teichmann.

Coleman took a different tack when it came to regrouping; once he was back stateside, he started the process of reinvigorating his life as a performer. By February he had organized a quartet that was set for a three-week engagement at London House. Gossip columnists' tongues wagged during Coleman's Chicago engagement, because he was seen frequently with Claiborne Cary, one of the actresses who had been let go from *Little Me* and who was appearing in a revue at the Happy Medium, the club owned by Marienthal brothers, who also ran the venue where Coleman was appearing.

If there was anything romantic going on between Coleman and Cary, it was a relationship that was ultimately upstaged by his professional obligations, starting with news in March that he and Johnny Mercer would collaborate on a show together. In 2004 Coleman remembered discussing the idea of working with the lyricist: "I once said: 'Johnny, why don't we do a show together?' but he never had that Broadway feeling. He said: 'Okay, Cy, just send me the tunes to California, and I'll write the words.' He used to do that for people like Blossom Dearie; Johnny was very generous in that respect. But [for a Broadway show] it wasn't going to work that way."[9]

The idea of these two men working together is an intriguing one. An undated letter from the lyricist that Coleman held on to until his death indicates that Mercer had received a melody from the composer but had not had time to outfit the tune with words. It was, as Coleman wistfully recalled, "a deep flirtation never realized."[10]

In later years, Coleman would also recall ruefully one other collaboration that never came to fruition: one with Alan Jay Lerner. The men weren't discussing working together in the 1960s, but rather twenty years later. Coleman described what happened: "Alan Jay Lerner called me when I was in London and he was doing a play, *My Man Godfrey*. He was working with someone; he wasn't happy. He said he would like to work with me. And we worked together a little bit, but we didn't really write anything. But the girl that he married, Liz Robertson, was in *I Love My Wife* in London. So we got over there, and he became very fascinated with me, and somehow he missed me in the lineup. Then, he said, 'I think we can write something more important.' And I said, 'Great,' and then he went to the hospital and he died. . . . I'm sorry about missing that opportunity."[11]

But in 1963 Coleman was still without a writing partner, so he turned to composing instrumentals, including a score for an American Airlines promotional movie, *The Masters*. Filmed by Bernard Hirschenson (who had just done *David & Lisa*), the short was intended to acquaint audiences with the ways in which the company maintained its fleet. It used almost no dialogue but rather coupled footage with jazz backing, and a reviewer in the October 18, 1963 issue of *Back Stage* wrote that Coleman's work was "good enough to tempt a record album release."

The album didn't materialize, but a single did. Just after the movie came out, Coleman, backed by an orchestra conducted by Billy May, recorded the film's seductively jazzy "You Turn Me on Baby" for a Capitol Records single.

The disc was just one pairing of Coleman and May during the year for the label. They also went into the studio to record Coleman's second Capitol LP, *The Piano Witchcraft of Cy Coleman*. Whereas his first outing for the label, *Broadway Pianorama*, had been essentially a cover album, featuring tunes by the likes of Irving Berlin, Frank Loesser, and Cole Porter, *Piano Witchcraft* was dominated by Coleman's own songs.

Furthermore, the albums were conceived on two distinctly different scales. *Pianorama* was an intimate affair, featuring piano, guitar, bass, and drums, while *Piano Witchcraft* showcased Coleman's work as a composer and pianist on a grand scale. It's an energizing album—particularly when May's brass section blows the roof off with "Hey, Look Me Over"—and for anyone who wondered about what the tune for "The Best Is Yet to Come" might have sounded like before it was slowed down for vocals, Coleman's deft playing here gives a pretty clear indication of the melody's original tempo.

These two recordings—there was a third, *Comin' Home*, recorded in 1963 but not released until 1987—were not the only albums Coleman had out during the early 1960s. There were also singles and albums featuring his work for three feature films that were released during the period, a level of activity that almost made it seem as if Coleman was abandoning Broadway for Hollywood.

His first foray into scoring a feature film came with the indie *The*

Troublemaker, released in the middle of 1964. Directed by Thomas J. Flicker (who shared writing credit with Buck Henry), the rollicking comedy, laced with social commentary, centers on Jack Armstrong (Tom Aldredge, a future Tony nominee for shows like *Sticks and Bones* and *Passion*), a chicken farmer from New Jersey who comes into Manhattan to open a coffeehouse. He quickly discovers, however, that before he can get the place opened he needs to grease the palms of both government officials and members of the mafia. He refuses to acquiesce, and so his pal T. R., a hotshot, womanizing attorney played by Henry, concocts ways of paying the bribes unbeknownst to Jack.

But the good-natured rube ultimately catches on and puts a stop to the payola, only to find himself crusading against a corrupt world, often to comically surreal effect. In one sequence, Jack arrives at City Hall to complain to the mayor about the graft, and as he does, he inadvertently leads a group of picketing latter-day Nazis into hizzoner's office. In another scene Jack finds himself committed to a psych ward in which it's difficult to tell the patients from the nutty doctors.

Developed improvisationally with members of the Off-Broadway troupe the Premise, the movie, which takes some of its cues from 1930s screwball comedies, also features Joan Darling as Denver, Jack's kooky love interest; James Frawley, in a trio of roles; and a bevy of Playboy bunnies playing T. R.'s various girlfriends.

Coleman didn't just compose the score for *The Troublemaker*; he also provided the arrangements and conducted the orchestra. And more than in any of his previous pop or theater work, his zinging melodic wit shines through. For Jack's arrival in Manhattan, Coleman wrote a twangy banjo solo that both establishes character and the collision of two worlds (country versus city) about to take place.

Once the film's comedy kicks into high gear, Coleman lavishly uses brass to give Jack's plight a sort of circus feel, and for the movie's main romantic theme he developed an Asian-sounding motif, inspired by the curious fifth-century Manchurian outfit that Denver wears when she slips into something "comfortable" during an evening with Jack.

Coleman's eclectic work, including the kazoo sections of the music, was preserved on an LP augmented by a quartet of covers of mainstream film hits of the time, along with a vocal rendition of one of the *Trouble-maker* tunes, "Here I Go Again." The number, performed by China Lee (one of the Playmates in the film), featured a lyric by Tommy Wolf, who also wrote "The Ballad of the Sad Young Men," a hit for singers ranging from Rod McKuen to Roberta Flack. Coleman obviously had some affection for the unusually ethereal melody, because he also had it outfitted with a lyric by Edward Heyman ("Body and Soul" and "Blame It on My Youth"), resulting in the unrecorded "Roses in the Sky."

While *The Troublemaker* was limited primarily to art-house theaters in metropolitan areas, Coleman's next film outing, *Father Goose*, was a big-budget mainstream film starring Hollywood luminaries Cary Grant and Leslie Caron. The lighthearted romantic comedy centers on Walter Eckland (Grant), an American who is drafted by an old pal in the British navy to watch over a Pacific island and finds himself sharing it with Catherine Frenau (Caron), the daughter of a French diplomat and tutor, who has in her care a septet of girls whom she has been attempting to take to safety from New Britain. Dissolute and self-involved, Walter, whom the British navy has given the galling code name of "Mother Goose," finds himself turning into a "Father Goose" for the girls, as well as Catherine, with whom he becomes romantically involved.

Coleman got the assignment after a phone call from Grant, whom he had come to know socially. Coleman set off for California not at all clear about what he would need to write, but during filming he got his primary inspiration. He found himself watching the lilt in Grant's step, and from this came the inspiration for the movie's main song and theme. Once he had written the melody, though, he knew he needed a lyric.

Even though they hadn't spoken since the *Little Me* opening eighteen months earlier, he called Carolyn Leigh from California and asked if she would consider doing a lyric. She agreed, and he flew back to New York, spent some time at her apartment playing what he had written into a tape recorder, and departed. A few days later Leigh came up with the lyric for the song, "Pass Me By."

The song itself, sung by English performer Digby Wolfe, who had just moved to America and was attracting attention for his work in cabarets on the West Coast, is heard during the film's opening credits and then used in variations as underscoring and as Walter's theme. Walter even hums the jaunty tune throughout the picture.

One way in which Coleman used the tune was actually suggested by Grant himself. As Coleman recalled during a *Music Makers* radio interview with Skitch Henderson, "[Cary] was very helpful, by the way, he's a really very astute man when it comes to films. He said to me, 'How would you like a good musical joke?' and I said, 'Well, sure, I'll take it where I can get it.' And he said, 'Well, I'm in this small boat that's being followed by this big boat. Now, when you see me in that small boat, you give me that funny little theme' (which was 'Pass Me By'), and he says, 'Play it very small.' And then he says, 'Afterward, when the big boat comes in, go very, very big with the music. That'll get you a big laugh.' I said, 'It will?' He said, 'Yeah, I'll guarantee it.' So I said, 'Okay, I'll do it.'"

Coleman's use of Grant's suggestion made it to the final cut of *Father Goose*, and the composer recalled the moment "when we came to the preview, and it was a big laugh. It really was."

So, too, was the song itself—not in Wolfe's version, but in a subsequent recording from Coleman's dear friend and soon-to-be writing partner Peggy Lee. Their closeness is best illustrated by a night right after her version of the tune was released; as Lee recalled: "We gave a big party there, hoping, to be truthful, to break the lease. Cary Grant was the guest of honor. . . . At some point, we put on my new recording of 'Pass Me By' from 'Father Goose' and played it at full volume and marched down the hall into the elevator, continuing to march in place, outside into the lobby, around the lobby, back into the elevator and back upstairs to the penthouse. Cary Grant was the drum major, I wore some Indian footbells; Cy was, at least, a couple of trombones. Not only didn't the landlord object, he loved the excitement."[12]

Coleman's next film was a grander and more challenging assignment: a score for producer Russ Hunter's big-budget comedy *The Art of Love*. Directed by Norman Jewison at the start of his career (he would eventually be the man behind films ranging from *Fiddler on the Roof* to *Moonstruck*), the movie stars Dick Van Dyke (fresh off his success in *Mary Poppins*) and James Garner (in the early days of a big-screen career after his five seasons as the title character on the television series *Maverick*) as a pair of Americans living in Paris.

Van Dyke plays Paul Sloane, who, tired of eking out an existence in the City of Light as a painter, decides to return to America and his wealthy fiancée Laurie (Angie Dickinson). Garner, as Paul's roommate and best friend, Casey Barnett, tries to dissuade his pal from the idea, worried less about losing a pal than about losing the meal ticket that Paul's provided, since the two men have been living off the money Laurie has been sending.

Before Paul leaves Paris, he and Casey get drunk and muse about how funny it would be if Paul were to commit suicide, blaming the establishment for his lack of success. Casey scribbles a fake suicide note for his pal, who wanders off drunk. As Paul lurches away, he sees Nikki (Elke Sommer) plunging into the Seine. He follows her into the river to save her, and the two wind up on a passing barge. When an inebriated Casey discovers Paul missing and later finds Paul's discarded jacket on the bridge, Casey assumes that his buddy has actually killed himself.

In short order, as word of Paul's tragic demise circulates, demand for his artwork skyrockets, and when he eventually returns to Paris Casey convinces him to hide out at a nightclub (run by a flamboyant woman played by Broadway legend Ethel Merman) so they can both capitalize on Paul's "posthumous" fame. Complications arise when the police, unable to find Paul's body, begin to suspect foul play and Laurie shows up unexpectedly.

Critics greeted the movie tepidly and at times dismissively. In the May 12, 1965 *Variety* review it was described as "a garbled mixture of coquettish comedy," and the review in the *New York Times* on July 1 announced that the film had come "straight from the assembly line" at Universal. These sentiments were even echoed by one of the film's stars: Merman referred to it in her eponymous 1978 autobiography as "a featherweight comedy that sank like lead."

Nevertheless, the antic comedy afforded Coleman the opportunity to display his virtuosity as a composer in new ways. From the opening animated titles, which lampoon the cartoon sequences from *The Pink Panther*, to Paul's climactic sprint through the streets of Paris as he tries to set everything right, Coleman developed tunes that bring the Gallic and Continental milieu of the film aurally to life, as well as ones that gently echo the satiric tone of the movie. For instance, for the French detective investigating Paul's death, Coleman riffs on the sounds of Henry Mancini.

Coleman also borrowed from the styles of comic capers from the silent era. He even performed the rapid piano underscoring in these sequences when the music was recorded.

There is also one song in the movie, "M'sieur," that Merman performs in the club her character owns. The number features a lyric by a new partner for Coleman, Don Raye, who had written such songs as "Boogie Woogie Bugle Boy" and "Irresistible You" with Hughie Prince and Al Kasha, respectively. The Coleman tune, which Merman's character delivers as her club's scantily clad performers parade in the background, started off with references to their alluring physical qualities, but Raye's lyric proved to be too risqué for Motion Picture Association of America censors, and in its final incarnation the song (delivered in a kind of pidgin French) makes almost no sense whatsoever.

The score for *The Art of Love* ended up being voluminous. There were as many pages to it as there were for Stanley Kubrick's epic *Spartacus* (which was more than twice as long as *Love*), and when the time came to develop an album for the movie, Dave Cavanaugh (the man who produced *Piano Witchcraft* and *Comin' Home*) and Coleman decided that rather than releasing a strict soundtrack LP, they would take the music and fashion it into an album of orchestral melodies.

The resulting record was deemed a "sparkling entry out of the Hollywood scene" by *Variety* on July 21, 1965, and, indeed, a listen to the LP (or its remastered incarnation on CD) satisfies tremendously, particularly when Coleman's fantastically nimble fingers hit the keys.

The score also spawned a number of singles, as Coleman's tunes were outfitted with words by a variety of lyricists. Raye added words to the title tune, which was recorded in several versions, most notably by Eartha

Kitt, who gave it a sultry spin on a Decca 45 that had on its B side the theme for Sommer's character, Nikki, with a lyric by Coleman's old friend James Lipton.

Murray Grand added a lyric to a third tune, "Kick Off Your Shoes," an insistent jazz waltz, which didn't get a recording until a year after the film's release. When it did, however, it shone brightly on Carmen McRae's *Woman Talk, Live at the Village Gate* LP.

Grand also put words to a fourth melody from the film, "So Long, Baby," and in mid-1965 Leonard Lyons reported that "'Bricktop,' the nightclub singer of N.Y., Paris and Rome, just made her first recording, with Cy Coleman—'So Long, Baby.'"[13] The track was never officially released, and Bricktop's session with Coleman has in subsequent years been mis-identified as having occurred in 1972 because of a slip of memory in the singer's autobiography: when talking about her return to New York in the early 1970s, she wrote, "I recorded 'So Long, Baby' around that time. It was the only recording I've ever done."[14]

Coleman was testing the waters with other wordsmiths as well. During 1963 and 1964 he worked with writers ranging from Allan Sherman (best known, of course, for "Hello Muddah, Hello Faddah") to crooner Buddy Greco to singing sensation Peggy Lee. The results were songs that ran the gamut from goofy ("The Aardvark Song," with Sherman) to forget-table ("Take a Little Walk," with Greco) to modestly successful ("I'm in Love Again," with Lee as well as Bill Schluger).

The two biggest and most enduring successes from this period are another that he wrote with Schluger alone, "Pussy Cat," and "Sweet Talk," which paired the composer with one of the lyricists he'd gotten to know during the mid-1950s and *Ziegfeld Follies*, Floyd Huddleston. This song got a recording from Lainie Kazan, a rising singer who would eventually become romantically involved with Coleman and figure prominently in one of his 1970s shows.

Coleman would ultimately write only a handful of songs with most of these men; with Lee, however, he would maintain an artistic and personal relationship that would extend for decades. Still, no writer in the mix was measuring up to Leigh, or maybe it was simply that there were too many other things on Coleman's plate to provide him with the time to build a lasting partnership.

Another reason for Coleman's inability to commit to anything long-term with the men might have been the fact that his work with Leigh continued to linger in his consciousness, for a variety of reasons.

First, there were details surrounding the London premiere of *Little Me*, which was in preparations during the second half of 1964. The production marked Coleman's West End debut, and beyond the usual details of casting, it required that he and Leigh attend to and approve certain changes because the musical had been reset in England.

In some instances the revisions, made by Neil Simon and Herbert Kretzmer (the man who would eventually outfit *Les Misérables* with English lyrics), were minor. Secondary characters, like Noble's school chums, were given the more British-sounding names of Cecil, Daphne, and Lydia. Similarly, place-names were changed to make the comedy more instantly recognizable for British audiences. Noble and Belle, for instance, had grown up at the opposite ends of Highgate Hill, rather than in Venezuela, Illinois.

Beyond the changes to the book, which Simon was on hand to oversee (giving him the chance to search for two English actresses for roles in his next play, *The Odd Couple*), there were slight revisions to Leigh's lyrics to excise any overly American references. In "The Truth," for example, a mention of American film star Mary Astor was dropped in favor of one to the more contemporary Elizabeth Taylor and Richard Burton. Even the show's most familiar songs weren't immune from changes, including "I've Got Your Number," where "I know you inside out" became "I've got you cut and dry."

In one particular instance, however, the changes to *Little Me* were more substantial. The producer decided that the phrase "the other side of the tracks" would hold no meaning in the United Kingdom. A new lyric was written, and Leigh initially vetoed it. She ultimately conceded to the change, but with one stipulation: the song could never be recorded. Thus, the program for *Little Me* in London lists the song as "At the Very Top of the Hill," while the cast album for the show contains the number as originally written.

The musical debuted at the Cambridge Theatre on November 18, 1964 and starred British comedian Bruce Forsyth (in the Caesar roles), along with Eileen Gourley and Avril Angers as the Younger and Older Belles, respectively. The company also featured Swen Swenson, who reprised his showstopping performance of "I've Got Your Number." Critics and audiences embraced the production, and it settled in for a run of almost a year, during which time it also picked up the Evening Standard Award for best musical.

It wasn't only details relating to the show that caused Coleman to glance back at his work with Leigh. A song they had begun working on before the breakup was picking up momentum. "When in Rome (I Do as the Romans Do)," which they had drafted for *Little Me*, resurfaced at the end of 1964, receiving recordings by Peggy Lee and Barbra Streisand.

But while Coleman may have been hesitant about establishing any sort of lasting relationship with a writing partner in the years immediately following *Little Me*, he was demonstrating little indecision about taking charge of his career and the business of managing it. In 1964, following in the footsteps of such composers as Richard Rodgers and Frank Loesser, he formed his own publishing company, Notable Music, meaning that he could guide how his work reached the public.

In addition, Coleman was voted onto the board of directors of the American Society of Composers, Authors, and Publishers (ASCAP). He had been a member of the group since the early 1950s, and the organization's mission—to protect the interests, both intellectual and financial, of composers and publishers alike—was important to Coleman both professionally and as a matter of personal principle. He fiercely believed in the organization's battles, and through the years he could frequently be found lobbying—particularly on copyright matters—in the offices of congressmen and testifying in front of the legislators.

But even with this heightened level of activity as a businessman, a trio of full-length films, and over a dozen songs, Coleman still sought out additional outlets for his music, finding one in the Ford Motor Company.

His relationship with the car giant was a substantial extension of his brushes with corporate America that began with his and Leigh's Newport cigarette jingles and continued with his work for American Airlines. He had even appeared as a spokesperson for Lucky Strike in the 1950s. For Ford, however, his work was more extensive than it had been for these other companies. Between 1964 and 1967 he provided full scores for two industrial shows that launched new lines of cars.

In the first year, Coleman, with advertising executive Ed Birnbryer serving as lyricist, wrote *The Sky's the Limit*, a minimusical that ran at New York's Coliseum for seven performances. The company spared no expense on the production, converting the building's exhibition hall into a theater seating 2,100 and boasting a stage comparable in size to Radio City Music Hall. Such expansiveness was necessary for a production that had an ensemble of nearly fifty performers. Eileen Rodgers, who had starred as Reno Sweeney in the Off-Broadway revival of *Anything Goes*, headlined, and at her side were Jack Goode, Bob Roman, and even the African American dance team the Three Tapateers. Coleman composed a specialty number for them and songs like "Station Wagon Ramble," "Mustang Ramble," and the title number.

Three years later Coleman and Birnbryer re-teamed for a second Ford show, *Excitement U.S.A.*, for which Coleman served up tunes that encompassed everything from New Orleans jazz (for a Mardi Gras sequence) to Latin dance (for a number that compared Ford's products to America's burgeoning space program).

Birnbryer's work on the show certainly has verve, but it's nothing compared to the sort of wordcraft that Coleman had become accustomed to working with Leigh and Joseph A. McCarthy Jr.. Similarly, Coleman had enjoyed some pop successes with others, but not the kind that he enjoyed with the two writers who had been his principal collaborators.

That would change in short order, however, thanks to a relationship with yet another lyricist that he began cultivating in early 1963. At that point there hadn't been a fitting project for them to work on together, and so they bided their time until the moment was right. It came just a little over a year later, and it would serve as the basis for a collaboration that would last ten years.

14

Sweet Charity Onstage

W ell before Coleman's sojourn in Hollywood, he had laid plans for what would become his next long-term collaboration. It started at a cocktail party on the Upper West Side for a group of composers and lyricists hosted by Dorothy Fields. Daughter of the vaudevillian Lew M. Fields, she had begun her own theatrical career in the mid-1920s, working with Jimmy McHugh. Among their first songs together was the classic "I Can't Give You Anything but Love," heard in *Blackbirds of 1928*.

Over the next three decades Fields wrote words for songs with melodies by some of the greatest writers of the early and mid-twentieth century, including Jerome Kern, Sigmund Romberg, and Arthur Schwartz, and her work with these men resulted in American Songbook standards such as "Close as Pages in a Book," "I'm in the Mood for Love," and "Pick Yourself Up," as well as "The Way You Look Tonight," which won the Academy Award for best original song in 1936. In addition, she penned the books for musicals; among her biggest hits in this capacity were *Annie Get Your Gun* (cowritten with her brother Herbert Fields) and the Tony Award–winning best musical of 1959, *Redhead*, for which she served as both lyricist (to Albert Hague) and co–book writer.

It was a body of work that placed her squarely among the elite in songwriting circles, and neither this nor the fact that she was twenty-three years older than Coleman daunted him when he approached her in 1963.

As Coleman recounted for one interviewer, "I was at a party . . . and I met Dorothy Fields. And she was a legendary woman; she'd done all those wonderful things with Jerome Kern and Jimmy McHugh and Burton Lane. She was a glorious writer. So I walked over, and I said, 'I'm Cy Coleman.' And she said, 'I know who you are.' And I said, 'If I'm not being too forward, how'd you like to write some songs with me?' She said, 'I'd love it! Thank God you asked.' And I said, 'Don't a lot of people ask you?' She said, 'No, they're either intimidated or whatever.'"[1]

Earl Wilson got wind of the conversation and reported in a late-August column that "Cy Coleman's now collaborating on songs with Dorothy Fields." After this, Coleman busied himself with recording and movies. About a year later he received a call from Bob Fosse, who had been attempting to develop a musical that would star his wife and terpsichorean muse, Gwen Verdon.

Working with producers Robert Fryer, Lawrence Carr, and Sylvia and Joseph Harris, Fosse, had come up with the idea for a pair of one-act musicals, tentatively called *Hearts and Flowers*. The first half of the evening would be a tuner based on the Federico Fellini film *Nights of Cabiria*, as adapted by Fosse himself; the second would have an original story and feature a book by Elaine May. Fosse hoped Coleman would provide the music for both.

In Fosse's adaptation of the Fellini movie, the action was shifted to New York, and instead of centering on a prostitute, Fosse's version would focus on a dance-hall hostess, a woman who toiled at night dancing with strangers for the modest fee of, as the saying goes, "ten cents a dance," or, as had become the case in the mid-1960s, about $6.25 per half hour. Always hopeful and always on the lookout for true romance, the character in both is an indomitable heroine and a rather pathetic victim.

For the second half of the bill, May developed a scenario about an ex–circus highflier (to be played by Verdon) and her husband, who had once performed a human fly act. Other characters in the musical, which would be about a botched robbery attempt, included former circus performers as well as members of the couple's family, including their teenage son.

Coleman said he would be interested in writing the music for the two pieces and suggested that Fields serve as his lyric-writing partner. Fields had previously worked with both Fosse and Verdon—as well as Fryer and Carr—on *Redhead*, so her presence on the team seemed like a perfect fit.

Casting notices in March 1965 announced that rehearsals would begin for the two-show bill in early August, but plans changed two months later, following a backers' audition at Delmonico's. At this point Fosse realized the *Cabiria* adaptation would need more stage time, so May's portion of the evening—still unfinished—was eliminated, and the musical became a full-length adaptation of Fellini's film.

With this decision Fosse returned to an idea he had early on in his conception of the show: working with a playwright on the book. He had started the process with Martin Charnin (who wrote the lyrics to Mary Rodgers's music for the Judy Holliday vehicle *Hot Spot* and who would later collaborate with Richard Rodgers on *Two by Two* and Charles Strouse on *Annie*). After completing a first draft, though, Fosse withdrew from the collaborative process and continued writing alone.

Among the authors he considered during the middle part of 1965 were Abe Burrows (responsible for *Guys and Dolls* and *How to Succeed in Business Without Really Trying*, two musicals that had examined the grittier aspects of life in New York), Paddy Chayefsky (a friend of Fosse's and the screenwriter of such working-class dramas as *Marty* and *A Catered Affair*), and Hugh Wheeler (then at the start of his career but later the book writer of such musicals as *A Little Night Music* and *Sweeney Todd*). Wheeler drafted his own version of the first seven scenes of the musical but ultimately decided that he was not a good match for the material and withdrew from the project.

Even as Fosse searched for a collaborator, he continued to expand and rewrite the show on his own. Casting notices over the summer help to track the changes he was making. In July available roles ranged from a Jewish newspaper dealer to a Broadway columnist "with a poor memory for facts."[2] A few weeks later a new role was added: a "male film star, not too young, vain, spoiled."[3]

During the spring and summer Coleman and Fields tackled the score, writing much of it in the Hamptons. Among the first songs they wrote was a group number for the women working alongside Charity at the dance hall. It would eventually become known as "Big Spender." Coleman recalled the impetus behind this number in later years: "One of the things

Fosse and I fought about on *Little Me* had been the way he would add accents to the music that I didn't intend and . . . open up the songs for dance breaks in places that I didn't like. . . . When we started work on *Sweet Charity*, I decided that I would write a song that was full of accents—but accents where I wanted them to be. I decided they'd be written into the music in such a way that they were locked in and couldn't be changed."[4] The result of this desire to beat Fosse was a vamp that was all accents, and the now-iconic introduction to the number.

With "Big Spender" in hand—as well as a few others, including the Latin-tempoed "There's Got to Be Something Better Than This" and "I'll Take Any Man" (a number written early on but never used)—Coleman and Fields went to Fosse, who responded, "Sometimes you people make me cry," as Coleman recalled for BBC Radio 2 in 2002. It was praise that both gratified and galled Fields. Coleman, in the same interview, remembered, "Dorothy used to hate to hear him say 'You people,' and she'd get up on her high horse and say, 'We are not "you people." I am Dorothy and this is Cy.'"

The story serves as a terrific example of Fields's sometimes prickly nature, which also informed her work with Coleman. An early riser by nature, Fields would accomplish most of her lyric writing just as the sun was coming up, and when she had written something she wanted to share with night owl Coleman she would phone him, waking him up. Coleman remembered, "She'd get this kind of funny tone in her voice, you know, imperious, it was the only time she was like that, and she'd say: 'You're still in bed?' And I would be furious."[5] Eventually the two settled on a schedule that was for the most part agreeable, but Coleman would often sense her disgruntlement at the arrangement, particularly when he discovered that hiding the phone under pillows could forestall his hearing an early morning call.

Still, Fields's sense of humor matched Coleman's remarkably well, particularly when they hit a snag. "We'd be staring at each other so that my only recourse was to go to the bathroom," Coleman recounted while recording an interview for the ASCAP Foundation *Living Archive Series*. "And I'd say, 'I'm going to the bathroom,' just to break it. And I'd wait there, and I always came back with an idea. And so it got to the point where it became a joke. Dorothy would say when we were stuck, 'Cy. Go to the bathroom.'"

Coleman chose not to share this anecdote in August 1965 when he was invited to write a story about *Sweet Charity* for Dorothy Kilgallen's national readership while she was on vacation. Instead, he used the opportunity to discuss the general vision he and Fields had for the show, in particular how his work on *Father Goose* and *The Art of Love* had affected his own approach to writing.

He had come to *Charity* knowing, for instance, that he wanted to develop a musical motif for the heroine, and as he told readers, "In this show, Gwen Verdon has her very own theme which is inherent in the character she plays and is heard every time she moves so beautifully on stage." Furthermore, his appreciation for the ways in which underscoring could cue audiences' reactions and perceptions had deepened during his time on the West Coast.

But his most important consideration was creating "as tuneful a show as possible," and he guaranteed readers that they would be "hearing top recording artists sing the songs on records even before the show comes out."

Nothing Coleman wrote was misleading or hyperbolic flacking. He had written a delicate lilting melody that followed Charity during her misadventures, and there was a generous supply of music that ran underneath the action. As for advance recordings, Coleman—now head of his own publishing company—would certainly do his utmost to make sure that the songs that he and Fields wrote were in circulation before the show's scheduled opening. Sheet music for all of the songs was printed, and they were packaged and distributed along with an LP featuring Coleman and other vocalists performing a dozen of them.

Fosse didn't have the luxury of a partner off whom he could bounce ideas while writing (but Verdon was on hand at all times to work with him on the dances), and though he managed to expand the book to a full two acts, he still sensed he needed assistance, particularly because he felt that the show was not funny enough. It was at this moment that he sent the script to Neil Simon, whose rise among the ranks of writers for the stage and screen had been meteoric since he last worked with Fosse and Coleman, on *Little Me*. In the years that followed that show, his comedies *Barefoot in the Park* and *The Odd Couple* had debuted on Broadway, and his first play, *Come Blow Your Horn*, had been made into a film.

Simon, at the time Fosse reached out to him, was in Rome, on the set for the movie *After the Fox*. Simon started reading as soon as the script arrived, and as he read he realized that "it *desperately* needed humor," so "I sat down and spent one long night removing the lines that didn't work and inserting new and what I hoped were funnier ones."[6]

He sent his changes to Fosse and soon received another call. Fosse liked Simon's work so much that he needed the writer to continue working on the script. Simon protested, citing his commitments to both the film in Italy and the forthcoming film version of *Barefoot*.

Fosse, however, wouldn't take no for an answer and flew to Italy to play Coleman and Fields's demo tapes for him. When he got to the house Simon was sharing with his wife, Joan, the choreographer started by describing his vision for "Big Spender." Then he played the couple the tape of the number. "It was Cy Coleman's music at its best, and with it were Dorothy Fields' great lyrics—tough, funny, and Brechtian." After this Fosse played "There's Gotta Be Something Better Than This," at which point, Simon remembered, "Joan and I burst into applause. Then she turned to me and said, 'If you don't do this show, you and I are through.'"[7] Simon acquiesced (willingly and eagerly) and began working on the script while on the set in Rome.

Concurrently the show got its title, *Sweet Charity*, and its Broadway home. The musical would open at the refurbished Palace Theatre, the premiere home for vaudeville from 1913 to 1932, as part of the Keith-Albee circuit; performers like Fanny Brice, the Marx Brothers, and Ethel Waters, along with Weber and Fields (the comedy duo that featured Dorothy Fields's father), had all played there. But the showplace had fallen into disrepair after years of serving as a movie house.

The Nederlander Organization, which at that point controlled numerous theaters in Detroit as well as two in Chicago, had bought the Palace in an initial effort to establish a presence in New York and was financing the renovation and improvements. So *Sweet Charity* snagged a prestigious theatrical venue, but the theater was mammoth. To help ensure that the musical had "an intimate atmosphere,"[8] the producers decided they would not sell tickets to the Palace's second balcony.

In one regard, however, playing the Palace did prove beneficial to the production overall. After it was discovered that renovations on the theater would take longer than anticipated, it was announced that *Sweet Charity* would play two tryout engagements instead of one, beginning in Philadelphia and then traveling to the Nederlander-owned Fisher Theater in Detroit. Ultimately, everyone involved with the show would use the additional time out of town to incorporate important changes that would not have been possible with only the Philadelphia engagement.

Casting was completed while Fosse was bringing Simon on board and Coleman and Fields were finishing the score. Verdon would be joined by Helen Gallagher and Thelma Oliver, who would play Charity's best friends, Nickie and Helene, respectively. In addition Gallagher, who picked up a 1952 Tony Award for her performance as Gladys Bumps opposite Harold Lang in the title role in a *Pal Joey* revival, and who appeared in other shows like *The Pajama Game* and *Hazel Flagg*, would serve as Verdon's understudy. Oliver, who was getting her Broadway bow, had a number of Off-Broadway credits, including the musical *Cindy*. In addition, she attracted considerable attention for her performance in the movie *The Pawnbroker*, which starred Rod Steiger.

The *Sweet Charity* cast also included John McMartin, who worked with Fosse on *The Conquering Hero* and *Pleasures and Palaces*, as Charity's love interest, the nebbishy Oscar; James Luisi (who'd just been on Broadway in Richard Rodgers and Stephen Sondheim's *Do I Hear a Waltz?*) as Vittorio Vidal, the Italian film star who shows Charity an evening of kindness after meeting her outside of a discotheque; and John Wheeler as Herman, the guy running the Fan-Dango Ballroom, where Charity works. The company also featured a former Miss America, Sharon Ritchie, as the film star's fiery on-again-off-again girlfriend and Ruth Buzzi (who would soon be known throughout the country through her work on Rowan and Martin's *Laugh-In*) in a variety of comic roles.

As rehearsals began, Simon was still in the process of revising the book. Thelma Oliver recalled, "Right at the beginning, there were a lot of line changes that came. Almost at every rehearsal we were getting new lines, and mostly for the principal characters, including us, Charity's sidekicks. There were actually three of us to begin with, and in a matter of a few days they whittled it down to just Helen Gallagher and myself."[9]

Simon's book revisions meant that Coleman and Fields were also changing and cutting their own material. One of the most notable alterations after Simon became involved was the elimination of a scene set at a carnival where a hypnotist took Charity back to her childhood. It was a scene Fosse had adapted directly from *Cabiria*, and Coleman and Fields had penned a charming number for it, "Pink Taffeta Sample Size 10," which poignantly underscored Charity's intrinsically hopeful nature.

Another song that was jettisoned as Simon reworked the book was "Free Thought in Action Class," an ensemble number set at the 92nd Street Y, where Charity went to better herself intellectually. When she got to the Y, she overheard Oscar ask which room his class was in and decided she'd follow him, but before she did, she wanted to know what it was about. The receptionist described a self-analysis discussion group in which people are pushed into saying whatever comes into their minds.

For this scene Coleman and Fields had written a comic choral number, but in Simon's revision to the script neither Oscar nor Charity reached the class. Instead, the playwright imagined, based on his own experience, that the two got stuck in an elevator, causing Oscar's claustrophobia to kick into high gear. The result was a new song entirely, "I'm the Bravest Individual."

Simon's earliest rewrites contained another new scene that inspired one of the show's signature numbers. When they read what Simon had written for Charity as she luxuriated in the apartment of the Italian film star, they wrote, in short order, "If My Friends Could See Me Now." Another early change to the score came without prodding from Simon. Coleman and Fields, realizing that "I Can't Let You Go," a number that they'd penned for Vittorio was overly syrupy, wrote a new one with more emotional and musical weight, "Too Many Tomorrows."

Such instincts for fitting the songs to the needs of the show was something that Oliver recognized from the first day of rehearsals: "That's when I thought, 'My god, this stuff is really soulful.' I was surprised that it wasn't typically showy show tunes. It had some real 'ummph' to it. . . . And it made it so easy for me to actually just sink into the character."[10]

But even with daily changes, rehearsals never became as tense as they were during *Little Me*. "[We] avoided almost all of the problems of musicals in trouble," Simon wrote in his memoir. Even when Fosse and Verdon would develop new routines ad hoc, a generous, collaborative spirit prevailed. As Simon described it, "Cy Coleman often sat at the piano improvising variations on the themes of the score so to fit Bob's need in creating a dance."[11] Performer Oliver, too, remembered Coleman's energy for whatever might be needed: "He was just an amazing light. He was always like that. He never changed. No matter what kind of changes he had to make. He just never stopped being that bundle of joy."[12]

An overall sense of congeniality did, however, vanish when it came time for the performers to don the lavishly conceived and delicately created costumes by Irene Sharaff, who had just picked up her fourth Oscar for the epic *Cleopatra* (Sharaff would eventually have five Academy Awards, her last being for *Who's Afraid of Virginia Woolf?*).

The stories about Fosse's reaction to some of these ensembles (and the fate they fared as the dancers performed in them) are legion. Perhaps the most famous involves what happened when the ensemble stepped onto the stage for "Rich Man's Frug," a number that had been conceived along the lines of "Rich Kid's Rag" to mock the upper classes at play. Fosse took his inspiration from watching people at the hot club of the time, Arthur's, which was run by Richard Burton's ex-wife, Sybil Burton.

For this number, dancer Lee Roy Reams remembered, "[The costumes] were different colors and different styles, as normal people would be in a disco, and they were beiges and browns, but they were silk mohair. And we started dancing that number and we did the first big plié and you just heard [makes the sound of fabric ripping]. All the seats of the pants went out. The jackets all ripped. And the girls, because of that step where they lean back, their dresses had all of this trim, they were getting their heels caught in the dresses, and they had hand-painted tights from Paris that were like paisley and everything. One plié and the knees came out. We finished that number and we looked like we had just gone through a war. The clothes were just all ripped, and Fosse was going crazy."[13]

Something needed to be done, and Verdon came up with the solution. During rehearsals, she had been wearing a black shift, a slip really, that would look chic and also be functional for the number. Again, one of the potentially apocryphal stories about the *Charity* rehearsals goes that she taught the seamstresses how to quickly whip up similar garments on their sewing machines.

When talking about his mother and the potential veracity of the tale, Verdon's son, James Henaghan, said, "She would do things like that. She knew that stuff. That's kind of the amazing thing about her. That she knew how to do the costumes. She knew what kind of shoes would work. She knew that if a costume designer brought in a costume and said, 'Here it is,' she would look at it, and if she knew the dance, she knew whether or not it would work. And she would be able to not just say, 'I don't like it, it's not going to work' but rather, 'You know you have to cut it this way, and the seam needs to be here.' So I can imagine the tale being quite accurate."[14]

With costume issues mostly solved, as well as the potentially thornier issue of who would receive credit for writing the book (it was given solely to Neil Simon), the musical departed for its first tryout engagement at the Shubert Theatre in Philadelphia. After three previews the show opened on December 6, and the following morning raves began to pour in. Among them was Jerry Gaghan's in the *Philadelphia Daily News*, where he wrote that it was "the most enlivening first night of the season." Of Coleman and Fields's work, he said that "[they] have turned out not only songs with chart potential . . . but they have furthered the action with bright patter numbers."

In the *Evening Bulletin* the day after the Philadelphia opening, Ernest Schier ended his enthusiastic notice with "'Sweet Charity' is a dizzy, dancing valentine and never mind that it isn't the right time of year. It's always the right time for a bright, cheerful show."

On the day these reviews ran, the rush on the box office was so great that police had to be summoned to control crowds at the Shubert, where, according to a report in the *Philadelphia Inquirer*, "two patrolmen stayed in the lobby to supervise the lines of buyers." Once the show had become a standing-room only event, the producers even stopped running ads, because there was no need to promote a show for which no seats were available.

Along with the praise the show received came some cautionary notices about its shortcomings. In his AP review Norman Goldstein wrote, "Hopefully the expected Christmas trimming for 'Sweet Charity' will make it a polished gem before it gets to the renovated Palace Theater in New York next month." Heedful of his words, the creators embarked on the task of honing the show.

The critics couldn't have known about one particular issue that needed to be addressed: the demands that the musical was placing on its star, who found herself onstage almost all of the time.

Verdon, who was never particularly assured of herself as a singer, was concerned primarily about the number of songs she had to deliver. She opened the show with "You Should See Yourself," sang and danced up a storm solo in "If My Friends Could See Me Now," and had two lengthy ballads, "Where Am I Going?" and the highly praised "Poor Everybody Else." In addition, she was part of the trio in "There's Gotta Be Something Better Than This" and shared two duets with McMartin.

The two ballads in succession were the biggest problem, and as Emile Charlap, the show's copyist, remembered, "Gwen said, 'I can't sing both of them.' She gave them a choice."[15] Initially Coleman was unwilling to let either of them go, but eventually he conceded to the need for cutting "Poor Everybody Else." But it was a tune that Coleman held on to, and during the course of the next six years he would return to it as he developed several other properties.

Something was needed to replace it, however, and Coleman and Fields set about developing a new number that would allow Charity to express her ebullience at finding Oscar. The result was "I'm a Brass Band," a high-stepping dance number that allowed Verdon to take center stage with minimal demands on her voice. By Coleman's estimate, he and Fields completed the song in just a couple of hours. Fosse staged it as soon as it was written, and, by the time *Sweet Charity* opened Detroit it had what would become one of its signature numbers in place.

Reams remembered the changeover between the numbers: "With 'Poor Everybody Else,' she was singing it to herself as she was packing a suitcase, and it was a nice song. But when they did 'I'm a Brass Band,' because it was a big musical number with dancing—a big production number—it was much more valuable to the show. . . . The amazing thing is to watch creative people create when you're there, and how they came up with that song and what it meant, and then watching Bob Fosse choreograph off the top of his head, and us being onstage while he was doing it. I was just overwhelmed by that."[16]

Coleman's facility at developing new melodies was nothing new to either Fosse or Simon, but Simon had never seen Fields at work on a lyric, and looking back on the evolution of *Charity* he singled her out: "She was tough, all business, and could meet a crisis with the best of them. . . . It was easier for her to rewrite a song than to fight for one. And took less time."[17]

The show faced other challenges in Philadelphia besides the material: an injury. One night, in the scene in which Charity hides herself in a closet while the Italian film star reconciles with his girlfriend, Verdon inadvertently inhaled a feather from one of the costumes onstage. She didn't notice it when it happened, but a few days later she began complaining of problems breathing, and in short order her voice became raspy and she was feeling incredible discomfort in her throat. It turned out that the feather had lodged itself around her vocal chords, and while it was removed and she was recovering, Gallagher, unrehearsed, had to take over the role.

Verdon returned to the show and played the final Philadelphia performances, and then the company moved to Detroit for the Christmas season. The show officially opened on December 19, and the following morning the company once again found reviews filled with accolades.

Louis Cook, in the *Detroit Free Press*, said, "There are moments during 'Charity' when one has that tingly feeling of being present at great instants of theater history." Jay Carr's notice in the *Detroit News* sounded a more cautionary note. He found much to admire in Verdon's work but noted problems with Simon's writing: "The book's strength lies in its impudence of viewpoint, but its level of immediacy lags behind that of the lively, spirited dancing." Interestingly, while both critics cited the numbers that they favored most, neither mentioned either Coleman or Fields by name.

Following the opening the creators set about making their final changes. The process included Coleman and Fields revisiting one of the first songs they had written for the show, "You Wanna Bet?"—a number that had, as Coleman put it in an interview with David Kenney on WBAI in 2004, "a real beat under it." Coleman said that when he first wrote the music, to be delivered by Oscar, "The guy was very brassy. He was more like a Sinatra character." But McMartin, who was singing the song, was "more of a shy, inhibited guy. So, Bob said, 'We've got to change it,' and Dorothy said, 'The song doesn't fit him now.' And I said, 'Fine, let's write a new song.' But Dorothy said, 'No, I like that melody.'"

Coleman's response was to suggest taking out the beat, changing the title from "You Wanna Bet?" to "Sweet Charity" (since both scan the same). Everyone agreed, and Fields returned with the new lyric in short order. Such quickness on the part of both Coleman and Fields was one of the things that had cemented the relationship between Fosse and Verdon and the songwriting team. As Verdon's son put it, "[My mom] felt like privileged in a way and honored to work with somebody like [Coleman]. And I think that Bob felt the same way in terms of that, maybe more so because of his professionalism that Bob saw. I mean, Bob saw that he knew what he was doing, and they liked to work with people who performed and who weren't just all talk."[18]

The last musical revision to the show in Detroit did not, however, come as easily. It centered on the number that opened the second act, a revival number called "Gimme a Rain Check." Coleman recalled, "It felt terribly old-hat. [Fosse] did ten versions of that number and not one of them worked." Coleman knew that it was a number that could sink the show by the time it reached the Palace, so he and Dorothy wrote a new one—"The Rhythm of Life." "It was inspired by Bach with a lot of interweaving polyphonic musical lines and was quite a challenge for Dorothy. She worked at it like a jigsaw puzzle and put the lyric together one phrase at a time."[19]

Once it was finished (and while Fosse was on a trip back to New York), Coleman taught it to the ensemble so that it was ready for Fosse to hear when he returned. Fosse, however, did not want to hear "Rhythm." He vowed he would make "Rain Check" work.

Coleman's reaction was fiery: "I was furious. Finally I left him a note, and I told him, 'I've given up. You're going to die with 'Rain Check.' You've died every time you put on 'Rain Check' and you are going to die some more with it. Have a good time. I'm through.'"[20] The ultimatum was enough to spur the director-choreographer forward. When Coleman arrived at the theater the next day, Fosse had already staged half of the new "Rhythm of Life" number.

It was the last change to the score before the company headed back to New York in January to prepare for both the show's debut and that of the newly refurbished theater it would be playing. Anticipation for both events, among both public and press, was high.

In the days leading up to the opening, the newspapers were filled with stories about what theatergoers could expect in the historic building, which was becoming New York's second-largest legitimate theater. The Nederlander Organization had hired scenic designer Ralph Alswang to create a new lobby, and under his guidance it had reverted to its origins: "You now have the original ceiling. We had to break through plaster to get to it. We found crystal chandeliers 5 feet wide, 7 feet high, in dressing rooms and they now hang in the lobby." In the theater's interior Alswang used red as the dominant color in another attempt to make the gargantuan theater appear more intimate: "We use color architecturally to make the volume of the space seem smaller."[21]

Beyond the restoration, the theater was also outfitted with an exhibition that drew from the Museum of the City of New York's Theater Collection. Mementos, portraits, and caricatures were on display throughout the theater's lobbies and foyers.

On opening night, January 29, 1966, the theater was jammed to capacity, filled with "black ties, perfume and Paris gowns."[22] The performance, set to begin at 7:00 p.m., didn't start until 7:30 and was followed by a sumptuous party at the Starlight Roof at the Waldorf Astoria Hotel, where Columbia Records, which had invested in the show, taped interviews with members of the glittering crowd and released them on an LP to help promote the company's cast album for the show.

When the reviews started to appear, the cast and creative team found that they had a sizable, if not unqualified, hit on their hands. There was almost unanimous praise for Fosse's work. Norman Nadel, in a review that appeared in both the *Sun* and the *New York World-Telegram*, said that Fosse told Charity's tale "in the crystal-clear language of the dance, individual and ensemble." Stanley Kauffmann started his notice in the *New York Times* with "It is Bob Fosse's evening at the Palace."

Verdon's performance, too, received undivided acclaim. It was described as "glowing" by Richard Watts Jr. in the *New York Post*, and John McClain in the *Journal-American* said, "She has never been in better form."

As for Simon, who already had two hits (*Barefoot in the Park* and *The Odd Couple*) running on Broadway, he received some of the reviewers' strongest criticisms. In the *New York Herald Tribune*, Walter Kerr wrote that Simon's book "skimped sorely and unexpectedly on the comedy, apparently because bittersweet is to be the mood of the hour." Watts quibbled with the ending, admitting that he only wanted to see good things for Verdon, and in *Newsday* George Oppenheimer found himself admiring the fact that Simon's writing was both "humorous and tender" but concluding that the overall book did "not add up to a happy total."

The songs, too, garnered wildly divergent responses. In the *Daily News* John Chapman found the score "considerably above average" and even made mention of how the songs were "deepened with fascinatingly modern internal rhythms by the arranger, Ralph Burns." But Kauffmann's review in the *Times* read, "Coleman here joins the company of the many current show composers who supply appropriate rhythms but no tunes that can be remembered." As for Fields's work, Kauffmann added that she had written lyrics that were "no more than serviceable."

One of the things none of the critics picked up on was an instrument that had made its way into the orchestra pit of the Palace Theatre. To give the show its mod sound during numbers like "Rich Man's Frug" and "The Rhythm of Life," an early synthesizer from the Chicago-based company Cordovox was being used. In some interviews later in his life, Coleman would claim that by using this device, "I brought electric into the pit for the first time."[23]

As for the theatergoing public, they seemed to read only the raves for the show, and lines began to form at the Palace Theatre box office immediately after the opening. Two weeks later *Sweet Charity* was doing standing-room-only business, prompting *Variety* to proclaim that it was "apparently due for a smash run."[24]

Equally poised for potential for hit status were Coleman and Fields's songs on their own, thanks to the myriad recordings that came out in tandem with the show's tryout and opening. Barbra Streisand recorded both "Where Am I Going?" and "You Wanna Bet?"; Tony Bennett released a single with "Baby, Dream Your Dream" on one side; Sylvia Syms waxed "There's Gotta Be Something Better Than This" and "Poor Everybody Else"; and Peggy Lee, who introduced "Big Spender" as part of her set at the Copacabana in November 1965, several weeks before the first public performance of *Sweet Charity* in Philadelphia, had gone into the studio to preserve her sultry rendition of the song.

The way in which Lee came to this number beautifully illustrates both Coleman's relationship with the singer and the way he actively promoted his work in the months before the show's opening. He would often tell the story of how he called Lee in the hope of getting her to record "You Wanna Bet," but as the conversation continued he came to realize that she wasn't interested in the song. She hedged by asking about how the show was going.

Coleman recalled that the conversation proceeded: "So I said, 'I'm working on a new song.' And she said, 'What's it called?' 'It's called 'Big Spender.' She said, 'That's an interesting title.' I said, 'Yeah, it's kind of an interesting song. It's a group number. All of the girls are lined up and they sing it. It's about boredom. It's about how it's this line that they throw out

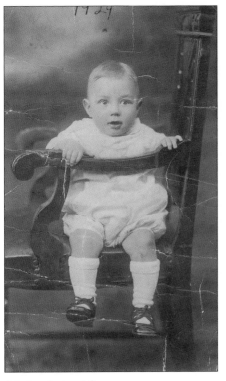

A baby photo of Cy.

Cy (*sitting, bottom left*) with his family, circa 1930. His mother, Ida, is standing at left; his father, Max, is at center.

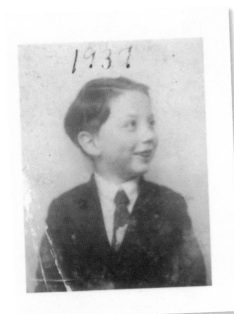

Cy—in a school photo, perhaps—in 1937.

Cy with his sister Yetta circa 1940.

Cy (*right*), with three friends, unwinds in the Catskills.

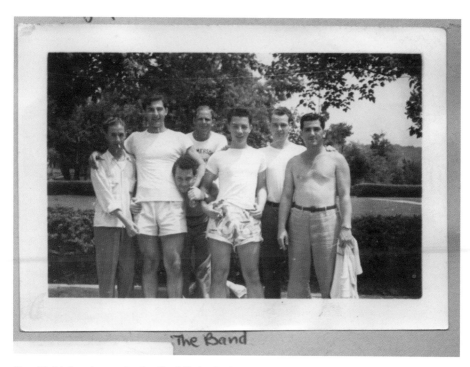

The Band

Cy with his bandmates in the Catskills in the late 1940s.

Cy takes part in one of the amateur shows at Kaufman's in the Catskills, circa 1953. Photo by Irv Roth.

Cy as he appeared on television screens on the morning program *Date in Manhattan*.

Cy (*standing to left of sign*) with the *Date in Manhattan* crew at Tavern on the Green.

Cy in his
apartment,
working,
circa 1955.

A promotional photo for the
Cy Coleman Trio—John
Cresci, Cy, Ernie Furtado—
circa 1956.

Table card for an appearance at the Mermaid Room.

Cy works with
his teacher, Adele
Marcus, on his
Sonatine in Seven
Flats, which he
wrote specifically
for her.

Cy (*standing,
far left*) attends
the wedding of
bandleader Herb
Gordon (*standing,
third from left*).
Seated (*left to
right*) are Cy's
songwriting
partner Joseph
A. McCarthy
Jr., Veronica
Lake, and an
unidentified
guest.

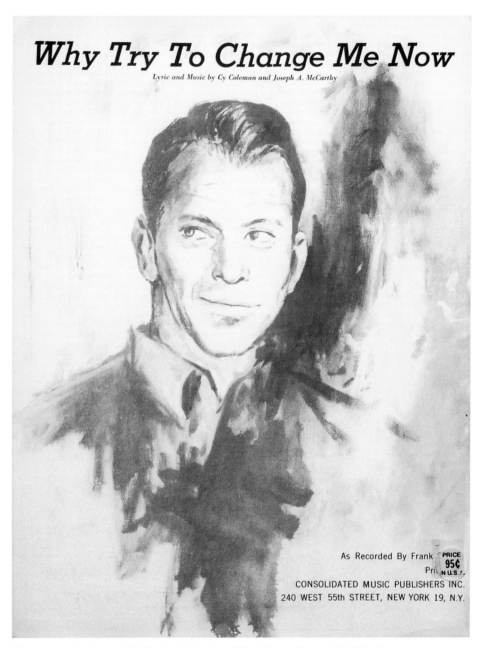

Sheet music for Cy and McCarthy's first hit, "Why Try to Change Me Now."

Sheet music for Cy and Carolyn Leigh's hit "Witchcraft."

every night: 'The minute you walked in the joint.' And it's being brilliantly staged by Bob Fosse.' She said, 'Sing me a few bars.' So I did, and she said to me, 'I could make a hit record out of that.' And I said, 'No. It's a group number. It isn't really a song per se.' And she said, 'Well, make it a song, and make a demo and send it to me.' So I did and she was right."[25]

Beyond the covers of the show's tunes, many of which were on the Top 40 Charts at *Billboard* for the first half of 1966, the sheet music from Coleman's Notable Music was selling briskly as the show opened. Estimates were that, before *Sweet Charity* had been open a full week, "1,200 and 1,500 copies of each of the 12 songs in the show" were sold.[26]

The cast album, recorded on February 6 and released within the month, helped to publicize the show further, spurred ticket sales, and, in one instance, compelled a critic to reconsider his initial opinion of the Coleman-Fields score. In a March 19 column in *Newsday*, George Oppenheimer wrote, "My first reaction to Mr. Coleman's music was not overly favorable. After hearing it a second, third, and numerous other times, I am prepared to eat copious crow, sprinkled, I hope, with Miss Fields' lyrics which I admired greatly then, now and always."

By spring, as the cast recording was moving gently up Billboard's Top LP Chart, peaking at number 92, more recordings of the score began to appear as Coleman's work attracted the attention of other musicians. Skitch Henderson released an album that put a big-band sound to the music. More important, this LP preserved in toto one melody that survived only in part as a small snippet of underscoring in the final *Charity* score. Coleman had originally composed this tune, titled "When Did You Know?," for a ballet that Fosse had at one point envisioned in the show. It was something that Coleman returned to nearly fifteen years later when writing *Barnum*. Outfitted with a lyric by Michael Stewart, it became "Love Makes Such Fools of Us All."

Along with Henderson's LP, a semi-studio cast album was released by the Roxy Theater Orchestra and Chorus, and later Bobby Hackett and Ronnie David released an LP with one side dedicated to *Sweet Charity* numbers. Somewhat ironically, this latter album paired the *Charity* songs with ones from Jerry Herman's *Mame*, which bowed at the end of May and which, along with *Man of La Mancha*, proved to be formidable competition for the Coleman-Fields-Simon show as awards season in New York kicked into gear.

When the Tony Award nominations were announced, it looked as if *Sweet Charity* could emerge as the winner of the season. The show received nine nominations, the most of any show that year, including two nods for Fosse (director and choreographer categories), while Coleman and Fields, Verdon, and Simon garnered a nomination apiece. Just behind *Charity* were both *Mame* (eight nominations) and *La Mancha* (seven nominations).

Charity ultimately won in only one category: Fosse picked up his fifth Tony for his dances. The other awards were distributed almost evenly between the chipper *Mame*, where Angela Lansbury, Beatrice Arthur, and Frankie Michaels were winners, and the serious *Man of La Mancha*, which received not only the much-coveted best musical award but also best score, best director, and best actor prizes.

Nevertheless, *Sweet Charity* remained one of the top attractions on Broadway and settled into a 609-performance run, evolving into a property that would become a successful business unto itself and require Coleman's attention for the next three to four years. Perhaps more important, however, was that the show had brought the composer together with another lyricist with whom he could enjoy a long-term partnership. As 1966 progressed, they found themselves very much in demand as one of Broadway's top songwriting teams.

15

"In Tune"

Before *Sweet Charity* opened, the pairing of Cy Coleman and Dorothy Fields struck many as incongruous, principally because of the difference in their ages. Furthermore, as Gwen Verdon's son, James Henaghan observed, "To me, she didn't look like the person who would write those kinds of songs. She looked like a kind of matronly lady."[1]

But as Coleman pointed out when asked how Fields stayed in touch with the pulse of the times—in both *Charity* and *Seesaw*—in a 1977 interview with Lynn Summerall for WBJC radio in Baltimore: "She was a philosopher and somewhat of a psychiatrist. . . . She saw aspects of life and the various staples of life, let's say, that don't change. For example, the song 'Where Am I Going?' I've had a lot of young people come over to me and say, 'That's my story.' And I tell them that the woman who wrote it was seventy years old, and they ask, 'How did she know that about me?' . . . I don't think she necessarily had to go to a discotheque or follow the charts at *Billboard* to know what's happening to do her lyrics. All she had to do was know the show and just write human nature."

It wasn't just Fields's commonsense approach to her craft but also her openness to the way theater was changing that allowed her to work so easily with Coleman. In the middle of 1966, just as *Annie Get Your Gun* (for which she and her brother Herbert had written the book) was being revived, she talked about how musicals had evolved since she began her career in 1928 and pointed to *Sweet Charity* as an ideal example. "The curtain closes just once through the entire show, at the end of the first act," she told syndicated reporter Joan Crosby, adding, "Now there are all kinds of pieces of elaborate mechanical devices which eliminate the need to close the curtains to change the scenery. This also means the secondary love story—the one that always took place before the curtain—has been eliminated."[2]

Fields's son, David Lahm, believed that on some levels his mother was "ready for it," by which he meant the chance to work as the business and styles were changing. "She was one of the lucky ones. Most of her colleagues by the time they had reached her age were on the shelf. They couldn't get a show. They could hardly work. But she found Cy or vice versa, so she had a chance to go around a whole second time." Lahm also noted that his mother's work with Coleman gave a certain symmetry to her career. "She'd started with Jimmy McHugh, who was something of an entrepreneur like Cy."[3]

For whatever reason, the Coleman-Fields team had clicked, and in mid-1966 they embarked on a second show together, *Keep It in the Family*, a musical adaptation of Samuel Taylor's play *The Happy Time*, which had enjoyed a healthy eighteen-month run on Broadway at the start of the 1950s. It revolved around a world-renowned photographer who visits his family in Canada, where he inspires his teenaged nephew with his free spirit. The show, to be produced by David Merrick, reunited Coleman with N. Richard Nash, who had written *Wildcat*, and according to the first announcements about the project the new musical would star French actor Yves Montand, who was riding the crest of his newly established fame in the United States thanks to movies like *Goodbye Again* and *My Geisha*.

Coleman and Fields took Nash's first draft and started conceiving numbers for the project. They were quickly able to provide a title song, since they had begun work on a sprightly number coincidentally called "Keep It in the Family" for *Sweet Charity*. Other trunk songs from this show fit easily into the new one, and by Nash's second draft the show had moments for both "Pink Taffeta Sample Size 10" and "Poor Everybody Else."

Coleman and Fields also wrote a trio of new songs for *Family*, ranging from a gentle jazz waltz ("Meat and Potatoes") to a lightly Gallic ballad for which they contemplated two distinct titles. In scripts the number is indicated by the name "In the Spring (An Old Man's Fancy)," but when Coleman wrote it out it bore the title "I'm Way Ahead." Years later he and Fields would write another, completely different song with the same name. The third song that they finished for *Family* was "So What Now?," a stirring anthem for Montand's character.

The project remained on the team's docket through the beginning of 1967, at which point they withdrew because they learned that Montand would not be available for the show for another two years. When this happened, producer Merrick brought in a new songwriting team, John Kander and Fred Ebb, who had just had their first show, *Flora, the Red Menace*, on Broadway in the spring of 1965. The project, under the name *The Happy Time*, eventually reached the stage with Robert Goulet as its star in 1968.

Given that Coleman and Fields wrote over two dozen tunes for *Charity* in just about eight months, the fact that they developed a mere fraction of that in the same length of time for *Family* may seem surprising; but it is important to note that there were still matters regarding *Charity* that required some of their attention.

Most notably, negotiations for the film rights had to be taken care of during the second half of the year. From the moment the show opened on Broadway, there was speculation about a film version. Initially, it looked as if Joseph E. Levine (executive producer of films ranging from *Godzilla, King of the Monsters* to *Long Day's Journey into Night*) would acquire the musical for Embassy Films. The company also happened to hold the rights to *Little Me*, and Levine was still heavily promoting his company's plans to produce it with double truck (two-page) ads in such industry papers as *Variety*. In short order, however, other studios expressed interest in the property, and eventually the rights went to Universal Pictures for $500,000.

Coleman never forgot the irony behind the musical's being bought by this particular studio. After all, he and Universal had a checkered history. As he remembered some years later: "They offered me a partnership deal where we would split everything down the middle, but the prospect of tying myself up for so long scared me to death so I reneged on the deal and wrote 'Sweet Charity.'"[4] After all, writing for the movies wasn't a match for him temperamentally. As he observed late in his career, "When I score a film . . . [I] come in at the end. Everybody's gone home and they've had all the fun."[5]

Along with speculation about which studio would bring *Sweet Charity* to the screen, rumors began to abound about who might play the role, and among the names that circulated through columns was that of Ann-Margret, who wanted the role "more than anything," according to Alex Freeman's May 17 column in the *Hartford Courant*. Shirley MacLaine flew to New York specifically to scout for shows that might become film vehicles, and it was she who ultimately snagged the part.

Universal put one of its top men in charge of production: Ross Hunter, the man who had also brought *The Art of Love* to the screen; and as news of the studio's deal and the movie's star became public, so too did the name of the movie's director and choreographer. Bob Fosse would make his Hollywood debut behind the camera, reprising his work in both capacities on film, which was considered by many to be one of the most important on the company's docket.

Even as tongues wagged about the movie, talk in columns in New York and beyond also included speculation about who might star in a national tour of the show and who might be a substitute for the seemingly irreplaceable Verdon on Broadway when she took her vacation. In one instance, this all started before the show opened on Broadway. Gretchen Wyler (who had followed Verdon in the role of Lola in *Damn Yankees*) hinted in a club act that she would be starring in a national tour; then, before the show reached its two-month mark, columnist Louis Sobol hinted that Mitzi Gaynor, who had won hearts for her work in films like *South Pacific*, was a possibility for both Broadway and on the road.

By April Robert Fryer was unwilling to confirm when, or even if, a national tour would be launched, citing the fact that a company crisscrossing the country could have a negative impact on the brisk ticket sales the production was enjoying in New York. At the same time, however, he was able to report on the progress that had been made for international companies. Chita Rivera (star of *West Side Story* and *Bye Bye Birdie*) had agreed to star in London as Charity. Rehearsals were slated to begin in late 1966 or early 1967. As for other international incarnations of *Sweet Charity*, Fryer had his eye on Jeanmaire (who had had a Broadway hit with *The Girl in Pink Tights*) to play the role in Paris, and he told the *New York Times* that he would be willing to "wait for years" to have her play the title role.[6] A German company that would play Vienna, Berlin, and Munich, according to Fryer, would be headed by film star Johanna von Kosczian (whose screen credits overseas included a 1957 remake of *Victor/Victoria* and *The Marriage of Mr. Mississippi*).

Fryer made all of this sound like a fait accompli, but within a few months plans changed, particularly with regard to *Charity* in the United States. The producers struck a deal to serve as "entertainment consultants for Caesar's Palace, the new Las Vegas hotel" and in this capacity would bring their two current New York hits—the other being Jerry Herman's *Mame*—there.[7]

The deal was unusual—and financially attractive. The hotel agreed to finance the entire venture and guaranteed a sixteen-week run for each new production. After this, should the hotel's management not exercise an option to continue either production's engagement, the producers would have a second full-scale incarnation of the show, theoretically ready for touring. But as Joe Cohen noted in the August 17 issue of *Variety*, the stage at Caesar's was "larger than will be found in most legit houses," meaning that there would be an expense related to downsizing elements of the physical production once a tour commenced.

Within a month the producers announced who would play Charity in Vegas: Juliet Prowse, who gave a breakout performance in the movie version of Cole Porter's *Can-Can* playing Claudine, the role originated onstage by Verdon. Subsequent to *Can-Can*, Prowse's credits stretched to several other films, including the Elvis Presley flick *G.I. Blues*, and numerous television appearances.

The full company came into focus quickly after this announcement. Elaine Dunn, who had been in *John Murray Anderson's Almanac* over ten years before, snagged the role of Nickie, and Paula Kelly, who was just beginning her stage and screen career, would play Helene, Charity's other best bud at the Fan-Dango Ballroom. Ronald Holgate, who had been in shows like *Milk and Honey* and *A Funny Thing Happened on the Way to the Forum* was cast as Vittorio; he played the role briefly on Broadway while the Las Vegas company rehearsed in New York. Similarly, the man cast as Oscar in Las Vegas, Peter Lombard, had done a stint in the Broadway *Charity* when he stepped in for a vacationing John McMartin.

The opening date in Las Vegas was set for December 29, but before the show could even start rehearsing there was one other issue involved with taking *Charity* to Vegas. The show had to be streamlined so that it could be performed twice a day and not distract gamblers from the action at the casinos. To this end Simon's book was drastically pruned and three of Coleman and Fields's songs—"You Should See Yourself," "Charity's Soliloquy" and "I'm the Bravest Individual"—were cut.

The revisions did not in any way dampen the critical and popular reaction to the show when it bowed in Caesar's Circus Maximus. When reviews began appearing during the first days of January 1967, Prowse, her co-stars, and the creative team were all garnering raves.

In the January 3 *Los Angeles Times*, John L. Scott wrote that the show was "90 minutes of uninterrupted enjoyable action" and that Prowse "seems to have limitless energy and scores particularly with her superb dancing." In the *Van Nuys Valley News*, John Cronan reported, "Caesar, who has brought an 'orgy of entertainment' to his Las Vegas strip palace, reached new highs with the Broadway musical hit 'Sweet Charity.'"

The January 11 *Variety* review echoed these sentiments, stating that the idea of bringing a Broadway show to Vegas was "paying off handsomely—firstnighters were enthusiastic in their praise and reservations are coming in far in advance." As for Prowse, the review stated: "This role will certainly carve a deep notch in her zooming career."

During the time before the Las Vegas opening, Coleman had also begun to refocus on his career at the keyboard; notable in this regard was a one-night-only appearance that he made in June at the request of producer Arthur Cantor at the American embassy in London. The event, called "A Very Informal History of the American Musical Theatre," gathered a starry crowd of theater and political notables and featured not only Coleman, who played some of his own songs, but also Barbra Streisand, who was then appearing in *Funny Girl* in London. Coleman's portion of the evening focused on contemporary songwriting, and during the course of his set he performed "Hey, Look Me Over" (sharing the story about his difficulty performing it) and a handful of tunes from *Little Me*. In conclusion, he described how singles released in advance of a show could serve as marketing and promotional tools, at which point he introduced Streisand, who opened with "Where Am I Going?" before delivering a medley of songs from *Porgy and Bess* and her hit from *Funny Girl*, "People."

Coleman also returned to the studio to record his own versions of "Rhythm of Life" and "Big Spender" for Capitol Records. The resulting single didn't gain any sort of real traction on the charts, but Coleman's honky-tonk piano work on "Spender" was impeccable, while "Rhythm," featuring some decidedly perky arrangements for orchestra and voice by Ray Ellis, offered, albeit briefly, a hint of an album that Coleman would record two years later in which he would push mod and classical sounds to sublime effect.

The effort was Coleman's goodbye to the label that had given him a trio of LPs, and as 1966 drew to a close he recorded a full LP, *If My Friends Could See Me Now*, for Columbia Records, which had stepped in as both investor and recording label for *Sweet Charity* after Capitol withdrew its support from the show. The album was the first that showcased Coleman as both pianist and vocalist and was made up entirely of his own creations. It featured ten of his best-known tunes along with one of his most recent ones: "Sweet Talk." Lainie Kazan had given this tricky jazz waltz a sizzlingly intense rendition in early 1966, but Coleman, as he did with many of the songs on the album, found its more dapper and teasing charms.

Coleman's work was greeted with accolades by industry press and in general-interest publications. It also proved to be a hit with the public. Columbia had to order a second pressing of it, and for a while it looked as if it would spur him back into a club career. There was talk, for instance, that he'd be making a return engagement at Chicago's London House before 1967 ended.

Coleman, however, didn't return to that venue, or any other, for a number of years, though he was back in the recording studio in short order for a pair of unique projects. The first was *Boozers and Losers* for his old friend, onetime band singer Claire Hogan. On this LP Coleman was credited for conceptualization as well as producing.

Hogan had been part of his circle of close friends (and sometimes interpreter of his songs) for over ten years. When Coleman opened Notable, she had volunteered to help out, and as Coleman wrote in his liner notes for the album, the notion "appealed to our collective sense of humor so we moved another desk into the office and Claire became my personal secretary, Girl Friday and good friend (still)."

As for Coleman's vision for the record, it came into focus at the opening-night party for *Sweet Charity* in Philadelphia. It was at this event that Hogan took to the floor to perform one of the songs they had talked about having her record, "The Whiffenpoof Song" (the signature song of the Yale a cappella group). "As she sang, the room started to quiet down until all you could hear was the soft piano and the voice."[8]

It was enough to give Coleman a comprehensive sense of what Hogan's album should be, and the result was an eleven-song recording that showcased her smoky, sultry vocals. Coleman commissioned Ray Ellis for the arrangements, which provided just the right backing for the singer and also contained some terrific surprises, such as an insistent, almost obsessive beat for the first measures of the Rodgers and Hart classic "Falling in Love with Love." Alongside this number and the two that Hogan and Coleman had already agreed on, they chose a little-known song by Fields and Arthur Schwartz, "I'll Pay the Check," and Charles K. Harris's "After the Ball," which Coleman outfitted with some new words.

Coleman's work was also represented by the inclusion of "I'm Gonna Laugh You Right Out of My Life" and "Here I Go Again." In addition, he and Murray Grand (a friend of both Hogan's and Coleman's) provided the jazzy torch song that gives the disc its title, which she delivers with smoldering elegance. On some levels it almost seems as if she and Coleman might have, intentionally or not, been paying tribute to one of his earliest interpreters, chanteuse Mabel Mercer.

Boozers ultimately displayed Coleman's artistic taste at one end of the musical spectrum—the quintessential art song—and in May 1968 his craft in this area was demonstrated by Mercer herself, along with Bobby Short, at a joint concert at Town Hall. People flew in from around the world for the event, and tickets were in such demand that crowds were accommodated by placing chairs on the stage behind the performers. They had all come, according to the *New York Times* May 20 report on the event, "to hear the specialized singing of Mr. Short and Mabel Mercer."

The performance, which generated a live recording and prompted a second concert a year later, featured Coleman's work heavily, and not just the songs he had written with Joseph A. McCarthy Jr. early in his career (the ones that Mercer had often originated). She also offered a tune from *Charity*, introduced one that he had written with Robert Wells ("Bad Is for Other People"), and tackled "Sweet Talk," all in her own inimitable fashion. Short's portion of the bill also contained a pair of Coleman numbers, and the two singers closed the show with "Here's to Us" from *Little Me*.

But even as this event and Hogan's album exhibited Coleman's work as an artful modern songsmith, he himself was involved with another recording project that cunningly utilized his affinity for—and facility with—classical music.

The album, *Ages of Rock*, featured Coleman playing works by Mozart, Bach, and Chopin, among others, accompanied by an ensemble playing rock settings and arrangements that he had created and that had been orchestrated by Larry Wilcox. In an interview with Skitch Henderson on the *Music Makers* radio program some years later, Coleman explained his inspiration for the fusion: "I was fooling around with the idea of 'rhythm.' You know when you sit down and you start getting theoretical about your work? And I was working in eighth notes and I kept figuring out different accents for it. And I said you take just one steady stream of eighth notes and you place the accent in different places, and all of a sudden you have a different style of music. And this theory started me off on this album."

The record's eleven cuts were the product of about two years' worth of work. Coleman described his process in his notes for the LP, saying that throughout it all he had to be aware of "keeping myself honest, not imposing myself on the music, but taking from the music. I remained in tempo and played the melodies straight. And the rock backgrounds, while remaining true to themselves, set up variations. It's a meeting of two honest commodities and if one is falsified both are immediately cancelled out." Coleman associated each finalized piece with a color, resulting in melodies with names like "Sonata in Shocking Pink" and "Pavane in Purple," and when the album was released, a March 3, 1968 review in *Billboard* lauded his success in "tearing down the barriers" between different musical forms.

MGM, which released this and Hogan's LP, promoted the album heavily with localized contests around the country and by releasing several 45s pairing selections from the album. Coleman participated in these and also made sure that Notable published the selections. Further promotion came through a series of humor-laced postcards that featured period illustrations and "endorsements" from the composers of the works Coleman had selected.

This album and the efforts surrounding its marketing were indicative of the new directions into which Coleman was moving as composer and performer, as well as businessman and entrepreneur. In this last arena there were other activities as well, perhaps most noteworthy among them his expansion of his company with the establishment of Portable Music, which was created so that he could publish and promote BMI songwriters like Bobby Hebb ("Sunny") and even songstress Blossom Dearie.

It was in early 1967, too, that Coleman made his first forays into serving as a lobbyist for ASCAP when he traveled to Washington to testify in front of the Senate Judiciary Subcommittee on Patents as it considered different provisions to include in the renewal of copyright law. ASCAP's choice of Coleman made perfect sense. He was the youngest of the organization's board members at the time. Furthermore, he was energetic and charismatic and could speak passionately to the issues at hand, namely per-play fees from both radio stations and jukebox operators.

As if all of this were not enough—and by this stage in his life, Coleman's modus operandi was to have myriad projects in the works at once—he was also finishing the score for his second industrial show for Ford Motor

Company, and there were individual songwriting projects, including a pair of seasonal tunes that he penned with Peggy Lee. In addition, he and Fields had begun drafting songs for a new musical that Alexander H. Cohen, the prolific producer who would eventually be responsible for bringing the Tony Awards to television, was developing for Broadway.

The show was to be based on Stefan Kanfer and Jess Korman's *The Coffee Lover*, a comedy that had its premiere out of town at Connecticut's Westport Country Playhouse in August 1966 in a production directed by Morton Da Costa. The play focused on Tom Gordon, a successful voiceover talent for television ads, who, believing that his life and career had become meaningless, has a mini-breakdown on air and promptly sells the home in Great Neck that he shares with his wife, Julie, to buy a derelict building in Greenwich Village that he plans on turning into a hip coffeehouse. His decision, unsurprisingly, rocks his marriage, but he still proceeds with his designs, aided (and sometimes distracted) by a colorful crew of characters from the downtown scene.

Before the comedy opened in Connecticut, there were rumors that it might transfer to Broadway, but lukewarm reviews from the local press and a similarly mixed notice in *Variety* scuttled these plans, and it was about a year later that Cohen acquired the rights for transforming the play into a musical.

Work on the show began during the last few months of 1967, with Korman and Kanfer adapting and expanding their work so that it encompassed more characters and locations. As they did this, the story line of the show grew to include a broader journey for the hero. He toyed with mysticism, club hopping, and even moviemaking with an Andy Warhol wannabe before turning to life as an activist. For Coleman, who had to deliver commercial messages throughout his early days on television, Tom's desperation for a change must have had a savory resonance.

As the script evolved, Tom's divergent escapes from the mainstream world became more central to the show, while certain details about his life changed. In a first draft, he and Julie had two preteen kids, but in a later draft they are just expecting their first child. With each draft the narrative for the musical becomes increasingly taut as the writers reconsider and restructure existing scenes and in some instances create new sequences altogether.

It was a process that required the songwriters to develop—or at least begin conceptualizing—a wide variety of songs. In two instances Coleman and Fields turned to their trunk. They found that "Poor Everybody Else" could function as a kind of musical red herring for Julie as she seemingly accepted the new world she shared with Tom. In one draft, too, they inserted "Meat and Potatoes," which they had developed for *Keep It in the Family*, its melody and lyric seemingly tailor-made to suit Tom's jaded worldview.

In all other instances, though, the musicalized *Coffee Lover* required new songs and dance music, which Coleman and Fields supplied over the course of the first portion of 1968, often after working meetings with Korman and Kanfer at Fields's Upper West Side home.

A few of the ideas they developed were ultimately realized as full-blown songs, including "After Forty, It's Patch, Patch, Patch," which was envisioned as a song for Julie—and her suburban friends—as she contemplates what her own existence might become as she moves into her middle years. Another completed song was "We've Got It," an exuberant duet for Tom and Julie as they settled into a seemingly happy existence together in the Village. For one of the secondary characters, Coleman and Fields came up with the seductive "You're in a Highly Emotional State," which helped spur Tom's exodus from corporate life, and finally, for a young woman who became a kind of surrogate teenage daughter to the couple, Coleman and Fields created a folksy ballad, "Whisper on the Wind."

Fields completed lyrics for an additional four songs, including "Yoga and Yogurt," for a spiritual guru to whom Tom turns for guidance; "That Does It," which, in addition to serving as a new title for the piece at one point, gave Tom the opportunity to express in song his resolve to start anew; "Daddy, Come Back to Scarsdale," a number that would have been performed by the couple's nine-year-old son; and "You Could Last Me a Lifetime," meant to be a parody of 1930s schmaltz that was used alongside one of a young film auteur's projects.

The various drafts indicate almost another dozen songs that the team planned to write, ranging from possible solos for both the principals and secondary characters to group numbers, including one possible cantata that would have been heard as Tom opened his new business. The scripts also indicate that Coleman might have been contemplating at least two different pieces of extended dance music, including one for a scene at a high-end restaurant frequented by executives looking to pad their expense accounts.

Korman remembered that the process was a drawn-out one. Coleman, overextended with so many different projects unfolding at once, would show up late to meetings and was often simply unavailable: "He was always out on the coast. You know, it was the period of *Sweet Charity*." Still, the writers were able to complete enough work that they could present a reading of the show "at Dorothy's for Alex. Neil Simon was also in attendance,"[9] as Korman remembered it. Unfortunately, the project stalled, and Coleman turned the majority of his attention to *Sweet Charity*, for which filming was about to commence.

16

Sweet Charity Onscreen

The variety of projects that Coleman undertook from early 1966 through the beginning of 1968, with the seeming hunger of an artist just at the beginning of his or her career, belied one small fact. He had a hit Broadway show that was turning into a big business. *Sweet Charity* on Broadway and beyond was taking on a life of its own in many forms.

On Broadway, the musical continued with Gwen Verdon at its center, but there were a few bumps as the run progressed. For instance, there were problems with the theater itself—not in the front of the house, where theatergoers were enjoying the renovated building's opulence, but backstage, where the company was roasting during the summer and freezing during the winter. "It got so bad once that a bucket of water had to be thrown on me,"[1] Verdon told columnist Earl Wilson.

Lee Roy Reams's memory of the theater and backstage in particular was that "it was dirty as hell. The house looked great, but backstage it was a mess. And they had torn up all of the carpeting and had it out in the alley and we had nothing to stand on but concrete floors. The dressers went out and pulled in some of the old carpeting for us to stand on. And they made quick-change rooms for us in the basement. They hung up sheets and took mirrors and taped them on walls for us."[2]

Verdon complained about all of this and more to both management and her union, Actor's Equity, and when her grievances appeared to fall on deaf ears, she took a bold stand, announcing that she would resign from Equity. The tactic worked. Conditions soon began to improve for the company, and Verdon remained an Equity member.

It was a threat that resonated with the union. One night six months later the theater's air conditioning failed. A representative from the performers' union was at the Palace the next day. He heard both the star's and the company's complaints and in short order informed the management that "it might be wise to cancel the show."[3]

But as *Sweet Charity* moved into its second full year, there was another, bigger snag. The show's demands were taking their toll on the star, and, at certain performances, in an effort to minimize the strain she was feeling from performing eight times a week, Verdon would inform the conductor before the curtain went up that she would be eliminating a number, often "Where Am I Going?," during the show.

According to Reams, it was a number that she had disliked performing from the outset. "Gwen hated singing 'Where Am I Going?' Hated it. I was there the day she broke down and cried, and said, 'Bobby, I don't want to sing this song.' She was very insecure just standing there singing the song."[4]

The decision to omit the number prompted an angry letter from one patron, who wrote to the star and demanded a refund. When she got the note, Verdon sat down and calculated how many minutes had been taken off the show when the song was omitted and sent the patron a refund check for that portion of the ticket. It came to forty-two cents.

Things went more smoothly with the Las Vegas *Charity* company. It settled into its run and played ten weeks longer than originally scheduled. By the time the show had concluded its six-month engagement, it had played to over 300,000 people (about 11,000 per week). In recognition of Prowse's drawing power, Caesar's management presented her with a Jaguar. Her success in Vegas ultimately led to her, rather than the originally announced Chita Rivera (who eventually starred in the show's national tour), taking on the role in the show's London production.

Prowse opened the show at the Prince of Wales Theatre on October 11, 1967, and, unlike *Little Me*, the musical arrived without substantial revisions. The next day critics embraced the show, its star, and its score almost wholeheartedly. John Peter wrote in the *Times* that it was "easily one of the best musicals to have come to London for some time," and in a follow-up Sunday review in the *Guardian* Ronald Bryden said that the show was "good, fast and loud." He also made sure to mention the man who had restaged Fosse's dances: Eddie Gasper, an original Broadway cast member who would eventually become Prowse's husband.

The production, which also featured Paula Kelly as Helene, Josephine Blake as Nickie, and Rod McLennan as Oscar, went on to enjoy a healthy run, and Coleman, Fosse, Fields, and Simon could share credit when the show picked up the Evening Standard Award for best musical of the year. The London production also spawned a new set of singles of songs from the show, most notably a swingingly hip incarnation of "Where Am I Going?" by Simone Jackson, who once had, during a concert in 1962, a rather impressive quartet as backup singers: the Beatles, just before the dawn of their global popularity.

The press that the various stage incarnations of *Sweet Charity* received was matched, and soon exceeded, by the coverage being garnered by the film version. Universal spent lavishly to acquire the rights and gave the title role to Shirley MacLaine, then one of Hollywood's top-drawing stars and at that point a three-time Academy Award nominee.

MacLaine had started her career as a Broadway performer and lived a real-life *42nd Street* tale while understudying Carol Haney in *The Pajama Game*. When Haney broke her ankle during the run of the show, it was MacLaine who performed the Fosse-choreographed "Steam Heat" number. One night film producer Hal B. Wallis spotted her and signed her to a contract with Paramount Pictures. Since that time she had been in movies ranging from Mike Todd's grandiose *Around the World in 80 Days* to Lillian Hellman's drama *The Children's Hour* to the musical *Can-Can*.

Given MacLaine's visibility, press about the *Sweet Charity* movie would have come naturally, but once the studio's publicity machine kicked into gear, the project was garnering stories and generating buzz even before filming began.

The first big news about the film, which was slated to start filming on November 1, 1967 for an October 1968 release, was the announcement that producer Ross Hunter, who was riding a crest of success with another film, *Thoroughly Modern Millie*, had hired I. A. L. Diamond to write the screenplay. Diamond had been responsible for movies like *Some Like It Hot*, as well as *The Apartment*, which also starred MacLaine, in one of her Oscar-nominated performances.

Diamond completed an outline for the film, which included a scene that provided a reason for using one of the cut numbers from the show, "Pink Taffeta Sample Size 10." It also indicated that there needed to be a new title song for the opening moments of the movie and provided a new twist to the ending. Charity would give Oscar her dowry to make a down payment on a business he had always dreamed of buying, but when it came time for them to meet and go away together, he wouldn't come for her.

Both of these changes would have made the movie version of *Sweet Charity* more like its source, Fellini's *Nights of Cabiria*, and the alterations sparked conflict between Diamond and Fosse, who was concurrently working on his own scenario for the way in which the romance between Charity and Oscar should unfold in the film. Producer Hunter stepped in, and within six weeks of announcing Diamond as the screenwriter Hunter replaced him with Peter Stone, who had picked up an Academy Award for another movie with Coleman's music, *Father Goose*.

This shift, just three months before filming was to commence, was an omen of the troubles that were brewing and the changes to come. In November, just as MacLaine was reporting for dance rehearsals for the film, Hunter withdrew as producer. "There were serious and irreconcilable differences . . . between the director and me,"[5] Hunter said in a statement.

One of the conflicts Fosse recalled was the tone and content of the film. "There was quite a fight," he said, "about whether Charity could say Up Yours [*sic*]. I felt that if she couldn't, then we might as well make Mary Poppins all the way. I get very upset about innuendos, not about Charity's straight talk."[6]

Universal replaced Hunter with Robert Arthur, who had worked with both Coleman and screenwriter Stone on *Father Goose*. Among his many other Hollywood credits were such hits as Fritz Lang's *Big Heat* and *Operation Petticoat*, which starred Cary Grant.

Some in the industry saw the shifting of control away from Hunter as a victory for Fosse, who, now with a delayed filming schedule, began reaching out to stage performers, rather than Hollywood A-list names, for the movie's central roles. Before Hunter's departure, potential actors had included Alan Alda, who had reportedly been offered the role of Oscar, and Mitzi Gaynor, whom Hunter was wooing for the project.

One of the first people Fosse contacted was Chita Rivera, who flew to Los Angeles for a screen test while she was playing Charity at Chicago's Shubert Theatre. Because of her stage commitments, she flew to California immediately following a Saturday night performance, rehearsed with Fosse on Sunday, and shot the test on Monday before flying back to the Midwest. Rivera recalled the experience: "These are the things you want to do in your life. You don't say I'll think about it."[7]

By mid-December Rivera had snagged the role she tested for: Charity's best friend, Nikki. Not long afterward it was announced that Paula Kelly, from the Las Vegas and London companies, would be reprising her portrayal of Helene.

As for the men, Fosse lined up other actors with theatrical experience, including John McMartin, who originated the role of Oscar. Other performers to whom Fosse turned had both stage experience and brought star power to the project, notably singing sensation Sammy Davis Jr. (who had done the Broadway musicals *Golden Boy* and *Mr. Wonderful*). He was offered—and in a matter of hours accepted—the role of Daddy Johann Sebastian Brubeck (or "Big Daddy"), the head of the Rhythm of Life Church. The film's cast also boasted the popular comic actor Stubby Kaye (Broadway's original Nicely-Nicely in *Guys and Dolls*), who took on the role of Herman, the owner of the Fan-Dango, and screen heartthrob Ricardo Montalban (who had starred opposite Lena Horne in *Jamaica*), who signed on to play Vittorio Vittale, the Italian film star.

For the ensemble, Fosse also brought a host of the performers with whom he had worked on Broadway, including Suzanne Charny (who danced the lead in "Frug" onscreen), Lee Roy Reams, and Bud Vest. Another member of the movie's ensemble was future star Ben Vereen, who was in the Las Vegas company.

As news of the major casting was slowly rolled out during the end of

1967 and the beginning of 1968, an important element of the film's creative team fell into place. Coleman was signed as musical director; as reported by columnist Joyce Haber in January 1968, he was to "write additional background music, as well as score the film." His duties, along with those of lyricist Fields, eventually grew to penning a trio of new songs, among them a new title number.

Coleman remembered the evolution of this last piece during a radio interview with David Kenney in 2004: "Fosse said, 'Maybe we can make [*Sweet Charity*] feel more contemporary. It is the title song of a movie.' And I said, 'Well, maybe I can put in a slow rock beat,' and he said, 'That sounds great to me.'"

Eventually, Coleman began to think that his revisions should have a new lyric, and when he approached Fields with the idea, she said, "'Oh! I've said everything I have to say about 'Sweet Charity' in that song; I don't have another word to say.'"[8] It was at this point that Coleman decided to change the music for the song entirely.

The new melody that Coleman created for Fields's lyric ultimately came to have a number of different purposes in the film. Coleman created a bouncy, mod variation on it that would be heard during the opening credits with background vocals. For these he turned to Nancy Adams, the wife of lyricist Floyd Huddleston, with whom he had collaborated occasionally.

Adams, herself a performer, had recorded several demos for Coleman in New York, including ones of "Sweet Talk" and another Coleman-Huddleston tune, "I'm Serving Out a Heavy Sentence Loving You." By the time work on the film was under way, the Huddlestons had moved to the West Coast. According to Adams, "Cy was really loyal, and he absolutely loved Floyd. When we moved out here, he got in touch with us regarding *Sweet Charity*. . . . I had done a lot of work, studiowise, with vocal groups for arranging and that kind of thing. And Cy knew that, and he called Floyd, and they contacted Ralph Burns [who was serving as the film's orchestrator] and asked him to hire me as vocal-group contractor, because that's what I was doing at the time."[9]

Burns agreed, and Adams put together a group of singers—including Sally Stevens, who would eventually tour with Burt Bacharach—to record background vocals that would be heard during the film's opening moments, at its midpoint, and then again at the end. According to Adams, "They wanted a young, pure kind of sound. . . . The open fifths and open fourths that they used during the '60s that were not Broadway at all. It was more of a record-company sound."[10]

The "oohs," "ahhs," and "bah-bah-bah-bahs" that are heard in these sections, which do indeed evoke the polished recordings of Bacharach's tunes, are not the only riffs on the new melody for the song "Sweet Charity" heard in the film. Coleman also used it for two significant pieces of underscoring: he conceptualized a pair of suites that were extended variations of the tune, each of which accompanied montages of still photographs of Charity designed to give audiences a sense of her life as well as the passage of time.

Beyond these various pieces, Coleman, with Fields, came up with an additional two songs for MacLaine before filming began. With "My Personal Property," they wrote a bubbly paean to New York that established Charity's innate ebullience during the movie's opening moments. "It's a Nice Face" was penned as a replacement for "I'm the Bravest Individual," the tune that Charity and Oscar performed together while stuck in an elevator. The gentle ballad provided Charity with a moment of introspection as she reflected on this new man in her life.

For MacLaine's songs, as well as the ensemble numbers, Fosse felt it was important that the singing sound as natural as possible, and to this end he vetoed the studio's idea that someone besides MacLaine perform her vocals.

Furthermore, when it came time to do the prerecord of "Big Spender," he took exception to the purity of the sound that the ensemble hired by the studio produced, so he pulled them out of the session. Louise Quick, who had been a replacement in the Broadway production and was a dancer in the film, remembered, "You know Bob . . . I can't remember if any of the studio singers stayed on any of 'Big Spender' or if he took them off completely, but [the dancers] did that. And we definitely did 'I Love to Cry at Weddings' and 'Rhythm of Life.'"[11]

Filming occurred on both Universal's sound stages and on location in New York. Coleman was present throughout, finalizing his thoughts for the intricate scoring and music cues that would eventually be part of the film. By July 1968 his precise notes on when music would start and stop during action—and dialogue—ran to nearly two dozen tightly spaced typed pages.

Because all the vocals had been prerecorded, Coleman found himself with down time, and there came a moment that became quite memorable for Quick. "I don't know what was going on, but we were not learning any new stuff, and we had already shot the master shot for 'Big Spender,' but only the master shot. So . . . we had a week of rehearsing 'Big Spender,' Monday through Friday all day." One day Coleman appeared where the women were rehearsing and offered an impromptu performance at the piano. Quick continued, "I was so impressed that Cy Coleman played piano for us. I don't know why. It seems like a wonderfully kind thing to do, because he really entertained us. . . . I was impressed with his laid-backness, because I had him up on this pedestal from his work. He was so warm and so open and so funny and so smart that we all had a wonderful time with him then."[12]

Quick's story gives a sense of a theaterlike family involved with the picture, and it's one that's supported by an anecdote from Reams about how he came to his costume for the "Rhythm of Life" number. "Gwen Verdon, Buddy Vest, Ben Vereen, and [I] went into stock wardrobe at Universal or one of the costume places. We went into the costume shop and we went through clothes and we picked out our own clothes. I remember this exactly because I remember my costume. I got a pair of paisley pants, and Gwen found a 'Sonny and Cher' fringed vest, and she said, 'Here. Lee Roy, put this on.' And I put it on and then I said, 'Oh, this red velvet shirt!' and I put that on. And desert boots! I said, 'Oh, I gotta have the desert boots!' And I said, 'I want to look like an Indian.' And Gwen said, 'Oh, good! We'll stick a feather in.' We were laughing so hard, and I said, 'I've gotta have long black hair,' and I used Liz Taylor's old *Cleopatra* wig. So I had Liz Taylor's old wig on. We were screaming. Edith Head was our costumer, but we picked our clothes out of stock at a costume shop."[13]

Even columnist Dick Kleiner sensed the happiness. He began one piece about the filming by almost grumpily announcing: "There was so much sweetness around the 'Sweet Charity' set, it was like dessert time at the candy convention. Everybody loves everybody."[14]

By late spring the filming of *Charity* on the West Coast had ended, and the company and crew came to New York for the location shots Fosse required. For Coleman, as both composer and publisher of the movie's songs, it was time to find singers who would release additional singles, particularly of the three new tunes.

Changing musical tastes, however, meant that gentle ballads like "It's a Nice Face" and the somewhat idiosyncratic "My Personal Property" were a difficult sell to performers. It was, after all, the age of Aquarius for musicals after the 1967 premiere of *Hair* at the New York Shakespeare Festival's Public Theater and that show's transfer to Broadway in April 1968.

Coleman talked about the emergence of the rock musical with *Boston Globe* reporter Harry Neville just before the premiere of *Sweet Charity*. Of *Hair*, which he labeled a revue, he said specifically, "It has lots of enthusiasm going for it, but the basic idea won't bear successful repetition."[15] Interestingly, his thoughts on the arrival of the rock musical on Broadway tellingly echoed what he had said about rock 'n' roll a decade earlier: "This probably has been the bleakest period in pop music history and it has now reached its peak."[16]

Regardless of his opinion of this music or rock in general, Coleman could grasp and appreciate some of the new sounds of the late 1960s. Perhaps the best indication of his ability to understand and enjoy the day's music is a story from Jess Korman about an afternoon when Coleman was late for a work session for *The Coffee Lover* at Fields's home off Central Park. Korman remembered, "He came in clutching a record, 33$^{1/3}$ LP. 'You all have to hear this,' says Cy. Dorothy gives me a look and I shoot her a look. Then Cy puts on *Sgt. Pepper*. He had just heard it."[17]

Of the songs that might be able to expand into this sort of musicality, the most obvious choice was the new version of "Sweet Charity." This number did get several unique recordings, including a terrifically funky rendition from Lou Rawls and a lightly trippy interpretation from the mod garage duo Jeff and Jerry, on which the flip side was the decidedly psychedelic "Voodoo Medicine Man." Another—and perhaps the most intriguing—of the singles from this period is one that was never released. The test pressing of it features an unidentified male vocalist delivering "Where Am I Going?" in a style that brings to mind Jim Morrison's work with the Doors.

There were more–traditional-sounding covers of the *Charity* songs to be found as the movie neared its premiere. Sammy Davis Jr. included a triptych of the Coleman-Fields creations, including "My Personal Property," on his album *I've Got to Be Me*. The other two, "Brass Band" and "If My Friends Could See Me Now," were also released as a 45. As for the movie's third new song, "It's a Nice Face," Shani Wallis, who starred as Nancy in the 1968 film version of Lionel Bart's *Oliver!*, included it on her album *As Long as He Needs Me*, delivering it with silky, almost sensuous aplomb.

For Fosse, the summer months were spent editing the film and coping with one major issue: the ending. He shot two versions. In one, Oscar jilts Charity just as they are about to get their marriage license. Brokenhearted, she wanders the streets of New York before returning late at night to the bridge in Central Park that had become her rendezvous spot with Oscar. For a moment, it looks like she may jump into the lake, but then the scene fades to morning and a group of flower children are found walking through the park, proffering daisies and "love" to the people they pass. They find Charity and wake her. Their presence and message is just enough to give Charity the strength to once again pick herself up, and at the end of the film she's seen walking into the sunrise as Coleman's last new melody plays, the buoyantly soaring "Rebirth."

The alternate ending Fosse shot gives Charity and Oscar a fairy-tale wind-up. He still jilts her at the city building, and she once again roams New York before arriving in Central Park. Fosse then cuts to Oscar's apartment, where his claustrophobia is kicking in. He races out and into the park and finds Charity on the bridge. Believing that she's about to commit suicide, he dashes to her, stumbles over her suitcase, and plunges into the lake. She dives in after him and while they float, he admits, "You're the only breath of fresh air I've ever had" before proposing. And even though this insurance actuary warns Charity, "The odds against us are at least a hundred to one," she joyfully and tearfully accepts the risk.

Each of these scenarios features one of the show's most recognizable numbers: MacLaine sings "Where Am I Going?" during Charity's late-night walk, and at advance screenings both versions received approximately the same reaction from audiences. Ultimately, Fosse gave Charity the less happy fate, and the film was ready for release.

Universal had opted to make *Sweet Charity* a road-show attraction, meaning that it would be seen in select venues around the country where patrons would buy reserved-seat tickets in advance, much as they would for any live musical performance. The sense of films such as *Charity* (or Barbra Streisand's *Funny Girl*, which was released almost concurrently) being like a theater piece was further enhanced by the inclusion of an intermission, and there were usually souvenir programs that patrons could purchase. The one for *Sweet Charity* even proclaimed in its introduction that the movie was "destined to be the musical motion picture of the 1970's."

The hyperbole was echoed in a *Variety* review that ran on January 29, 1969: "For the director, the star and the producer, 'Sweet Charity' is a professional triumph. . . . For the public, it is a rare experience of entertainment-plus." As for Coleman and Fields's work, the critic mentioned all of the songs written for the movie by name without passing judgment, merely remarking that they were "plot-enhancing if not memorable at least on first hearing."

But even with this complaint the review amounted to an essentially unqualified rave. Unfortunately, as the film rolled out, reactions among critics in the general press would become increasingly less enthusiastic. Things started well when the movie premiered in Boston on February 11. The *Boston Globe*'s Marjory Adams wrote, "It looks to me as if everybody in the film, whether from the original theater production or not, decided to make the Universal film a success and did their best work when they saw the vivacious star challenging Miss Streisand as musical sensation of the year."

The film's second engagement was at the Pantages Theatre in Los Angeles, where praises continued to flow. Critic Charles Champlin announced in his March 23 *Los Angeles Times* review that the movie was "vivid, exhilarating, funny, contemporary, superbly alive, and mobile, and, if sad, then sad in a bittersweet, sentimental, defiantly optimistic and non-depressant way."

After this, though, positive reviews were difficult to come by. On March 28, *Chicago Tribune* reviewer Terry Clifford took a swipe at everything from Fosse's direction to MacLaine's performance to the score, which he said was "consistently anti-hummable (including the three added starters which contribute little except running time)." And as the movie was beginning its Big Apple run at the Rivoli Theatre, Vincent Canby, who had covered the musical's opening at the Palace, wrote in the *New York Times* that the musical "has been so enlarged and so inflated that it has become another maximal movie: a long, noisy and, finally, dim imitation of its source material."

For the most part the reviewers' complaints centered on Fosse's direction, which is filled with gimmicks and cinematic sleights of hand. In hindsight, the movie does have a certain first-time clumsiness, but at the same time there's something curiously prescient about it. The film's fast cuts and steep, awkward camera angles all anticipate the grammar of musical narrative that Fosse would employ to more optimal effect in the movie *Cabaret*, techniques that would ultimately become an industry standard with the launching of MTV in 1981.

For Coleman, the score for the film fared better once it was divorced from the visuals. A capsule review in *Billboard* on February 22 opined that it would be difficult "to find a bouncier, more rhythmic score," and in the March 7 *Lowell Sun* William E. Sarmento anticipated: "You will be clamoring at your record store to get the album."

Sweet Charity garnered Coleman his sole Oscar nomination, for best music, best score of a motion picture (original or adapted), but he lost to Lenny Hayton and Lionel Newman, who adapted Jerry Herman's *Hello, Dolly!* But even before the Academy Award nominations were announced in February 1970, Coleman had sprinted forward in new directions.

17

"After Forty, It's Patch, Patch, Patch"

Coleman's duties for the *Sweet Charity* film extended to frequent television appearances on talk shows and jaunts around the country as the road-show film made its bow in different cities. None of this, however, prevented him from broadening his company's scope in a variety of ways, especially the formation of Notable Records. The label would allow him to record his own work as well as that of the artists the company published, including Blossom Dearie and two newly signed talents, Hod David and Tom Paisley. His vision for the material was that it would be contemporary and modern in tone. In addition, Coleman announced that "We will have an open-door policy for young producers and encourage them to submit their ideas and products."[1]

Beyond this work as a businessman, there were reports that he would collaborate on a musical with playwright Arthur Kopit, who had burst onto the scene six years earlier with the provocative comedy *Oh Dad, Poor Dad, Mamma's Hung You in the Closet and I'm Feelin' So Sad.* Coleman was also said to be working on a movie musical with comedian David Steinberg, who had become a fixture on programs like *The Tonight Show* and who was something of a comic renegade, particularly after a controversial appearance on *The Smothers Brothers Comedy Hour* in 1968.

Nothing came of the rumors, but they indicate how Coleman was attempting to adapt to changing tastes in popular culture as he aligned himself with two cutting-edge artists whose work would appeal to a generation that was adopting Jack Weinberg's "don't trust anyone over thirty" as its motto.

Another fascinating indication of how Coleman, who had just turned forty, was working to ensure that he and his work would be perceived as "with-it" was a change that he began to institute in the company's publishing practices. Concurrent with the creation of the new label, he announced that all of the covers for his company's sheet music would be designed by famous artists and be suitable for framing. It was an effort to attract female buyers, who he believed would be attracted by the pop-art covers for decorating purposes.

Remo Bramanti, an abstract painter who had also begun designing the covers for LPs, was the first artist he commissioned, albeit for a surprising piece of music: "50 Stars," a patriotic choral anthem that had a lyric by Coleman's old partner Joseph A. McCarthy Jr. and a melody by Joseph Meyer. Coleman intended to use the tune for the debut of another new label under the Notable rubric: Generation Records.

Given that the Vietnam War was at its midpoint, antiwar protests were taking place around the country, and the seminal Woodstock festival had put a new face on and given a fresh voice to the era's music scene, Coleman's decision to launch both of these initiatives with a song that in its tone and sentiment could rival Irving Berlin's most flag-waving work was a surprise.

Even more interesting is the reception that the 45 (which had a robust, freshly scrubbed rendition of Coleman and Fields's "Keep It in the Family" on the B side) got from *Billboard*. In the August 16, 1969 issue of the industry paper, the disc from New York University Choir and Chorus was called "an auspicious debut" for Generation Records.

Unsurprisingly, the song was rapidly embraced by the Armed Forces. Just a week after the review of the 45 appeared in its pages, *Billboard* reported that a new arrangement had been made for the Navy choir and that copies of the record and sheet music were being sent to Armed Forces glee clubs across the United States with the suggestion that "'50 Stars' become part of their portfolio."[2] The record's success led to talk of a follow-up LP, *Songs for Everybody's America*, but like many of the diverse projects attributed to Coleman during this period, the album never materialized.

One reason might have been that Coleman was taking the first steps in managing and promoting a singer, Steve Leeds, whom he met in the late part of 1967 or early part of 1968. Leeds came to Coleman's attention when his cousin Norm Blagman (who composed a pair of songs, including "Put the Blame on Me," that Elvis Presley recorded) and Nick Meglin (who would become an editor at *Mad* magazine) were auditioning a song they had written for Coleman; Leeds arrived with the writers to perform it.

The next day, Leeds recalled, "I got a call saying that they would like to have me sing on the demonstration records for *Sweet Charity*. They needed to show these tunes to Shirley MacLaine and Sammy Davis, etc. etc. So obviously, I said, 'That's great. I'd love to do it.'"[3]

Leeds did the recording session, and then, when Coleman formed Notable Records, he got a second call: "Cy loved my singing, and he decided to sign me to a two-year recording contract and a managing contract."[4] Coleman put Leeds on the first release from the new label, a 45 on which Leeds delivered the new *Charity* title song and "It's a Nice Face," with the appropriate alterations made for a male singer.

Coleman's arrangement for the A side walked a fine line, managing to sound pop and Broadway concurrently with Leeds's breezy and sunny vocals, supported by equally cheery background singers, pushing the tune toward the former. On the B side, Coleman's uptempo arrangement, heavy with electronic instruments, turns the gentle ballad heard in the film into a more insistent piece of music.

Leeds believed that Coleman created these versions of the songs in an attempt to help them compete against Burt Bacharach and Hal David's "Raindrops Keep Falling on My Head," which, as recorded by B. J. Thomas, was an enormous hit at the time. They might also have been one last attempt by Coleman part to create buzz and awareness of the tunes so that they would be considered as best song possibilities for the Academy Award nominations.

Coleman himself became the second artist to be featured on Notable Records, with the release of a 45 offering his own "Russian Roulette." This instrumental piece sounded a bit like one of the Monkees' chipper tunes—the group was at the height of its popularity at the time—slowed down to eerie, dissonant effect. On the B side was a decidedly funky version of an older Coleman tune, "Sweet Pussycat." A review in the December 10 issue of *Variety* commented on the "offbeat" sound of both offerings, noting that it could mean that they might have "novelty impact."

In tandem with this record, Coleman launched an extensive advertising campaign in the trade papers for the disc. It featured him at his sartorially hippest, with longish hair and bushy moustache and sporting an embroidered turtleneck pullover that might have been found in London's Carnaby Street. There was not only a grooviness but also a creepy playfulness to the full-page ads: they featured Coleman, revolver in hand, with two other men, seemingly dead and lying across the studio control board. The copy for the advertisement included a list of the artists "who gave their lives" recording the piece. In the text, too, Notable Records extended "deepest sympathy to those who have not heard ['Russian Roulette']."

Coleman returned to a less "out there" sound for the next two records for the label, which included his own cover of Bobby Hebb's "Sunny." It's a full-bodied orchestral take on the soulful tune that features several nimble and speedy piano solos from Coleman, and in a May 23 review *Billboard* commented on the "powerful workout" he gave the song and predicted it would chart. Against songs like Guess Who's "American Woman," Chicago's "Make Me Smile," and the Beatles' "The Long and Winding Road," Coleman's "Sunny" failed to climb into the paper's rankings.

Between Coleman's two releases there was one from another artist, blues singer Jimmy Huff, whom Coleman had also signed to Notable and who took on songs from two of Notable's songwriters, Hod David and Tom Paisley: "The Lonely Young Girls" and "I'd Love Making Love to You." Both tunes were the most decidedly rock of the four releases, though both were tinged with a slight country feel. Huff's raw, plaintive vocals imbued the songs with an emotional urgency that helped to garner modest sales attention. The record spent four weeks on the "Looking Ahead" charts in *Cashbox* magazine but never managed to break into the publication's Top 100 charts. Still, this release demonstrated the synergy that Coleman was developing with his multifaceted business practices, which were beginning to mirror those of his mentor publisher, Bud Morris.

Back when Coleman was first starting out, he saw that Morris knew the value of publishing the songs from Broadway and Off-Broadway shows. By creating a recording arm at Notable, Coleman was able to expand on Morris's business practices by both printing sheet music and ensuring that the public knew the company's music through the singles he released. The songs that Huff had performed, in fact, came from one such property, David and Paisley's musical *Cities*.

This show never made it to production in New York, but another one for which Coleman had also acquired publishing rights was on its way to the stage during the course of 1970: *Sensations*, a rock musical based on Shakespeare's *Romeo and Juliet*. It had lyrics by Paul Zakrzweski and music by Wally Harper, who was then just starting out but would go on to a multifaceted music-theater career, perhaps most famously serving as Barbara Cook's musical director for nearly thirty years.

Unlike *Cities*, *Sensations* made it to a full production and opened October 25 at Theatre Four in midtown Manhattan. In his *New York Times* review the following day Mel Gussow complained that the show lacked cohesiveness, but he also wrote that it was "challenging, original, ambitious, and overflowing with artistic riches." Perhaps most important (particularly for Coleman), Gussow found that Harper had composed "one of the best rock scores I have ever heard—complex, richly textured, even hummable—a perfect answer to anyone who thinks rock is not melodic."

Other reviewers were less charitable regarding the weaknesses of the show's book but still admired its music. A November 18 *Variety* review said the composer had written "an interesting score, even if major portions sound as abrasive as William and Jean Eckart's largely pop art setting looks."

Before the reviews were out, Mercury Records committed to a cast album, to be released as a double LP, and also recorded several singles of songs from the show, including one of "Lying Here" from Leeds. The record was released in tandem with the musical's debut, and in a *Billboard* review of the recording Coleman was heralded for having discovered someone who would eventually become "a chart winner."[5] Coleman understood the potential in Leeds and demonstrated his commitment to his client when he took out a full-page ad in *Billboard* to toast him and the single.

Mercury also recorded a cut of Coleman himself singing the show's title song. When the show closed after only sixteen performances, neither this, the cast album, nor the many other singles that were touted prior to the show's opening hit stores. According to an October 21 story in *Variety*, Coleman had "racked up singles from the score." Among the artists who were theoretically committed to record *Sensations* tunes were Shirley Bassey, Sammy Davis Jr., and Robert Goulet.

Also unreleased were the final two songs Coleman had written with Murray Grand specifically for Leeds—"Now" and "Holes in My Shoes." Demos of the two reveal that neither Coleman and Grand's work nor Leeds's was subpar, so it's difficult to understand why Coleman chose to keep them off the market. It might have had something to do with the fact that Coleman was probably having a growing sense that his work with Leeds was about to come to an end.

Looking back on this period, Leeds said, "I wasn't receptive [to what Coleman was doing]. I was too busy with a relationship with a woman back in the Bronx, a childhood girlfriend, getting married, and my drinking career started there. . . . My priorities were all screwed up." As an example, he pointed to what happened when Coleman enrolled him at the Stella Adler Studio of Acting: "His idea was to kind of launch my career through the soap operas. . . . I went to a couple of classes, but I just kind of went through the motions."[6]

The professional ties between Coleman and Leeds were severed as 1970 turned into 1971, but the two remained friends for the remainder of Coleman's life. Regardless of the difficulties that arose between Coleman and Leeds during their work together, it was a time when Coleman was squarely in one of the places he liked best as both an artist and a businessman: the recording studio.

Leeds recalled Coleman's demeanor in the studio and enjoyment of the process of recording: "Cy would say, 'Why don't you phrase it this way,' and I'd be very nervous, and he'd be kidding around, and I'd be thinking, 'This must be costing him a fortune having all of these strings in here.'"[7]

It was during this time that Coleman came to know recording engineer and producer Tony Bongiovi, who was making a name for himself in New York after several successful years working with Berry Gordy at the Motown Studios in Detroit. Bongiovi, who would eventually cofound the cutting-edge Power Station studios, looked back on meeting Coleman: "I got Cy Coleman there one time. I didn't know who he was, and we recorded [some songs from] 'Sweet Charity'. . . . He liked what I did with the recordings when I'd say 'Let's try this and let's try that,' and so I participated beyond my normal job, which is to sit there and make sure everything is recorded properly."[8]

Bongiovi's almost improvisational approach to recording appealed to Coleman, and when Coleman returned to the studio for his own and Huff's subsequent sessions, Bongiovi remembered, "Cy always asked for me to work with him, because of the way I interacted with him."[9]

The rapport was mutual. "Cy was very easy in the studio. He'd let it happen. He'd let the arranger and the musicians work it out, and if he was critical of anything, maybe he'd go out and say, 'No. No. This is the chord here, not that.' That's why we became good friends; there was no arrogance. He wasn't demanding. . . . He was one of the few people in New York who was a professional and a success whom I became friends with."[10]

A measure of Coleman's success, just as Bongiovi was coming to know him, could be found in the growing number of appearances Coleman was making as a celebrity performer at fund-raising benefits. He had always been an active champion of causes, particularly ones with a liberal agenda, but as the 1960s drew to a close and the 1970s dawned he was featured almost monthly as part of the entertainment at events for organizations ranging from New York's public television station to the Muscular Dystrophy Association.

Assisting such worthy causes provided Coleman with an outlet that his work as a businessman and a recording artist could not: he was able to return to live performance without having to commit to a two- or three-week period in a specific venue.

Coleman's accomplishments also paid financial—and, by extension, personal—dividends. In August 1971, after years of summer rentals in Amagansett, he bought a two-level home in Southampton. It would be both a haven and a workspace for the remainder of his life. His love of the beach and this place even inspired him to write one of the few songs for which he supplied his own words, "September's Coming," which went unrecorded until *It Started with a Dream*, a late-life CD from Coleman himself. In the liner notes he wrote: "I didn't start out as a beach person, but at a fairly young age turned into one. That, coupled with my fondness for autumn and my strong feeling that September is when exciting things start to happen, inspired me to write this tone poem."

Coleman's busy workload also included searching for properties for a Broadway musical to work on with Dorothy Fields. There had been *The Coffee Lover* just before the start of filming on *Sweet Charity*, and there were also rumors of other shows, such as one from early 1967, when Jack O'Brian reported that he had uncovered the project the writers had "been cloaking in such secrecy."[11] It was a musical version of the 1941 movie *Hold Back the Dawn*, which had starred Charles Boyer and Olivia de Havilland. The idea for this project most likely came from Fields, who had for a while in the mid-1950s toyed with the idea of using some of Jerome Kern's unpublished melodies as the basis for a musical version of the film. Nothing from Coleman or Fields ever materialized for it, however, and though the success of *Charity* prompted many offers, the team turned them down.

At the end of 1969 Coleman and Fields did find a property to musicalize: a prizewinning play by Jerome Coopersmith, who received a Tony Award nomination for his book for the Sherlock Holmes musical *Baker Street* and who also contributed to the book of the musical *The Apple Tree*. Coopersmith had recently taken first prize in a Massachusetts State College drama competition with a biodrama about Eleanor Roosevelt; it focused on her young adulthood at the dawn of the twentieth century as she struck out to forge a life on her own and found herself being wooed by the man who would become America's only four-term president, Franklin Delano Roosevelt.

As originally envisioned, the piece would contain songs. Coopersmith's conceit had Eleanor repeatedly returning to a central musical theme and literally trying on different hats as she attempted to create her identity.

Coleman took an unusual step with regard to the project. He optioned it himself, and his decision to start work on it—without the benefit of an outside producer—demonstrates that he was trying to gain more control over his work and career. Now, in addition to serving as producer of his own records, publishing a growing catalog of music, and managing performers, he was considering the possibility of serving as his own theatrical producer, thus gaining the ability to completely shepherd a show as it was being developed.

In the first story about the project, *Variety* made special note of the new role that Coleman and Fields were taking. They would be "proceeding without a producer for present. They'll most likely coproduce it with an outside management."[12] With the announcement, which projected that the show could potentially reach Broadway within the 1969–70 season, came one other significant detail. A director had been signed to stage the production: Morton Da Costa, who after his work on both the stage and film versions of *Auntie Mame* and *The Music Man* had developed something of a spotty track record, thanks to shows like *Sherry!* and *Maggie Flynn*, both of which had brief runs (fewer than a hundred performances) on Broadway.

Coleman, Fields, and Coopersmith worked on *Eleanor* throughout the course of 1970, but according to Coopersmith it was a rocky collaboration from the outset: "Dorothy was ill-tempered and negative about my work from the beginning. She wanted to throw out my concept entirely and start from scratch to write a musical play about the Roosevelts. I had to remind her what the situation was: namely, that the play was already written and I thought being considered for musical adaptation."

Coleman attempted to defuse the situation: "At one point, she went into the kitchen to get coffee and cookies for all of us. When she was gone, Cy whispered to me, 'Watch out for her. She's half monster, half Jewish mama.'"[13]

Despite the differences between Fields and Coopersmith, he did begin making changes so that the book for the musical focused more on the
romance between Eleanor and Franklin. But the goal of having *Eleanor*
reach Broadway before summer 1970 was not met. Instead, it began to
appear among the shows being touted for the 1970–71 Broadway season.

By this point not only had Coopersmith given the show a new title—"If
There Were More People Like You"—but Coleman and Fields had also
outlined some seventeen songs that would be part of it, including the
trunk songs "Keep It in the Family" and "After Forty, It's Patch, Patch,
Patch." Coleman and Fields also completed work on another nine numbers, and the show was in good enough shape that they offered a reading
of it to Alexander Cohen, who came on board to serve as producer.

The team also began looking for stars and found the performers they
believed could play the central roles. For the future president they turned
to Ken Howard, who recalled, "Dorothy Fields, and maybe Cy too, liked
me a lot from *1776*, and maybe she'd seen me in something else, and she
had it in her mind that she wanted me to play the young Franklin Delano
Roosevelt. And I said, 'I'm a little tall and I'm a little young.' She didn't
care."[14]

For the title role, they set their sights on Jane Alexander, who had
earned raves for her performance opposite James Earl Jones in Howard
Sackler's *The Great White Hope*. Years later Coleman remembered, "Jane
Alexander, who later did 'Eleanor and Roosevelt,' was somebody I was
working with for that role."[15]

The team redrafted the work once Cohen became involved, and plans
started for a Broadway bow in the spring of 1971. In January of that year,
however, Cohen withdrew from his involvement. Coleman later recalled:
"We couldn't get it produced. Everybody disliked the book. . . . But the
book writer didn't want anybody coming in and changing anything,"
Although Coleman attempted to do some more fund-raising himself, he
was, according to columnist Hobe Morrison, "unable to get the project in
motion."[16]

Eventually, the show was abandoned, and for the rest of his life Coleman would often say that it was a score of which he was particularly

proud. Houston Huddleston, Floyd and Nancy Huddleston's son, recalled that when he was a young adult working to get his start in the film business he spent some time with Coleman, who, no matter how busy, would always find time for his friends and their kids. When Huddleston asked the songwriter about his career, Coleman told Huddleston that *Eleanor* had "the best score I ever wrote that no one will ever hear."[17]

The difficulties with getting *Eleanor* to the stage might have contributed to a shift in Coleman's focus on writing partners other than Fields during this period. Perhaps most surprisingly, and even though they hadn't worked together in any substantive or genuinely collegial way in nearly ten years, Coleman started working with Carolyn Leigh again.

Their renewed collaboration resulted in a single song, a curious bit of specialty material, "Feathers," which has a slight 1920s bounce to it. Its sound may indicate that they intended it for a production that producer Arthur Whitelaw announced at the end of 1971: a full-scale revival of *Little Me* that would feature a revised book by Neil Simon and new songs by Coleman and Leigh. But, like *Eleanor*, the project never got further than the drafting stages.

A similar fate lay in store for one other show to which Coleman and Leigh were attached during their trial reunion. In early 1972 Alexander Cohen announced that he would produce a new version of the topical revue *Hellzapoppin*, which had enjoyed a nearly three-year run in the late 1930s. It took over four years to bring this production to the stage, and when he did it featured only one song from Coleman and Leigh: a cutout from *Wildcat*, "Bouncing Back for More." The songwriters, however, would never see the day when this tune would debut on Broadway. *Hellzapoppin*, which starred film comedian Jerry Lewis and stage and screen star Lynn Redgrave, closed during its out-of-town tryout.

The troubles that Cohen had in getting *Hellzapoppin* to the stage were indicative of changes that were taking place in the paradigm of bringing a new musical to Broadway. No longer could producers simply announce a show and have it arrive within the span of a year. The cost of bringing a show to Broadway had risen too steeply. For instance, Coleman's first show, *Wildcat*, required an investment of $450,000 (or, in 1976 dollars, roughly $850,000). In comparison, when *Hellzapoppin* closed out of town in 1976, it cost nearly $1.3 million.

It was a trend that Coleman took seriously and attempted to address throughout the remainder of his career. He always had at least three or four different shows, with different collaborators, in process at any given moment. One musical that would be part of his life through the end of the decade was born alongside these other projects.

It was a show that Coleman developed with his longtime friend and sometime collaborator James Lipton, who had provided lyrics to one of Coleman's melodies from the score of the movie *The Art of Love*. By the time it was announced in the fall of 1971, the musical the two men had written was known as *Beautiful People*.

The tuner centered on a forty-eight-hour marathon group encounter session. During the course of the show, all of the patients—from an unhappy Westchester housewife to a repressed gay man to a woman who had once been a centerfold model for a *Playboy*-style men's magazine—stripped away their repressed feelings and desires to emerge as relatively cleansed souls.

For *Beautiful People* Coleman worked in a pop vein, supporting Lipton's tale. It was one that aimed at being as frank as possible about life in 1971, covering not only issues of sexuality and sexual identity but also the strictures that society was placing on the group participants.

Coleman and Lipton's work attracted producer Herman Levin, who was responsible for bringing *Gentlemen Prefer Blondes* and *My Fair Lady* to Broadway and at the time was enjoying another very different success with the drama *The Great White Hope*. Levin's plan, during the final months of 1971, was to produce Coleman and Lipton's show on Broadway the following spring. However, simultaneously with Levin's acquisition of the rights, Coleman and Fields finally found the property that they had been seeking for two years. *Beautiful People* would have to wait.

18

Seesaw

With their new project, a musical version of William Gibson's two-character play *Two for the Seesaw*, Coleman and Dorothy Fields found themselves returning to both a milieu and character types that had helped inspire them during their first outing together. This portrait of a conventional man from Nebraska and a decidedly unconventional woman from New York falling in love despite their differences bowed on Broadway in 1958 starring Henry Fonda and Anne Bancroft. With its backdrop of New York City and its slightly kooky heroine, who yearns for a man with whom she can share her life, Gibson's play had more than a passing similarity to *Sweet Charity*, and the fact that the film version of it starred Shirley MacLaine (opposite Robert Mitchum) only reinforced the sense that Coleman and Fields were returning to familiar territory.

The first inkling that the intimate piece was being turned into a musical came in September 1970 in a season preview in *Variety*. The show, like *Eleanor*, was expected during the course of the next seven months. At the time, however, producers Joseph Kipness and Lawrence Kasha—whose most recent productions were *Applause* (the musical adaptation of *All About Eve*) and the rock musical *Inner City*—could not release any information about who the creators might be.

For the next year the project disappeared from the news. Stories about the spring 1971 season didn't mention it, and when previews of the 1971–72 season ran, a musical version of *Seesaw* was not among the shows anticipated. Then, in November 1971, Jack O'Brian led his column with the news that Coleman and Fields would be creating the score and that

Michael Stewart (who wrote the book for the Tony-winning musical *Bye Bye Birdie* and picked up a Tony Award for his book for *Hello, Dolly!*) would write the show's book. O'Brian even added a bit of Shubert Alley gossip: "Liza Minnelli can have the role originated by Anne Bancroft."[1]

The Minnelli rumor went no further, and she wasn't mentioned at all when the *New York Times* carried a story about the show in January. Fascinatingly, however, the piece did remind readers that another musical version of Gibson's play had once been in the works. In 1967 Hillard Elkins, who produced the Sammy Davis Jr. musical *Golden Boy*, with a book by Gibson, announced that he had convinced the playwright to write *Gittel*, a musical that would "weave a brand new script" around the heroine.[2]

This plan evaporated when Gibson grew "reluctant" about the idea, and it was only after the success of *Applause*, which starred Lauren Bacall, that Gibson allowed Kipness and Kasha to option his play for musicalization. When the *Times* story was published, Stewart had already been working on the adaptation for nearly six months, and he told the paper, "I hope I've kept the spirit of the play without swamping it."[3]

By May *Seesaw* appeared to be picking up steam. The producers announced that they had engaged Robert Moore (who'd helmed *Promises, Promises*) to direct and that they anticipated the show would arrive on Broadway by Christmas, after tryout engagements in Washington, D.C., and Detroit. But by July it seemed as if these announcements had been premature: a *Variety* article about Broadway productions for the coming season made no mention of *Seesaw*. Its omission might have struck insiders as particularly peculiar, since the story outlined plans for numerous other and much more speculative projects, such as the Coleman and Leigh–scored *Hellzapoppin* and *Eleanor*, which still had Coopersmith as book writer, along with a new set of producers and a songwriting team that had yet to be named.

The omission of *Seesaw* from this article might have stemmed from the fact that Kipness and Kasha had to find a new director: over the summer Robert Moore withdrew. In his place came Edwin Sherin, who had been steadily establishing himself as a director of nonmusicals, particularly at Arena Stage in Washington, D.C., where he had served as associate producing director. Among his credits were classics like Bertolt Brecht's *Galileo* and Shakespeare's *Macbeth*, as well as new works, perhaps most notably Howard Sackler's Pulitzer- and Tony-winning *The Great White Hope*, which marked his Broadway debut as a director. Sherin (who married *The Great White Hope*'s star Alexander in 1975) was a bold choice that underscored the fact that both the producers and creators felt *Seesaw* had the potential to be something other than a run-of-the-mill musical comedy.

While Kipness and Kasha were working on nailing down the specifics of the production, which by August had been delayed to March 1973 and booked for the Palace Theatre, Coleman and Fields worked steadily at outfitting Stewart's evolving book with songs. Because of the similarities between Gittel and Charity, the team had a pair of trunk songs that easily fit into the show. They found a spot not only for "Poor Everybody Else," which had briefly been used in *Sweet Charity*, but also for "Big Fat Heart," which had never been performed.

The songwriting team also looked to their most recent collaboration for material as they contemplated the *Seesaw* score, and they found places for "If There Were More People Like You," "We've Got It," and "It's Not Where You Start, It's Where You Finish," from *Eleanor*. They were even able to use one song from *The Coffee Lover*, the teasing "You're in a Highly Emotional State," in this new project.

They augmented these songs, which with the exception of one were for the central characters, with another fourteen during *Seesaw*'s development and rehearsal process. Coleman worked in a variety of musical vernaculars to bring a genuinely contemporary sound to the show and to emphasize the multiethnic landscape that Stewart was building into his book. Before going into rehearsals, Coleman and Fields completed a rousing Latin-infused ensemble number, "Spanglish"; a gospel solo for one of Gittel's best friends, "Ride Out the Storm"; and a semi-funkadelic paean to Manhattan, "My City."

Alongside these were other songs that brought a smooth pop sound to the show. "Pick Up the Pieces," "He's Good for Me," and "Loveable Lunatic" all coursed with the sort of energy and rhythms that were associated with performers ranging from Neil Sedaka to Dionne Warwick.

Coleman's knowledge of pop and his facility with any number of styles uniquely suited him not just for a show like *Seesaw* but also for the changing musical landscape of Broadway. After all, he'd brought in a synthesizer for *Sweet Charity* in 1966. Since then such landmark shows as *Hair*, *Jesus Christ Superstar*, and *Godspell*, as well as lesser-known ones like Melvin Van Peebles's *Ain't Supposed to Die a Natural Death* and *Don't Sell Us Cheap*, had radically changed the sound of Broadway musicals. In his work on *Seesaw*, Coleman was attempting to bridge the divide between a "golden age" sound and a pure rock score.

With the particulars for the production in place and the script and score being finalized, casting began. For the leading man, Fields suggested the performer she had wanted to play young Franklin Roosevelt, Ken Howard, and after a pair of auditions he had the role of Jerry Ryan.

For Gittel Mosca, there had been some big names floated in columns (generally by Jack O'Brian, who after stumping for Minnelli, suggested both Barbra Streisand and the original Gittel, Anne Bancroft). The role eventually went to Lainie Kazan, Coleman's longtime friend, whose career as both a singer and actress had been steadily on the rise since the mid-1960s. She recalled how she got the part after seeing an announcement of the show in a trade paper: "I called [Cy], and I asked him if I could come in on my own dime and audition for them. And he said, 'Of course,' and so I flew in and I auditioned for Ed Sherin and Cy and Dorothy and Michael Stewart, and from that I won the role."[4]

As casting continued through the latter part of 1972, the company grew to include Bill Starr, who would play Gittel's good friend and dance teacher, Larry; and Joshie Jo Armstead, who played her best female friend, aspiring actress Sophie. Tellingly, both performers came to *Seesaw* after having worked in musicals that featured a pop sound. Starr had been in *Via Galactica* (a short-lived rock musical by Galt MacDermott, who had written *Hair*), and Armstead had been seen in one of Van Peebles's musicals. The company also featured another *Galactica* vet, Richard Ryder, along with Chris Wilzak, who was making her Broadway debut, as the couple who ran Gittel's favorite health-food restaurant. Playing Jerry's Latino neighbors were Gloria Irizarry and a very young Giancarlo Esposito.

Via Galactica not only provided *Seesaw* with some of its players but also with a home, the Uris Theatre (later renamed the Gershwin), which was left vacant when the former show closed after a mere seven performances. With the new theater came a new opening date, February 27, 1973.

The casting of Starr and Ryder—who were performing in *Galactica* until December 2—indicates how tight the rehearsal process was for *Seesaw*, which was slated to begin previews at the Fisher Theatre in Detroit on January 8. Sherin, along with choreographer Grover Dale, had been able to do certain amounts of work with the principals and the dancers, but the company had only the month of December—and a short month at that, because of the holidays—to get the musical in shape for audiences.

A further sense of how *Seesaw* was coming together at the eleventh hour came from musical director Don Pippin, who had a long string of Broadway credits on shows like *Irma La Douce* and *Mame* and had won a Tony Award for his work in this capacity on *Oliver!* He recalled how he was hired for the new show: "I was called by the producers a few days before rehearsals, and I just happened to be free, so I said, 'Okay. Fine.' As a favor." A few days later Pippin, who had never met Coleman, had his first meeting about the score with the composer. "After about an hour of our first meeting, knowing I had to get vocal arrangements done before rehearsal, which was only three days away, I suddenly realized we were never going to get through the material, because there were so many different ways his mind kept going about everything."[5]

It was, Pippin recalled, an indication of Coleman's "nimble, fast mind. . . . It wasn't a question of any of them weren't very interesting, but you had to choose one of them." Eventually, Pippin decided, "I had to start making very fast choices, so I could get out of there and start doing my work."[6]

Neither Howard nor Kazan recalled time being an issue as they rehearsed, but there were others. Howard remembered that Sherin "sort of wanted to deal with this great *Two for the Seesaw* story and leave the singing and dancing to the others. Somebody like Robert Moore [with whom Howard had worked on *Promises, Promises*] can do that with a certain amount of style and say, 'Listen, as far as I'm concerned, a key is something you open a door with.' He would defer to others, but he had a sense of what the whole musical was." He added, "I got the feeling that Michael Stewart, right from the beginning, wasn't happy with Lainie, so there was a little bit of an edge."[7]

Kazan remembered, "I had been studying with Lee Strasberg and Sanford Meisner, and I was very much the method actress, you know? And I was trying to be pure in my approach to the role, and I became Gittel Mosca."

Because of Sherin's background, she said, "he understood my approach to the role, where no one else did because they were all from the musical theater. You know, 'Hit your mark,' 'Say your lines,' and 'Sing out, Louise.' I was going deep into the role. I was carving this role out and knowing where it would end up but getting there in a different manner. The impatience for success from everyone was so immediate that they didn't allow that kind of work."[8]

It all came to a head one afternoon when Stewart exploded and Kazan ended up in tears. At this point, Howard recalled, "I left. I just didn't want to be part of it. This was a disaster. You could just sense it. It was all wrong." Producer Kipness, who owned a nearby restaurant, Joe's Pier 52, saw what had happened and stopped Howard, saying, "C'mon kid. Let's go to my place and have a drink." Over a couple of shots of Jack Daniels, Kipness assured the leading man, "Don't worry, kid, you're doing fine. We'll see what happens on the road," to which Howard replied, "Joe, no. I don't want to get in the middle of this back and forth."[9]

But Howard didn't want to leave the show, particularly because he was enjoying his work with the songwriters so much: "That was always a joy and nothing less than really, really helpful. Cy was—I don't think I was so square—but Cy was cool. He really knew how to kinda swing it."[10]

Yet the tension continued to concern him, and a few nights later he ran into producer David Merrick at a theater district restaurant. Howard and the producer had worked on a number of shows together, not only with the touring company of the musical *Promises, Promises* but also with the Broadway production of Robert Marasco's thriller *Child's Play*, for which Howard won a Tony Award.

"I tell him what's going on and that I'm nervous. He said, 'All right. This is what's going to happen.' He said, 'Just do what you do. Don't get embroiled in all of this. You'll be fine. They'll replace the role of Gittel. It will be one of four actresses.'" Howard said he remembered Merrick specifically named Linda Lavin, Brenda Vaccaro, and Michele Lee. Howard also recalled that Merrick's forecast continued: "And I think Michele Lee might be the smartest choice."[11]

According to Howard, the conversation continued. "And then [Merrick] said, 'They'll have to bring in a new choreographer. It'll either be Ron Field or Michael Bennett.' . . . And then he gave me his phone number and said, 'If things really become troublesome, call me. This is my private number. And I'll advise you whether you need to go into a hospital with nervous exhaustion.' He was trying to protect me."[12]

The tension extended to the music department, on one day at least, when the orchestra assembled to play through Larry Fallon's orchestrations for the first time. Much to Pippin's surprise, Coleman stopped the musicians with surprising frequency. "I know from years of work that not only is it a terrible way to work; you never get an overall pattern about how something is. Musicians absolutely hate it, because they want to get a feeling of what is this piece like and what are the demands of this piece. And you can't get that if you're stopping every few bars," said Pippin.

Pippin tried to stop Coleman, but to no avail. "I was so annoyed with him, and he wouldn't stop. And I thought, 'I've got to take a strong stand,' and the only way was to not go back to rehearsal after lunch. And so they came looking for me, and they said, 'Cy's upset that you're not there. We should get going.' And I said, 'Please tell Cy we are both not needed.' That was the strongest message. And then he apologized to me, and I explained to him why I did that, and I said, 'Cy, I cannot work this way. The orchestra hates it. They hate you, and we cannot get a feeling of what your music is like.' And then he stopped and he backed off."[13]

The company eventually left for Detroit for a week and a half of previews, where during the first few performances the show ran over three and a half hours long. Before opening on January 17 it had been trimmed to just under three hours, mostly with cuts to tighten the book, although some of Coleman's interstitial music, which used snatches of recitative and short reprises, was also excised.

The morning after the opening the reviews from the dailies came in. Lawrence DeVine, writing in the *Detroit Free Press*, was particularly hard on the show, labeling it a "mess." His chief complaint was that the two-character show had been too aggressively expanded. He observed that Gibson's original title "has been pared down 75 percent," and then added, "But everyplace else the scheme has been to add and then add some more."

The *Variety* review one week later echoed Devine's sentiments: "It's not bad enough that Gittel Mosca has a bleeding ulcer. In 'Seesaw,' they've put her in a busy, cluttered musical and surrounded her with 57 other characters more or less representing New York's low-level theatrical world."

Jay Carr, in the *Detroit News* on the morning after the opening, took an entirely different view of how the musical had expanded upon its source material. He praised the fact that "the affair between a dancer named Gittel and an about-to-be-divorced lawyer from Omaha named Jerry is minor compared to the passion between Gittel and New York."

And while the critics took aim not only at the deficiencies of the book but also at Sherin's direction and the performers, particularly Kazan, Coleman and Fields's contributions to the show received generally high marks. DeVine said that it had "a cantering, lyrical score" and Carr described the music as being "suavely eclectic."

More than the local reviews, it was the *Variety* review that provided advice on what should be done next with the show: "Gittel and Ryan need more time alone to develop their characters and their plight. They should not be interrupted by a Puerto Rican street theatre presentation of 'Hamlet,' no matter how quaint."

Given the notices, producers Kipness and Kasha decided that the show needed a new director, or at least an artist who could come in and doctor it, providing advice on how to improve it without necessarily unseating the existing director. They approached Jerome Robbins, but he turned the project down. When the team called Michael Bennett, he flew to Detroit to assess what might be done.

At this time, Bennett was just on the cusp of what would become his extraordinary career as a director-choreographer, the force behind such musicals as *A Chorus Line* and *Dreamgirls*. Despite the fact that these shows were still in his future, he had already established himself as a formidable presence on Broadway. In 1972 he had just picked up a pair of Tony Awards for his work on *Follies*, one for choreography and one for direction (which he shared with Harold Prince). Among his other credits were Tony-nominated work on Burt Bacharach and Hal David's *Promises, Promises* and Stephen Sondheim's *Company*.

After Bennett saw the troubled show he met with the producers and outlined what they would have to agree to before he would consent to working on *Seesaw*. Some of his demands involved money for new sets and costumes. Beyond this, Pippin recalled, "He made it quite clear that he would come in, but only if he had dictatorial—and that was the word he used—dictatorial control of that show. He said, 'There is no time to meet with people, discuss it, argue about it, anything.' He said, 'We only have time to do what I feel I can do with the show. Period.' And that's the way it worked. And no one was allowed to interfere with him at all."[14]

The producers agreed, and within a week of the opening Ed Sherin was let go from the production. Bennett put out phone calls to longtime friends and colleagues, asking them to come to Detroit to help him with the overhaul of the show, which was only four weeks away from its scheduled New York opening. Bennett knew that he would not be able to do all of the needed work on his own.

In short order, Bob Avian, Baayork Lee, Thommie Walsh, and Tommy Tune were in Detroit. Tune recalled how he came to the show: "I'd just gotten back to this country from making *The Boy Friend* over in London, and Michael Bennett was going to let me stay in his apartment for a while 'til I could find a place to live. . . . So, as I'm going into Michael's house— he left the key under the mat—the phone's ringing. So I answer it, and it was Michael, and he said, 'Don't unpack. Come to Detroit. I'm taking over on a show called *Seesaw*, and I need you to choreograph some numbers for me."[15]

Sherin wasn't the only person who was fired from the show. Leading

lady Kazan was also let go and replaced by—as Merrick predicted—
Michele Lee, who had gotten a phone call from Kasha asking her to read
the script and consider the part. She did so, agreed, and was soon on her
way to Michigan.

As for Kazan, she recalled: "I remember [Ed Sherin] taking me out
to dinner and saying, 'I've been fired, but you're going to be great. Just
stick with it and roll with the punches. It's going to be a wonderful success, and I leave you with love.' It was very sad. And then, when Michael
Bennett came in, oh my God. He didn't even say hello to me. He didn't
even acknowledge me. And one night I called him and said, 'Please, Mr.
Bennett. I would just like to have you hear me and see me in what I do,
and then if you don't like what I'm doing you can tell me. I'll change it. I'll
do whatever you want. I'm an actress. I can do it.' And he sent a message
back to me, I swear to God, with his assistant, and he said, 'Tell Ms. Kazan
I'm too stoned to come down to see her.'"

In looking back on what happened in Detroit, Kazan called it all a
"nightmare" and remembered that even Coleman, to whom she had been
so close ten years earlier, was not available to her. "I guess his business
hat was on more than his affection for me. . . . It was as though he couldn't
allow himself to be soft to me or open to my problems because he had
problems of his own. And I didn't understand that. That's where it ended
for a while. But, you know, we came back together as friends and spoke,
but it was a distant relationship after that."[16]

Despite being fired, Kazan continued to perform while Bennett
worked with Howard, Lee, and the company (which was also being radically reconfigured) during the day on a new version of the show. Lee
recalled, "I don't know how Ken survived. I mean, the brain. Forget it.
He would do the show at night with the songs and dialogue as they were,
and then during the day we'd rehearse the 'new *Seesaw*' changes, which
weren't just changes in scenes and some characters but also in the musical numbers."[17]

This grueling schedule for the performers and the creators continued
for two weeks as *Seesaw* finished its engagement at the Fisher. For Coleman, suffering from the London flu, which had hit the United States in

epidemic proportions that winter, it meant not only writing new songs but also providing new dance arrangements.

Among the first of the new numbers that Coleman and Fields wrote was "Welcome to Holiday Inn," which replaced "You're in a Highly Emotional State," a song for Gittel just before she and Jerry might spend their first night together. It wasn't only the song that changed but also the scene in which it was delivered as Bennett began reshaping the musical. Instead of having a bittersweet tone that closely mirrored Gibson's play, it became one that was both direct and filled with a bit of comic romance, thanks to the new song. The change to this section of the show did not mean, however, that "Emotional State" was lost entirely (at least at this point). Bennett shifted it into another scene, and had Jerry deliver it as "I'm in a Highly Emotional State."

Such repurposing extended to other numbers, such as "Ride Out the Storm," which Sophie originally sang after nailing an audition. This scene in the second act, which featured her delivering a hefty section of Shakespeare's *Antony and Cleopatra*, was cut entirely, and the song was shifted to the first act and performed during a party that Gittel attended when she was supposed to be meeting some of Jerry's business associates.

Just as Bennett had Stewart trim the book in Detroit, Coleman and Fields's score was also truncated, with "Pick Up the Pieces" and "More People Like You" among the songs that were jettisoned entirely.

Changes also extended to the orchestrations and arrangements for Coleman's music, which had originally been done by Larry Fallon, who had only minimal experience in musical theater but a lengthy string of credits in the world of popular music, including working with Coleman on singles for pop records. Larry Wilcox, a veteran of five Broadway shows, came in to reorchestrate the show. As music director Pippin remembered it: "Wilcox, who was a fabulous orchestrator, came in and changed a lot of the orchestrations and did some of the new ones. . . . He did some great work in that show." Pippin also recalled, "Another major orchestrator, Jonathan Tunick, came in and did a couple of numbers too."[18]

As for the dance arrangements, Coleman always preferred to do them himself, and during rehearsals Coleman spent time in Grover Dale's studio watching as he created various numbers with his assistant and future wife, Anita Morris, as well as Michon Peacock, who was in the ensemble and also the show's dance captain.

Despite the flu and the need to write new songs with Fields, Coleman still wanted to work on the dance arrangements in Detroit, and they were at the center of Tune's first meeting with the composer. "I needed dance music, of course. And I said, 'I'm different than other choreographers. I like to dance to the melody.' That made him so happy because usually a dance arranger comes in and does variations on the theme. But I really like to dance to the melody, if it's a good melody. If it's not, then you sort of have to tamper with it. So we hit it off great, and then he wrote a countermelody for me for 'It's Not Where You Start,' because even he didn't want it played over too many times."[19]

But Coleman couldn't redo all of the dance music himself, and so another artist, Marvin Hamlisch, was brought in. "You know a lot of people helped," said Howard, "But I think of Marvin Hamlisch more because he was right at the piano as we were adding phrases and more music that we needed. He was a big part of it."[20]

By the time the show reached New York, it had been radically trimmed. It also had a new leading lady and featured a largely new ensemble, which included Dale's assistant Morris as well as Bennett's associates Walsh and Lee. And there was one new principal, Tune himself, whose facility with the dances led to his assuming the role that had been played by Bill Starr. "Michael said, 'I love these numbers, but I like the way you do them better than the guy playing the part; so I'm firing him and I'm putting you in."[21]

It was all part of an overall vision to transform the show, which Peacock described as having been originally "like *In the Heights*. There was a feel like being in the 'hood, being in the barrio, the *real* barrio." Bennett's vision she described as "slick city, hot stuff. I mean he went all the way. It just went from one far extreme to another far, far extreme."[22]

Still, Bennett had not finished with his work on the musical, and he also needed to make some changes to the theater itself. Howard recalled, "I remember Michael Bennett coming into the Uris Theatre and saying, 'I'm not opening this show with white walls.' So he made them paint the walls a darker brown. He tried everything he could to make the place kind of warm."[23]

Previews finally began on February 19, but there was still work ahead for Coleman and his fellow creators, and some of the changes that Bennett still wanted finally pushed book writer Stewart to the brink. He took his name off the show, and in a last-ditch effort Neil Simon, who had already earned the nickname "Doc" because of his ability to diagnose and fix the problems of flailing shows, was called in to make recommendations about how to improve *Seesaw*.

Among Simon's suggestions was a new opening number for Gittel, one that would better explain the story. In short order, Coleman and Fields produced "Nobody Does It Like Me" to replace "Big Fat Heart." Simon also recommended that Bennett cut an appearance by Jerry's former wife (a role played by Amanda McBroom, the singer-songwriter who would go on to write "The Rose"). "Neil said, 'Look, she's very good. There's nothing wrong with what she's doing. But in the audience's mind, she's not an equal. She's not a threat. If it were a movie, you'd need somebody like Dina Merrill. What you're going to have to do is let Amanda McBroom go, and I've written this scene, a very funny phone call in which the audience imagines the likes of a Dina Merrill . . . that will solve the problem."[24] McBroom wasn't let go, but her speaking role was eliminated.

One final piece of principal casting changed while the show was in previews at the Uris. Joshie Jo Armstead, who had been playing Gittel's friend Sophie, left the company and was replaced by Cecelia Norfleet. Armstead did not, however, leave the show behind entirely. She released a single version of the song she'd originated in the production, "Ride Out the Storm." According to columnist Leonard Lyons, the right to record it had been a "going-away present" from Coleman and Fields.[25]

Beyond the work on the show's material, there was another issue looming: given Stewart's departure, who would be credited as having written the book? Coleman and Bennett discussed the issue and ultimately decided that giving Fields the credit would make the most sense.

In the early 1980s, Coleman described to Paul Lazarus in an interview on *Anything Goes* on WBAI Radio what happened next: "So we called up

Dorothy and said, 'You must do this Dorothy, for the good of the show.' And she said, 'I don't know. I don't know. I did not write that book. I've written a lot of books.' And we said, 'That's precisely why. You're the only one that can. You're the only one who has real credibility, since you're the only one who has written books here.'"

Fields was not unaware of the importance to the show of the credit, so she considered the request carefully for several days. She ultimately declined, saying, "I cannot do it. I cannot put my name on something I didn't do."[26] Given Fields's decision, the only other logical choice was to give the credit to Bennett. He was, after all, the man whose vision had transformed the musical.

There was one more change Coleman and Fields decided on before opening. They wanted to make Gittel's closing number, "I'm Way Ahead," a stronger statement about the character's journey. They expanded the number, and when it was done, Lee related, "Cy picked me up in a cab, and in the back seat he handed me all of this music and said, 'This is the new 'I'm Way Ahead' finale.' We went upstairs to the rehearsal studio, and on this very old, out-of-tune piano, he played me the new 'I'm Way Ahead' finale, which we put in the show that night."[27]

Finally, on March 18, after extending the show's preview period by nearly two weeks, *Seesaw* officially opened to reviews that were, for a show that had gone through such turmoil, remarkably positive.

Coleman and Fields's contributions were generally well received. Richard Watts's review the following morning in the *New York Post* said that it was "steadily agreeable and tuneful," and several weeks later in a *Time* magazine review, T. E. Kalem said, "Cy Coleman's music is amiably melodic and Dorothy Fields' lyrics ingratiatingly intelligent."

Coleman received the highest praise from Martin Gottfried in a March 20 *Women's Wear Daily* review, not for the score itself but rather for his overall talent. "It is not his finest score—Coleman could doodle more interesting music on a ticket stub—but it sure as hell is melodic and singable."

The artist who received almost unanimous praise was scenic designer Robin Wagner, who had devised a series of moving screens onto which still images could be projected. In his opening-night review in the *New York Times*, Clive Barnes wrote: "The American musical theater has for long [*sic*] neglected projection techniques in its production, and in this way was far behind dance company [*sic*] such as the Alwin Nikolais or even certain opera productions. 'Seesaw,' which has scenic design by Robin Wagner and media art and photography by Sheppard Kerman, makes a determined effort to catch up, and with its projections of sky-scrapers and cityscapes it really does look very good."

What Barnes and his colleagues didn't realize, though, was how Bennett had transformed the use of the screens and the projections, which had originally been relatively static. As Wagner described it, "We discovered that if you put the projection on first against a black background and then the screens came into them, it looked like a moving projection. It was like watching movies. So when Michael saw that, he started building numbers around that. So suddenly he was choreographing the screens, which was a whole brand-new idea."[28]

As positive as the critics had been, they were not—as they're called in theater circles—"money reviews," and the production, which had been struggling at the box office during previews, needed help fast to spur ticket sales.

One of the opening-night attendees had been the city's mayor, John Lindsay, and at the party that followed he had trouble containing his en-thusiasm for the musical. Bennett latched on to this, as well as the strik-ing resemblance between Lindsay and leading man Howard, and hatched an idea. What if, in this musical about New York City, the *actual* mayor made a walk-on appearance? Bennett had Lee call, Lindsay agreed, and on March 23 he showed up in the opening number, in which "he played straight man to half a dozen chorus girls."[29]

This widely reported stunt was followed by another welcome infusion of publicity when Walter Kerr's Sunday review of the show appeared in the *New York Times*. It bore the headline "'Seesaw'—A Love of a Show," and it was simply a valentine, a rave through and through. Slowly ticket sales started to increase—but not nearly to the extent that was necessary to ensure the production's longevity.

A healthy, extended stay on Broadway required more than reviews and stunts (like an appearance by the company at City Hall in downtown Manhattan in late April). What was needed was a concerted advertising campaign that would raise the visibility of *Seesaw* and awareness of the positive reviews it had gotten. Unfortunately, however, the producers didn't have the money for such a push, and in fact Kasha and Kipness had misrepresented the production's financial health. Things were so bad that "at one point they had to lock the doors of the theater, because they had not turned in the tax money to the government," according to Pippin. "That was cleared up pretty fast. We didn't miss a performance; it was cleared up before that evening."[30]

Coleman, who had been taught well by his original publisher, knew that getting the music into public consciousness could help a show, and he had worked concertedly to get popular artists to record individual songs from the score. At one point it looked as if Tony Bennett would record "She's Good for Me" and that Peter Duchin would take on "Spanglish," but neither project materialized.

Coleman did convince singing legend Bing Crosby to return to the studio to record "It's Not Where You Start," but Crosby's version of the song was released only in the United Kingdom. And in a telling sign of how tastes in music had changed since Coleman had had over a dozen recordings in advance of *Sweet Charity*'s opening on Broadway, *Seesaw* ultimately spawned only two other singles: Armstead's "Ride Out the Storm" and a version of the title song recorded by the Cy Coleman Co-Op, an ad hoc singing group that had been created at London Records.

These records gave listeners only a limited sense of the show. Coleman knew that a cast album was needed, but in absence of a record company willing to bankroll such a venture, it fell to the producers to underwrite an LP. Once again, the limited funds that Kipness and Kasha had on hand meant that an original cast recording had to be financed some other way.

Eventually, Coleman, Kipness, Bennett, and Fields pooled money to get a studio session for the company. To keep costs low, the actors and musicians all agreed to work for scale. The LP hit stores by mid-June, and though well received, it was certainly no panacea for the show's box-office woes.

Ironically, the delay in opening—which had allowed the creative team to effect the final and important changes that Simon had recommended—also precluded its being eligible for the Tony Awards, which would have given *Seesaw* a much-needed jolt of publicity. Still, *Seesaw* attracted award attention that spring. Lee won Drama Desk and Outer Critics Circle Awards, and in New York Drama Critics Circle voting the show placed second, losing out to *A Little Night Music*. And when the 1974 Tony Awards rolled around, *Seesaw* received seven nominations, including one for best musical and one for Coleman and Fields's score. It won two, for Bennett's choreography and Tune's performance in a featured role.

Those awards, however, were not handed out until April 1974, and in the interim the show struggled. More cash was infused, and in June 1973 Jack O'Brian reported: "'Seesaw' needs more than its last-week gross of $66,000 to break even—even with all of the writers foregoing royalties—and even lyricist Dorothy Fields and composer Cy Coleman losing more than royalties—they helped out with fat five-figure donations each to keep it alive."

Within a month of this story came the news that *Seesaw* would go on hiatus in New York to play a weeklong engagement at the St. Louis Municipal Opera (familiarly known as the Muny), then return to New York and resume performances. In the process, the musical gained a new leading man, John Gavin. The show did indeed return to New York—but not to the Uris Theater: it reopened at the less cavernous Mark Hellinger Theatre.

Its return, however, did not spark ticket buyers' interest, and just a month later a closing notice was posted. This news, however, did attract buyers, and the production managed to stay open through the beginning of December, having played a total of 296 performances.

As with *Little Me*, which had been well received but never caught fire among theatergoers, Coleman would muse in later life about what might have contributed to the closing of *Seesaw*. At one point, he opined, "We should have stayed out on the road for two more weeks, but we didn't have the money. I think the negative rumors [about what happened in

Detroit] influenced New Yorkers. . . . The show turned around and they weren't ready for it yet."[31]

The closing on Broadway didn't mean the end of the show, though. A national tour was planned for the spring of 1974. The road company would star Lucie Arnaz, along with Gavin and Tune. In addition, it would feature a new song, "The Party's on Me," an edgily funky number written specifically as an ensemble number to replace "Ride Out the Storm."

This song turned out to have the last lyric Fields would ever write. She died on March 28, 1974, shortly before the tour was slated to launch. But she did get to see the company perform it. After Bennett had choreographed it, Tune said, "We got the number together and showed it to Dorothy. The lyrics were 'Everybody drink up. Everybody drink up. Drink up. The party's on me,' and she saw it in the afternoon. . . . Dorothy went home and died. So the last lyric she wrote was 'Drink up. The party's on me.' It was stunning. We got the news the next day, and it was so ironic that she had seen that number done and she was finished. She was finished with it."[32]

Two weeks later Ken Howard introduced Lee at the Tony Awards and paid tribute to Fields, saying, "Her death two weeks ago has left a hard-to-fill void in the musical theater."

19

"Bouncing Back for More"

For other musical theater writers, such as Richard Rodgers, who spent a majority of his career working with just two primary lyricists, or Alan Jay Lerner, whose main body of work was written with one composer, the death of a partner like Dorothy Fields might have resulted in a period of inactivity. But unlike these authors, Coleman had maintained and cultivated a host of different collaborative relationships since he and Fields first explored working together in the early 1960s, and his workload in the months following the opening of *Seesaw* was typical of how he juggled work with different partners while also creating opportunities for himself as a performer.

In May 1973 it looked as if Broadway would be welcoming a new Coleman musical before the end of the year: *Beautiful People*, the tuner about a marathon group encounter session that he and James Lipton had completed in late 1971. Herman Levin had originally planned on producing it, but after *Seesaw* started heading for the stage, he moved away from the project, making way for an unexpected producer, Warner Bros., which announced its intention not only to bring the show to the stage in the fall of 1973 but also to turn it into a feature film.

The company's investment in the show and its wide-ranging plans for the property fueled almost immediate interest in the musical among the general press, and soon details about the musical were fodder for columnists. Jack O'Brian became one of the first (and then most frequent) chroniclers of the aborning show when he reported that *Beautiful People* had a "fat role for a slender beauty that should make her a star. Agents have hundreds of clients lined up. The character's named Miss January because she's so-named in a Playboy centerfold."[1] In a subsequent column he teasingly told readers, "Eighteen roles are up for grabs in the Cy Coleman–Jimmy Lipton musical 'Beautiful People' and you'd be amazed at the stars fighting for them."[2]

Not to be left out, Earl Wilson used his column to tout the show over the summer: "None of the actresses up for Miss January in Cy Coleman's new musical, 'Beautiful People,' mind the nudity in one scene—what scares them is the torrid lesbian action."[3]

The section of the musical to which Wilson was so luridly referring was a dance sequence in which one of the women in the group became entranced by the sexuality being expressed by Miss January and one of the male group members, and in the process a heterosexual pas de deux transformed into a homosexual one.

Tellingly, neither these general-interest columnists nor reporters from industry press speculated about who might stage the work during the course of the summer, and in the absence of a director, there was no mention of when *Beautiful People* might be reaching the stage. As the 1973–74 season progressed, the show's title was never touted even as a dim possibility for production.

Glimpses of the show would be caught in articles over the next seven or eight years when the title would surface periodically on Coleman's slate of in-process projects. In most instances, however, the show was merely mentioned in tandem with another project that was in rehearsal or already in production.

Still, Coleman, who had gotten Tony Bennett to record one ballad from *Beautiful People*, "It Was You," for the 1972 LP *The Good Things in Life*, sustained his efforts to promote songs from his pop-heavy score for the show, and Carmen McRae recorded the bluesy torch song "Would You Believe" as part of her 1976 album *Can't Hide Love*. Furthermore, she included it in her act that year. One of her performances was preserved on *Live at Ratso's, Vol. 1*. The recording demonstrates the rich complexity of Coleman's melody, which strategically uses syncopation to underscore hairpin emotional turns in Lipton's lyric.

Beautiful People, though never produced, would carry with it one additional legacy. In late 1975 it became the center of a lawsuit that Coleman brought against director-choreographer Michael Bennett, with whom Coleman had shared both the script for the musical and a film treatment that he and Lipton had written about a group of Broadway chorus performers, also known as "gypsies." Coleman's contention was that Bennett had used the two projects as inspiration for his landmark hit *A Chorus Line*.

Terrie Curran, Coleman's aide-de-camp from this period until his death, recalled, "Cy and Jimmy were working on a thing called 'Gypsies,' and they liked Michael's direction after he'd stepped in on *Seesaw*. And apparently they invited him out to Southampton and told him the whole story, and he said he wasn't interested. Then, a little bit later, he came out with *A Chorus Line*, and Cy said, 'That's mine and Jimmy's idea.'"[4]

While generic elements from the two Coleman-Lipton projects, such as the audition process itself, surface in *A Chorus Line*'s tale of dancers vying for a coveted place in the chorus of a new Broadway musical, it contains nothing—either in terms of plot or character—that links it substantively to Coleman and Lipton's work. In his defense, Bennett denied that he ever saw either the script or the treatment. He eventually agreed to an out-of-court settlement.

Looking back, Nicholas Dante, who with James Kirkwood wrote the book for *A Chorus Line*, said, "Michael claimed he never read Cy's script, but I think he did, because he was so nervous about the case. I didn't see why, because the material in the show came from the tapes and the other interviews, and Jimmy and I never saw Cy's script."[5]

The details of what, if anything, transpired between Coleman and Bennett regarding *Beautiful People* must remain the source of speculation. There is, however, certainty about their plans to collaborate on another project: a new musical that, like *Beautiful People*, looked like it might reach Broadway during the 1973–74 season.

This show, known as *Pin-Ups*, was one that Coleman undertook with Fields as well as with book writer Leonard Gershe, whose play *Butterflies Are Free* had enjoyed a nearly three-year Broadway run and who also wrote the book for the musical *Destry Rides Again*. The *New York Times* described it as "a history of pin-ups, roughly from the time advertisers began using girls as sex symbols." Bennett didn't only plan to direct and choreograph *Pin-Ups*; he was also going to produce the multi-decade show, which he envisioned as "employing five or six top fashion designers to create the costumes."[6] This extravagant vision ultimately proved too costly, however, and Bennett abandoned the idea.

The loss of *Pin-Ups* as a new project and the ongoing difficulties in getting *Beautiful People* produced did not mean, however, that Coleman was stalled professionally. He began to create other opportunities for himself as a writer, initiating projects that would be on his docket for the next five to ten years and accepting offers for unexpected jobs as they came along. Most notably, he returned to New York's cabaret scene in late 1973 with a two-week engagement at the Rainbow Grill, the intimate venue adjacent to the fabled Rainbow Room atop Rockefeller Center.

Coleman's two-week stint was billed as "Cy Coleman and His Music," but unlike his first nightclub forays, when he fashioned a jazz trio, Coleman assembled a sextet of artists to appear alongside him: four musicians and two female backup singers. His program, as the title promised, was made up of his own songs, which he played and sang, along with one work that paid a nod to his earliest days of performing: a piece by Mozart.

Critics responded warmly to Coleman's return to performing after an absence of ten years. An October 24 *Variety* review called the show "a highly informal and entertaining act," and John S. Wilson, in his write-up in the *New York Times* on October 22, described him as "a lively, puckish singer."

It was an engagement affectionately recalled by Coleman's friends and colleagues, including Tommy Tune, who remembered how Coleman singled him out the night he attended the show: "He introduced me from the audience as 'that Dancing Devil, Tommy Tune.' It was the first time that had ever happened."[7]

Coleman's assistant Curran even held on to one of the lesser-known songs that Coleman included in the show: "Cy did a song that has one of my favorite lyrics, a song called 'Suddenly.' It was this song about New

York, and one of Jimmy's lyrics was 'There's a lemony snap in the air.' It was just a clever turn of words." In thinking about her boss's relationship with the lyricist, she added, "Cy was very loyal, and he would always use people he liked, and he liked Jimmy."[8]

And though Coleman ruefully told columnist Leonard Lyons that by returning to the cabaret scene "I feel like I'm opening an old can of peas,"[9] the Rainbow Grill experience set the stage perfectly for a new opportunity that was to come in 1974 just months before Fields's death: working on a solo show that Shirley MacLaine was preparing to open at the MGM Grand in Las Vegas.

Coleman recalled how he became involved with this project during a 2002 interview for a BBC Radio 2 documentary: "She was given a lot of money to do a nightclub act in Las Vegas, but she hadn't the slightest idea of how to go about it." He remembered her saying, "I don't know what I'm going to do," to which he responded, "For one, you do this, and then, you do this and this."

Coleman hadn't anticipated doing much more than offering some phone advice: "I had no intention of getting involved. It was just 'Here I can help you, take it and be well and any time you need something call me.'" Eventually, however, Coleman found himself composing new music for the show and consulting on the production with its writer, Bob Wells, as well as Alan Johnson, who staged the piece.

When MacLaine's show officially opened in July 1974, she received rapturous reviews, and before the end of the year Coleman, with Wells and John Bradford, had adapted the act for television. The special, *Shirley MacLaine: If They Could See Me Now*, aired in December 1974 and went on to score five prime-time Emmy nominations, winning one for Coleman in the category of outstanding writing in a comedy-variety or music special.

Coleman's work with MacLaine in this vein would continue over the next two years, starting with a second TV special, *Gypsy in My Soul*, which aired in January 1976 and which Coleman coproduced with Fred Ebb and executive producer William O. Harbach. The program, written by Ebb, paid tribute to MacLaine's roots as a Broadway chorus dancer (i.e., a gypsy). It was actually performed for an audience of working dancers and also featured *Wildcat* star Lucille Ball. The program used a number of Coleman's existing songs, including "Bouncing Back" (one of the cut *Wildcat* songs) and "It's Not Where You Start, It's Where You Finish," as well as one new one, "Bring Back Those Good Old Days," a number that managed to evoke old-style New Orleans jazz while also sounding like a chipper contemporary pop tune.

Gypsy in My Soul was even more widely acclaimed than MacLaine's first special, and after calling the show a "delight" in his January 20 *New York Times* review, John J. O'Connor predicted that it "should devour every musical Emmy Award they have next year." His expectations were partially met. The show garnered numerous nominations—including one for Coleman's music and one for the specialty material he and Ebb provided. Yet it picked up only two wins. One was for Tony Charmoli's choreography, and, more important, one named it "Outstanding Special— Comedy-Variety or Music," an award that included Coleman among the honorees.

Following its air date MacLaine took a stage version of the show on an international tour, garnering raves in London, and then brought it back to the United States, playing at Caesar's Palace in Las Vegas. *Gypsy* eventually served as the vehicle that brought MacLaine back to Broadway, and she opened it at Broadway's Palace Theatre in April 1976.

MacLaine's one-woman show did not, however, give Coleman his first post-*Seesaw* Broadway credit. That distinction went to a drama, Peter Shaffer's *Equus*, which opened on Broadway in October 1974 after an acclaimed run in London's West End. The play, a mystery of sorts, centers on a psychiatrist who is trying to find out why an adolescent boy for no apparent reason blinded a group of horses.

Coleman's contribution to the show was an original composition that played during a critical moment in the young man's treatment, when he relives an evening in which he and the young woman he's interested in go to the movies to take in a "skin flick" that's all the rage. Audiences didn't see the sexually explicit film that the two characters were watching, but they did hear the insistently rhythmic instrumental that Coleman had created as its soundtrack. Beyond crafting a melody with an unquestionable drive,

Coleman had also written one that was disturbingly creepy, and his work was made oddly futuristic thanks to the electric guitar work of Vinnie Bell, who hit the charts in 1970 with a similar-sounding solo for the love theme from the movie *Airport*.

Coleman's eye toward the future on this brief (under six minutes) piece of music presupposed his next theatrical outing, one made with old friends but new collaborators, Betty Comden and Adolph Green. The two had written lyrics for Leonard Bernstein's music for *Wonderful Town* and *On the Town* and had worked with composer Jule Styne on shows like *Bells Are Ringing* and *Do Re Mi*.

The friendship between the writers dated back to the 1950s (Comden and Green were guests on the debut episode of *Art Ford's Greenwich Village Party*, where Coleman was the regular musical artist), and through the years the relationship deepened to the point that Green's wife, actress-singer Phyllis Newman, recalled the countless evenings they had all spent together at the Greens' Central Park West apartment, where music and humor intermingled freely.

"The performing thing was a big thing. It's all one memory of Cy at the piano underscoring what you were saying as a joke," Newman remembered. The results of Coleman's impromptu songwriting about topics as simple as a lost dog would leave the group "screaming on the floor."[10]

In late 1974 Newman was approached by Wynn Handman, who was the artistic director of American Place Theatre Off-Broadway, an organization committed to nurturing new talents. Handman had, as Newman described it, "a very good idea for a revue about our future and knew I loved to put things like that together. I love the challenge of that sort of thing." Handman had already talked to some writers about contributing to the show, and Newman began to discuss it with people she knew, including Peter Stone. Eventually, Newman recalled realizing "I need songs. And then, I thought Cy and Betty and Adolph; they've never done anything together. So I talked to them all, and they said, 'Sure!'"[11]

During this first-time collaboration, the trio developed the working habits that would be their norm for nearly twenty years. They would always work closely together, experimenting with ideas in a free-form way.

"Cy's improvisations were insane," Newman recalled, adding, "Adolph would say that they would have to say, 'Stop, Cy. Play that again.' Because so much came out of him. So much music and such original stuff that they took to having a tape recorder around, telling him, 'Play it once more for the tape recorder.'"[12]

Newman added, "Because it just came bubbling, bubbling, bubbling out of him—the music—that's why he was such a great musical performer, jazz performer. He was filled with it. I've never seen anything quite like it. I know a lot and have known a lot of great, great composers, and most of them have a lot of that, but he had that extra performing thing."[13]

Eventually the writers came up with a trio of songs for *Straws in the Wind*. The most unusual, at least for Coleman, was "Simplified Language," a meditation on what a future without gender in people's vocabulary might be like. The underpinning of Coleman's melody is one of his favorite styles, a march, but it's written to be performed at double tempo to match Comden and Green's linguistic playfulness, resulting in what might be considered the composer's first patter song. The other tune that made it into *Straws* was "The Lost Word," a driving, melancholy waltz, in which Coleman's knowledge of and facility with Viennese traditions resulted in a superlatively moving lament to another notion that might disappear in the future: love. The trio's third song for the show, "Goin' Home," found them working in yet another vein as they crafted a comedy tune that might have been perfect for Al Jolson, had he ever needed to play an extraterrestrial leaving Earth for his home planet.

Straws in the Wind eventually grew to include numbers by Stephen Schwartz (then of *Godspell* fame and later the man behind *Wicked*), Billy Nichols, and the team of composer Galt MacDermot (*Hair*) and lyricist Ira Gasman, who would, because of this show, come to be one of Coleman's collaborators.

Between songs, *Straws in the Wind* had traditional revue sketches from not just Stone but also future Oscar and Tony Award winner Marshall Brickman, as well as sequences more literary in style, notably an extended monologue from novelist Donald Barthelme.

The show enjoyed a monthlong run, but Newman opted to not have it open to the press (an option available to all artists working at American Place Theatre). "It was my call, which to this day I rue, not to allow critics in," Newman mused. "It was so full of talent, but I did not feel that I had done my job well. Not that it wasn't well directed. I just didn't think it hung together, and that's the problem with a revue, and I was a fool because it was so full of wonderful stuff. But at that time, I guess I was vulnerable enough not to do it."[14]

Despite the lack of critical assessment at the time the songs debuted, they would later come to garner praise once the lyricists included them in their show *A Party with Comden and Green* in early 1977. At this time, as critics assessed some of their most famous numbers, they also admired the show's lesser-known titles, like "Simplified Language" and "The Lost Word." A *Variety* review deemed these two "outstanding."

Beyond resulting in three specific numbers, *Straws in the Wind* gave Coleman yet another avenue for future Broadway collaborations in a post–Dorothy Fields world.

20

I Love My Wife

After *Straws in the Wind* concluded its limited Off-Broadway engagement, Coleman spent time pursuing a career as a soloist with symphony orchestras. He made his debut with the Milwaukee Symphony in November 1974 and followed it with an appearance in New York at Town Hall with the American Symphony. Similar engagements in 1975 took him to work with pops groups in Syracuse as well as Pittsburgh, where he appeared with legendary conductor Arthur Fiedler. He also took part in a series of New York concerts that were part of the world-renowned Newport Jazz Festival.

He also returned to the studio to record his first LP in eight years. The album, *The Party's on Me*, took its title from the last song he'd written with Dorothy Fields, and as the LP's cover art—a woman dancing hip to hip with the silhouette of another figure in front of what looks to be a mirror ball—seemed to indicate, much of the music on the album drew inspiration from America's latest craze: disco.

In addition to a funked-up incarnation of the song that had been added to *Seesaw* for its national tour, the album contained covers of Jim Croce's "Time in a Bottle" and Neil Sedaka's "Love Will Keep Us Together," along with a couple of original Coleman tunes: a Muzak-y "Cote d'Azure" and a number that he was prepping for the next Shirley MacLaine special that he was working on, "Bring Back the Good Old Days." This latter tune, paired with "Chloe," a disco cover of the 1920s tune from Gus Kahn and Neil Morét, was released as a single by the album's label, RCA. Coleman's impeccable piano work and the sharply intelligent arrangements he and

Mike Berniker had created for the "Chloe" sparked with both listeners and dancers, putting the single briefly on *Billboard*'s "Disco Action" chart and later into the paper's Easy Listening Top 50.

In many respects Coleman's work on this LP seemed to be setting the stage for his next Broadway project, which began to come into focus just as "Chloe" was charting. The musical, slated to bring Coleman back together with Michael Stewart and producer Joe Kipness, would be an adaptation of a hit comedy from France: Luis Rego's *Viens chez moi, j'habite chez une copine*, which translated roughly to "Come Up to My Place, I'm Living with a Girlfriend."

Stewart, who had a house in the south of France, had traveled to Paris to see the show and was struck by what he saw there: "I found a packed house and a very mixed audience. There were families, kids, some very elegantly dressed people, others in jeans, and even a half row full of nuns, which surprised me, as I'd heard the show was about two ordinary middle-class couples (the guys were moving men) who live in a small suburb on the outskirts of Paris and decide that the four of them [want] to try a communal marital relationship."[1]

Stewart was impressed not only by the diversity of the audience that had come to see what he described as "a musical comedy about sex that wasn't in the least bit sexual. It was completely a family show." Furthermore, he was taken in by the production overall. "The musical numbers were handled in a very unusual manner. Not so much to forward the plot but to comment on it. Whenever they'd come to a musical number, one, two, or three of the guys would bring on their instruments, whoever was singing the number would go to either the right or left portals, unhook two microphones, they'd do the number almost as a sort of vaudeville presentation, and then go smoothly and lightly back into the plot."[2]

Stewart was so enamored of the show that he "called up Joe Kipness, one of Broadway's most adventurous producers . . . and persuaded him to come to Paris and see the show. Kippy doesn't know a word of French, but he could understand all of the laughter around him and agreed to get things moving."[3]

With Kipness involved and having determined to adapt the show for American audiences, creating "an X-rated musical for the entire family,"[4]

Stewart then turned to Coleman, who came on board because the idea of it appealed to him. "It used a revue format but it wasn't really a revue."[5]

That spring Stewart and Coleman completed work on the adaptation, resetting the action in Trenton, New Jersey. They also rethought the plot, so that the musical centered not on two couples' communal life together but on their attempts to join the ranks of the sexually liberated with a little wife swapping. "There's an innocence in these four people," Stewart said, "like all of the people I've ever written about."[6]

And as the piece evolved, the importance of the musicians in the show expanded. They weren't just a group who were called onstage to accompany the characters when a number began. In Stewart and Coleman's adaptation of Rego's script, they became characters in the show, old high school pals of the central characters who, along with playing music, delivered lines and sometimes served as stagehands.

The show's plot, style, and setting gave Coleman the chance to write a score that spanned the gamut of music, similar to what might be found by spinning a radio dial from one end to the other. Coleman himself said that the show's music was "a hybrid," adding, "But a hybrid is what I am. Beethoven, jazz, Broadway, TV—it all mixes up into who I am."[7] Indeed, the score to *I Love My Wife* has something for just about all musical tastes, from country ("Someone Wonderful I Missed") to light contemporary pop ("Love Revolution") to barbershop quartet ("A Mover's Life") to honky-tonk ("Hey There Good Times").

In a couple of instances Coleman looked backward to his previous work when developing the score. One song, "By Threes," was actually one of his old jazz instrumentals from the 1950s, "One-Two-Three." Another, "Scream," used a melody that he originally devised for *Eleanor.*

Eventually, the show had a bountiful seventeen songs, each in a different style yet seemingly cut from a similar piece of musical cloth thematically. And in Stewart's first outing as both book writer and lyricist, Coleman found a partner who, as he said, "didn't worry about writing like everybody else. He was fearless and smart."[8]

While the men worked, the search for a director was under way, and by August Joe Layton had been signed to direct and choreograph. Layton's career on Broadway stretched back to the early 1950s, when he made his debut as a performer in the original cast of *Wonderful Town*. Since then he had established himself as a choreographer and director, working on shows ranging from *The Sound of Music* (where he provided musical staging) to *Bette Midler's Clams on the Half Shell Revue*, which he entirely staged. Along the way Layton picked up a pair of Tony Awards for his dances, the first for Richard Rodgers's *No Strings* and the second for *George M!*, a bio-tuner about George M. Cohan with a book by Stewart, John Pascal, and Francine Pascal.

Once script, score, and director were in place, casting began, and by September the eight-member company had been assembled. The actor-singers for the show were two Broadway veterans, Lenny Baker and Ilene Graff, who played husband and wife Alvin and Cleo; and two performers making their Broadway debuts, James Naughton and Joanna Gleason, who played the other couple, Wally and Monica.

For the musicians Coleman assembled a group that included bass player John Miller (who had worked with Coleman on the LP *The Party's on Me*), guitarist Michael Mark, pianist Ken Bichel, and drummer Joseph Saulter. Because of the demands that would be placed on them, the musicians had to go through an audition process similar to that of the actors: reading lines, singing sample numbers, and even performing some simple dance steps. Miller joked about his memories of the audition. "They wanted us to do what in the business one would call choreography, but with musicians. I think they just wanted to know that we knew what our left leg was and what our right leg was."[9]

Miller, who had been specifically called in by Coleman, remembered being offered the gig of bass player and music director at his audition and later asked Stewart about his hiring: "I said to Michael Stewart, 'Michael, why did you guys give me the gig?' He said, 'It's very simple. When I had envisioned the role of Harvey, I envisioned a kind of short, kind of balding guy with glasses and a beard. Kind of above it all, within it all, and kind of like a jazz sage kind of guy. When you walked out on the stage, I turned to Cy, I said, 'I don't have to [see anyone else], even if this guy can barely carry a tune, can barely speak, he's the perfect guy.'"[10]

Once the company was formed, however, the production hit a snag. The cast was told that a backer had withdrawn support of the show's relatively small—just $350,000—capitalization, and that the tryout, which had been set to begin at Philadelphia's Forest Theatre on December 20, was scrubbed. All of the performers were asked to put a hold on their schedules until new financing could be secured. They agreed and even took part in backers' auditions for the show, which were held in Coleman's and Stewart's apartments.

After the show opened, Coleman described the process of raising money for the production: "It turned out to be the hardest thing I've ever done. Michael Stewart and I took this show to producers. Nobody was interested. Somebody would open a wallet on a street corner, and we'd stand and sing the songs. We had dinners all over Manhattan."[11]

By the beginning of 1977, however, their efforts had paid off. Terry Allen Kramer and Harry Rigby (who had backed *John Murray Anderson's Almanac*, the show with Coleman's first Broadway song in it) signed on as the show's producers, and a new timeline for the musical fell into place. Following a four-week rehearsal period, *I Love My Wife* would play a three-week engagement in Philadelphia before opening on Broadway in March.

Sadly, once rehearsals were under way, *I Love My Wife* had to overcome another hurdle: the loss of director-choreographer Layton. "One day we came in to work, and they said, 'Joe has been in an accident,'" Graff recalled. "They said that he had fallen from his loft and broken all the bones in his body and would not be continuing and that we were going to get a new director and a new choreographer."[12]

"I remember that morning terribly well," said Naughton. "It was 10 o'clock in the morning down at the Ukrainian Hall on the Lower East Side, and all of a sudden we didn't have a director. . . . We hung around trying to figure out what to do. Finally, an hour or two later, and I was sitting next to Cy as he was trying to find someone to come in. He put in a call to Gene Saks, who was living in California then with his wife, Bea Arthur. And, in fact, it was very funny. If you remember, Bea Arthur had a very deep voice, and Cy rang. . . . I remember him going 'Hi Gene, it's Cy!' And then he said, 'Oh, hello, Bea.'"[13]

Saks had a reputation for his work in comedy, having directed the film versions of Neil Simon's *Barefoot in the Park* and *The Odd Couple* and such light Broadway fare as Bernard Slade's *Same Time, Next Year* and Simon's *California Suite*. In addition, he had helmed the original production of Jerry Herman's *Mame*, with Angela Lansbury.

After the phone call, Saks flew to New York to take a look at the piece. He later told reporters, "I'd been working with Cy on another musical that's still in development. . . . I thought I owed him at least a trip to New York to listen." Saks looked at what the company had worked on so far and, as he recalled, "Something happened to me when I saw the four young performers and four musicians who are the cast. I couldn't get them out of my mind."[14] It was enough for him, and soon he—along with choreographer Onna White, with whom he'd worked on both *Mame* and the musical *Half a Sixpence*—were on board.

It was an awkward time for the company. "None of us was really off book yet, and we had a long way to go," Naughton said, "but all of a sudden we were in the position of having to audition what we were doing, what we had, for prospective directors."[15]

Nevertheless, a bond between Saks and the performers developed quickly, and by the end of the rehearsal period the cast had gained tremendous respect for Saks and his work. "He was heaven. Gene was one of those directors who makes you feel smart and funny because he responds to what you are doing. He laughs. To make him laugh is a great pleasure," Gleason explained. "Gene also knows comedy and timing down to the millisecond, and Gene knows what is true to a character and what isn't true to a character. He knows when you need to respond and when you don't need to respond, even physically. His comedic gifts are prodigious."[16]

Graff looked back on the process of working with Saks and one particular contribution he made in the use of the musicians: "It was Gene's idea to put them in the wacky costumes, so in my number, in 'Love Revolution,' they were devils, because they were the ones who were putting all of these naughty ideas in my head. And it was terrific."[17]

Graff's respect for Coleman and his work was equally profound. "Cy was a musician. He knew everything there was to know. And I'm not a good musician, but I come from music, and so there was a kind of respect for my—as much as it was, which was not great—musicianship. But he knew that I came from music and that I understood what he did was good and that it was special and that if we needed to change a chord, we didn't have to go to the arranger and say, 'How do you do that?' He knew how to write a great melody. The chords were interesting, the rhythms were fascinating, so you got the whole package."[18]

Miller's memories of Coleman's musicianship echoed Graff's. "What was so interesting for musicians playing Cy's music is that what would seem so complex a harmonic structure, how you're in one key and then, all of a sudden, without anything jarring, you're in the key that's the diminished fifth of the beginning chord. So, for musicians playing his stuff, there would always be this—especially when we'd hear Cy play it the first time—there'd always be this look we'd give each other, 'How did this guy get from here to there, having it seem so bloody seamless?'"[19]

As rehearsals progressed, Stewart honed sections of the book and Coleman tweaked the music. Unlike Coleman's previous shows, there wasn't any furious writing of new material. And only one song was jettisoned, a bit of Christian pop that was to have been performed as the two couples ate their Christmas Eve meal before the anticipated exchange of spouses.

Eventually the show reached Philadelphia (after a two-week delay to accommodate the transition between directors), and it offered two preview performances at the Forest before officially opening on March 22.

Reviews were supportive, if not overly enthusiastic. One in *Variety* on March 23 offered, "Where everybody ends up is hardly a surprise, but amusing single entendres and ingenious production gimmicks get you there."

Compared to Coleman's previous experiences out of town, his work on *I Love My Wife* in Philadelphia was relatively easy. There were no substantial rewrites, just judicious pruning and gentle revisions, and after the show's three-week tryout, *I Love My Wife* returned to New York and the Barrymore Theatre, where it opened on April 17.

It had been a particularly hard year for musicals, and for most of the season Broadway houses had been filled with special engagements featuring performers such as Shirley MacLaine, Debbie Reynolds, Bing Crosby, and Barry Manilow. New musicals had been disappointing, and even revivals of seemingly indestructible titles had lukewarm receptions. New productions of both *Guys and Dolls* and *Fiddler on the Roof* failed to last for a full year.

Broadway was eager for a hit, and in *I Love My Wife*, with its gentle, audience-friendly take on the sexual revolution, critics and audiences alike found a tuner they could embrace. The morning after the opening the love notes to *Wife* started to arrive, starting with Clive Barnes in the *New York Times*, who called it "bright, inventive, amusing and breezy" before singling out the importance of the show's conceit: "What Mr. Coleman and Mr. Stewart have done is breathtakingly simple, but no one—so far as this aging memory can recall—has ever done it before. . . . The musicians are welded into the play, as a kind of Greek chorus."

In the *Daily News* Douglas Watt offered similar accolades before concluding, "Musical comedy is back. Hooray!" And in the *New York Post* Martin Gottfried, though not necessarily as charmed by the show as some of his colleagues, devoted space to discussing the fact that Coleman had written the show's orchestrations and arrangements: "Orchestrators can, and too often do apply their own sounds to composers' music and make them sound common. Coleman's orchestrations are exactly in his music's spirit, of course, and bring out just what he was trying to do."

And, indeed, Coleman's work was meticulous in this regard. A few months after the show's opening, he described how he built "Hey There Good Times" to emphasize its feel-good qualities: "I began with the bass because the bass is the bottom and gives you the tone. Then I added the banjo, which gives it a nice old-time feeling of nostalgia and comfort. The next thing I thought necessary was rhythm—you want that beat to get stronger, so I brought in the drums. Last was the piano, to emphasize the melody."[20]

There were those who had troubles with the show, notably once the weeklies came out. In his review in the May 2 issue of the *New Yorker*, Brendan Gill took issue with the whole affair, calling it "a monotonous and mildly unsavory series of variations on a single witless joke." In his *New York Magazine* review Alan Rich decried it as being "a tepid knee-slapper."

Perhaps the difference in the tone of the reviews was a matter of timing: when the critics from the dailies reviewed the show, many hadn't taken in the musical that opened within days of *I Love My Wife*, the mega-hit *Annie*, which bowed on April 21. In the face of this genuinely family-friendly tuner, the genial and even schmaltzy sexuality espoused in *Wife* must certainly have been a bit of a head-scratcher. Even the dailies had noted that *I Love My Wife* seemed to be a bit behind the times; after all, *Bob & Carol & Ted & Alice* had brought the idea of wife swapping to movie screens around the country in 1969, and even the sitcom *All in the Family* had tackled it in 1972 when that show's female lead answered a personal ad, not understanding what was meant by the word "swingers."

The *I Love My Wife* cast members recognized the good fortune they had in the timing of their opening. "Fortunately, we opened just before *Annie*," recalled Naughton. "*Annie* sort of sucked a lot of air off of the street in terms of PR and so on, but we got in just under the wire and declared this kind of terrific little hit."[21]

And it wasn't just the show itself that was a hit. So was its title song, thanks to a record cut by Frank Sinatra backed by a sumptuous Nelson Riddle arrangement, that was released well before the production opened. The single did so well that *Billboard*'s review of *Wife* began with a reference to how it had opened "riding a crest of pre-opening publicity created by Frank Sinatra's tuneful version of the title song."[22]

Sinatra wasn't the only one crooning the tune. It became part of several cabaret performers' club acts during the first months of 1977, and Coleman's work as publisher-promoter resulted in a couple of other singles, including another of the title song from guitarist Tony Mottola and one of "Hey There Good Times" from pianist Michael Corey. Coleman also worked to get other recordings, and just before opening, *Billboard* reported that "Everybody Today Is Turning On" was "being recorded separately by Pearl Bailey and Ethel Merman."[23]

Neither of these ever made it to stores, nor did a proposed version of

"Someone Wonderful I Missed" that Peggy Lee was reportedly scheduled to release, but the show did get a cast album, after some furious bidding (theoretically) inspired by the 30,000-plus copies Sinatra's single sold. Eventually Atlantic Records released the LP, and Coleman lavished extra time and money on it, paying the cast for two sessions to create an album that "could compete with any pop album on the market."[24]

His exacting work paid off and spawned a new slew of praise for the music. "Cy Coleman's score and Michael Stewart's lyrics come across even brighter and wittier than they do on the stage," was Jerry Parker's response to the LP when he reviewed it in *Newsday* on November 20, 1977.

John S. Wilson's lengthier assessment of the album in the *New York Times* on October 10 noted: "The singers gain in vocal presence [on the record] and, in the process, several songs emerge in clearer terms than they do on stage. . . . There is a deeper, warmer charm in the country flavor of 'Someone Wonderful I Missed' . . . and the easy, 1940's pop style of 'Lovers on Christmas Eve.'"

Unlike Coleman's previous shows, most of which had opened in the winter, *I Love My Wife* opened in the spring, just weeks in advance of the awards season for theater, so it wasn't long before *I Love My Wife* could be advertised as one of the year's Tony Award–nominated musicals. In all, the show picked up six nominations, including Coleman's fourth for best score, and when the prizes were handed out in June, director Saks and performer Lenny Baker won in their respective categories. Other honors came in as the show settled into its run at the Barrymore. Gleason nabbed a Theatre World Award for an outstanding debut performance, and with the Drama Desk Awards Coleman received the award for outstanding music and the production's musicians were honored as a whole as outstanding featured actor in a musical.

On the heels of its opening came word that *I Love My Wife* would be produced in London's West End, and in October the show opened at the Prince of Wales Theatre (where *Sweet Charity* had played ten years before), marking the first time that Coleman had a show simultaneously playing on both sides of the Atlantic. Saks and White reprised their duties as director and choreographer for the production, which featured Ben Cross (a few years before his *Chariots of Fire* fame) and Liz Robertson (who had starred in the West End *A Little Night Music*) as Wally and Monica and Richard Beckindale (a favorite on British television thanks to shows like *Rising Damp* and *Porridge*) and Deborah Fallender (who would go on to have a substantial television career) as Alvin and Cleo.

The London critics were less enthusiastic about the show overall than their American counterparts, but Coleman's work continued to receive accolades for its diversity and unity. Robert Cushman wrote in the *Observer*, "Through rock, country, cod ballad, straight ballad, military march, buck and wing, and barrelhouse sing-along, Mr. Coleman manages to keep faith with each convention while adding to it a beat, a lilt, a rhythmic pattern or a sense of fun that is entirely his own."[25]

The U.K. production of *Wife* only managed to reach 401 performances, at which point the Broadway production was still enjoying its healthy run, thanks in part to the arrival of two stars, the brothers Tom and Dick Smothers, whose work on television, notably their own comedy show in the mid-1960s, had made them household names. They were joined by two new female leads. Barbara Sharma, who had been in both *Little Me* and *Sweet Charity* as featured dancer, took over the role of Cleo, and Janie Sell, whose credits included a recent revival of *Pal Joey* and Stewart's *George M!*

The Smothers Brothers' presence didn't translate only to ticket sales. It also meant that the show underwent some changes. They brought their knack for improvisational comedy to the production, and there were moments when they would simply ad lib. "'We don't do it as often as we could,' Dick Smothers said, 'but we try to draw on our own relationship, and use it to set up a relationship between the characters.'"[26]

Similarly, the addition of performers who were not necessarily singers into the show meant that it also began to change musically, and Miller noticed. "The Smothers Brothers came in, and you know with their experience there were certainly musical ideas that they had that they knew were going to work for them." Concerned, Miller called Coleman, saying, "I'm calling as the music director. It's my job to tell these people 'No.

Here's the way it goes, and here's the way it has to be sung.' I kind of assume that's what you entrusted me to do as music director."[27]

Miller recalled Coleman's response: "Cy said something like, 'I trust the music director to let the Smothers Brothers have the show run for six more months. Let them do whatever they want to do.'"[28]

Miller did, and the Smothers Brothers continued with the show into the spring of 1979 and later toured extensively with it. When it came time for a new Broadway cast, the producers opted to take the show in a new direction and announced that Jimmie Walker (who had become an instantly recognizable star thanks to his portrayal of J. J. Evans on the sitcom *Good Times*) would head an all–African American cast.

Walker eventually withdrew during rehearsals, but the idea of an all-black cast took hold, and as *I Love My Wife* entered its third year at the Barrymore, it boasted a new above-the-title star, Lawrence Hilton-Jacobs, who had played Freddie Washington on the sitcom *Welcome Back, Kotter* and was making his Broadway debut as the goofy Alvin. At his side were Broadway vets Hattie Winston as Cleo, and Marjorie Barnes and Larry Wiley as Monica and Wally.

The reconfiguring of the show's ethnicity unfortunately did not spur ticket sales, which even with the Smothers Brothers in the show had begun to dwindle. Shortly after the new cast took over, *I Love My Wife* closed after 857 performances. By that point it had spawned productions in cities such as Madrid, Johannesburg, and Tokyo, among others. But more important, during the show's two-year run another Coleman show reached Broadway, winning him his first Tony Award. He also watched a second musical collapse while wending its way to New York and was at work on a third that looked as if it would be ready for production by the end of the year.

21

On the Twentieth Century

When Michael Stewart approached Coleman about collaborating on *I Love My Wife*, the composer was also in talks with Betty Comden and Adolph Green about an idea that would allow them to continue the collaboration that had begun with *Straws in the Wind*. They were all eager to do a full musical, as the lyricists remembered: "The first time we sat down to write something with him things started to happen. He had imagination, individuality and a head full of exciting musical ideas."[1]

In 1976 they were still in the process of brainstorming, but there was one idea to which they kept returning, albeit reluctantly: Ben Hecht and Charles MacArthur's 1932 comedy *Twentieth Century*.

The farce, set aboard the fabled train that whisked passengers from Chicago to New York in the span of sixteen hours, centered on a onetime giant of the theater, producer Oscar Jaffe. Down on his luck, desperate for a hit, he boards the train with the intention of convincing Lily Garland, a screen star whom he had catapulted to fame on the stage, to make her return to the theater in his next show. The fact that they had had a prickly romance when they originally worked together doesn't help matters any, nor do a host of complications that arise en route.

Comden and Green were the ones who initially gravitated toward the material, but Coleman demurred: "I knew there was a certain perception that the show should have a 1920s score. I didn't mind doing a period piece, but it was not a period that I wanted to do. I felt it was too boxlike and confining musically."[2]

They discussed a number of other properties that might make sense and even considered creating a completely original musical, but somehow *Twentieth Century* kept coming up as they talked. Nevertheless, Coleman remained resistant to the idea.

Then, according to Comden and Green, "One day, working with Cy, we improvised a musical sequence that was highly flamboyant verging on the operatic. We laughed, dismissed it as 'too much,' and then suddenly realized that that was really the way Oscar and Lily should sound. In fact, it was the way the entire show should sound. We felt we had the key."[3]

Having moved beyond the hurdle of what the show should sound like, the process of adapting the original began. Comden and Green, working as the show's book writers as well as its lyricists, knew they had to streamline the original: "It seemed wildly verbose with a lot of subsidiary characters."[4]

They cut out some roles entirely, such as a pair of actors from Oberammergau who were passengers on the train, refugees from a lost production of that city's legendary history of a seventeenth-century passion play. But with the excision of these roles, they had to enhance another character that would provide Oscar with the necessary inspiration for luring Lily back to the stage. So they built up the role of a religious fanatic who was also en route to New York. They changed the character from a man to a woman and gave her the fanciful name of Letitia Primrose. It was through her presence that Oscar hit upon the idea of having Lily make her theatrical comeback as Mary Magdalene. Another terrific bit of recrafting was the name change they made for Lily's dim boyfriend from Hollywood. In the play he'd been an agent named George Smith. For the musical Comden and Green turned him into a preening young leading-man type named Bruce Granit.

By May 29, 1976, just three months after announcements had been made about the show that would become *I Love My Wife*, Jack O'Brian reported in his syndicated column that Coleman was at work on musicalizing *Twentieth Century*, and within a month the project even had its producers, Cy Feuer and Ernest Martin, the men who brought *Little Me* to Broadway.

For the rest of 1976 Coleman worked on both *Wife* and *On the Twentieth Century*, and by the time the former show was in rehearsals, Comden and Green were able to tell reporters during press junkets for their own show, *A Party with Comden and Green*, about their work with Coleman: "The new score is just glorious. It's given us a new enthusiasm for working in the musical theater again."[5]

Coleman was equally galvanized. Writing in this overblown style took him back to his days as a classical pianist, when he had loved playing Rossini as piano duets. The score, he remembered, "literally poured out. As a matter of fact, I was writing it so fast, I wouldn't have time to put it on paper,"[6] and as Green's wife, Phyllis Newman, remembered, Comden and Green were once again diving for their cassette recorders.

As Coleman rehearsed *Wife* and Comden and Green performed on Broadway, they also began the search for a director for their new show. To fill this role they turned to a man who was a legend in theatrical circles: Harold Prince. He had begun his career as a stage manager working for director George Abbott, eventually graduating to producing and then directing. Among the shows that producer Prince shepherded in the 1950s were *The Pajama Game*, *West Side Story*, and *Fiorello!* Shows like *She Loves Me*, *Cabaret*, and *Zorba*, all produced and directed by Prince, were among the impressive additions to his résumé in the 1960s, and then, with the dawn of the 1970s, he formed a relationship with Stephen Sondheim that resulted in *Company*, *Follies*, and *A Little Night Music*.

By the time Coleman, Comden, and Green were looking for a director, Prince was coming off his most recent Sondheim show, *Pacific Overtures*, in which he had lost some of his own money. Since then he had admittedly "shopped around for assignments."[7] One of these had been the film version of *A Little Night Music*. He soon got the call about possibly staging the trio's new show.

Prince was intrigued and went to Coleman's apartment to discuss the project. He arrived aware of the piece's history. He knew that his theatrical mentor Abbott had directed the original production. Prince had not been around to see that staging, but he had seen the film that it had inspired. Additionally, he had taken in the 1950 Broadway revival starring José Ferrer and Gloria Swanson. "I didn't think it was a great movie, and I didn't think the revival was great, but I thought it was fun."[8]

After he heard Coleman, Comden, and Green's work, he thought that the dimension they had added "was brilliant. They'd made a modern operetta out of it. The score was not a Broadway score. It was larger than life, like Oscar Jaffe. And I thought, 'That's interesting, what they have done.'"[9]

Beyond the songs, the project held an additional appeal for Prince: "I thought the best part of it is that you have to do a musical on a train. That's a challenge. Sort of the same thing that challenged me when I did *Kiss of the Spider Woman*, a whole musical in a jail, for God's sake. Well, a musical on a train, how the fuck do you do that? And that was tempting, plus the three of them are all quintessential professionals and good and the spirit of it was fun. So I said yes."[10]

It was an unusual move for Prince, who had built his reputation on musicals that were darker in tone. Beyond this anomaly, Prince also said, "It's the only time in my life that I did a show that was finished already."[11]

Casting notices for the show started to appear just weeks before *I Love My Wife* opened on Broadway. Then, in June, the production hit a stumbling block: Feuer and Martin pulled out as producers. A new team came in almost immediately: the newly formed Producers Circle 2, a consortium of theatrical backers with a fascinatingly diverse set of backgrounds. One member had considerable theatrical experience, Robert Fryer, who had coproduced *Sweet Charity* and was now managing director of Center Theatre Group in Los Angeles. The others ranged from Martin Richards, who had started his career as a singer, went on to work in casting at Twentieth Century–Fox, and subsequently graduated to production. Also part of the Producers Circle was Mary Lea Johnson, heiress to the Johnson & Johnson medical-products fortune, and a former actor, James Cresson. The group's work was not limited to theater; they were also backing films at the time, notably *The Boys from Brazil* and *The Shining*.

One of the reasons for Feuer and Martin's departure was a disagreement over casting. They wanted a star for the role of Oscar Jaffee, as he was now called in the musical, along the lines of Alfred Drake, Broadway's original Curly in *Oklahoma!*, or Danny Kaye, who had starred in musicals like *Lady in the Dark* and *Two by Two*, while Prince was leaning toward a performer with more of a background in nonmusicals.

One actor he considered was Alan Bates, who did indeed audition for the team. "We had a private call at Cy's apartment," said *On the Twentieth Century* choreographer Larry Fuller. "Cy played for him. It was just Betty and Adolph and Hal Prince and me, sitting in Cy's living room with Cy at the piano, which makes it more nerve-racking for the actor, as opposed to being at an aesthetic distance on a stage or in a big rehearsal room where you're not right on top of them. You could hear—well, not literally—but it seemed like you could hear the change in his pockets shaking, he was so nervous."[12]

The team had to pass on Bates because he wasn't up to the score's vocal demands. A similar fate was in store for an actress who auditioned for the role of Lily Garland: Meryl Streep, who had yet to make the transition from her stage career—which included having just starred on Broadway in the Kurt Weill–Bertolt Brecht musical *Happy End*—to her incredible one onscreen. Fuller recalled their post-audition discussion of the future star: "She didn't have the high Cs, and Betty and Adolph wanted the operetta voice, and so they were very disappointed to have to say, 'No, we can't use her.'"[13]

Eventually the role of Oscar went to John Cullum, who had picked up a Tony Award nomination for his portrayal of the psychiatrist in *On a Clear Day You Can See Forever* and had won a Tony for his performance in *Shenandoah*. Madeline Kahn, who had been an early favorite for the part, was cast as Lily. Kahn had begun her career on the stage, appearing in the last of Leonard Sillman's *New Faces* revues in 1968; Richard Rodgers's musical about Noah, *Two by Two*; and David Rabe's drama *In the Boom Boom Room*. Since this last show she had worked primarily as a film actress, notably in Mel Brooks's *Young Frankenstein* and *Blazing Saddles*. Her screen successes had been followed by a period of self-assessment. "I went into seclusion for . . . well, let's see now . . . about a year, in 1975, and it lasted a year and a half. I was very confused. I called a stop to everything. I had to see where I was."[14]

When *On the Twentieth Century* began rehearsals, the company also included Kevin Kline, who had been a member of John Houseman's company of Juilliard graduates, the Acting Company, and had appeared on

Broadway in the short-lived musical *The Robber Bridegroom*, as Lily's boy-friend. For Letitia Primrose, a role that for a while was rumored to belong to Mildred Natwick, Prince lured comedienne Imogene Coca, a staple of 1950s and '60s television, back to the stage.

Supporting roles in the musical were filled by a host of Broadway vets. George Coe and Dean Dittman played Oscar's protégés, Owen and Oliver, and George Lee Andrews (who would eventually have an extraordinary run in Prince's production of *The Phantom of the Opera*) got one of his first Broadway credits in the small role of a theatrical producer who was working against Oscar. Prince also cast Judy Kaye (an actress with whom he had been hoping to work for some time) in the relatively minor role of Lily's maid, Agnes. In addition, Kaye was on hand to serve as Kahn's understudy.

As for the design team, it included scenic designer Robin Wagner, who was responsible for giving *Seesaw* its innovative look, and costume designer Florence Klotz, who worked with Prince on his last three Sondheim musicals, winning Tony Awards for each. Wagner was responsible for bringing the art deco majesty of the train to life, creating an ingenious progression of units that allowed the show to shift seamlessly to spots both in its interior and exterior. He even devised a way in which audiences could experience, as if from a distance, the train's journey on the tracks. Wagner's gleaming sets were complemented marvelously by Klotz's detail-rich costume designs, which had period flair and made the glamour of the central characters palpable.

The creative team also included a new collaborator for Coleman: orchestrator Hershy Kay. Kay had been working on Broadway for over thirty years, and his involvement with shows like Leonard Bernstein's *Candide*, Marc Blitzstein's *Juno*, and Jerome Moross and John Latouche's *The Golden Apple*—all of which were operatic in nature—made him the ideal choice for this new show.

Given the size, scope, and technical intricacy of the production, rehearsals for the principals were conducted on an exact replica of Wagner's set, which was installed in one of two rehearsal rooms inside the Minskoff Theatre. Cullum vividly recalled, "It had all of the dimensions and the levels, and the train was there, and all the compartments were there, so we had a perfect set to work with."[15]

Prince had the principals on this recreation of the set on the first day of rehearsals, and at the same time Coleman began to work with Kahn on her songs. Larry Fuller remembered, "So, the first day of rehearsal, I happen to be in earshot when Hal told Cy to take Madeline in the small vocal room at the rehearsal studios . . . and go over her part of the score, which was considerable.[16]

Fuller continued, "I think that was in the morning. Anyway, a few hours later, when Cy had done this, I again happened to be standing with Hal when Cy came out of the rehearsal room and came over to us, and Hal said, 'Well, how did she do?' And Cy said, 'She won't sing above a G.' And Hal said, 'What do you mean? I thought they hired her—we hired her—because she could sing high Cs whenever needed.' And he said, 'Well, she can, but she's afraid she can't do that eight times a week.'"[17]

Eventually, Fuller recalled, a compromise was reached. "There were maybe three numbers where she had to sing the high C. They made alternate endings to each one of those numbers, so if she didn't feel vocally strong enough that day, she would do the lower note."[18]

It was the beginning of what Cullum called a "fraught time" as all of the creators, from Prince to Coleman to Comden and Green, struggled to hone the show, in particular the sections that illuminated the backstory of Oscar and Lily's relationship.

When the show went into rehearsal, Comden and Green's book included a series of flashbacks to Oscar and Lily's earliest days together, first as her theatrical star was rising and then the moment when she broke off with him. It came after she discovered that he was being unfaithful to her while she was touring in a production. For this section of the show, Coleman had written "Oscar Jaffee," a song that brings to mind the burlesque revelries featured during a birthday celebration for Orson Welles's character in his film *Citizen Kane*.

By the time the show reached Boston, these scenes, which moved back and forth between the action on the train, had been integrated into one extended sequence that took theatergoers through Lily and Oscar's stormy relationship. In the revision, Oscar wasn't unfaithful; rather, he deliberately undermined her in front of other producers as she was attempting to secure a role in a new play by Eugene O'Neill.

For this section the songwriters devised a new song, "This Is the Day," a Rudolf Friml–like aria in which Lily expressed her delight about the new prospects on her professional horizons. Coleman even wrote a small snippet of recitative for Lily and Agnes that harked back to the sorts of exchanges between maid and mistress in such operas as *The Barber of Seville.*

During the course of rehearsals, Prince took out two other numbers. One, "Lucky Lily," preceded the flashbacks to Oscar and Lily's personal life, and the other was a comedy piece for Oscar's aides-de-camp, "Show Biz Is the Lowest Biz There Is." He also had Coleman, Comden, and Green write one more new song, "Mine," which gave Oscar and Bruce a chance to preen in front of mirrors in two adjoining compartments on the train.

Prince recalled Coleman during rehearsals, saying, "I knew that he was more site specific than anyone I've ever worked with, and I've worked with a lot of people," adding, "When I direct, I do not let the authors come to the rehearsal. They come after I've put stuff on the stage. It's very difficult for authors to understand that, but I'm at a point—well, I have been for a long time—where I say, 'Let me do it. You come in in the afternoon and see it, and if I didn't do it right, I'll do it right the next day, but I can't have you sitting at my elbow.' That was hard for Cy, really hard. And I knew it. But he's the only one it's ever been hard for in all of my experience, including Lenny [Bernstein]."[19]

In looking back on his work with Coleman, Prince also said, "[Cy] was fun to work with. So knowledgeable about music. I'm not. I'm knowledgeable about theater. . . . He really knew everything there was to know about orchestrations and all of it. He was taking more responsibility than anyone I'd ever collaborated with before, including Sondheim or Bernstein really. Bernstein, no, I guess not. I don't know, because Lenny wrote a show and then just kind of went away and then came back once in a while. Cy was there all the time."[20]

Coleman might not always have been able to be at Prince's side while the director was staging the piece, but his involvement in the show was palpable, particularly for Kaye: "I really got to know Cy in the rehearsal process. Madeline, I don't know if she didn't like to rehearse or if she was afraid. Something was going on that I really couldn't tell. But I wound up being asked to sing a lot of stuff during the rehearsal process, and I had a couple of private work sessions with Cy, and it was like a match made in heaven. It was so much fun. It was just me going over to his office and working on music."[21]

Fuller remembered how he, too, worked with Kaye during rehearsals. "I would stage a number with Judy and the men, and when I had it more or less set, then I would teach Madeline separately, so that she didn't have to learn in front of anyone."[22]

With the rewrites that were happening and because of his work with Kahn and Kaye, Coleman didn't have as much time to spend with leading man Cullum, a fact that the actor regretted, particularly because he had gotten to work closely with the composer before rehearsals began.

Cullum had one particular memory of a meeting that took place in Coleman's apartment: "We discussed what would be the pleasant and convenient and doable notes that I could use in songs that he was going to have me sing, and I remember him saying, 'What are you comfortable with on a high note?' And I said, 'Well, I can hit an F-sharp, but I'm better off with an F.' And he said, 'No. What is your real comfort level?' And I said, 'Well, an E. I can sing that very well, and that's a good high note for me.' And he said, 'No, what are you really comfortable with?' And I said, 'Well, I can sing an E-flat all night long.' And so that was what he put into his brain, and I remember in certain songs, for instance, in 'The Sextet,' where I had about thirty-two E-flats all in a row."[23]

Similarly, Coleman crafted "Mine" for Cullum's and Kline's voices. Kline recalled that before the number was added, "They called me in during the second week of rehearsals and asked me to sing scales for them."[24]

Cullum said that ultimately "I didn't have that much to do with Cy during rehearsals, because there were so many other problems." What's interesting is that while he was aware that the show was going through a rough rehearsal period, he was not aware of specific difficulties with Kahn until the company was about to leave for Boston and Prince came to him to talk about her. "When Hal came to me and said that there might be a problem, it was the first time I knew it. And it was the last week of rehearsal in New York, and I said, 'Madeline Kahn is my leading lady. You are not going to get me to say anything against my leading lady, because I love her and I love what she does and I'm just not going to run her down.'"[25]

Whatever problems Kahn might have been having during rehearsals, either personal or professional, did not stop her from putting on a brave face for the press as the show neared its tryout run at Boston's Colonial Theatre. In mid-December 1977 she told *Boston Globe* reporter and critic Kevin Kelly, "My real dream's at hand, a big Broadway show, a really big Broadway show, 'Twentieth Century.'" Yet she did admit to him that she had concerns about being back onstage. "I know when I step out on that stage on opening night that I'm there to be judged, and that, truly, is what I detest."[26]

It wasn't only Kahn who was worried about the critics. Prince was too, because, as he remembered, "She could not sustain a performance night after night. She was used to doing Mel Brooks movies. She's hilariously funny. She had a nice operatic sound, but she tired easily. . . . I could not get a consistent performance out of her."[27]

Boston critics noticed something was wrong when the show opened on January 11. Kevin Kelly wrote in the *Boston Globe*, "Madeline Kahn is still outside Lily Garland, edgy in the first act, oddly restrained in the second." Beyond concerns about the performance, reviewers cited the extended flashback sequence as one of the show's most problematic points.

But, there was praise too, particularly for Coleman's score. Kelly might have felt that there was too much of it, but he called it "wry, precise, comically apt, and/or romantically appealing," and a January 18 *Variety* review called the score "suitably bouncy, matching the literate, amusing lyrics by Comden and Green."

In the days that followed the opening, Prince began to further refine the show, and when it came time to tackle the section that dealt with

Lily and Oscar's early days together, he took a draconian measure. After spending a day working on the scene, Cullum remembered that "the next day Hal . . . cut the entire scene, taking out a whole major set and leaving a big void in the play." The excision meant that the show might have lost one of Coleman's most lush ballads, "Our Private World," but Coleman, Comden, and Green managed to revise the book so that it was sung "not really as a duet, but rather as Oscar singing to himself and Lily singing to herself," said Cullum, who added, "Thank God Cy put that together and we were able to integrate it into the train scene. It was done in the compartment. It's one of the loveliest moments in the play as far as I'm concerned, and I was afraid we were going to lose it."[28]

Not only did they not lose this number, but the show gained "Life Is Like a Train," a song for four Pullman porters that served as a coda to the first-act finale in Boston and came to open the second act in New York. Coleman also significantly extended Kahn's act 2 musical soliloquy, "Babbette." As originally written, the song served to illustrate how torn Lily was between taking the role Oscar was offering, Mary Magdalene, and an offer to star in a stock drawing-room comedy that had come from another producer. With Coleman's addition of a mock British jazz extension, the song also came to solidly demonstrate that Lily chose the latter.

Fuller remembered that the book and music changes were driving Kahn "crazy," adding, "I was surprised at how resistant she was to doing new material with hardly any rehearsal, since she came from the stage and Broadway and that's the way they did it in those days, especially when they'd say 'That doesn't work? Well [makes the sound of murmured rewriting], here, do this now.'"[29]

Still, Coleman found ways to make the revisions fun. Wagner recalled how Coleman had mused about wanting some sort of special effect in the overture. It wasn't long after, according to Wagner, that "[Cy] brought in a train bell, and suddenly a train bell was coming out of the pit. And the next thing, we had fire extinguishers firing behind the wheels."[30]

With the book streamlined and the score revised, the production shifted back to New York and Broadway's St. James Theatre, where, according to Cullum, it was during "the last four previews in New York, on a Thursday, [that] the show worked. And it only worked, not because of the performers, but because the set worked. The set finally worked. And when that worked, the show worked."[31]

When opening night arrived on February 19, Kahn gave the performance Prince had been hoping for. "I rushed up to her dressing room, and I said, 'You finally gave me the performance I want! Thank god you did it!' And she looked in her mirror, in the dressing room, and she said, 'I hope you don't think I can do that every night.' And my heart sank, and I thought, 'We are in terrible trouble.'"[32]

Most critics had not seen the opening-night performance but rather the press previews that were given just before the official opening. Regardless, the notices that appeared on February 20 praised Kahn highly. In the *New York Daily News* Douglas Watt described her work as "lovely and spirited," and in the *New York Post* Clive Barnes called her performance "marvelous": "She is a consummate performer who can always do too much with taste, and skillfully vary it as too little with energy. A mystery encrusted with realism."

Additionally, Coleman received some of the strongest notices of his career. In his *New York Times* review Richard Eder wrote admiringly: "There are grandiloquent and amusing suggestions of everything from Tchaikovsky through Puccini and Friml and up through Kurt Weill. Mr. Coleman is witty and inventive, and though much of his energy is spent in serving the comic-theatrical mood of the production, a number of the songs stand beautifully on their own. The title song, with its eight-note motif like a trumpet flourish and its exuberant chorus, is one of the best."

Similarly, in his February 21 review for *Women's Wear Daily* Howard Kissel wrote: "The title song is less a song than a fragment, which makes it easier to remember. It is so infectiously harmonized that you can't wait for it to come back and you can't help singing it as you leave the theater. Apart from its bright period charm, the strength of Coleman's score is its tongue-in-cheek formality, its bravura, which is very much in the style of Ben Hecht and Charles MacArthur's play."

Not all of Coleman's reviews were so glowing. In *Newsday* Allan Wallach complained, "Many of the songs seem to be mock-operetta numbers that make you wonder just what they're mocking." There were also reservations about the book. "Miss Comden and Mr. Green are not writing at the top of their form," said Edwin Wilson in his February 22 *Wall Street Journal* review.

These and similar criticisms may have contributed to a curious ambivalence expressed in many of the reviews, and most explicitly in *Newsday*. "'On the Twentieth Century' . . . blends old and new with Broadway professionalism, yet the show never achieves that magical fusion of laughter, story and songs that a truly satisfying musical comedy needs."

One aspect of the show that received unanimous raves was Wagner's scenic design. In the *Daily News* Douglas Watt wrote that it was "an ingeniously versatile Art Deco setting . . . that practically cheers itself." Wagner's work was so notable, in fact, that it ended up spawning features, such as one in the March 12 *New York Times* that was emblazoned with the headline "On Broadway, the Spectacle's the Thing." In it Leticia Kent not only reported the cost for the set—$196,500 (about $750,000 in 2014 dollars)—but also described how theatergoers "clap for it as if for a star."

The irony, of course, is that after working on the quintessential modern-sounding mini-musical *I Love My Wife*, Coleman had, with his collaborators, created what could be seen as a forerunner of the mega-spectacle poperas that would arrive from Britain in the 1980s.

Shortly after opening, Prince recalled, "[Kahn] got sick. Started to not come in. The handwriting was on the wall. We put Judy in. Judy knocked the ball out of the park, night after night after night. She would have been a superstar if she had opened on Broadway. As it is she's won a couple of Tonys and she's a terrific performer. But that night would have made her a superstar."[33]

Kahn's absences continued. One of them remained vivid in the mind of Coleman's assistant, Terrie Curran. On this particular night, she and he had dinner at Trader Vic's at the Plaza. Afterward they were walking in the lobby, and Curran remembered: "As we turned, coming around the corner was Madeline and a friend. She looked at Cy. He looked at her. He said, 'Madeline.' She said, 'Cy,' and we went on, and he was furious because she wasn't sick."[34] Curran remembered that it wasn't long after this encounter that Kahn left the production.

Another tale from the weeks leading up to Kahn's leaving *On the Twentieth Century* came from choreographer Fuller, who remembered the events on the day that the show's cast album was recorded. "We had the recording session the old-fashioned way, where everything was done in one Sunday. Madeline came in after the ensemble had done their stuff. And she did some of her stuff with them, but none of the high endings. And then everyone left, except Madeline. And I stayed, because Hal wasn't there, and I felt like somebody from the creative staging staff should just be here. So I stayed with Cy and the guys in the recording booth."[35]

They worked on Kahn's solos, and then "they'd play up to the last sixteen bars or so to lead her into being able to sing the end of the number," Fuller said, adding, "And she did them. Every one of them—I think there were three but I'm not sure—without a problem. She'd do it maybe two or three times for each song. And she came into the booth and Cy was just gushing over her, trying to be so encouraging. "Oh, listen to this. It just sounds wonderful.' And she said, 'Yeah, well, I guess it's okay, but my throat feels really rather raw. I don't know.' And she left in this state of emotional upset again."[36]

Kaye, who had played Lily ten times, officially stepped into the role full-time on April 24, just two months after the show opened. The announcement of the casting change in the *New York Times* included the statement that "Miss Kahn, who was supposed to appear in the musical until October, said she was withdrawing because of damage to vocal chords."[37]

Despite the backstage drama, *On the Twentieth Century* proved to be a total triumph for Coleman. He picked up his first Tony Award for best score when the prizes were handed out on June 4. The show also earned awards for Cullum and Kline as best actor and best featured actor in a musical, respectively; Comden and Green won best book; and scenic designer Robin Wagner was honored for his fabulous recreation of the luxury train.

The show had garnered an additional four nominations, including one for best musical, which it lost to the Fats Waller revue *Ain't Misbehavin'*.

Kahn was also nominated, even though the producers had campaigned for the nomination to be given to Kaye. (There was a precedent for this. In 1970 Larry Kert, who had replaced an ailing Dean Jones, was nominated for the musical *Company*.) Kaye did, however, earn a Theatre World Award for an outstanding performance and a Drama Desk Award. Coleman also earned a Drama Desk Award for score (his second), and, even more impressive, he received his first nomination for induction into the Songwriters Hall of Fame just after *On the Twentieth Century* opened (an honor he would receive two years and two shows later).

As the musical settled into its run, Coleman, as publisher of the score, began to consider how to promote its songs. He hit upon an unusual idea. Having seen Linda Clifford's success with a disco version of "If My Friends Could See Me Now," Coleman decided to give some of the *On the Twentieth Century* songs the same treatment. He turned to his old friend Tony Bongiovi, who recalled that throughout their long relationship the composer would frequently come to him and ask, "Which of my songs will fit the new genre?"[38]

Coleman and Bongiovi settled on two songs: "Never" and "Our Private World." The former was given a treatment that brought to mind the work of Gloria Gaynor (with whom Bongiovi frequently worked), especially "I Will Survive." With the second, a vaguely Middle Eastern vibe was layered onto the lush ballad.

As news of his plans for his songs reached the media, there was talk that leading lady Judy Kaye would be the featured vocalist for the new versions, backed by the actors who were playing the Pullman porters. Ultimately, the new incarnations of the songs were recorded by the Body Shop and released both on a 45 single and as an extended dance mix on a $33^{1/3}$ single.

Billboard described Coleman's first foray into disco—the 1976 recording of "Chloe"—as having "made minor waves." These two new tracks didn't cause a ripple, but they do keenly demonstrate Coleman's determination to navigate the changing tastes of American music buyers.

A fate similar to that of these covers of *On the Twentieth Century* songs lay in store for the show itself, which never caught fire at the box office, although while it was running Coleman could boast for the first time in his career that he had two shows simultaneously on Broadway. And even before *On the Twentieth Century* ended its run at the St. James Theatre on March 18, 1979, it looked like Coleman might actually be on his way to having a trio of musicals playing concurrently on the Great White Way.

22

Home Again, Home Again

During the months that followed the acclaimed opening of *I Love My Wife*, Coleman and his forthcoming projects were profiled extensively. At the time he had on his docket not only *On the Twentieth Century* but also the still-in-waiting *Beautiful People* (or *Encounter*, as it had been retitled), a project with Christopher Gore, and another one that would feature a book by *New York Times* columnist Russell Baker and lyrics by Barbara Fried.

When Coleman talked about having four shows all in various stages of readiness for production, he said, "I wouldn't want to give the impression I'm grabbing off a lot of projects all of a sudden. . . . They've all been around from seven to two years. But you simply cannot just sit around and wait for people to raise the money, to wait for a director or something else."[1] Indeed, the Baker-Fried project had been on Coleman's docket since the early 1970s, not long after he and Fried first met.

Fried had spent much of her career working as an editor of music and psychology books at W. W. Norton, and she had turned to lyric writing only in the late 1960s, when she was approached by some friends about collaborating on a children's musical. During her initial foray into the field, she discovered that the process and work suited her and began to take on other projects.

It wasn't long after this that she found herself at Notable Music with composer John Morris, who did the dance arrangements for *Wildcat* and went on to write the musical *A Time for Singing*, an adaptation of *How Green Was My Valley*. Fried and Morris had just completed work on a musical with the working title *The Ways of My Youth*, which was based on her book, *The Middle Age Crisis*.

"We had a producer who brought us to Cy," Fried recalled, "and Cy liked it, and he took the show to publish it." Before it could go into production, however, Morris got a call about writing music for one of Mel Brooks's movies. "John went to California to work, and I was bereft," said Fried, who then took an approach to finding a new collaborator very similar to Coleman's own when he embarked on his relationship with Dorothy Fields. Fried simply went to him and asked, "'Do you want to work with me?'" And his answer, she said, was "Sure."[2]

Coleman and Fried's first two songs—not intended for a musical— were released in mid-1972, just as Coleman was embarking on a new relationship with London Records. When *Billboard* announced the deal, which gave Coleman an outlet different from his own with Notable Records, it was described as being one that would "bring a contemporary approach to melodic music . . . geared for the top 40 market without competing with the current rock groove."[3]

The London releases featured Coleman and a group of backup singers collectively billed as the Cy Coleman Co-Op. The first effort for the label was a single that had his setting of Christina Rosetti's poem "What Are Heavy?" on the A side and his and Fried's "When It Comes to Lovin'" on the B side. It was an unusual pairing of tunes. Coleman's music for "Heavy" bordered on the liturgical, while his melody for the song with Fried had a spry R&B vibe to it. The *Variety* review of the 45 deemed the first song "interesting," implicitly preferring the second by calling it "neatly swinging."[4] In the hipper publication *Melody Maker*, the sound of the record was snarkily described as sounding like "some old ladies [*sic*] choir."[5]

Regardless of the recording's critical reception, "When It Comes to Lovin'" demonstrated that Coleman had found a lyricist who could provide erudite and tricky rhymes for his music.

Coleman and Fried's second song together was "Think Love"; it was featured on the B side of a London Records release of Coleman and Sheldon Harnick's "Theme from *The Heartbreak Kid*." This happier pairing of tunes resulted in a more cohesive, contemporary sound.

About a year after these records had been released Fried got a phone call from Coleman. He wondered if she was familiar with a writer for the *New York Times*, Russell Baker, whose "Observer" columns pointedly and humorously tackled the topics of the day, from the Watergate scandal to the growth of militant movements to the inferiority of coffee making in the United States. Beyond his initial question, Coleman wanted to know if she thought Baker's columns might serve as the basis for a musical. She said, "I think so."[6]

Fried then wrote a series of lyrics based on Baker's columns, and Coleman set them to music. Eventually they had enough to show a producer, so she and Coleman took the songs to Herman Levin, who, for a while, had been considering producing Coleman and James Lipton's *Beautiful People*. During the meeting Fried recalled, "Herman said, 'You need a book writer. Why don't you ask Russell Baker?' So we asked Russell Baker." At the time Baker had just relocated from Washington to New York, and Fried had the sense that he, as she had been several years before, "was looking for something else to do."[7]

Baker recalled the events leading up to his hearing Coleman and Fried's work differently: "I had a call from the producer Herman Levin."[8] Levin told Baker of Coleman and Fried's efforts and then asked if he would be willing to come into the office to hear them play their songs.

Baker knew of Levin's success with shows like *My Fair Lady*. Furthermore, "Cy Coleman was also a big Broadway name to me. Also, I used to come up to New York from Baltimore in my Baltimore Sun days back in the 1940s and I remembered hearing Coleman playing cocktail music, at the Sherry-Netherland I think it was, and thinking he was pretty good."[9]

Thus, via a phone call either from Coleman and Fried or from Levin, Baker found himself in Levin's office in early 1975, where he "listened to Cy play and sing the songs with Barbara. It was exciting and inflating. The theater bug had bit. Pretty soon I was working on a primitive script designed to provide a setting for the songs."[10]

By July 1975, while Coleman, Comden, and Green were discussing what they might do as a follow-up to their collaboration on *Straws in the Wind*, and well before *I Love My Wife* was on the horizon, there was enough to the work with Baker to warrant a complete feature about the gestating show.

Baker admitted to *Newsday* writer Leo Seligsohn, "I feel quite innocent about the musical, like a boob in the big town. But, it's something to do, a challenge."[11] He noted that this was particularly true given that while the show would stretch from the Depression years through Watergate, he was used to writing columns that were only seven hundred words long.

Fried remembered in particular one instance of the difficulties Baker was facing as he shifted into the realm of writing dramatically: "He once said to me, 'I'm having a terrible time with this problem.' He had gotten to the point where [the show's protagonist] had grown up and become a reporter. He meets this girl and they fall in love, and he said, 'I don't know how I'm going to get to his three teenage kids.' I said, 'Russell, you have him turn to the audience and say, "These are my children." That's all you have to do.' It would never have occurred to him."[12]

Eventually Baker's script took shape as a book musical, and after he shared it with Levin, Baker said that the producer "seemed, I thought, unenthusiastic."[13] Levin's response, as well as the songs that Coleman and Fried had already crafted, led Baker down a new path, and what emerged was something more episodic: a journey through a man's life from birth to middle age as well as an investigation of the metamorphosis—or devolution—of the American Dream from the 1920s to the 1970s.

Baker began the show with a scene in an amorphous void somewhere in the universe where past and future collided as the musical's protagonist, Philip (as he was known in early drafts), was learning from his deceased father, known just as Witherspoon, that he was about to be sent to Earth to be born in 1926. The wry tone of the show could be summed up by Witherspoon's reverie about the state of the country, which came in the middle of the song "America Is Bathed in Sunlight": "We had bootleg whiskey and those great gangsters Legs Diamond, Al Capone." It was a sentiment that stood in stark contrast to Coleman's melody, a pastiche of a pleasant, leisurely tune from the early twentieth century, the sort of thing that families might have sung together repeatedly around an upright piano.

From this opening the show moved on to a huckster's number, performed as a song in front of the curtain, extolling the portrait of the American Dream that was about to unfold as Philip's life eventually encompassed an existence in the suburbs with a wife and three children. Once they reached maturity, one son was drafted and sent to fight in Vietnam, while the daughter became a hippie, forcing her folks to confront her involvement with drugs and her promiscuity.

Along the way, songs—many inspired by Baker's columns—commented satirically on how the foundations on which the couple had built their lives were shifting and crumbling. From a piece about the homogenized worlds of gargantuan supermarkets and shopping malls, the songwriters wrote "Superland," a buoyant march. A column about the failings of industry inspired "America Don't Know How Any More," an ironically chipper ditty to be sung by four presidents.

But despite the impressive buildup the *Newsday* preview had given the musical in mid-1975, it wasn't mentioned in print again for over a year. Then, in a September 11, 1976 *Billboard* article, Radcliffe Joe included it in a story about shows that might be part of the 1976–77 season, The article also gave the musical a name: *Baker's Dozen*. Again, though, the show disappeared from view, eclipsed by Coleman and Michael Stewart's *I Love My Wife* and the news of *On the Twentieth Century*.

Then, just as speculation about the actor and actress who would star in the latter show was kicking into gear, columnist Jack O'Brian brought up *Baker's Dozen*, noting that the marriage of Baker's columns and musical theater might not be a happy one before adding: "But if anyone can turn this mess of reportage into tunefully successful shape, it is its producer, the immaculately tasteful Herman Levin, who gave us 'My Fair Lady,' 'Gentlemen Prefer Blondes,' 'No Exit' and other carbonated smashes all the way back to 'Call Me Mister' some 20 years ago."[14]

Unfortunately, after O'Brian's touting of Levin's ability to shepherd *Baker's Dozen* to a successful Broadway bow, the producer retired, and the writers, as Baker described it, "plunged mindlessly on, without a producer and no director in anybody's minds."[15]

For a while it looked as though the former problem would be solved by the Producers Circle, which added the show to its slate of upcoming productions immediately following *On the Twentieth Century*. When the group's involvement was announced in June 1978, Mary Lea Johnson told the *New York Times*'s John Corry that "it's a little difficult to describe. . . . It's a little like 'Our Town.'" She went on to describe the physical production that was envisioned, despite the fact that the show had neither an official director nor a designer. Johnson said the musical would have "big sets, like *Saturday Evening Post* covers, many primary colors, sunflowers, and gingham."[16]

The Producers Circle, however, did not end up being the official producers of the show. Instead, Irwin Meyer and Stephen R. Friedman took up the task, under the umbrella of their company, Regency Communications.

The two men owned Broadway's 46th Street Theatre (later renamed the Richard Rodgers Theatre), as well as the Helen Hayes and the Morosco, two theaters that were later demolished to make way for the Marriott Hotel and Marquis Theatre between Forty-fifth and Forty-sixth Streets in Times Square. In addition to their work as theater operators, they served as producers on a couple of shows, most notably the megahit *Annie*, as well as the musical *Working*. Their real-estate holdings and their success with *Annie* conferred a terrific pedigree on Meyer and Friedman. Their importance as players in the entertainment field was further enhanced just before they came to the now renamed *Home Again* when Warner Bros. infused their company with capital, making Regency one of its many subsidiaries.

As Friedman and Meyer came on board, so too did a director and choreographer. Gene Saks and Onna White, who had scored a success for Coleman when they stepped in at a moment's notice for *I Love My Wife*, would, respectively, direct and choreograph *Home Again*, which was on schedule for a Broadway opening in late February or early March 1979.

Saks and White quickly began assembling the cast, which came to have three above-the-title stars. Ronny Cox, who was an ensemble member in Arthur Kopit's *Indians* on Broadway in 1969 before embarking on a television and film career that would grow to include feature roles in

Total Recall, *RoboCop* and *Beverly Hills Cop*, was cast in the leading role of Thomas Jefferson (TJ) Witherspoon, the character that had previously been named "Philip."

To play TJ's father and other patriarchal figures in his life, the creators turned to Dick Shawn, an actor who had Broadway credits ranging from *A Funny Thing Happened on the Way to the Forum* to *Fade Out/Fade In*. He also had a significant amount of film and television work on his résumé, notably Mel Brooks's *The Producers*, in which he played Lorenzo St. DuBois (LSD for short), the leading man in the musical-within-the-movie, *Springtime for Hitler*.

Also above the show title was Mike Kellin, who had proven that he could handle both musicals and dramas on Broadway with credits ranging from the sweetly simple Hazel in Rodgers and Hammerstein's *Pipe Dream* to Dribble in the original Broadway staging of Eugene Ionesco's *Rhinoceros*. He shifted from Broadway to Hollywood in the 1960s and since that time had, like Shawn, become a familiar face from roles on television and the big screen.

Alongside these three men was an impressive trio of Broadway vets, including Lisa Kirk, who was Broadway's original Lois Lane/Bianca in *Kiss Me, Kate* in 1948 and who more recently had been featured in Jerry Herman's *Mack and Mabel*. The show also boasted Teri Ralston, a veteran of Sondheim's *Company* and *A Little Night Music*, and character actor Rex Everhart, whose credits included *Tenderloin*, *Skyscraper*, *How Now, Dow Jones*, and *1776*.

Home Again began rehearsals in January 1979 in anticipation of a single week's tryout in Connecticut in early March and a lengthier one that would follow in Toronto. The show was scheduled to arrive at Broadway's Mark Hellinger Theatre for a first preview of April 19 before an April 26 opening.

By this point both the book and the score had undergone significant alterations. It still was charting TJ's life through fifty years of the twentieth century, but it had become slightly more traditional, giving TJ a concrete aim through life. *Home Again* was now charting how he attempted to make it through life as a good guy, only to find himself thwarted at almost every turn, either by characters played by Shawn or by the pair of seemingly ageless gangsters (played by Kellin and Everhart). With this revision, the show began to resemble Richard Rodgers and Oscar Hammerstein II's musical *Allegro*.

Beyond the two gangsters, another new role had been added: that of Helen's free-spirited mother, Andrea, the role assumed by Lisa Kirk. It was a part that was created, as Fried recalled, "[because] Cy insisted on Lisa Kirk being in the show. It was one of those things where they had been friends for years and years and years. . . . So he made Russell write that part. And we did a song for her, called 'Traveling Together.'" Kirk also got the interpolated song "When It Comes to Lovin'," one of Coleman and Fried's first tunes. Fried admitted, "It's not a good song. It doesn't even make any sense. It was the first thing we'd done together, and I was not the writer I later became."[17]

Coleman and Fried's output prior to rehearsals was significant. In addition to the new tune for Kirk's character, they also wrote several more traditional book songs for TJ, which required that others they had created for the show early on be cut. Among the songs that never made it to rehearsal were "Honky," a vaudevillesque number for the Witherspoon character about his growing sense of being marginalized in society, and "Hello Again," a bittersweet tune for TJ and Helen's daughter as she explains her free-love philosophy.

To create the environment in which this semi-experimental tuner could unfold, the producers hired scenic designer Peter Larkin, who nearly twenty years before had designed Coleman's first show, *Wildcat*. Larkin created a concept that ideally suited the show's nontraditional underpinnings. Stage manager Craig Jacobs recalled, "The rule for the show was that all of the scenery had to come in in unconventional ways; so, for instance, the desks for the office scene were all bicycles, with a single wheel in the back and double wheels under the desks themselves. The young lawyers and such would ride themselves and their desks onto the stage. Same thing when you went into a restaurant in act 2; the tables were bicycles."[18]

For a scene set in a Chinese restaurant, a huge dragon, of the sort used in Chinese New Year parades, was brought on with six men from the ensemble inside. Jacobs explained what happened next: "It came down to the front of the stage, and with the dragon facing the audience, the mouth opened and there [were] a table and two chairs inside of it."[19]

The centerpiece of Larkin's design was "a big fan that opened up during 'America Is Bathed in Sunlight' and then would be able to change colors." In an ominous move, however, the piece was removed from the design to save money. "The budget kept getting cut . . . that was one of the first things that was cut. So we had a cyclorama in the back that was lit, but it didn't have the same effect," Jacobs recalled.[20]

The financial difficulties were kept from the cast as they rehearsed, and by all accounts putting the show on its feet was a collegial—and sometimes fun—affair. Ensemble member D. Michael Heath looked back on the weeks leading up to the first leg of the show's tryout fondly: "We were having a great time. You always wanted to go to work."[21] Ralston also recalled the time warmly, particularly her sessions with Coleman: "Cy taught me all my music, and the thing I remember most was his smile. He'd always be playing with this big smile."[22]

The high spirits of the rehearsal process were dampened, however, once it was time for the show's initial tryout engagement at the American Shakespeare Theater in Stamford, CT, where the first performance was cancelled after the sets failed to arrive on schedule. When the curtain did rise on *Home Again*, it ran an unwieldy three hours.

Jacobs recalled that certain sections worked beautifully, notably the "Superland," which, he recalled, "stopped the show,"[23] but overall the musical's mixture of homespun charm and biting satire bewildered audiences. The dichotomy of tone might have had something to do with the fact that at the time of *Home Again*, Baker was also beginning to contemplate his sepia-toned memoir, *Growing Up*, about his family's surviving the Great Depression. Looking back on the show's development, he felt that the gestating work "surely influenced me in shaping the musical's plot, if plot it could be called."[24]

Indeed, a number of specifics that ultimately were part of the Pulitzer Prize–winning book can be found tucked throughout *Home Again*. One anecdote from Baker's past, in fact, seems to have informed a song in the show. In *Growing Up*, Baker relates how an uncle got his first job as a reporter at a newspaper in Pittsburgh. During the interview, the editor asked, "Young man, how do I know you're not a damned fool?," to which Baker's uncle replied, "That's a chance we'll both have to take."[25] In *Home Again*, TJ returns from fighting in World War II and also applies for a job as a reporter, and when he's asked why he should be hired, he replies with a similar level of moxie, proclaiming in song "I'm Your Guy."

The combination of gently wistful and sardonic tones that were part of Baker's book extended to the score as well, further confusing the message the show was sending to audiences. It was filled with some of Coleman's sweetest melodies, but the lyrics with which Fried outfitted them were frequently tart.

Home Again's problems were exacerbated by an ill-advised marriage of director and material. "Cy decided he wanted Gene Saks," Fried remembered, and added, "He was persuaded to be the director. He did not understand the show, in the sense that it should have been extremely impressionistic."[26]

When the reviews began to appear, they ran the gamut from supportive to scathing. The March 15 review in the *Hartford Courant* fell into the former category, with Malcolm L. Johnson writing, "There is much to like in this original musical. . . . At the outset in fact, 'Home Again' really sings, evoking a clever collage of say, 'The Music Man,' 'L'il [*sic*] Abner,' and even 'Oklahoma.' Too soon, however, it becomes more like a 'Candide' of the American heartland—the original Lillian Hellman version, that is, which suffered from fragmentation and longueurs."

On the dismissive side was the March 21 review in *Variety*, which began, "It's difficult to be constructive about a show as mediocre as 'Home Again.' To use the old phrasing, there's nothing wrong with the show that a new book, score, cast, direction, choreography, sets and costumes wouldn't help." The piece even made reference to the fact that *Home Again* "suggests an impoverished rerun of the 1947 Rodgers and Hammerstein experiment, 'Allegro.'"

In the face of the critical and audience reaction, the creators panicked.

To quickly shorten the show, Lisa Kirk's role was eliminated. "After the fourth performance in Connecticut," Jacobs said, "Cy came up to me during the last part of the show and said to me, 'When you get a chance, get your script and figure out how we can cut Andrea's part out of the show,' which was Lisa Kirk." Jacobs later explained to Coleman and his collaborator what removing the part would entail: cutting just two scenes and two songs. "And bingo. She was out of the show."[27]

There wasn't time during the one week of performance to do much else that was substantive in terms of integrating rewrites, but the process had begun. Coleman, never at a loss for melody, started writing new numbers to replace ones that were being cut or curtailed. Matching him was Baker, a neophyte to the tension-filled world of a musical's out-of-town birthing pains, who worked on adjustments to the book.

According to Ralston, during the weeks that followed in Toronto, "It felt like they didn't know what they were doing," but, as she also pointed out, "I had done *The Baker's Wife*, so I had been on the road in a show that was in trouble for eight months. . . . That was such a horrendous experience, I kept saying, 'Nothing could touch that. This is a breeze. It's okay. I can get through anything.'"[28]

Jacobs said that all of the changes that happened in the next few weeks stemmed from the creatives' being "desperate,"[29] while Fried noted that some changes were made for personal reasons. She said that "Superland" (which had been landing well with audiences in Connecticut) "was taken out because Onna White, who was the choreographer, said to me, 'I've done this kind of thing many times. And I don't want everybody saying that I can only do one thing. So I want to get rid of this number.'"[30]

Eventually the Toronto papers weighed in on the show, and the reaction was no better than it had been in Connecticut. In his March 21 review in the *Globe and Mail* Ray Conlogue said, "You expect with a Broadway-bound show that somebody will still be caulking the leaks, hoping even for something buoyant, but those who bet today on 'New York Times' columnist Russell Baker's 'Home Again' would have bought tickets on the Titanic yesterday."

In her *Toronto Star* review the same day, Gina Mallet gave the still-evolving show the benefit of the doubt, despite her dismay about the actual narrative. "I think this is what happens" was how she introduced her description of the musical's plot. What she admired was that in her opinion *Home Again* was "a rarity these days, a musical that defies anyone to take it seriously. It's slight, funny and throwaway." Concluding her review, Mallet compared sections of it to lunatic Marx Brothers films and then pondered the show's future: "Can the show make sense and still keep that spirit?"

At this juncture, the creators had three weeks in Toronto to fix *Home Again*. Coleman and Fried's contributions included "The Daily Rag," a cynical song about the newspaper business, which White choreographed as a tap number; "President," an amusing tune about the travails of the commander-in-chief, inserted and then quickly cut; "Call Your Daddy," a droll lullaby for one of the father figures played by Shawn; and "I Don't Remember When I Didn't Love You," a gentle country ballad for TJ that, according to Fried, "we wrote downstairs in the basement of the theater."[31]

Baker's rewrites encompassed not only building scenes to accommodate the new songs but also revising sections to help clarify the story and the show's objective. In looking back on the experience, Baker realized that he would never have escaped one problem with the show: being "committed to the absurd task of writing a book for a Broadway show for which the music had already been written. I was too ignorant about theater to know that this couldn't possibly produce anything but disaster, probably even with Hammerstein writing the book."[32]

Another revision to the show came at the suggestion of "some misguided corporate thinker," according to Baker. There was a problem with the title. "He had run a poll and found it didn't fetch the public, which, he went on, had responded happily to a title that included the phrase 'sunshine mountain.' Cy and the rest of us wasted an evening wrestling with this until I pointed out that there was a fine old Protestant Sunday school hymn titled 'Climb, Climb Up Sunshine Mountain.' After which we decided to change the title from 'Home Again' to 'Home Again, Home Again.'"[33] In public, producer Meyer explained the change by saying, "We thought the new title would be funnier, and give someone a laugh."[34]

Still, the writers, Saks, and White persevered, incorporating more changes. But the strain began to show. Even Ralston, who believed she would be impervious to the pressure, given her laborious experiences on the road with *The Baker's Wife*, snapped. "I had been so strong and just dealing with everything, and one day I just broke down crying onstage. And Gene said, 'I can't believe I've made Teri Ralston cry.'"[35]

At the same time, however, Ralston understood what the team faced and admired what they were trying to accomplish. "With the money involved, it was huge pressure on Gene. . . . They had a point of view, certainly, with what they believed about the American Dream and good versus evil. They just couldn't get it together on how to tell a story. . . . So they kept reaching around, trying different things."[36]

In this regard Coleman did something quite unexpected. Baker related, "Cy got his New York psychiatrist on the phone one afternoon and must have started discussing the psychological makeup of the main characters in our floundering play. This was absurd, of course, since the chief characters were little more than bloodless stage cartoons. It became sillier, however, when Cy switched the shrink onto a conference call so he could lecture Barbara, Gene, and me on our failure to grasp the psychic ordeal our characters were undergoing."[37]

Overall, said Fried, "it was really like a Warner Bros. movie."[38]

As all of this was happening, both the company and creative team began to sense that Meyer and Friedman might opt to close the show out of town. Fried recalled, "Irwin and Steve were not there, and when they were there they were not helpful, and they were always complaining about how much money we were costing them."[39]

The producers assured the team that the show would play Broadway, and yet they were not doing anything to promote it there. In the weeks leading up to the scheduled first preview, April 19, there was no advertising until April 1, when the producers took out a full-page ad in the *New York Times* to promote both *Home Again, Home Again* and another show they had on its way to Broadway, Ira Levin's *Break a Leg*. The ad promised that the Hellinger box office would be open for business the following day, but "when people went down to the box office," Fried said, "there weren't any tickets for sale."[40]

Subsequent to the ad, the producers ran no more advertisements and even eschewed placing the show in the theater listings until April 15, less than a week before previews were set to begin. At that point they opted to insert a small listing, which, confusingly, announced that the box office would be opening for business the following day. Even more telling is the way in which the producers were promoting their other show, giving it a continual albeit minimal presence in the *New York Times* theater listings. (*Break a Leg* did eventually make it to Broadway, where it lasted a single performance.)

Jacobs believed the producers, whom Baker described as "two shrewd Brooklyn street kids,"[41] never intended to bring the show in. "Actually, one of the mothers of one of the kids called the box office in New York to order tickets [and none were available]," Jacobs recalled.[42]

Meyer and Friedman were in Toronto during the final week of performances there. "They had a series of conversations with Cy, and with Gene and with Onna, to which we were not privy, or . . . I was not privy," said Fried. "Russell didn't know anything about it either. Then they told us we were closing. Well, Cy and Gene had a fit. Neither one of them was used to failure."[43]

A few years later, when Coleman was being interviewed by Paul Lazarus for the WBAI radio program *Anything Goes*, he described his feelings about the folding of *Home Again, Home Again*: "That was my first show that ever closed like that. But what was heartbreaking about it was to leave a show that's playing and the audience is howling with laughter. So the timing was off."

The company was informed of the producers' decision on April 12, when there were just two days left in the Toronto run. Ralston recalled, "I wasn't surprised. I didn't think we would go in. There was disappointment that we weren't able to get it together, but I also knew that we'd get killed if we went into New York. We knew it wasn't good enough. So I was not surprised. I wasn't relieved like I was when I found out *The Baker's Wife* was closing. There I jumped for joy."[44]

After the closing notice was posted, news came out that Warner Communications had withdrawn from its agreement to finance the theatrical projects that Meyer and Friedman were developing through their company, Regency Communications. The *Variety* story on April 18 about the closing and the producers' troubles also mentioned that the two men were "defendants in a Federal civil suit brought by the Securities & Exchange Commission alleging securities violations in connection with a coal mining tax shelter venture." The paper printed a retraction the following week, saying that they were no longer defendants in this suit; however, by the end of 1981 they had pled guilty "in Federal court to charges of conspiring to help investors file false tax returns" in conjunction with tax-shelter fraud.[45] The men ultimately received six-month sentences.

Almost immediately after the word hit that *Home Again, Home Again* would not be arriving in New York, Coleman announced, "The authors are revising the show and intend to seek other management auspices for a production next season."[46] A few years later Coleman was still talking about his plans for the show, telling Paul Lazarus on WBAI, "I'll just have to thank those producers for giving me a wonderful workshop. Because we're going to do it again."

Home Again, Home Again would never materialize as a show unto itself, but Coleman, Fried, and Baker would eventually resurrect material from the musical. Before that, however, and true to form, Coleman was off on another project that would require most of his attention for the first few years of the 1980s.

23

Barnum

oleman's habit of having myriad projects in various stages of development was instrumental in helping him rebound from the disappointment of *Home Again, Home Again*. Only five months after that show's closing out of town, he had another on its way to Broadway as the first casting notices for his newest musical, a look at the life of circus impresario P. T. Barnum, began appearing.

Coleman first encountered the project in the mid-1970s, when Mark Bramble, a young writer whose day job was working for producer David Merrick, brought the book for *Barnum* to Coleman and asked if he would consider writing the music.

"I have no idea why Cy agreed to see me, because he didn't know me from Adam, except that I said I am working in the Merrick office. And that may have gotten me in the door," Bramble recalled. "Cy read it, and he asked me to come and see him again, and he said, 'I'm not going to do this.' And he talked a little bit about it. Not a great deal. But as I was leaving, he said, 'But if you can't find anybody else, you can come back.'"[1]

After *Barnum* became a success, Coleman looked back on his first impressions of the idea when talking with Robert Viagas for the book *The Alchemy of Theatre*: "The circus part was interesting but there was no story. Barnum got married and started a circus. That was it."

Despite Coleman's rejection, Bramble persevered and approached other composers. "I tried every living composer who had ever done a Broadway show, and they all said the same thing: 'This is a terrible idea.' Except Jerry Bock. He almost did it, but he had decided to retire, well he was retired. He was tempted to come back and do it with Lee Adams, but in the end, he said, 'No, I'm done.'"[2]

Bramble went on to other projects, such as cowriting—with Coleman's frequent collaborator Michael Stewart—the book for Jerry Herman's musical *The Grand Tour*, which opened on Broadway in January 1979. It was during this show's San Francisco tryout in late 1978 that Bramble found himself talking with Merrick, who was then in Hollywood, having produced such films as *The Great Gatsby* and *Semi-Tough*. Merrick asked about the status of Bramble's Barnum project. "Well, I can't get any traction on it. I just can't get anybody interested in it," Bramble told Merrick.[3]

Bramble remembered the veteran producer's unexpected response: "He said, 'I'll do it.' And I said, 'What?!?' He said, 'I'll produce it for you. I want to come back to the theater. I'm tired of the movies. I'll produce it.' So he optioned it."[4]

Merrick did have one condition: Bramble had to agree to casting Jim Dale, who had been the toast of Broadway in 1974 thanks to his bravura performance as the roguish title character of *Scapino*, an adaptation by Dale and Frank Dunlop of Molière's seventeenth-century comedy *Les fourberies de Scapin* ("Scapin's Deceits"). *Scapino* came to New York from London for a limited engagement at the Brooklyn Academy of Music and, thanks to Dale's performance, proved so popular that it moved to Broadway. In addition to attracting glowing notices, the show inspired many theatergoers to see it repeatedly, including Bramble, who recalled, "You fell in love with him. He was just so adorable."[5] So he readily agreed to Merrick's casting suggestion, and Dale was on board, realizing that the show "was what I had been waiting for. 'Scapino' was the training ground for 'Barnum.'"[6]

It was at this juncture that Coleman reentered the picture. Stories vary as to the specifics of how he became involved with the musical. Bramble remembered that Merrick asked him who he wanted as a composer, and "I said, 'Cy is the one, but Cy has turned it down,' and [Merrick] said, 'You call Cy and tell him that I'm producing it and that Jim Dale is starring in it, and he'll do it.' So I called Cy. 'David Merrick is producing. Jim Dale is set to star.' And Cy said, 'I'll do it.' So I went back to Merrick, and he said, 'Now, who's going to do the lyrics?' And I said, 'I want Michael to write the lyrics, but he also turned it down.' And he said, 'You tell Mike that I'm producing it. Jim Dale is starring in it. Cy Coleman's composing, and unless he wants to be left out of a good thing, he better sign on now.' Which he did."[7]

Coleman offered a different version of being reapproached about *Barnum*. "Michael Stewart called me up and said, 'I think we can do this.' A lot of people had talked about doing Barnum's life in the past, but that was all. I thought there was something intriguing about a circus show. Then I called Michael, after a sleepless night, and said, 'If you can put this show in the middle of a circus ring, I can bring in all kinds of chases, to keep it going, and I love to write chases.'"[8]

It wasn't long after Coleman and Stewart had come on board as Bramble's collaborators, however, that the question of who would produce *Barnum* was reopened. The problem arose because of another project that was on Merrick's docket, a stage version of the 1933 movie musical *42nd Street*. This show, like *Barnum*, was to have a book by Stewart and Bramble, and Merrick was struggling to find a director. Gower Champion had been involved but had backed out. Merrick was coming to realize that putting *42nd Street* together was going to require all of his time and concentration, and so he went to the *Barnum* team and announced he wanted to postpone the show, at least until *42nd Street* was up and running.

But, as Bramble recalled, "Cy didn't want to wait to do *Barnum*. Cy said, 'No, we're ready to go,' and David, very graciously, said, 'You can have it back.' I will assign you the contract I have done with Jim Dale, and if you return the advance, you can have it back.' And that's what happened."[9]

Coleman, who was still stinging from the shoddy managerial oversight on *Home Again, Home Again* and also recalled the way in which *Seesaw* struggled because of its undercapitalization, decided that Merrick's withdrawal from *Barnum* was an opportunity to ensure that he would be better able to control how the musical reached the stage, so he stepped in as producer and convinced Michael Stewart to serve as his coproducer.

Stewart's involvement in this capacity was relatively short-lived, however, and so Coleman turned to Judy Gordon, who had produced *2 by 5*, a revue of John Kander and Fred Ebb's songs at the Village Gate, and gained her first credit as lead producer of a Broadway show in 1978 with Christopher Durang's *The History of the American Film*. Self-described as "an aspiring and ambitious young producer,"[10] Gordon introduced herself to Coleman at a party just after the revue opened and suggested that she would like to do something similar with his music. Nothing had come of this idea or several others that they explored before *Barnum* came into the picture, but in the process of investigating the feasibility of different projects, a solid relationship was built.

Gordon recalled how, after Stewart backed away from producing, she got a phone call. "Cy said, 'Come over and hear the score, and if you like it, then you can produce it, and I'll do it with you.' . . . It was a great opportunity for me and a big deal."[11]

With the partnership established, Coleman and Gordon set about raising the capital for the show. Gordon described watching the writers as they performed for potential investors. "There was nothing like seeing Cy and Michael Stewart do a backers' audition. I mean, if you wanted to raise money, you did it with the two of them. They were just captivating. I mean, our largest investors, Maurice Rosenfield and his wife, Lois, originally had no interest at all." The Rosenfields' reticence to invest in *Barnum* came, Gordon said, because, "They had put a little money into a show [a revival of Herb Gardner's *The Goodbye People*, which had lasted all of one performance] and lost it. So they had decided they had had it with Broadway."[12]

Knowing the impact that a performance by Coleman and Stewart might have, Gordon decided to persevere with the couple. As the writers were preparing to do a performance of portions of the show, she said, "I just decided to call [the Rosenfields] again, and it turned out they were going to be in New York on that date, and so I said, 'Just come over to Cy's and you'll enjoy it anyway.' And that was what did it. Lois just fell in love with Cy, and they ended up putting in half the money, half the budget."[13]

But it wasn't only the financing that needed to be secured; a director had to be found. At one point, Coleman thought of Harold Prince and sent him the script and score. After he had read and listened to it, Prince had a meeting with Coleman and Stewart, telling them, "You guys. You're all rich. You've all got hits on Broadway, and you're all going to be successful your entire lives. Why don't you put this show in a brown paper bag and stick it on the shelf? And come back to it in a few years and see if you really want to do it?" When they asked why, Prince responded, "I just don't think it's any good at all."[14]

A director who did see potential in the script was Joe Layton, and he took on the show, serving as both director and choreographer. He also made a bold decision about what his approach would be in staging it. Bramble explained, "The concept was that we were going to use circus elements to tell the story and that there was not going to be any choreography per se. . . . Joe said, 'I'm not doing any steps.' He said everything that would be choreographic should be replaced with something to do with the circus. And he was very, very true to that and stayed very much on point with that."[15]

Layton's vision for the show could be seen in the first casting notices, which appeared in late September 1979. They said that anyone auditioning "must have some special ability that could be used in the circus."[16]

One performer who eventually landed a role in the show was Andy Teirstein, who, in addition to having a music degree from Bennington College in Vermont, had studied with a master mime in Mexico and toured that country with a circus. When Teirstein heard of the *Barnum* auditions, "I thought, 'What the hell? I'll try.' I went to Woolworths to get a dollar mug shot from one of those photo-booths and took it to the audition." When he went to the call he found "a patchwork of performers there, and they lined us up across the stage and went down the line, each proclaiming his or her circus skills and instruments."[17]

Eventually it came time for Teirstein to perform his solo, and "I was terrified. I stepped out onto the stage in whiteface, in my bare feet. There were murmurings . . . 'Is this his picture?' someone asked. 'Where's the résumé?' But Cy said, 'It's all right.' He stood up, introduced himself, and asked me to play something. From the first moment, everything was going wrong. I opened my violin case and the fiddle fell out. The music stand fell over. But Cy laughed. I tripped over my hat. He bellowed. I looked at his face and saw encouragement, warmth, camaraderie. Cy said, 'That's great. Can you sing?' I had prepared the first song I would ever sing in public, a Fred Astaire thing entitled, 'A Fella with an Umbrella.' I sang through it and left, ushered out by audition assistants, and feeling sure I would never be back."[18]

Teirstein left the theater but remembered that he had been advised that after an audition a performer should always shake hands with the director, so he returned, only to find that the auditions were over and Layton was unavailable. Undeterred, Teirstein sneaked into the balcony in the hopes that he might figure out a way to pay his respects to Layton.

"From there, what I saw on stage I will never forget," Teirstein said. "Cy Coleman was prancing back and forth excitedly, merrily banging out chords on an upright and the next moment rushing downstage gesticulating to his creative team about his vision of their new show. Watching him on his feet, possessed with the excitement of his ideas, I felt that I was receiving a gift, a glimpse of how a show comes to life. And then I heard him say, 'Here's where that white-faced fiddler steps in. He'll do this little waltz with Charity Barnum; it's like he's her own muse, or he's Barnum's inner spirit.' From there Cy moved on to other ideas, igniting his collaborators in a dialogue about each character. I picked up my fiddle case and sailed home feeling as if I had swallowed the moon. Here I was, a street performer with no résumé, and they were going to put me on Broadway."[19]

The waltz Coleman described that day was part of the script by the time rehearsals for *Barnum* began a month later, and the moment—which comes just after Barnum has learned that his American Museum has burned to the ground—remained a part of *Barnum*. By the time the musical began performances at the St. James Theatre, Teirstein was also an integral part of the preshow entertainment that director Layton devised for his environmental staging.

Barnum actually began on the street in front of the theater as one actor welcomed theatergoers and performed magic tricks while they entered. Inside, ticketholders were greeted by another member of the company, who guided them through memorabilia about Barnum's life that had been loaned to the production by two other members of the producing team, father and son Irvin Feld and Kenneth Feld of Ringling Bros. and Barnum & Bailey Circus. Inside the auditorium, audiences enjoyed performances by Teirstein and Bruce Robertson. Another member of the company was also in the house as audience members filed in: Glenn Close, at the start of her career and playing Barnum's conservative wife, Chairy, as she was familiarly known. She was seated in one of the theater's boxes, deeply immersed in a knitting project, above and apart from the merry happenings taking place.

It was a comprehensive vision meant to evoke the grandeur of a big-top entertainment, and one that greatly expanded on what Bramble had originally envisioned: a vest-pocket musical intended for a company of three principals and an ensemble of nine. In fact, Gordon remembered that originally "they wanted to do it in a very small way, like at the Brooks Atkinson. I remember that was one theater we looked at, rather than a regular musical theater house. . . . It was supposed to be small house, big concept that would be just like a circus exploding out of the theater. And then it evolved into a bigger show."[20]

To bring this larger show to life visually, the creators originally turned to Oscar and Tony Award–winning designer Tony Walton, who had a friendship with Coleman that dated back to the early 1960s, when Coleman's first musicals were being produced on Broadway and Walton's first wife, Julie Andrews, was astonishing audiences in shows like *My Fair Lady* and *Camelot*. In addition, Walton was the scenic and costume designer for *Bette Midler's Clams on the Half Shell Revue*, which Layton directed.

At the time Walton was working on two films and did not believe he would be able to add a theater project to his docket, but he agreed to a meeting with the director. Walton recalled, "Joe said, 'I just need to sit down with you and describe the show, because it's going to be the simplest musical you've ever had to tackle in your life." During the course of the meeting, Walton had an assistant take notes as Layton described the show and its requirements, and as Walton remembered it, "[My assistant] had just completed a whole yellow pad by the time Joe arrived at the end of the first act. So I said, 'Joe, would it be alright if I just did the poster?'"[21]

David Mitchell, whom Layton had chosen as the scenic designer of *I Love My Wife*, would ultimately be the one who created the flexible circus-inspired environment for *Barnum*, enhancing the audience's sense of the musical's immediacy by extending the stage of the St. James out over the orchestra pit.

Even Coleman's music seemed to reach out and surround theatergoers. Not only did members of the orchestra file into the aisles during each performance, but also two pianists were placed in boxes on either side of the stage. Ted Kociolek, who began his relationship with Coleman's shows on *I Love My Wife*, for which he joined the production as second pianist and later helped assemble the bands for the show in other cities, remembered what it was like to be a musician working on *Barnum*: "I just loved playing it. Because you're right there in the audience's lap. There were other people, literally, in the boxes."[22]

For costumes Layton turned to Theoni V. Aldredge. At the time she was one of Broadway's most sought-after designers because of her astute ability to combine elegance, showbiz flair, and down-to-earth naturalism, qualities that were in evidence at the time in her designs for *A Chorus Line* and *Annie*. For the show's orchestrations Coleman once again turned to Hershy Kay, who served in the same capacity for *On the Twentieth Century*.

As for the company beyond Dale and Close, it included, in other principal roles, Terri White, a vet of Broadway's *Ain't Misbehavin'*, who played Joice Heth, one of Barnum's first attractions; Marianne Tatum, who made her Broadway debut as a teenager in *Half a Sixpence* and went on to a career that encompassed other Broadway and Off-Broadway work, as well as seven seasons at the Houston Grand Opera, as Jenny Lind, the Scandinavian singer whom Barnum billed as "the Swedish Nightingale"; and Leonard John Crofoot, who had toured with Carol Channing in *Hello, Dolly!* and appeared on Broadway in shows like *The Happy Time* and *Gigi*, as Barnum's superstar, General Tom Thumb.

Beyond these five the show was filled with young artists, many of whom, like Teirstein, came to the show with circus experience and were making their Broadway debuts. Among the future headliners in the company were Terrence Mann, who would go on to starring roles in *Cats*, *Beauty and the Beast*, and *Les Misérables*, and Sophie Schwab, who, billed as Sophie Hayden, ten years after *Barnum* would win accolades while starring in a Broadway revival of Frank Loesser's *The Most Happy Fella*.

The company assembled for rehearsals in February and found that Coleman and Stewart had outfitted Bramble's book, which had changed in subtle but significant ways since the composer first saw it, with fifteen numbers. For this show, more than for his past three, the composer drew liberally, and admittedly, from his trunk. The tune of Jenny Lind's arialike "Love Makes Such Fools of Us All" was "When Did You Know?," which was to have been a ballet in *Sweet Charity* but ultimately was only heard as a piece of underscoring. One of Barnum's biggest numbers, "Out There," used a driving melody that Coleman had written for "Charge," a duet sung by the strong-willed title character of *Eleanor* and her bombastic uncle, Teddy Roosevelt.

Additionally, Coleman expanded on snippets of music from his work on *Compulsion* as well as from an unused idea for *Little Me* and even a cut song from *On the Twentieth Century*, which has the beginnings of "Join the Circus" running through it.

But the *Barnum* score wasn't merely a patchwork of unheard or little-known Coleman. It contained a wealth of music that Coleman wrote specifically for it, ranging from "Black and White," an extended ensemble number that evoked memories of songs by both Fats Waller and the songwriting team of Eubie Blake and Noble Sissle, to the John Philip Sousa–like march "Come Follow the Band," to the George M. Cohan pastiche "Bigger Isn't Better," with its direct musical sampling of "Yankee Doodle Dandy" (the tune that Coleman had played over thirty years before when he made his radio debut).

The show also contained music specifically created for the talents of its performers, particularly leading man Dale. "I remember telling him and Mike that in the script there was mention of Barnum's Museum in

Lower Broadway, and wouldn't it be great to list as many items as possible in a patter song," Dale recalled. "I told them that I would be able to sing the song very fast, as I had once been a pop singer and had done some 'scat' singing in my early days. I then sang a very fast number to them made famous by Annie Ross called 'Twisted.' Two or three days later they came up with 'The Museum Song.'"[23]

Barnum, nontraditional to start with, given its environmental and circus nature, needed a similarly unconventional rehearsal period, starting with where the company worked on the production: the unused ballroom at the then rundown McAlpin Hotel at Herald Square. It was a space that was large enough and high enough to allow for the performers to not only work on the scenes and songs but also the show's circus elements.

Furthermore, the cast took part in actual circus training. "One of the first days of rehearsal, we went over to Big Apple Circus and actually worked on real circus trapezes and ropes and things," recalled Tatum, who also remembered that Layton insisted that "everyone else in the whole company had to learn how to juggle, and I remember being very grateful that I was exempted from that."[24]

After the training away from the McAlpin, Layton also instituted "play time," when, according to White, the members of the ensemble "all pulled out their toys, their single ladder and passing clubs, and so on." Layton, along with Coleman, would watch what they were doing, and then White recalled, "Joe would say, 'Cy, I need music for a scene change going into Susan B. Anthony,' and then Cy, just watching the flow of the passing and how the clubs moved, began connecting the music to the movement on stage." It was in this manner that Coleman wrote music, based on the opening number "There Is a Sucker Born Every Minute," to create the underscoring for a crossover into a restaurant. White marveled, "It was just craziness as far as I was concerned."[25]

Coleman's ability to improvise on the songs he had written was demonstrated time and again during rehearsal and then in the theater itself one day during a lunch break, when sound designer Otts Munderloh asked him to go to the calliope onstage and begin playing. White was in the house when it happened: "He just sat there and played the entire score like circus music. It was like magic on the stage, and him just glowing being able to do this. . . . He never stopped or said, 'Now I'm going to try this.' He just went from one song to the next to the next to the next, and then, after like fifteen minutes, he got up and said, 'Okay. I'm done.'"[26] Munderloh captured what Coleman had performed, and it became the preshow music.

Layton also infused the process with a liberal dose of improvisation. "Joe was someone who wasn't a great planner. I mean, he planned but not in the way that Gower Champion planned. Joe did a lot on his feet. And often the things that he did on his feet were the best," recalled Bramble, who pointed to Layton's handling of Chairy's death in the second act as a particularly apt example.[27]

Bramble had written the scene so that it included a duet reprise of "The Colors of My Life," during which Barnum charmed his dying wife by magically producing enough flowers to create a bouquet. After this she was simply led offstage by the White-Faced Clown. One day, Bramble recalled, "something popped into [Joe's] head as he was doing it. He said to the stage manager, 'Go get me the jugglers. Go get me anyone who can juggle.'"[28]

Layton then proceeded to stage the reprise so that while Dale and Close sang, the ensemble members appeared and began to juggle. Late in the song Chairy, who had long eschewed Barnum's profession, took three of the balls and began juggling herself, suggesting that she had finally understood her husband. Then, as the song ended, "She tosses the balls to Barnum who begins juggling as Chairy and six jugglers exit."[29]

In the process of adding a circus-performance aspect to the song, Layton had found a metaphorical way of bringing the couple closer together spiritually than they had been throughout the rest of the show, which only made her exit from Barnum's life all the more poignant. Bramble looked back on Layton's work with this scene admiringly: "He created that moment, which was just gorgeous."[30]

Not everything about rehearsals and the company's arrival at their preview period was as much fun as "play time." One exceptionally difficult day was the first orchestral play-through, the moment when the company hears for the first time the score as it will be played in the theater. As Bramble recalled, "It's usually the most thrilling moment on a musical. And we went to Carroll Music and the orchestrations were unusable. Hershy Kay had had a stroke, unbeknownst to any of us. . . . It was all 'Turkey in the Straw' and demented. It was the work of a damaged mind. When it finished, everybody was just so heartbroken."[31]

Coleman scrambled to salvage this portion of the show. Bramble remembered, "Cy called every orchestrator who was in the metropolitan area that weekend and just handed out the songs, and said, 'This is what we have, and this is what the lineup is.' It was Bill Byers. It was Phil Lang. It was Larry Wilcox. It was Michael Gibson. I can't think if there were others."[32]

These rush reorchestrations occurred in the days leading up to what was to have been the first preview on April 5, but this performance, as well as several subsequent ones, were canceled. When the cancellations were announced in the *New York Times* on April 4, the reason cited was: "A spokesperson for the production said the transit strike had delayed completion of the work on the production."

Indeed, *Barnum* was facing problems beyond the orchestration debacle. Gordon recalled, "The costumes weren't ready for our first preview, because the workers couldn't get to their workrooms to work on the costumes."[33] But even with the delay, some of the clothes didn't arrive at the theater on time.

Bramble described what awaited audiences when the first performances were offered: "Most of the musicians sat in view of the audience (because the band was onstage) and holding their instruments for most of the performance. . . . As the arrangements were finished, they went into the show, but we started with a lot of the show being played with two pianos and half costumes."[34]

There were other problems as well, notably the show's length: two and a half intermissionless hours. "The show, I originally wrote it in one act, and I still believe that it could play more effectively in one act than it does in two because the story isn't that big. It's not a strong enough plot to take the break at the interval and come back and do a second act. But I had to give in on that because there was just too much else going on. But we did play the first preview—we played a few previews—with the show in one act."[35]

Barnum might have been shortened during rehearsals, but according to Bramble, there were numbers that "Cy wasn't willing to cut until he saw how they played."[36] Coleman eventually gave in, not just on the song that he had hoped might become a stand-alone hit, "At Least I Tried," an anthem that Barnum delivered just after he realized his affair with Lind had been a mistake, but also on "Now You See It, Now You Don't," a tune that showed how he outschemed a rival to acquire the American Museum. "Share and Share Alike," a slight number performed by conjoined twins that was intended to illustrate how inextricably linked Barnum's life was to the circus, also went.

When it came to one other song, however, it wasn't Coleman who was resisting a cut; it was Stewart. He wouldn't let Layton remove "That's What the Poor Woman Is," an extended sequence with an oom-pah-pah polka rhythm that comically brought to life the battle of the sexes in the mid-nineteenth century. Bramble described it as "the biggest number in the show. It was clowns doing a women's rally for equality. And it just went on and on and on. And Michael Stewart loved it, because he had some wonderful lyrics in it and the music was good. . . . But it was way too late in act 1 for this thing that had nothing to do with nothing."[37] Ultimately, Stewart acquiesced to having this song removed from the show.

As Coleman faced these usual—and unusual—complications with mounting a new musical, he also coped with the details of the show's business health. Gordon and he had taken steps to ensure that they would be able to work together closely by renting space in the Fifty-fourth Street building where his offices were to serve as the base of operations for *Barnum*. "We had a direct phone line between our office and Cy's office, so that worked out very well. I was more involved with the day-to-day things with Jim Walsh, our general manager, but I never decided on any kind of real decisions without talking to Cy about it."[38]

There did come a point when Coleman "was very immersed in the show, as well he should be. We had a major crisis with one of our investors, which I had to deal with and he didn't because he was just too busy with the show. One of our investors got very crazy and threatened to put an injunction on the show, but Cy wasn't really that involved with that because he was busy with the show and I didn't want to bother him with that."[39]

It might have been a bit worse than Gordon remembered, because there came a point when producer Cy Feuer was invited to see the show. As Bramble explained, "It was a mad moment when we considered not opening in New York after we had started previews here and going to play the Civic Light Opera subscription in San Francisco and L.A. It was an insane idea, but the show was really struggling." The notion was abandoned, but not before Feuer pointed out to Bramble that he recognized one of the songs back from the days when he was producing Coleman's second show: "'Oh, there's that song that we threw out of *Little Me*. He won't let it die.'"[40]

Finally, there came a night when, Gordon recalled, "there was just a totally different feeling in the audience. Like the show was working, and you just felt magic when Jim came out on the stage, because all of the extraneous stuff was cut out and Jim's performance shone."[41]

Gordon wasn't alone as she watched that performance from the back of the St. James. At her side was producer David Merrick, who, because of his vested interest in the show—after all, he needed Stewart and Bramble for *42nd Street*—had made it a habit of watching *Barnum* in previews. Gordon remembered, "That night Merrick said to me, 'You're going to have a hit.'"[42]

Merrick's prediction was almost met when the reviews began to appear on the morning after the show's official opening on April 30. The notices for Dale were certainly glowing. In the *New York Times*, Frank Rich declared, "This man can create magic—the magic of infectious charm—even on those rare occasions when he's standing still." In the *New York Post*, Clive Barnes began his review by announcing, "Jim Dale is a one-man, three-ring, four-star circus in *Barnum*."

But while critics could agree that Dale was the star attraction of this event and the main reason for taking it in, other aspects of the show, including Coleman's score, received mixed reaction. Rich said that Coleman was "in top form. Having flirted with operetta in 'On the Twentieth

Century,' he has now returned to the snazzy showbiz idiom of 'Little Me' and 'I Love My Wife.' 'Barnum' simply bursts with melodies." Barnes wrote, "Coleman is a permanent gem in Broadway's musical crown. His music is so effortless and yet honeycombed. . . . His songs always clinch into their dramatic pace and place." Other reviewers, however, were not so taken, particularly *Newsweek*'s Jack Kroll, who said in his May 12 review, "Cy Coleman's score is a doleful disappointment."

Reviewers were similarly conflicted about Layton's direction. Douglas Watt, in the *Daily News*, said that the show had been "joyously staged," and Associated Press critic Jay Sharbutt echoed that sentiment when he said that Layton had "brilliantly staged" the musical. Rich's accolades went so far as to say that the director had made "a cast of 19 seem about a hundred strong."

But even as reviewers were praising his work, they were noting that he was straining against what they viewed as the weaknesses of Bramble's book, which was labeled "sketchy" by Watt and described by Barnes as "a library of good intentions." Rich wrote simply that the show "doesn't have a book."

The mixed critical reaction did nothing, however, to diminish theatergoers' enjoyment of or interest in the show, and it settled into what would become a two-year run. Within the first few weeks after the reviews appeared, ticket sales skyrocketed, and for the next year *Barnum* played to near-capacity and sometimes even standing-room-only houses.

As with *I Love My Wife*, *Barnum* arrived just prior to the cutoff date for 1980 Tony Award eligibility. When the nominations for the prizes were announced, *Barnum* had scored a total of ten, just one shy of the eleven received by its biggest competitor, Andrew Lloyd Webber and Tim Rice's *Evita*. In addition to one for best musical and one for Coleman and Stewart's score, the show garnered a pair of nominations for Layton (as both director and choreographer) as well as ones for Dale, Close, and Bramble. In the long run, *Barnum* couldn't overpower *Evita* in many categories, but it still won a respectable trio of prizes: for Dale as well as for designers Mitchell and Aldredge.

Any marketing boost that the awards gave *Barnum* at the beginning of

June was enhanced a month later when Columbia Records released the cast album. A new slew of raves poured in, particularly for Coleman's music. Frank Rich's assessment of the LP ran in the *New York Times* on July 4, and after noting that the music "may be right up there with his scores for 'Little Me' and 'Sweet Charity,'" he said that the album was so strong that it made it "hard to resist the urge to march down to the St. James and see the show again." Rich even noted Coleman's work in the studio on such recordings: "Since Mr. Coleman helps produce his own cast albums, the results are invariably first-rate. His scores for 'Seesaw' and 'I Love My Wife' sound far better on records than they did in the theater."

Coleman also got his first multiply recorded hit from a show since *Sweet Charity* when "The Colors of My Life" started receiving cover versions from artists ranging from such legends as Perry Como and Teresa Brewer to other talents like Vera Lynn and Richard Hayman. In addition, Coleman went into the studio himself and, in a toast to the old days when full LPs of jazz covers of a show's songs were plentiful, he recorded *Cy Coleman Presents "Barnum,"* on which he was even able to preserve the cut song "At Least I Tried."

As *Barnum* was entering its second year on Broadway in 1982, Coleman spoke candidly on Marian McPartland's *Piano Jazz* radio show about how the record business had changed since he began his career: "You know, when you used to do a show, you used to have a tune come out and you used to get a lot of people to record them. But now it's not the same kind of thing. You've got to fight for the record, but when they do come around, they're nice."

Before this he had been less magnanimous about the business and much more pointed when he told Associated Press writer Jay Sharbutt, "[The record companies] don't have the same faith (in the tunes) they once did. . . . They're willing to lose money on 100 rock groups in the hope that one hits."[43] It was a public forthrightness from Coleman that hadn't been seen since his earliest days in the limelight, when he had announced, "On last week's 10 top tunes list, there was not one song that made any sense, either melodically or lyrically. Not one that couldn't have been composed by my nephew. He is ten."[44]

With McPartland, he described how such bluntness was problematically magnified while *Barnum* was running. When a reporter asked him what it was like producing a show, Coleman remembered, "I said, 'Well, being a producer is like being a garbage dump. Everybody just comes and dumps all their stuff in your lap.' I said, 'I'm not crazy about it at all. I'm only a producer to protect my music and protect the show. But other than that, it's really the garbage dump.'" Coleman then related, with both chagrin and amusement, that when the article was printed "the caption in the picture [read] 'Cy Coleman says "producing is like a garbage dump."'"

Coleman may have had his problems with being a producer, but it didn't completely undermine his work on the managerial side of *Barnum*. Gordon described him as "a really good businessman." She did add, however, "I think that he was first and foremost an artist and a composer, and the show was his baby, and so he wasn't really a producer. It was a side profession, and so if it was a financial decision, and it was something he really wanted as the composer, but as a producer it wasn't really a good idea budgetwise, he would push for the artistic rather than the financial."[45]

Similarly, Bramble believed that the strain of both writing and producing had stretched Coleman too thin, pointing to the incident with the show's orchestrations as one example: "[Cy] should have been paying more attention, but he was so busy trying to gather money that he wasn't paying attention to Hershy."[46]

Other incidents would arise during the 854 performances that *Barnum* played on Broadway, including a conflict between the writers about Dale's replacement. Yet the fact remained that Coleman, like composers before him from Richard Rodgers to Jule Styne, had established himself as a producing presence with *Barnum*, a show that would go on to have two American tours (one headed by Stacy Keach) and an acclaimed run in London, with the future star of *The Phantom of the Opera*, Michael Crawford, as well as productions in France, Spain, Holland, and Australia.

As Coleman moved into his fifties, the boundless energy that had propelled him with meteoric intensity during the first three decades of his career wasn't enough to keep his momentum of having one show a year reach full production. The theater world had just changed too dramatically, and though Coleman would never be lacking for work or projects in the 1980s, it would be nine years before he had a new show reach the Broadway stage.

24

"Some Kind of Music"

With *Barnum*, Coleman had brought his fourth full musical to the stage in just as many years, and even before it went into rehearsal, he was touting what his next one would be, a tuner called *Atlantic City*. He had begun the project in 1975 with lyricist Christopher Gore, who penned the lyrics for the flop that preceded *Seesaw* at the Uris Theatre, *Via Galactica*, and who would also go on to have markedly greater success with his screenplay for the movie *Fame*.

Coleman put *Atlantic City* to the side after he and Gore began it because of his workload on shows that were reaching production, but by February 1980 he was ready to refocus his energy on it. His first step in moving the musical from the page to the stage was to be a two-LP concept recording that Columbia Records would release during the summer. Once the album was on the market, Coleman felt that the show—which had Bob Fosse attached as director and choreographer and which was on the Producers Circle's docket—would wend its way to the stage.

In announcing his plans for the LP, Coleman described the musical as being one that would "combine the old elegance and the Miss America atmosphere with the gambling of the modern city," adding, "It's a black, dark musical."[1]

At this juncture in its history, the show's book was being penned by Jack Heifner, who had written *Vanities*, a play that had enjoyed a three-year run Off-Broadway. As the 1980s dawned he was working with Carolyn Leigh on the musical *Smile*, and it was the lyricist who introduced the playwright to Coleman.

Heifner, however, was not the first person Coleman spoke to about the show. That distinction belonged to John Guare, who at the time was known for such plays as *The House of Blue Leaves* and the book for the musical *Two Gentlemen of Verona* and who would go on to write the Pulitzer Prize–winning play *Six Degrees of Separation*. Guare's work had demonstrated his keen ability to capture the quirks of the seamier side of life with humor, sensitivity, and a sense of danger, and as Coleman began to formulate his concept for *Atlantic City*, the playwright's aesthetic seemed to make him a natural candidate.

In later years there would be rumors that the conversations the two men had about the show inspired the playwright to write the screenplay for his successful film of the same name. But Guare denied the causal effect, noting that even before their talks he had had his own fascination with the place and the stories of its denizens. Furthermore, he said, "I also felt, having gone down there, that Atlantic City is impossible to capture on the stage."[2]

Coleman then approached journalist Pete Hamill about the project, but as with Guare, nothing came to fruition. In Heifner, however, Coleman finally had found someone with whom it seemed a genuine collaboration was possible. Coleman gave Heifner the songs that he and Gore had written, after which Heifner scheduled a series of meetings with Fosse to discuss the show. Heifner recalled, "I can't say that there was a great deal of guidance there. I was sort of off on my own, trying to come up with a story. . . . I went down to Atlantic City (you know, before it changed), so it was fascinating."[3]

At this point Heifner began writing, but he found it frustrating, as "we were trying to fit something together that was already written."[4] Wittingly or not, Coleman had placed the writer in the same position that Russell Baker had found himself in with the musical *Home Again, Home Again*.

But Heifner did not allow the confines of working with a preexisting score to impede him, and from his conversations with Fosse he developed a concept for the show that set the Coleman-Gore tunes into a time-bending theatrical collage about the famed seaside resort. The slightly surreal and dark funhouse tone of Heifner's book beautifully matched Coleman's uncharacteristically dour but still attractively tuneful songs.

Overall, *Atlantic City* seemed tailor-made for Fosse's directorial and choreographic edge, but Heifner sensed that it wasn't an ideal match: "I felt from the very beginning Bob wanted to do something, and he wanted to do something new, but that he was not interested in this."[5] Perhaps Fosse's disinclination had something to do with the fact that he was starting to focus on another project, a musical version of the Italian film *Big Deal on Madonna Street*, a property that he had optioned back in 1967.

After Heifner turned in his draft, *Atlantic City* went into a kind of limbo. He recalled, "I don't remember a final meeting or us discussing 'We're not going to do this.' It was just one of those things I worked on and worked on, and then it was just we're not working on it anymore."[6] In hindsight, the demise of *Atlantic City* might have been caused by timing. By the time Heifner's draft was completed, the film *Atlantic City* was on the horizon and scheduled to open in early 1981.

Although the show was never produced, some of its songs did enjoy some life in the public ear. Tony Bennett included the bittersweet ballad "On the Day You Leave Me" on his 1986 album *The Art of Excellence*, and when Coleman recorded the CD *It Started with a Dream* nearly two decades later, he included not only the show's mournful title number but also the gently sultry "I Really Love You" and the Latin-infused "Nothing to Do but Dance."

Among the other nine songs in the *Atlantic City* score were a sly R&B tune, "Toyland," a curious paean to the town's sex shops; and a comic vaudeville number that puts a surprising spin on infidelity, "When Jill Is Gone." Overall, the score reveals another, rather startling side to the composer, particularly after the ebullience of the Americana-infused music he wrote for *Barnum*.

On some levels, there's a bravado to these songs that might be seen in a younger writer. It's interesting that as Coleman was working to make *Atlantic City* become a reality, he was also revisiting, with Heifner, the first musical that he had written with Carolyn Leigh: *The Wonderful O*. The property came up in conversation while Heifner and Coleman were talking about ideas for an original musical they might write together.

All three writers met about the project, and Coleman and Leigh played the songs for Heifner. "I remember them saying, 'This is one of the first things we wrote when we were like kids in Greenwich Village' or something. Whether that's true or not, I don't know. And it had that feeling to me. The music. It was young and just wonderful."[7] Unfortunately, they discovered that the rights for the Thurber book were still unavailable, and so the project was shelved.

For Coleman, who had music "bubbling, bubbling, bubbling out of him," as Phyllis Newman once remarked,[8] it seemed that during the first few years of the 1980s he could not have enough projects happening at once. Alongside all of this work, he also began conceiving two new musicals with Michael Stewart. One was splashy enough to attract attention from the press for almost a full year: a musical based on Mickey Spillane's famed private eye, Mike Hammer.

Coleman was the first to broach the idea by saying to his old producers Cy Feuer and Ernest Martin, "I'd love to do a musical based on the jazz of the 1950s." Feuer recalled talking with Coleman about it more. "We hit upon the idea of Mickey Spillane and thought we'd see if we could use one of his Mike Hammer stories."[9] They decided to call it *Oh, Mike!*, and after meeting with the author, Feuer, Martin, and Coleman walked away not only with a commitment for a completely new detective yarn, but also with a book writer. Spillane had decided he would write it himself.

When the show was announced, Spillane said he found the entire idea of writing a Broadway show "kind of wild," adding, "I like the title. Any title with punctuation is fantastic. I'm writing a typical Mike Hammer story—beautiful blondes and a great, great ending."[10]

The other collaboration that Coleman and Stewart embarked on was with Mark Bramble: a musical adaptation of James Montgomery's 1916 comedy of manners, *Nothing but the Truth*. The plot for this featherweight piece involves a New York businessman who is bet that he cannot go for twenty-four hours without lying. The wager complicates his romantic and professional life, as well as the lives of everyone around him.

The play inspired two film versions, one in the earliest days of the talkies and one in the early 1940s with Bob Hope as its star. Harry Rigby, one of the producers of *I Love My Wife*, had a fondness for both the piece and the period (after all, he had been the producer of the acclaimed revival of the 1925 musical bonbon *No, No, Nanette*) and approached the writers about adapting it as a musical.

They agreed with him and began discussing the piece in mid-1981, but a few months later they hit a snag in their professional relationship when it came time to choose the replacement for Jim Dale in *Barnum*.

Since Dale had established himself as a bona fide star in the show, the prevailing thought was that he should be replaced with a marquee name. Nevertheless, one unlikely candidate cropped up: Mike Burstyn, who had appeared on Broadway in the late 1960s in *The Megilla of Itzik Manger* and subsequently spent much of his time performing in Israel, as well as in Holland, where he had a variety show.

It was through the Dutch television program that he met Chita Rivera, who thought he would be good for the role and recommended that he contact Coleman directly when she learned of his interest in playing it. Burstyn recalled calling the composer and saying, "I love this show, and I know that I could do this. I'm willing to fly in at my own expense, but it's an expensive thing, coming into the United States from Israel. I'm willing to do it, but I understand you may be looking for a name." Coleman responded, "'If you're what we're looking for, we'll make the name."[11]

With that encouragement, Burstyn booked his flight to New York. His audition was held on the stage of the St. James, and he performed for Coleman, Stewart, and Bramble, along with producers Judy Gordon and Maurice and Lois Rosenfield. At the end, Burstyn remembered, "Cy asked me, 'There's one thing we need to know. Will you be able to walk a wire?' And my answer was 'Mr. Coleman, if I could learn Dutch in three months, I can do anything.' I had a lot of chutzpah, and I found out later, Cy told me, that answer and that chutzpah was what convinced him."[12]

Burstyn's gutsy response, however, did not convince Coleman's writing partners, and the actor was eventually informed that he had not gotten the part. Within a few days, however, he received a telegram telling him that he would indeed be replacing Dale. "I found out later that Michael Stewart was the holdout. That Michael wanted Bert Convy. . . . Michael had had a case similar with a show that he had done where the star was replaced with a non-star and the show closed, and he was afraid the same thing would happen here."[13]

Just after the announcement that Burstyn would be taking over in *Barnum*, Stewart, who had threatened to close the show if Burstyn was cast, informed Coleman that he would no longer be working on the projects they had in development. It wasn't until five years later, when tempers had cooled and wounds had healed, that work began again on *Nothing but the Truth*.

Intriguingly, in the months before Coleman dove into making *Atlantic City* a reality and embarking on two new shows with Stewart, he told Associated Press writer Jay Sharbutt, "My problem is that sometimes I don't want to write. I like to do other things, too. But it seems to me lately that I write all the time."[14]

Indeed, even as he worked on his post-*Barnum* projects, Coleman was enjoying activities beyond composing, principally performing. Not only had he cut his first album in years—the jazz album of *Barnum* songs—he also stepped up his work in political circles. He became active in former mayor John Lindsay's campaign for the United States Senate and performed as part of *Broadway for Kennedy*, a fund-raiser for Senator Ted Kennedy's bid for the White House, held at the Shubert Theatre during the Democratic National Convention in August. For the event, Coleman put a political comedic spin on one of his most famous songs, "Big Spender." Sally Quinn reported on his plans in the *Washington Post*: "He has announced [it] is Billy Carter's song to Qaddafi." Coleman also told Quinn that while he was playing, "Betty Bacall dances playfully around the stage."[15]

Perhaps most tantalizing among the other appearances on Coleman's docket that year is a concert he was scheduled to give with the ninety-three-year-old composer-pianist Eubie Blake to raise funds for Boys Harbor in East Hampton. The two extraordinary pianists were to play duets; unfortunately, illness sidelined Blake, resulting in a solo show from Coleman.

The need to perform, kindled in him at a young age, and the need to compose, which he came to while in his teens, created a yin-and-yang sort of pull in Coleman that was only exacerbated by his desire to take on myriad different stage projects, all of which contributed to his sometimes being less than available for his collaborators.

"[Michael Stewart] always said [*I Love My Wife*] got written in 'Cy, I just need five minutes of your time. Just give me five minutes,'" Bramble said. Because Stewart lived near Coleman's offices, "Cy would say, 'Okay, okay. Just come around.' And then, of course, it would go into a work session. But I think Mike had to plead with him to get time. Once he got into it, he was totally into it. But Cy was doing a million things, always. And *Barnum* was the same way of 'We just need five minutes.'"[16]

Coleman's admission about his need to do things other than compose and the frustrations that Stewart and Bramble had with him (which echoed Leigh's from the late 1950s just before work on *Wildcat* began) make it slightly ironic that Coleman found himself working closely with her during this period—not only on the abortive attempt to bring *The Wonderful O* to the stage but also on a full-scale revival of their second show together, *Little Me*.

At the time, Coleman said, "It's not a revival like so many of the successful musicals are these days. . . . What we're doing is practically a new show."[17] Indeed, Neil Simon had rewritten the book for the 1962 tuner, dividing the male roles, all originally played by Sid Caesar, between two performers. Furthermore, he removed the character of George Musgrove, the childhood friend of heroine Belle Poitrine, substituting a character that had been in an early draft of the show, gangster Frankie Polo. The other major reworking involved the musical's framing device. No longer did Belle look back on her life from a world of affluence but rather from a seedy bar in New Jersey, where, washed and thoroughly liquored up, she retold her life story.

This last change indicates how drastically Simon had shifted the overall tone of the musical. No longer a lighter-than-air comedy, it was cynical and slightly bitter. Belle now hailed not from the obliquely humorous burg of Venezuela, Illinois, but rather from the crassly comic Twin Jugs, Illinois, and instead of the Steinbeckian "Drifters Row," Belle found herself living in the bluntly named "Dump Town."

YOU FASCINATE ME SO

To complement Simon's changes, Harold Wheeler was brought in to provide new, contemporary-sounding orchestrations, and Coleman rewrote the show's vocal and dance arrangements. More notable, however, was the addition of two new songs from the team of Cy Coleman and Carolyn Leigh, the first tunes they had written together for a musical since *Little Me* premiered.

The first was a brassy honky-tonk tune for the older Belle, "Don't Ask a Lady," which opened the show and necessitated the excision of "The Truth," the song that Coleman had rewritten so often for the original production. The second was "I Want to Be Yours," a silky ballad almost in the style of Jule Styne that was delivered by the younger Belle and a new beau, Philip Randolph Worst, whom Simon had created for the revision. Two songs were also jettisoned for the revised *Little Me*: "Be a Performer" and "Dimples," tunes that had come to the musical from Coleman and Leigh's *Gypsy* trunk.

Hopes were high for the production, which brought James Coco back to the stage after an absence of more than a decade, during which time he had established himself as one of Hollywood's most reliable comics. Coco was to play the older men Belle encountered in her life, while Victor Garber, who was just coming off the original *Sweeney Todd*, in which he played the sailor Anthony, would portray the younger men Belle knew, including the love of her life, Noble Eggleston.

As the "little me" of the show's title, Simon's new script retained the original conceit of having the part played by two actresses. Mary Gordon Murray (who had been a standby for both roles in *I Love My Wife* and eventually played each as a replacement) was the heroine in her prime, and Jessica James (who was a standby for Elaine Stritch in the original cast of *Company* and who played the eccentric Bunny Weinberger in the original cast of the long-running comedy *Gemini*) was on hand to play her in her later, blowzy years.

Robert Drivas, who guided the original production of Terrence McNally's farce *The Ritz* to acclaim in 1975 but had not had a similar hit since, helmed the production, which had choreography by Peter Gennaro (a member of the original *Little Me* company who moved on to a successful career creating dances for the film version of *The Unsinkable Molly Brown* and for the Rockettes at Radio City Music Hall).

The new *Little Me* opened at the Eugene O'Neill Theatre on January 21, 1982 to primarily negative reviews. In the *New York Times*, Frank Rich called it "a spotty, sloppy substitute for the zestier and grander 'Little Me' of 1962," while the *Variety* review that appeared a week after the show opened forecast that "the revival seems a questionable prospect to last more than a few weeks."

Indeed, the show ran a mere thirty-six performances before shuttering. In 1994, when Coleman talked about the revival with Michael Barnes of the *Austin American-Statesman*, he reflected, "That version was a mistake on all our parts. We tried something new—we split up the roles among several actors (brash Sid Caesar played all the male leads in the original). The whole thing was created as a tour de force. We made bad cuts, and the scenery was cartoonish. We tried to do a different production instead of just 'Little Me.'"

Still, it was enough to reunite Coleman with both Leigh and Simon, and as the year progressed, they started in on an entirely new show together, a stage version of the 1972 film comedy *The Heartbreak Kid*.

Written by Simon and directed by Elaine May (who, after years of being Mike Nichols's partner in comedy, had established herself as both a writer and a director), it was a property with which Coleman had more than passing familiarity. After all, he wrote the movie's theme song, "You're Going Far," with Sheldon Harnick, the man who had been the lyricist on numerous Broadway shows, most prominently *Fiddler on the Roof*. It was actually May who thought of Coleman and Harnick (to whom she had been married in the early 1960s) for the movie, but as Harnick recalled, "She felt very awkward about calling me directly, so she called Cy and he called me."[18]

Coleman set up the meeting, and Harnick described what happened: "She said, 'I need this song. Can I have it tomorrow?' That's what she said, and we looked at each other and said, 'No.' We said we'd do it as quickly as possible, and I think we did it in about two or three days."[19] The assignment, however, wasn't just a straightforward song; May wanted something that could have dual meanings.

Harnick explained, "What she wanted was a song that when you heard it at the beginning of the film it would register one way, and when you heard it at the end of the film you would hear it with great irony, knowing what the film had been. It was not possible to do something like that in three days, but we came up with a very nice song."[20]

May wanted the dual meanings in order to underscore the relatively static journey that the movie's central character, Lenny Cantrow, takes in learning that the grass isn't always greener on the other side. For the proposed musical, Simon kept this premise: Cantrow marries one woman, who, like him, is a Jewish New Yorker, only to jilt her on their honeymoon for another woman, Kelly, who is his wife's antithesis: younger, Midwestern, and Christian. Lenny struggles to win Kelly, but once he has, he discovers that life with her will be filled with the same compromises that he would have had to make with his first wife.

Leigh and Coleman began drafting a half dozen songs, all of which had the sort of wit and sophistication that typified their earlier work combined with a musical fizziness that had become part of the pop world in the intervening years.

By mid-1983, however, the creative team for the show went into flux. First, there were reports that the lyricist would be not Leigh, but rather Tim Rice, lyricist for Andrew Lloyd Webber on *Jesus Christ Superstar* and *Evita*. Then came the news that Simon had turned to another composer, Burt Bacharach, who had worked with Simon on the 1968 musical *Promises, Promises*. Eventually Simon shelved the project and moved on to what could be termed the second act of his career. He began working on darker and more introspective plays: his autobiographical triptych *Brighton Beach Memoirs*, *Biloxi Blues*, and *Broadway Bound*.

Even if Simon and Coleman had not begun talking about different collaborators during the first part of 1983, they would have had to turn to a new lyricist by the end of the year, after Leigh's unexpected death from a heart attack. She was only fifty-seven.

"Mr. Coleman hailed Miss Leigh yesterday as one who strove endlessly for perfection and worked at her craft very hard," read her obituary in the *New York Times* on November 21. Coleman also described her to the paper as a "poet" who "had a great feeling for music."

The affection and appreciation that Coleman expressed at the time of Leigh's death was moderated years later when he discussed her passing with a sense of anger. "She'd had a heart attack, and it was not diagnosed properly, so it was one of those terrible stories where her doctor said, 'Well, take a couple of aspirin.' And, you know, Carolyn was a big woman. I mean really big, so she was tall and big. And I always thought about that. How could you tell somebody like that to take a couple of aspirin? But it was very sad, and it was just a shame that her career was nipped in the bud like that."[21]

Her death dovetailed with a return that Coleman was making to some Hollywood work. In fact, he and Leigh had one assignment on their docket, a pair of songs for the film comedy *Blame It on Rio*, about a middle-aged man who, during a monthlong holiday in Brazil, is seduced by his teenaged daughter's best friend. Coleman needed a collaborator who could work quickly, so he turned once again to Harnick, with whom he'd written "You're Going Far" in just two days.

"I got a call from Cy, and it had to be done immediately, because they were behind schedule. He recorded one, gave it to me, and then he went off to Cincinnati or some place to do a gig," Harnick recalled, and then added, "It truly was effervescent. It is a wonderful song." Harnick was speaking of the film's title song. Once it was done, the two men completed "I Must Be Doing Something Right."[22]

Harnick didn't mind Coleman's approaching him at the last minute for things like this. "Anytime he called, professionally, I was delighted, because I knew that it would not only be fun to work with him but that the result would be something that I'd really like."[23]

During the early 1980s Coleman also began working with director Sidney Lumet, whose recent films had ranged from the Oscar-nominated *The Prince of the City* and *The Verdict* to the less than critically acclaimed *Deathtrap*. The first outing Coleman had on one of Lumet's films was the bittersweet comedy *Garbo Talks*, which centers on a man who, when his mother is diagnosed with an inoperable and fatal brain tumor, sets about making her dying wish—to meet Greta Garbo—come true.

Starring Anne Bancroft and Ron Silver as the mother and son, the movie (thanks to Larry Grusin's screenplay) never swerves into the realm of maudlin sentimentality. Instead, it uses the woman's illness to explore the son's midlife coming-of-age story as he discovers new things about himself (and his mother) while he searches Manhattan and beyond for the reclusive star.

Given that the film uses sequences from Garbo's pictures, notably *Camille* just after the opening credits, Coleman had to create a score that could evoke and blend with movie music from the 1930s while also supporting the picture of life in 1980s New York that was central to the film. To this end Coleman developed a main theme that was a waltz with a decided Viennese sweep and yet the simplicity of a delicate music-box air. He went on to develop a second theme that had an edgier quality and found ways to blend the two to underscore several of the montages showing the son as he researches and searches for Garbo.

Perhaps most impressive was the way in which Coleman eventually expanded the central melody for a scene in which the son narrowly misses meeting the screen star as she leaves her house on Fire Island, flying off in a sea plane. Before it has taken off, he rushes into the ocean, shouting in the hopes that he will manage to at least delay her; as he does so, Coleman's score swells as the tide surges and the plane zooms. The combination of action and music perfectly capture the marriage of high drama and extravagant music that was typical of the films of Hollywood's Golden Era.

Over the course of the next five years, Coleman would provide the scores for two additional Lumet movies: *Power* and *Family Business*. Neither of them proved to have the popular success of *Garbo*, but in each Coleman demonstrated a shrewd and delicate hand in the art of scoring.

In *Power*, a drama about a media consultant (played by Richard Gere) who, while juggling several political campaigns, has a crisis of conscience about his practices, Coleman's music blends the percussive rhythms of "Sing Sing Sing" (made a classic by Benny Goodman and a favorite tune of the movie's hero) with the staccato clicks and whirs of the then just emerging personal computer. The result is a subtle set of brief interludes that gracefully capture the mounting tension Gere's character feels as he sees a political campaign being undermined by an unscrupulous lobbyist.

The music in *Power* is so distinctive that it garnered the attention of one critic. In a January 31 review in the *Hartford Courant*, Malcolm L. Johnson commented on how "the jazzy, up-tempo scoring by Broadway's Cy Coleman" helped to keep "juices flowing, even when David Himmelstein's screenplay makes a clumsy move, or Lumet overstates a scene."

Coleman's final outing with Lumet was the 1989 movie *Family Business*, a dark comedy about three generations of con men (played by Sean Connery, Dustin Hoffman, and Matthew Broderick). While *Power* uses an existing swing song for its opening credits, *Family Business* has an original Coleman theme that evokes the era of Goodman, Ellington, and Dorsey even while sounding entirely contemporary. The latter quality is the result of an insistent vamp reminiscent of John Kander's work.

Beyond this central melody, from which the composer builds a series of intriguing variations, the *Family Business* underscoring contains elements that evoke his work in 1960s Hollywood, particularly during the movie's heist sequence, when the avant-garde orchestrations of *The Troublemaker* sound as if they've met Coleman's musical impersonation of Henry Mancini from *The Art of Love.*

As playful as Coleman could be in his film scoring, it didn't allow for the sort of collaboration that he enjoyed most and could be readily found in theater. So, even as he began contemplating the music for *Rio* and *Garbo*, he was still actively creating new theater work.

Sheet music for "Firefly," written on spec for the musical *Gypsy*; the song was a hit for Tony Bennett.

Cy with Carolyn; inscription from a later date. On the reverse she wrote, "The 'Donny' and 'Marie' of yesteryear? Hah!"

Album cover for Cy's jazz album featuring songs from Harold Arlen and E. Y. "Yip" Harburg's musical *Jamaica*.

Lucille Ball and Keith Andes take a bow at Cy's first show on Broadway, *Wildcat*.

Cy works with dance arranger John Morris during the Philadelphia tryout for *Wildcat*.

Album cover for Cy's jazz covers of his own Broadway score for *Wildcat*.

Hugh Hefner (*left, with pipe*) and Cy in the recording studio.

Cy (*left*) and Johnny Mercer lobby for ASCAP in Washington, D.C.

Promotional album from Cy's company, Notable Music, for the musical *Sweet Charity*.

Left to right: Lynn Lane (Mrs. Burton Lane), Richard Rodgers, Dorothy Fields, and Cy, circa 1966.

Cy at the beach in the late 1960s or early 1970s.

Cy atop the Eiffel Tower in 1985.

Cy vacations in Hawaii, circa 1982. Photo courtesy of Susan Agrest.

Cy celebrates his 53rd birthday in Australia as his musical *Barnum* opens. Photo courtesy of Susan Agrest.

Cy with Betty Comden and Adolph Green. Photo courtesy of Phyllis Newman.

Larry Gelbart, Cy, and David Zippel celebrate their Tony victory for *City of Angels*.

Cy with Tommy Tune.

Left to right: Pierre Cossette, Adolph Green, Cy, and Betty Comden accept their Grammy Award for the original cast recording of *The Will Rogers Follies*.

Cy rehearses with the kids at Paul Newman and A. E. Hotchner's Hole in the Wall Gang camp.

Left to right: Chuck Cooper, Pamela Isaacs, Cy, and Sam Harris celebrate twelve Tony nominations for *The Life*. Photo by Joseph Marzullo.

Cy and Gwen Verdon at a 1996 Drama League event. Photo by Joseph Marzullo.

Cy with Shelby on their wedding day.

Cy with his daughter, Lily Cye.

Cy (*center*) celebrates the opening of *Grace* in Amsterdam.

Cy on a family vacation with his wife, Shelby, and daughter, Lily Cye.

Cy celebrates his return to cabaret at Feinstein's, October 2004.
Photo by Keith Meritz.

25

"Good Intentions"

ven for Coleman, who seemingly was capable of juggling musicals with the ease of a circus performer, the end of 1983 was a particularly busy time, with two new shows going into performance in different cities: New York and Chicago.

In New York, the production was *Peg*, a show that starred his old friend and sometime writing partner, singing great Peggy Lee.

The thought of doing the show came to Lee in 1980 while she was in Michigan performing in the revue *Side by Side by Sondheim*. She liked the theater, and furthermore, she found herself inexorably pulled to a melody that she heard one of the production's accompanists, Paul Horner, playing during a lunch break. When she discovered that the tune was Horner's own and that he had written it hoping she would pen a lyric for it, a collaboration developed.

They started writing together, conceptualizing the show that would become *Peg*. As Lee recounted in her autobiography, "We wrote thirty songs for the score, and when it was finished, we began having backers' dinners at my house."[1] One such event wasn't necessarily intended as an audition; it was a party at which hoteliers Irv and Marge Cowan were present during which Lee and Horner offered an impromptu performance of the score. The Cowans liked what they heard and promised to help get the show produced. They eventually brought on Zev Bufman, who had among his producing credits *The Little Foxes*; *Private Lives*, with Elizabeth Taylor; and the Andrew Lloyd Webber–Tim Rice musical *Joseph and the Amazing Technicolor Dreamcoat*.

By 1982 Lee herself had penned the book for the show. "Eschewing the one-woman-show format filled with her best-known hits, Miss Lee preferred 'to bring my own little contribution to the theater,' she said in a telephone interview," wrote Susan Heller Anderson in an August 18 *New York Times* article about the production. At this point, the producers were envisioning a show that would have twenty-two performers and were budgeting it at $2.5 million.

As for the show's format, Lee told Anderson, "I'll be in the show substantially . . . with someone to play the younger Peg." Lee also indulged in some fantasy casting about one of the central figures in her life, jazz musician Dave Barbour, whom she had met while performing with Benny Goodman's band and married. As she thought about the show, Lee said, "Dustin Hoffman would be a lot like Dave."

At this juncture *Peg* was simply a collaboration between Lee and Horner, but as it continued to evolve, the creative team for it grew. First, William Luce, who wrote *The Belle of Amherst*, the acclaimed biodrama about poet Emily Dickinson, was brought on board to work on the show's book. Then Coleman, much as he had for his pal Shirley MacLaine when she was working on her solo show in the early 1970s, signed on as artistic consultant to work with the man hired to direct the piece, Robert Drivas, who had helmed the ill-fated *Little Me* revival.

Luce kept Lee's original multicharacter conceit for the show as well as the concept of having the star played by different actresses, and in early 1983 Lee was seemingly content with the idea. She told *Chicago Tribune* reporter Larry Kart that she would be "coming into and out of [the action] all the way through."[2] Eventually, however, the idea of multiple actresses playing her went to the wayside. "She always wanted to play herself," recalled producer Irv Cowan.[3]

There were conflicts not only about the way the piece should be constructed and cast, but also about the music it would contain. Lee and Horner had written enough material for two musicals, so Lee would not need to perform any of her hits. Nevertheless, there was a push to include some of them in the show.

Eventually Luce was removed as book writer, and though the show had been intended as "a kind of impressionistic piece,"[4] it gradually transformed into an essentially standard-issue evening of autobiography and song.

Coleman attempted to shape the production, but as Mike Renzi, the pianist who had come to it at Coleman's insistence from Lena Horne's successful one-woman show, recalled, "Cy's forte was Broadway. . . . [Lee] recruited him, and he decided he'd give her creative input. They were such good friends anyway, right? So we're rehearsing at Minskoff Studios, me and Grady [Tate, the show's drummer], no bass. Well, she'd never done a Broadway thing in her life, and she's fighting Cy all the way. Cy is saying, 'Peggy, I'm telling you—I know this is what we should do.' And then she would listen and she would say, 'Yeah—but no.' One day he got so fed up he walked out on her."[5]

Coleman and Lee made up, and during the show's two weeks of previews at the Lunt-Fontanne Theatre (the original home of *Little Me*), they would revise things, but bassist Jay Leonhart felt they focused on the wrong things: "A show like that is almost a vanity project, it's gotta be perfect, and in the end, she didn't have the energy for the rewriting it needed."[6]

What emerged was a show that had a smattering of original dialogue (prose voice-overs from other characters in Lee's life and autobiographical poetry) combined with fourteen of Lee and Horner's songs and eleven of the songs familiar to theatergoers from her long career, including Coleman's "Big Spender," which was heard late in the second act, alongside two Leiber and Stoller tunes, "I'm a Woman" and "Is That All There Is?" There was also one Coleman original in the show, "I Never Knew Why," which has a melody that could be counted among the most downbeat of any that he ever wrote. The song, with a lyric by Lee, allowed the performer to reflect, with brazen superficiality, on the demise of her relationship with Barbour.

The show opened on December 14, and the reviews were dismal. Frank Rich wrote in the *New York Times* that the piece was "nothing if not a religious rite . . . most likely to excite those who are evangelistically devoted to both Peggy Lee and God—ideally in that order." Of Drivas's and

Coleman's work, he said, "The staging is efficient, but these experienced theater men can only take their star so far." The December 21 *Variety* review not only echoed Rich's sentiments when it said *Peg* was "clouded by awkwardly written, mawkish autobiographical material that veers close to self-glorification," but it also appeared three days after the show had abruptly closed after just five performances.

While *Peg* was rehearsing and previewing, Coleman was also busy with an out-of-town project, *Shecago*, a show that would debut at a new cabaret venue in Chicago that had an unusual name: the Institute for Advanced Studies and Bar & Grill. The place was the brainchild of Arnie Morton and Victor Lownes, the men who, with Coleman's old friend Hugh Hefner, founded the Playboy clubs.

The show that went into this space actually had its origins in Coleman's conversations with Judy Gordon prior to their work on *Barnum*. She wanted to do a revue of his songs, but, she remembered, "He said that I had to have a concept for the show. . . . So I got in touch with Tommy Tune, who at that time was at the beginning of his career, and said, 'What about doing a show of Cy's music?' And he said, 'Oh yeah!' And so the three of us had a meeting in Cy's office, and Tommy came up with the idea of doing Crazy Horse in New York."[7]

Alain Bernardin had opened the club that Tune was talking about in Paris in 1951, creating a venue in which he could explore his artistic vision and showcase his love of beautiful women. Over the years it had established itself as one of the world's preeminent homes of avant-garde cabaret and burlesque. At the center of the Crazy Horse shows were numbers performed by scantily clad or nude women, with magic and variety acts interspersed.

Coleman immediately latched on to the idea, and the three began scouting for locations in which such a show could be produced. "We looked at all of these defunct nightspots," Tune recalled. "The El Morocco was gated up, and we went to look at whether we could work in there and different places. He wanted to call the show *Quail*, because that's what musicians of a certain period called girls. In England, they called them birds."[8]

Their plans were put on hold because of other projects (and New York City's restrictions on public nudity). Then, in 1983, Coleman, now with Joe Layton as director and choreographer, resurrected the project when Morton asked that they come up with a show for his new venture. The ads for the auditions—at one point a half page in the industry casting bible *Back Stage*—featured not only a Picassolike drawing of a woman in a provocative pose but also a blunt statement of what was required of potential cast members: "You must be able to dance or move very well, and must have both a beautiful body and good looks to be able to qualify for this extraordinary job."[9]

These requirements caught the eye of columnists Michael Sneed and Cheryl Lavin (both women) in the *Chicago Tribune*, who followed the project with raised eyebrows and a healthy dose of sarcasm. On November 25, after the first auditions had been held, the writers revealed that the creators had not been able to fully cast the show and then reported that "[Lownes] has, if you'll pardon the expression, broadened the requirements" for potential cast members.[10] He upped the eligible age cap for dancers who wanted to audition from twenty-two to twenty-six and lowered the height requirement from five feet nine inches to five feet six inches.

Once the show was cast, the company members, which included the women and three men (two dancers and a magician), found themselves performing to roughly two dozen of Coleman's songs. The selections, which were all prerecorded, encompassed the entirety of Coleman's career, from "Isn't He Adorable?," with its lyric by Joseph A. McCarthy Jr., to numbers from *Barnum*. In between were hits from his shows, such as "Real Live Girl" and "Big Spender," both of which fit easily into the piece's conceit. There were also tunes that had gone unperformed, such as "I'm Watching You," written for *The Wonderful O*.

Ted Kociolek, who after serving as associate conductor and one of the pianists for *Barnum* became the musical coordinator on *Shecago*, remembered how inventive Layton's staging was for even the most familiar of tunes, like "The Colors of My Life": "In this number, one of the guys was a painter, with Day-Glo colors on a canvas. They also had one of the ladies

dressed in a Day-Glo unitard of various hues, but it was covered completely in black Velcro, so the guy would take his paintbrush of neon color
and do a splash at her. At which point somebody would rip off a piece of
the Velcro to reveal a Day-Glo pink, for instance. And thus the woman is
'painted' by ripping off the Velcro."[11]

Kociolek also recalled how a dreamy, ethereal rendition of "You Fascinate Me So" became a "quasi-Sapphic encounter" as two of the women
"crawled up and over a jungle gym–like [set piece] in almost Cirque du
Soleil or balletic fashion."[12]

None of the sequences, according to Kociolek, was "salacious," and
indeed, when Larry Kart's review appeared in the *Chicago Tribune* on
December 20, he dubbed it "moderately entertaining, mildly erotic, and
probably of interest mostly to conventioneers." Kart also took great pains
to describe how much the show had improved since he first saw it, at
what was supposed to have been a press preview but turned out to be a
performance to which reviewers had been disinvited.

On that night, Kart wrote, "everyone (onstage and in the audience)
was wondering whether these people were going to fall down." What had
happened during the course of the week, Kart reported, turned an event
that had been "ludicrous" into "a decently indecent piece of entertainment."

Unfortunately, the show never caught on, with either Chicagoland
natives or tourists, and by the spring of 1984 *Shecago* shuttered. In the
wake of its relatively quick demise, Cheryl Lavin, one of the two *Tribune*
columnist baiting Morton and Lownes from the beginning, provided a
postmortem of the show to the London *Observer*. In her April 22 report
she cited a number of missteps made by Morton and Lownes and also
found fault with the director and composer. "Coleman and Layton were
too big for the job. They each had more important, more exciting projects
to worry about." Layton, she wrote, "flew back and forth from Chicago to
Los Angeles, where he was directing a video for Lionel Ritchie." Coleman,
she said, "managed to get to Chicago only twice."

Kociolek remembered that a good deal of his work with Coleman had
indeed been done by phone and FedEx before the show opened, but he

said that Coleman was on hand and added, "To be fair, though, there would have been little for him to supervise in Chicago, since there was no singing or live music."[13] Another point Lavin failed to acknowledge was the relatively short period of time that the two men were given to move the show from rehearsal and into performance—essentially three weeks. Casting wasn't completed until the end of November, and performances began on December 8.

Following the critical and popular failures of *Peg* and *Shecago*, Coleman, curiously, turned his attention to another show of his that had fared badly. In early 1984 he, writer Russell Baker, and lyricist Barbara Fried were all taking a second look at *Home Again*, their musical that closed on its way to Broadway in 1979. They were not, however, trying to figure out a way to revive the prospects of the show. Instead, they were writing a new musical, using their experiences from the *Home Again* tryout period to create something new.

Scenic designer Robin Wagner remembered that the genesis of the new venture came about after he and Coleman had been talking about Wagner's fondness for the score: "One day, Russell Baker was in town, so Cy said, 'Why don't you come up and let's have a conversation with him.'" The three men met, and Baker admitted that "he'd never made a nickel in the theater, but he still liked it."[14] Baker also alluded to the fact that he'd been thinking about writing something satirical about his experiences on *Home Again*, and from this a new show, a bit of metatheatrics extraordinaire, was born. Baker would write a book for a musical about a show that was having a rough time of it on the road. The musical-within-the-musical would use songs from the earlier Coleman-Fried-Baker collaboration, and for sequences about the creators of the fictional musical Coleman and Fried would write new material.

First announced as *Baker's Broadway* in October 1984, the show would go through another three titles over the course of the next three years; its final working title was *13 Days to Broadway*. During that time Coleman and Fried developed a dozen or more new songs for the project even as they reworked some of their previous efforts.

In the latter category was "America Is Bathed in Sunlight," the wistful and leisurely paean to life as it once was that opened *Home Again*. For the new show, the song once again was a focal point, but in the most ironic of ways. As the fictional creators of the musical-within-the-musical struggle to figure out what's going wrong, they identify this number as the one that's killing them. They shift it around from one act to another, and then, in a fit of desperation, decide that it's just the wrong style. So the fictional composer reworks it. For this Coleman wrote "America Variations," recasting the song as a gospel number, a stylized version that might have been composed by Philip Glass, and, in a fit of desperation, a song to be intoned by a barking dog.

The new songs, which were among some of the most musically jocular that Coleman had turned out in several years, included "Ain't Show Business Grand?," an ironic toast to the industry that fused the sounds of pop with the Golden Age of Broadway; "Critics," a delicious patter song about the men and women who pass judgment on shows; and "Money and Manure," a paean to the art of producing that, by combining elements of country music and Alpine yodeling, musically captured both the lowbrow origins of the show's backers and their highbrow aspirations. This last song was also a bit of an inside dig at the men who produced *Home Again*. As Fried recalled, during the tryout period of the show, "Irwin [Meyer] had been going to Switzerland a lot."[15]

By the end of 1984 the new musical had gained a director, David H. Bell (then artistic director of Ford's Theatre in Washington, D.C.), who would be staging a workshop production of it. By the spring of 1985 it was on track for a Broadway premiere in the fall. "The workshop production this winter was very successful. We're just waiting for the Securities and Exchange Commission to clear us so we can raise the money," Coleman said.[16]

As Coleman had by now discovered time and time again, the matter of raising the money proved to be more difficult than he expected, and after his optimistic announcement that the show would be on Broadway before the end of the year, it went into stasis for nearly two years. During this time he, Baker, and Fried—and Wagner, who had signed on as a coproducer and director—continued to refine and workshop the show.

13 Days to Broadway resurfaced in mid-1987. At that point it was to have a tryout at the Drury Lane Theatre just outside of Chicago; after this, under the direction of Coleman's longtime collaborator Layton, *13 Days* was set to transfer to Broadway. Unfortunately, as Wagner recalled, "We got in with some crazy lady whose name I can't recall, who kept promising like a quarter of the dough, and we were all working to raise money," adding, "Finally, it came down that we got our portions. . . . But she never did."[17] It was at this point that the production got shelved.

In the midst of this process Coleman was back on Broadway with a revival of *Sweet Charity*, which had been restaged and rechoreographed by Bob Fosse and starred Debbie Allen in the title role. Allen got her start in Broadway shows like *Purlie* and *Raisin* and went on to achieve national celebrity thanks to her work in both the movie and television series *Fame*, playing the sensitive but stern dance teacher Lydia Grant. The show had what *Los Angeles Times* writer Paul Rosenfeld called a "dry run for a possible Broadway return" at the Dorothy Chandler Pavilion in Los Angeles during the summer of 1985.[18] It was during this time that Coleman began to work with Fosse on changes for the production that was roughly marking the twentieth anniversary of the show's debut.

"Bob felt that a revival should not just be a museum piece but should have some surprises in it for the audience," recalled stage manager Craig Jacobs, who added, "and while the original *Sweet Charity* was three hours long, he wanted this version to be two and a half, which is why ["Charity's Soliloquy"] was cut."[19]

Fosse's work, as well as that of Allen, received glowing reviews in Los Angeles, and in January 1986 the official word came that *Sweet Charity* would be returning to Broadway. "We think it has Cy Coleman's best score and that it was a little ahead of its time originally," said Joseph Harris (who had been one of the musical's original producers and was also a backer of the revival) when the announcement was made.[20]

By the time *Sweet Charity* opened on April 27, the changes to Coleman's score were not substantial, but they were distinct. Besides omitting "Soliloquy," Coleman substituted the film version of the title song over the version that had originally been heard on Broadway, and there were some new orchestrations. Fosse and Coleman discussed one other change to the music—a wholesale revision of "Rhythm of Life," the song Fosse had fought in the original production—but that idea was dropped during the course of rehearsals.

The show opened at the Minskoff Theatre to favorable if not glowing notices on April 27. As they had for the original production, the raves went to Fosse for his dances and, generally, to the show's star. Critics continued to have problems with Neil Simon's book: in the *New York Times*, Frank Rich called it a "hapless script."

As for the score, reviewers admired both Coleman's music and the ways it had been tweaked for this new production. In his May 20 *Wall Street Journal* review, Edwin Wilson wrote, "Cy Coleman's driving, upbeat score is probably his best, and he has made subtle changes in the orchestrations that update them without in essence altering them."

When it came time for the Tony Award nominations, the show garnered five, including ones for performers Michael Rupert and Bebe Neuwirth, who played, respectively, Charity's beau Oscar and her best pal, Nickie. It ended up winning four, including best reproduction (play or musical), and settled into the Minskoff for a run that lasted just under a year.

Following its Broadway closure, the production embarked on a national tour with a new star, Broadway veteran Donna McKechnie, who had won a Tony Award for her portrayal of Cassie in the original *A Chorus Line*. The venue from which the tour launched was the National Theater in Washington, D.C. Fosse and Coleman traveled to supervise the final rehearsals for the show. Shortly before the curtain went up on the production, Fosse suffered a fatal heart attack while walking from his hotel to the theater. He was sixty years old.

It was an extremely hard blow for Coleman, who said, after learning of Fosse's death, "Bobby was too alive to be dead."[21] That night Coleman went out with stage manager Jacobs, producer Harris, and some other members of the show's business team. Jacobs remembered, "We all went to Levitt's Grill and told Bob Fosse stories. Cy was very moved that night. He broke down a couple of times at the bar."[22]

Coleman's assistant Terrie Curran recounted the two men's close, jovial relationship. "They were always arguing about putting an act together, and Fosse would say, 'Feet and Fingers.' And Cy would say, 'Fingers and Feet.' It was always an argument about what the title would be."[23]

She also described how deeply Coleman felt Fosse's passing. "About a year [after I had started working for him], his mother died. And that was the first time I ever saw him cry. And there was that once and only one other time I ever him saw cry again—and now it wasn't sobbing, it was just tears—was when Fosse died."[24]

Unfortunately, it was a loss made all the more intense by the fact that it came just three days after Coleman's longtime friend and collaborator Michael Stewart died of pneumonia. By this time Stewart and Coleman had reconciled, and with Bramble they had begun work again on the musical *Nothing but the Truth*. In fact, the three men had completed a draft of the show, replete with eleven new songs.

At the time there were no plans for moving forward with the project, and Bramble recalled that after Stewart's death, "it just got put away. And then Cy said, 'You know, we really ought to look at that again,' and that would have been sometime after 1997."[25] It was a gap of ten years, which was becoming a standard in the development of some of Coleman's musicals—a sign of changing times in the ways in which shows reached Broadway and the evolution of Coleman's workload.

26

Welcome to the Club

During the course of the nearly yearlong run of the revival of *Sweet Charity* on Broadway, the *New York Times* profiled Coleman in an article titled "Cy Coleman, Composer with a Knack for Juggling." Journalist Dena Kleiman outlined the multitude of writers with whom he was currently working and also talked to a number of them, including Betty Comden, who commented on his propensity for working on multiple projects: "It's maddening at times," she said, but added, "When he is doing something, his concentration is total."[1]

Coleman never made it to the point of total concentration on one other project from the first half of the 1980s, a musical about Julian Eltinge, an exceptionally brilliant female impersonator who was the toast of New York—and later Hollywood—during the earliest years of the twentieth century. In fact, in 1912 his success in Manhattan resulted in the Liberty Theatre's (later incorporated into the AMC Theatre Complex on Forty-second Street) being rechristened the Eltinge Theatre.

Coleman first conceived the show in the early 1970s, and as he was formulating his ideas, he met, through Carolyn Leigh, a young playwright, Allan Knee, who would go on to pen the book for the musical *Little Women* and the play *The Man Who Was Peter Pan*, which served as the basis for the film *Finding Neverland*. At the time Knee was working with both Leigh and Lee Pockriss on a project, and like them, Coleman recognized potential in Knee. When the composer asked him if he might be willing to draft a book about Eltinge's life, Knee agreed.

Knee completed the script, sent it to Coleman and then heard—nothing. That is, until the early 1980s, when Coleman called to talk about the show. "I said, 'This is embarrassing, Cy. I no longer have a copy of what I sent you.' I had lost faith in it when he didn't respond to me." Coleman told Knee that he still had a copy, and Knee picked it up in Coleman's offices. "I was afraid to read it. What had I written ten years ago?" As he read it on the subway, Knee realized that he still liked what he had written. "So I called him up and said, 'Yeah, I'd love to come in and talk to you.' So I went in, and he said, 'I'd like to commission you to write the book for the musical.'"[2]

Knee accepted and began reworking his original script. Then, as he recalled, "I would come in like once every two weeks with expanded material, with developments. I would read the scenes aloud, and he would start improvising. This was all terrific. And I've never met anyone who wrote as magnificently as he did. He wrote a musical theme for Julian that was so beautiful and so full of pain at the same time."[3]

Coleman planned to treat this theme as a motif for the title character, varying it throughout the course of the musical. Alongside this instrumental, Coleman sketched out how the rest of the show would be built. It would be a combination of book songs and diegetic music-hall numbers, the latter actually being sung by the characters as part of their lives.

Despite his meticulous planning, however, Coleman never wrote anything beyond this central melody, and Knee grew frustrated. "I would do all of this work from this meeting to that meeting, and he would have done nothing. What he would do when I would get there is his noodling, and then, when I'd get there for the next meeting, he'd be in the same place."[4]

Coleman did set up a meeting with lyricist Sheldon Harnick to discuss the possibility of his joining in on the show, but Harnick, despite his fondness for working with Coleman, declined. Coleman also reached out to a young lyricist, David Zippel.

Originally trained as a lawyer, Zippel had been writing lyrics with various partners for years at this juncture, notably Wally Harper, who had had his musical *Sensations* published by Coleman, and in 1977 the two men had brought a song they had written to Notable Music for publication. Beyond this contact with Zippel, Coleman had been told about Zippel's talents from both his attorney, Albert DaSilva, whose son had been a friend of Zippel's at school, and *Barnum* coproducer Judy Gordon. Both DaSilva and Gordon thought the two men should be working together.

Zippel recalled, "I think Cy kind of felt their fingerprints and them pushing pretty hard, and Cy tended to like things to be his idea, so there was some resistance there." Eventually, however, Coleman did call Zippel to arrange a meeting to talk about a project. The lyricist accepted the invitation, and "I was thrilled that Cy called me, because he was my hero and someone I admired so much. And I desperately wanted to write with Cy Coleman. It was a lifelong dream from the beginning. Everything he wrote was so good."[5]

After hearing about *Julian*, however, Zippel said, "I was kind of crestfallen when I heard what he wanted to write with me. It was after *La Cage*, so it kind of felt to me like we'd been there already. But I thought, 'I'm certainly not going to turn him down. Yet.'"[6]

At a second meeting, however, Zippel did tell Coleman that he felt he was not right for the project but suggested that there might be another show for them to work on together. Coleman demurred, and Zippel departed.

Knee remembered that after Coleman was unable to bring a lyricist on board for the show, "he turned to his trunk and started bringing out numerous, I mean numerous, trunk songs,"[7] among them, "Pink Taffeta Sample Size 10" from *Sweet Charity* and "That's What the Poor Woman Is" from *Barnum*. But Coleman wasn't producing any new material.

After about a year Knee, frustrated about the show from both an artistic perspective and a business one (he still had no written agreement with the composer), confronted Coleman: "'Cy, I need a contract.' And he shouted to his secretary, Terrie, 'Where's Allan's contract? Why doesn't he have his contract? Why don't you pay him his money?' He did that three or four times, and I realized he wasn't going to give me a contract. He wasn't going to pay me anything for this. This isn't going to happen. I began to feel as if I was filling in time until he got something going that was going to be lucrative and possible for him."[8]

Knee recalled that the exchange became more heated. "I said, 'All right, Cy, I'm pulling away from this. I'm not doing any more work.' And then he really screamed. He really got furious at me. I said, 'You're never going to pay me. You're never going to give me a contract. You're just going to waste my time.' And he screamed, 'If you ever do anything with Julian Eltinge, I will sue you for everything.' And I said, 'Do what you want to, Cy. You're lying to me. There's not going to be a contract.' And he never said, 'Well, there is.'"[9]

What Knee didn't know was that Coleman, who had written the score for his first Broadway musical in just four months, had developed the habit of allowing musicals to gestate for years. Furthermore, and sadly, Knee hadn't known what Comden and Green learned early on: when Coleman turned to the piano, having a tape recorder at the ready was de rigueur, because, having spent so many hours with notebooks notating music as a child, he had grown to hate writing out his music. To preserve his ideas, an audio recording was absolutely necessary. Thus, the melody Knee so fondly recalled was never captured.

Coleman retained all of the research on the *Julian* project as well as Knee's scripts, but he didn't continue with it at the time, nor did he ever return to it. Instead, he turned to other projects and shows, and in the months before Fosse and Stewart died, Coleman was tending to one show—which he had written with A. E. Hotchner and which had its roots in the late 1960s—as it received two important workshop productions.

Hotchner and Coleman had met in the late 1950s, when the composer and actress Sylvia Miles were dating. Over the years the two men had remained close, and ultimately Hotchner shared a play he had written, *Let 'Em Rot*, with his pal. Coleman immediately saw musical potential in the script.

Hotchner based the play on his experiences as a lawyer handling divorce cases in St. Louis. He took the horrible, petty, and sometimes silly fights that he had witnessed couples embroiled in and attempted to mine the events for both comedy and drama, telling the story of a group of men who found themselves in jail because they had not paid their alimony. To Coleman's mind, it contained "the perfect situations for writing a score: They're emotional, comic, and comically heavy."[10]

Throughout the years they continued to discuss the project even as both men went on with their own work, Coleman penning musical after musical and Hotchner writing such books as *Papa Hemingway* and *The Man Who Lived at the Ritz*. Then, in the early 1980s, they decided to work on adapting the play into a musical in earnest.

Their first step in the process was opening it up so that it included more female characters and took audiences beyond the jail where the men were being held. What emerged was a show about four very different guys: a Jewish druggist, an African American insurance salesman, a sensitive writer, and a yuppie businessman. To bring women into the picture, Hotchner devised fantasy sequences and flashbacks that featured their wives. Another female character was added to the mix as well, a country singer who eventually joins the men because of her own financial delinquency with her ex.

With the reworked story in hand, Hotchner and Coleman began to contemplate whom they should have as a lyricist, and they were about to ask Carolyn Leigh to join them when she died unexpectedly. At this juncture, Coleman remembered, "We decided to begin pulling out ideas for lyrics ourselves. They started to develop and became so organic to the book that we decided to keep going." The men would not try to write a song per se but rather began to craft numbers out of existing situations, almost like dialogue, and as Hotchner recalled, "Cy, who knows song form so well, was able to shape the songs as the lyrics evolved."[11]

By early 1987 the show had reached a point where they needed to see how it played in front of an audience, and so they scheduled a workshop production at the Actors Studio Writers and Directors Wing. There were three performances. The event attracted the likes of Bob Fosse, Gene Saks, and David Merrick, all eager to experience Coleman's first musical as both composer and co-lyricist.

Also among the audiences at the workshop were representatives from Lucille Lortel's White Barn Theatre in Connecticut, which was founded in the mid-1940s as a place for artists to hone their work free of the pressures of the commercial world. Based on what was onstage at the Actors Studio, it seemed like *Let 'Em Rot* was a perfect candidate for the theater, and so the piece was put on the White Barn schedule for the summer, where a group of artists worthy of a Broadway production came together for a series of three performances.

Directed by Morton Da Costa (who been mentioned as a possible Coleman collaborator ever since *The King from Ashtabula* in the late 1950s), the company for the White Barn presentation included Marilyn Sokol, an actress-comedienne whose versatility had been demonstrated both on Broadway and off, as well as in films such as *The Goodbye Girl* and *Garbo Talks*; and William Parry, whose Broadway credits stretched from *Rockabye Hamlet* to *Sunday in the Park with George*.

Given that Coleman was a member of Broadway's establishment, it may have seemed curious for an institution like the White Barn to be developing his work. To forestall any criticism, press representative Richard P. Pheneger made it clear that the show fit squarely into the theater's mission. He told the *New York Times*, "The show needs work and they wanted a place to try it out without critics—to get some indication as to what it needed to make it viable for Broadway."[12]

Once again the workshop attracted some heavy hitters in the American theatrical community. Theater owner James Nederlander took in a performance, as did some members of the artistic and management team of the Coconut Grove Playhouse in Florida, which specialized in the development and presentation of new musicals. They too were impressed by the potential they saw in the tuner and began the process of adding it to the theater's 1987–88 season.

Let 'Em Rot eventually was slated for a late-winter run in Coconut Grove. A new director, Frank Cosaro, helmed this production, and it had choreography by Baayork Lee, who had been brought into *Seesaw* by Michael Bennett and later was one of the central performers in *A Chorus Line*. Corsaro came to the production with an impressive string of Broadway credits. He staged the original production of Tennessee Williams's *The Night of the Iguana*, starring Bette Davis. In the realm of musicals, he was the man who brought Scott Joplin's ragtime operetta, *Treemonisha*, back from obscurity with a production that debuted at the Houston Grand Opera and then transferred to Broadway.

The company in Florida once again included Sokol and Parry, along with another actor who had been appearing in the workshops, Ron Orbach, who was just beginning his career. New to the company were Martin Vidnovic, who won a Drama Desk Award for his work in the musical *Baby* and received a Tony nomination for his work in the 1981 revival of *Brigadoon*; and Cady Huffman, who, like Orbach, was at the start of her career. Huffman would eventually win a Tony for *The Producers*.

In Florida, the show was for the first time open to the critics, who were less than charmed. The March 2 *Variety* review described it as having "tunes and lyrics [that] strive for the slickness of cocktail-party satire. The gloss is an inconsistent veneer used to hide the show's vaudeville and locker room underpinnings." Furthermore, the critic pointed toward a sexist tone that ran through the show, noting that only after rewrites would it be possible to "minimize Hotchner's failure to beat a sex discrimination rap."

The reviews did nothing to stop audiences from showing up at the Coconut Grove. Business was good, and after the theater's subscribers had seen the show, single tickets sold briskly. Nonetheless, there were reports saying that the notices were "prompting talk of major revisions following the show's close [in Florida]."[13]

Hotchner and Coleman did start the process of revisions, going so far as to give the show a new name, *Welcome to the Club*. "We changed the title because we thought the first was a bit too abrasive," Hotchner said, adding, "Of course, people collapsed laughing when they knew what the show was about. . . . But if you didn't know, it sounded tough."[14]

With the announcement of the show's new name came the schedule for its Broadway debut. The writers believed that it would be playing in New York by the fall of 1988, featuring many of the performers who had been working on the show from the beginning. Then came delays.

"The Coconut Grove people were going to co-produce, but they were so busy with their season," Coleman said,[15] so he and Hotchner began the process of producing it themselves, hosting backers' auditions.

One person who attended one of these events, held at Coleman's townhouse, was Bill Rosenfield, who was just beginning his career at RCA Victor, where he would eventually rise to the level of senior vice president. "Cy put on an extraordinary presentation. You would have thought that

Welcome to the Club was the wittiest, most urbane, smartest, most melodic, fantastic, funniest musical ever written, because he (and I saw how he did this over the years with other shows) compressed it down to twenty-eight minutes, and it was all boom-boom-boom-boom. And if you're two and a half feet from watching Cy Coleman's hands on a piano, you think, 'This is Michelangelo.'"[16]

Getting *Welcome to the Club* to Broadway was not, however, a matter of just giving Coleman a chance to display his virtuosity at the keyboard; it was also a matter of demonstrating the finesse with which he was adapting to the changing route that a show took to Broadway. Ever since *A Chorus Line* was developed through a series of workshops at the New York Shakespeare Festival, stagings where the writers could revise on the spot or overnight were taking the place of out-of-town tryouts, where so much revision work was traditionally done. They weren't just happening in New York but around the country at other nonprofit theaters, which were looking to find the one musical that would provide financial security during lean times and underwrite their production of less-mainstream work.

It was a new dynamic, and one that Edwin Wilson examined in the *Wall Street Journal.* In his story he pointed specifically to two of Coleman's shows, *Club* and *13 Days to Broadway.* "Mr. Coleman has a number of projects in the works, but two in particular illustrate the circuitous and improvisational thing that a Broadway 'tryout' can now become." Wilson even went so far as to describe Coleman's and other writers' shows as projects that were "circling in the hinterlands like so many airliners stacked up above a permanently fogged in Kennedy Airport."[17]

Coleman might not have used the airport analogy to describe the dexterity with which he was navigating the changing landscape of producing a musical, but he certainly would have agreed with Wilson's use of the word "improvisational." He was doing everything and anything to get the production on, recognizing that things had changed dramatically in the thirty or so years since *Wildcat* premiered: "People used to be able to buy you on reputation, but they don't anymore. So you have to play the piano in your living room."[18] Elsewhere he remarked about *Welcome to the Club,*

"Ironically . . . it's easier to get backing for a $5 million musical than one that costs $1.5 million."[19]

A trio of men did ultimately join Coleman and Hotchner as producers of *Welcome to the Club*, which was budgeted at $1.5 million, about one-fifth of what new musicals on Broadway were costing at the time. To Coleman, working on a tight budget was a good thing. "You're watching every expenditure. . . . You know that old phrase about counting coffee cups? Well, we're counting coffee cups. But because of that, everybody works harder."[20]

Its funding secured, the show booked a theater (the intimate Music Box, built by Irving Berlin to house his own revues) and set an official opening date. It also got a new director, Peter Mark Schifter, who had made his Broadway debut with Albert Innaurato's offbeat comedy *Gemini* in 1977; it went on to have a run of over four years, after which Schifter established a career directing television and opera; with *Welcome to the Club*, he was returning to the Broadway fold.

The show also had a new headliner: Avery Schreiber, the popular comedian, who, after a start in Broadway shows like *How to Be a Jewish Mother*, became a fixture on television in everything from *Love, American Style* to *The Love Boat*. He took over the role previously played by Parry. Of the performers who were in the previous incarnations of the musical, only two remained: Sokol and Sharon Scruggs, who played the part of the country singer in the White Barn production. Other new members of the company were Jodi Benson, whose voice would achieve international fame with the release of the animated feature *The Little Mermaid* at the end of the year; Terri White, who had been in Coleman's *Barnum*; and Scott Waara, who would go on to win a Tony a few years later for his work in a revival of Frank Loesser's *The Most Happy Fella*.

Both rehearsals and previews for the show were, as White called them, "hard." She cited a number of factors that made the process problematic: "I think there were difficulties between A. E. Hotchner and Cy, and they were competing about who would make the story work."[21] Coleman himself, touting the show just before its opening, was even willing to say that the process had been rough: "I have never done a show that wasn't made in the preview period. Never. This is when we work. This is when it happens. This is where a show is pulled together. This period is for people who do not panic under fire."[22]

Throughout the workshop process Coleman, as both composer and co-lyricist, had been adding and deleting numbers from a score that had become as eclectic as the one he had written for *I Love My Wife*. Just as that show referenced everything from barbershop quartets to the gentle sounds of 1970s pop, the music in *Welcome to the Club* traversed a wide range of musical genres. There was one of Coleman's sly Latin numbers, "Rio," for the druggist's fantasy about escaping to Rio to be rid of his wife and his debts. For the insurance salesman and his wife Coleman penned "Piece of Cake," a red-hot-mama number worthy of Sophie Tucker.

Coleman continued to refine his score during the three weeks of Broadway previews. Four songs were cut, including the original title number, "Let 'Em Rot." Another four new songs were inserted, and Coleman finally found a spot for "Love Behind Bars," a bluegrass number that he had written for the show but never used.

Making the show work meant changes not only to the material but also to the cast itself. During previews actress Scruggs was let go. As Sally Mayes, who was hired as a swing, remembered, "As I was going into rehearsals, it became apparent to me and I think everybody else that I was really right for the part that I was swinging." One day Schifter called for an understudy rehearsal, and Mayes, who was doing her first Broadway show, didn't realize it was unusual. She remembered being warned by one of her fellow swings, "You better know your shit."[23] Indeed, the rehearsal was an audition of sorts to see if Mayes could assume Scruggs's role. Mayes proved herself and took over.

In addition to extensive rewrites and this one piece of recasting, *Welcome to the Club* faced a leadership crisis, epitomized by what happened when Mayes first went on. After the performance, Mayes remembered, "Director Peter Mark Schifter, God bless his soul, came into my dressing room and gave me about twenty pages of notes. The next day I went onstage, and I didn't get one laugh and nothing worked." Mayes remembered what happened afterward when Coleman visited: "Cy said, 'Did you get a lot of notes?' And I said, 'Yeah.' And he said, 'Throw them in the trash. Do what you did before.' So I did, and the laughs came back."[24]

Throughout it all, stage manager Craig Jacobs recalled, the crises were showing "Cy at his best, as always. If you wanted a new song, it was there in five minutes."[25] Coleman's willingness to do whatever it took even extended to performing. According to music contractor John Miller, "For the first week of previews, we didn't have an overture. When the house lights would go down, Cy would run into the pit, and he would just improvise for about three to five minutes on some unbelievable, great version of all of the tunes. And each time it would be completely different, and each time it would be better than the time before."[26]

Welcome to the Club, finally with an overture, opened at the Music Box Theatre as originally scheduled on April 13, and the reviews were generally as dire as they were when the piece was known as *Let 'Em Rot* in Florida. In his *New York Times* review, Frank Rich wrote, "[The show] is embarrassingly out of touch with the present-day realities of men, women, sex, marriage, and divorce. . . . Mr. Hotchner's book seems to have wafted down from a mysogynist [*sic*] time warp where women are all castrating kvetches and the ideal marriage resembles the one embalmed on top of a wedding cake."

Ironically, in a season that also included Peter Allen's *Legs Diamond*, a musical about the gangster that lasted only sixty-four performances; *Senator Joe*, a musical inspired by the life of Senator Joseph McCarthy, which closed in previews; and *Chu-Chem*, billed as the first Chinese-Jewish musical, which eked out sixty performances, *Welcome to the Club* was heralded by Clive Barnes in the *New York Post* as "the best completely new musical of the season." But he quickly added, "There have been bad seasons for the Broadway musical in the past. . . . But this is ridiculous."

Nonetheless, critics were able to get past the show's book to appreciate Coleman's music, even if the compliments came backhandedly. In *Newsday*, Linda Winer wrote, "It has music by the ever-engaging tunesmith Cy Coleman. Under the cover of sweet, old-fashioned melodies, however, lurks a show that, for starters, is really stupid about women." Similarly, Rich opined, "This Coleman project has a better score than the material merits."

A notice announcing that the show would close on April 15 was posted but then withdrawn. After one more week, however, *Welcome to the Club* shuttered on April 22, having played twelve regular performances. On some levels, Coleman saw its short run coming. He knew that in the event of negative reviews, they didn't have the money for advertising, and that then "you hope that word of mouth will do it."[27]

By the time the Tony Awards were announced, the lackluster season prompted the elimination of both the best book and the best score categories, meaning that neither Coleman nor Hotchner could even receive a nod for their work. The show was remembered in a pair of categories: Scott Wentworth was recognized as a featured actor, and Schifter received a nod for his direction. In a season that included two hit revues, *Jerome Robbins' Broadway* and *Black and Blue*, neither man won.

After this, *Welcome to the Club* lapsed into the kind of obscurity that's afforded to Broadway musicals that last less than a month. In hindsight, cast members contemplated what might have caused its failure. Actress White hypothesized that there was a conflict between the subject and the way in which it was presented: "I think the problem with the show was alimony jail. It's a subject that no longer exists, but they were trying to do it in the present day. But no one even knows about alimony jail anymore, so it was battling against itself from the very beginning."[28] Mayes recalled, "I was kind of green, so I didn't really realize quite how misogynistic it was," and then added, "If it had been done in the '60s, it would have been a different thing. . . . It would have been better received."[29]

As for Coleman, the idea of the show and his score stuck with him for the next decade or so, and it was a work to which he would return. Before that, not surprisingly, there were other tuners that needed his attention, and these had happier endings than the one that met *Welcome to the Club*.

27

City of Angels

Coleman didn't have much time to worry about the quick demise of *Welcome to the Club*, because he had another show that was already hurtling toward its opening. "It's all signals go for the musical-comedy thriller" was the way Enid Nemy characterized the pending arrival of *City of Angels* on July 29, 1989, in the *New York Times*. In fact, things were so certain for this musical that Nemy was able to report the date of its first preview (November 14) and the theater it would play, the Virginia (later rechristened the August Wilson Theatre).

When the announcement was made, Coleman had been working on the musical for over two years with two men: book writer Larry Gelbart and lyricist David Zippel. For Coleman, of course, the idea of a detective musical had its genesis a bit further back, when he, Michael Stewart, and Mickey Spillane had discussed the possibility of doing a musical with sleuth Mike Hammer at its center.

The composer had put the project aside for a while but then revisited it, eventually reaching out to Gelbart, who recalled in his memoir *Laughing Matters* that he received a call from Coleman in 1987 about the project. It must have come earlier, however, because in the January 29, 1986 issue of *Variety*, a report on Gelbart's many upcoming projects included a mention of the musical he was working on with Coleman: "Gelbart has also completed the book, Cy Coleman the music, for the Broadway legiter 'Death Is for Suckers.'" Regardless of when the call came and how far in the writing process either man was at the time of the *Variety* story, Gelbart believed that Coleman's concept for "a musical based on the private eye movies of the forties . . . was the perfect idea."[1]

By the time Coleman turned to Gelbart, the playwright and screenwriter's deft comedy skills were recognized on both coasts. In New York he and his cowriter Burt Shevelove had picked up a Tony Award for the book for *A Funny Thing Happened on the Way to the Forum*, and *Sly Fox*, Gelbart's adaptation of Ben Jonson's comedy *Volpone*, had enjoyed a healthy run on Broadway in the mid-1970s, starring, among others, George C. Scott.

In Los Angeles and Hollywood Gelbart's work had garnered him two Academy Award nominations (for *Tootsie* and *Oh, God!*) and a host of Emmy Award nominations—along with one win—for the television series *M*A*S*H*. And even though they had not worked together, there was a mutual admiration between the two men before Gelbart wrote his first words or Coleman his initial notes.

Gelbart had first encountered Coleman in the 1950s during the heyday of his work as a nightclub pianist. In a 2002 BBC Radio 2 documentary, *The Cy Coleman Story*, Gelbart recalled, "What struck me about Cy's playing, then as now, was a slyness in his music, a humor. The music was surprising in the way that humor is. Chord changes seemingly within chord changes. His was an arresting mind in terms of how he heard music internally and then expressed it outwardly." For Coleman, Gelbart was an ideal collaborator, because "a lot of people don't have the same feeling [as I do] for music, and Larry's exceptional in that. He was a musician, a clarinetist and a saxophonist."[2]

Zippel came to the project after Gelbart and Coleman had begun. The lyricist had campaigned to be a part of the team back when Coleman suggested they collaborate on the aborted *Julian*. Zippel told Coleman he didn't feel he was right for this show, but having read a report about the detective musical, he also said, *"That* is the perfect thing for me."[3]

The lyricist recalled that Coleman responded, "Well, we're talking to a lot of big shots for that one, but I'll think about it." After this, Zippel said, "We didn't talk for a couple of months, and then I got a call saying if I wanted to come in and write on spec that we would sit down and talk about the show. Then, Larry, he, and I would start, and we would write three songs, at the end of which we would decide whether or not we would all move forward together."[4]

Zippel agreed to these terms, and the three men met. Zippel said, "Larry had outlined the detective part of the show. At that point, he hadn't come up with the idea of telling two stories at once, so Cy wrote a complete melody, which he gave to me. The scene that we imagined it would be a part of was the scene where the missing girl was found naked in the bed of the detective. And the first thing I did was write the lyric to the melody of 'Lost and Found.'"[5]

Both Coleman and Gelbart liked Zippel's work, and so they moved forward. Zippel recalled the next lyric-writing assignment was for "a song for the detective's girlfriend to sing in a nightclub. The idea was that it was one of those truly romantic torch songs, and I had the idea that she was singing the lyrics but they were reflective of how the detective felt about her. And they liked that idea. Cy sat down at the piano and just played what became 'With Every Breath I Take.' While we were in the room, I heard the title line [in Coleman's melody] and I said, 'With every breath I take,' and he loved the idea, again very enthusiastic."[6]

Zippel penned a lyric for this song quickly but then thought, "Oh my God. That came too easily," so he wrote numerous other versions just to be safe. When it came time for Coleman to consider them, Zippel made sure the first one he had written was on top of the sheaf of lyrics he presented. The composer played through the melody using Zippel's initial version and immediately liked it. Zippel remembered, "Cy just said, 'This is terrific! Let's call Larry and play it for him!' And from then on, I was in. There was never a look back."[7]

As the collaboration progressed, Zippel recalled, "Cy and I started to get a little ahead of Larry, and we had a meeting where Larry said, 'I love where you guys are going. I love where the score is going. It's innovative. It's different. But I feel like I'm just writing a spoof of a detective novel, and I think I can come up with something that would make it more interesting, and it will give me a chance to break some new ground in the way that you guys are. So give me a couple of more months.'"[8] Gelbart characterized the block he was feeling at the time slightly differently. "However affectionate of a parody of a private-eye show it was, it wasn't even holding my interest."[9]

Coleman and Zippel agreed, and Gelbart returned to his home in California. A few months later, he called and said, "I'm ready. Come out to California."[10] The songwriting team flew out, and Gelbart told them about his idea of telling two stories concurrently. One would be the private-detective tale that they had been working on. The other would center on the process that a novelist was going through to get this private-eye yarn turned into a movie in 1940s Hollywood; as Gelbart put it, the musical would be "the private life of a private-eye writer."[11] Coleman believed that it was once Gelbart hit on this idea that "Larry had discovered a way for him to have as much fun as I was having doing the music."[12]

Energized by the turn the project had taken, the trio spent the next ten days working the plot and the story out. What emerged was the story of a writer named Stine who had written a novel about a detective named Stone. Stine's book was being turned into a film, and in the process it was being altered. Despite Stine's gut reactions against what was happening to his book, he was constantly agreeing to the changes, even when they damaged the integrity of the tale.

Beyond the dual storytelling, the team came up with a scheme for double-casting the show, so that the people in Stine's life were also the characters in the book and its film version. Stone's secretary, Oolie, for instance, would be played by the same actress who was playing the secretary to the Samuel Goldwyn–like movie producer with whom Stine was working. Similarly, the actress playing Stine's wife would also portray Stone's girlfriend.

With their new outline a bicoastal collaboration began. Gelbart faxed new scenes to New York and Coleman and Zippel sent tapes to Gelbart. Sometimes, in a burst of enthusiasm, they couldn't wait for a tape to cross the country, so they would simply play what they'd just written to Gelbart over the phone.

Once they had completed the new two-tiered version of *Death Is for Suckers*, the men began to contemplate who would produce and who would direct. For the former category, Coleman approached an old friend, Nick Vanoff, a television producer with a long line of credits in variety shows like *The Sonny & Cher Show*. Vanoff had also been behind the television specials for the Kennedy Center Honors, and he came to the table with some Broadway experience, including a couple of comedian Jackie Mason's shows in the mid-1980s. Zippel recalled that "Cy pitched the idea to Nick, and he liked it immediately."[13]

Another man who came on board early to produce was Roger Berlind, who had Broadway credits dating back to the mid-1970s, when he was an associate producer on Richard Rodgers's *Rex*. Since then the shows that he had brought to the Great White Way ranged from dramas like Peter Shaffer's *Amadeus* and Edward Albee's *The Lady from Dubuque* to musicals like *Sophisticated Ladies* and *Nine*.

Before the show reached opening night, it would gain another three producing partners, including two of the three theater owners on Broadway: the Shubert Organization and Jujamcyn Theaters. It marked the first time that the companies had worked together.

In addition, and in a sign of how corporate influence was infiltrating the world of Broadway, the name of the Japanese company Suntory International was also above the title. The show was one of four that the liquor company would invest in during the season as it sought to carve a niche for itself both in the United States and Japan, backing Broadway shows as well as supporting nonprofits ranging from Carnegie Hall to the Audubon Society.

As for the director, the men knew that they would need someone who could handle not just the musical aspects of the show but also its intricate plot line. The name they eventually came up with was that of Michael Blakemore. They thought of him primarily because of his work on Michael Frayn's *Noises Off*, a play that has come to be regarded as the quintessential backstage farce, in which audiences experience—to hilarious effect—how the personal travails and petty bickering between the actors and the technicians of a small theater company affect what takes place when they are working onstage.

What the creators did not remember was that in addition to *Noises Off*, Blakemore, early in his career, had directed Peter Nichols's *The National*

Health. Like the musical they had written, Nichols's play followed two story lines as it skewered the British health-care system, placing events unfolding in a real hospital alongside those in a soap opera that glamorized the medical system.

They sent a copy of the script off to Blakemore, who recalled, "So the book arrived, and it was called *Death Is for Suckers*, and I thought this was such an appalling title." Beyond his dislike of the title, Blakemore admitted, "I was also skeptical about whether a private-eye musical could work at all."[14] Nevertheless, based on his respect for and knowledge of both Gelbart's and Coleman's work, Blakemore started to read and didn't stop until he had finished the entire thing.

Feeling the show was "infinitely wittier and more intelligent than the books of most musicals," he then let his agent know that he would be interested in pursuing the idea of directing the show. The four men met in New York, and after this preliminary meeting Coleman and Zippel, eager to secure Blakemore's services, flew to London so that they could play the score for him. Blakemore remembered how "they hired a hall in West Hampstead with a piano, and I went up there and sat on a bench or a chair while the two authors (composer and lyricist) sang me the score." The director also joked that it was at this moment "I felt at last I'm in show business."[15] It was enough to bring Blakemore on board to the noir musical.

Even though he had officially committed only after Coleman and Zippel's performance, Blakemore recalled that he had already begun to visualize what he could do with the musical: "Often with scripts you like an awful lot, you really start directing them the minute you start reading them."[16]

One notable instance involved a scene in which audiences would see the author at work on his screenplay side by side with the scene he was writing. When the author makes revisions, Gelbart indicated, the actors in the detective story should start over. Blakemore drew inspiration from his experience doing sound editing on a film to expand upon that idea: "They used to do a thing called 'rock and roll,' where they'd run the film forward and then, in order to do it again, they have to run the film backward." When this would happen, Blakemore explained, "the actors move backwards and they speak the dialogue, so it comes off like some kind of weird Scandinavian. And so I thought we could do that there, and that's indeed what we did, and it got the first really deep laugh in the show."[17]

Beyond such specifics, Blakemore had a vision for the overall look of the show: "When I read the book for the first time, I immediately thought that I could do the film in black-and-white and I could do the Hollywood part of the story in color."[18] Ironically, this was something that had occurred to the writers as well, but as Zippel recalled, "Another interesting thing was, we had the idea of doing the black-and-white and color. But we didn't pitch it to him because we wanted to see what he would come up with."[19] It was a harbinger of the unity of vision that would shape the entire show, down to its title.

Blakemore's objection to the title *Death Is for Suckers* was profound. "What I thought was so awful about *Death Is for Suckers* is that in the Raymond Chandler books that Larry had pastiched quite brilliantly, Chandler would never make a joke about death. Death was the ultimate reality. Death was the big sleep. It wasn't something anybody evaded. So *Death Is for Suckers* was kind of a silly title, really, and that's why I didn't like it."[20] For a few months the show had an interim title, *Double Exposure*, before a casual conversation in a car between Coleman and Blakemore yielded *City of Angels*.

"We were driving back to New York from Southampton," recalled the director, "and *City of Angels* came up, and I thought that was far and away the best title, because it was an ironic title because the babes in it were so poisonous. It was very noir. It was an ironic title, but it wasn't a send-up title."[21]

Once this issue had been settled, the men turned to the show's overall look. Who could create two worlds onstage that could alternate between black-and-white and Technicolor? For this, they turned to designer Robin Wagner, who, as he had for *On the Twentieth Century*, created an elaborate and visually stunning period world for the show. Wagner's set simultaneously allowed Blakemore to realize the filmic aspects of the musical, providing the means for cross-fades between scenes and even the stage equivalent of tracking shots, where audiences sense they are seeing the action from a character's perspective.

As for the casting, Blakemore took an unconventional approach, particularly for a musical, but it signaled that he was treating the show as something fairly serious. Actress Dee Hoty, who played Chairy in the national tour of *Barnum* and eventually won the dual roles of the film producer's wife and the femme fatale of the noir fiction in *City of Angels*, recalled, "The first call was a meeting, an interview with Michael Blakemore. He probably just wanted to get a vibe from people, knowing Michael as I once did. So, it was an interview and very British."[22]

More traditional auditions (or callbacks, as some people called them) were held after such meetings at the Virginia Theatre, and during these the close collaboration between Coleman and Blakemore could be felt. Hoty recalled how, while Blakemore was asking for adjustment in her musical material from her, Coleman called out from the house, "She's great. I don't need to see any more. She can belt."[23]

Randy Graff, who snagged the roles of Oolie and Donna, remembered the active role Coleman took with her during the process. "After I had sung my two songs, he said to me, 'Do you know a song called "Nobody Does It like Me"? And I said, 'Why, yes. It was my big audition song when I had just graduated college.' To which he replied, 'Now you're making me feel old.'" Graff also admitted that she wasn't entirely sure that she would remember Dorothy Fields's lyric for the *Seesaw* tune. So Coleman helped out from the darkened theater. She started singing and "he was shouting the words at me from the house."[24]

The casting was completed over the course of the summer of 1989, and the company grew to include James Naughton, who was in the original cast of *I Love My Wife*, as the detective, Stone. Gregg Edelman, who had been steadily making a name for himself on Broadway since the early 1980s in shows ranging from *Anything Goes* to *Les Misérables*, got his first chance to originate a role on Broadway when he was cast as writer Stine. For the non sequitur–spewing producer who was in the process of turning Stine's book into a movie, the creative team turned to René Auberjonois, who had earned a Tony Award in 1970 for his performance in *Coco*, the musical about fashion designer Chanel, and also had a string of Hollywood credits that encompassed television and film work.

The show required two additional leading ladies. Kay McClelland, who had recently made her Broadway debut in *Into the Woods*, was tapped for the roles of Bobbi, Stone's chanteuse girlfriend, and Gabby, Stine's pragmatic wife; and Rachel York, like Edelman, got the chance to be an original cast member of a Broadway show when she was cast as the "bad" rich girl whom Stone was hired to find and the Hollywood starlet who was hired to play her.

Beyond these principals, a key component of the show was a vocal group dubbed "the Angel City 4." This quartet, plus a lead singer known as Jimmy Powers (played by Scott Waara, a *Welcome to the Club* veteran), was on hand as a kind of 1940s pop-music Greek chorus, delivering both songs that were being heard by the characters as if in real life and material that commented on the action. The arrangements for these songs were tight, intricate harmonies devised by vocal arranger Yaron Gershovsky (principally known for his work with the vocal group Manhattan Transfer) in consultation with Coleman. They were the kinds of numbers that Coleman believed could only be delivered by studio singers.

Unfortunately, and in a foreshadowing of the sort of battles the entire creative team would face over a production that had been quite frugally budgeted, there was a push to hire Broadway singers so that the members of the Angel City 4 could also be cast in other roles. Coleman was adamant on this issue, however, and as the show's musical director and conductor Gordon Lowry Harrell recalled, "Cy really dug his heels in on this one. He kept saying, 'They have got to be studio singers. They can't be Broadway people pretending to be studio singers. They'll never pull it off.'"[25]

Coleman described why such singers were needed just before the show opened: "[They] are not trained in theater or dance, but they know how to sing from a dissonance to a consonance on sight," he said, adding, "This intricate approach, with intricate harmonies and lyrics singing scat, along with a hot 22-piece orchestra, has never before been done quite like this on Broadway. In fact, I hadn't done it before myself."[26]

Gershovsky recalled how surprised the show's orchestrator, Billy Byers, a man who had been around the sort of music Coleman had written since his days as a trombonist with Benny Goodman, was by what the quartet was being required to do. "I remember Billy Byers asking, 'Did you really harmonize that?' and I said, 'Yes.' And he was like, 'Amazing.'"[27]

For Blakemore, Coleman's ferocity on this issue of how the Angel City 4 was to be cast proved that "he was a battler. You crossed him at your peril, but once he was assured of your good faith, once he knew you were both working on the same show, he couldn't have been more supportive or nicer. I was full of admiration for him, and I got very, very fond of him."[28]

Because of the way Gelbart, Coleman, and Zippel had constructed the show, there was no need for extensive revisions to the material during the rehearsal process. But that is not to say that any of the writers were idle. Gelbart honed his book constantly, eliminating extraneous material; but, as he pointed out just before the show's opening, "This is not the kind of show where you can put the second act song in the first act or drop that scene and write a new one. We've had to make all of the adjustments on the basis of what the show is. We've done a lot of work anyway, but it's been refining and clarifying."[29]

Among the notable refinements that emerged during rehearsals was the elimination of the interior monologues sung by many of the characters. A few remained, principally during Stone's first scene with Alaura, the wealthy woman who hired him, but what had been a series that ran through the musical's opening scenes was decidedly curtailed.

In other instances the score was gently augmented during rehearsals. To showcase Edelman's range, Coleman and Zippel added a cadenza at the end of "Double Talk," a tautly syncopated riff that establishes Stone's and Stine's characters. Another adjustment that came during rehearsals was in the early duet for Stine's secretary and Stone's wife. As Graff remembered it, "The riff that happened at the end of 'What You Don't Know About Women' was written during rehearsals. I remember Cy calling us over and teaching us that."[30]

Graff also remembered a more significant addition to one of her songs, "You Can Always Count on Me," which came during technical rehearsals: "We were on a break, and Cy said, 'Randy, come on down to the piano' (in tech the piano is always down in the house). I sat down next to him, and David was there. And David had written the lyrics out, like on a scrap piece of paper, and he said, 'Listen to this,' and he played me the verse and he said, 'That's what was missing to the song, a verse!'"[31]

Graff recalled how Coleman, who was himself also a performer, helped her perfect her delivery: "Working with him was heaven. He taught me how to sing that song, and every time I sing it, I still remember the phrasing that he taught me. It's just in my bones. And he'd just say, 'Think of Sophie Tucker.' And he would say things like 'Men don't give a waaaar-antee.' Just little phrasing things that have stayed with me." Graff, who would go on to record an entire album of Coleman's songs, said what was remarkable about his work on *City of Angels* was that "he wrote on you. . . . He wouldn't write a song and say, 'Come to me,' because he knew if you were comfortable, it was only going to make his music sound better."[32]

Music director Harrell commented that Coleman's work with the actors in this capacity was just one of the many talents he brought to any show. "Cy was a self-contained package. He could be a music director. He could be an arranger. He could be a composer. He could be a pianist." Of Coleman's work with the performers, Harrell said, "Cy was also a wonderful vocal coach. And he had no problems at all putting on a different hat. If a singer he was working with needed vocal coaching, he'd put on his vocal coach's hat. He knew how to do that impeccably, and not as the composer enforcing his will on him or her, but as an accompanist and a coach, drawing the song out of them."[33]

Even as Coleman was working with the performers and with Zippel on changes, the composer was also writing copious amounts of underscoring for the movielike production. "He was so enormously fecund as a composer. He had music coming out of every pore in his body. And you wanted something and he gave it to you," Blakemore remarked.[34]

Harrell remembered turning to Cy frequently with requests for such material. "I'd go to him and say, 'They need some music there Cy, to cover forty-five seconds for the transition of the black-and-white set to the color set.' And then he'd go and do that. Sometimes he'd pull in an actor, like Jimmy Naughton, and have them read the scene for him so he could get the feel of it, where are the actors taking this, because he wanted the music to go along with that and, in some cases, lead and take them there."[35]

With each piece of orchestral transition music, Coleman was drawing on his own experiences with and expertise in scoring films. Lowry described the work admiringly, saying that in each instance Coleman was creating non-songs that were meant to "make a dramatic moment. It was definitely not scene-change music. It was a dramatically structured non-vocal that got everybody to some place."[36]

As with Coleman's last two Broadway shows, *Barnum* and *Welcome to the Club*, and as was becoming increasingly the norm for new musicals on Broadway, *City of Angels* did not have an out-of-town tryout but rather opened "cold" in New York—although that term is somewhat loose, given the length of the show's overall rehearsal period, which ultimately stretched to an extravagant nine weeks.

The complexity of having two stories unfold side by side was one reason the show rehearsed for so long. The production simply needed a longer-than-average technical-rehearsal period. It was during this time that the producers' desire to cut corners was felt most keenly: "[They] hadn't taken the advice of the brilliant designer Robin Wagner and got the builder that Robin wanted. They had gone to someone else, with the result that when we got into the theater, the set was only half finished," said Blakemore.[37]

When pieces did arrive, the director remembered, "Something was always wrong, so I would get to the theater immediately before lunch and be told we couldn't possibly start until eight o'clock in the evening. The technical dress rehearsal went on forever. We scheduled about ten days and I think it went on for about a month." The construction decision was indicative of what Blakemore felt about the producers' overall attitude toward the show: "We got a lot of obfuscation and skepticism in the producing side of it, except perhaps from Roger Berlind, who I think always saw the merit of it." As a result, "Larry, Cy, and David and I bonded very closely, and we formed a kind of military square. And just drove it through without listening to anybody."[38]

The show eventually started its preview period on November 21, a week later than originally planned, and when there was also a delay in the show's opening (which was pushed from the desirable day of Thursday,

December 7, to the less advantageous Monday, December 11), some of the producers' lack of faith may have seemed justified. Beyond the delays, their fears may have also been exacerbated by the negative buzz that had begun to circulate about the show. Bill Rosenfield, who was at RCA and involved in the discussions about the company doing the show's cast album, recalled, "The first early word on *City of Angels* was that it wasn't working, and they hadn't found the tone and such."[39]

When opening night did finally arrive, scenic designer Wagner remembered: "At intermission, the producers were all out in front of the theater, saying, 'Anyone want to rent a theater?' They were all so certain it was a flop. And I never forgot that. And Michael was very insulted by that, because he heard it too. By the end of the show that night, there was a standing ovation."[40]

Once the reviews began appearing, it became clear that many critics had been as taken with the show as the opening-night crowd. In the *New York Times*, Frank Rich lavished praise on the show: "This is an evening in which even a throwaway wisecrack spreads laughter like wildfire through the house." As for Coleman's score, Rich said it was "a delirious celebration of jazz and pop styles sumptuously orchestrated by Billy Byers," adding, "The effect is like listening to 'Your Hit Parade' of 1946, except that the composer's own Broadway personality remakes the past in his own effervescent, melodic style."

Clive Barnes wrote in the *New York Post*: "Taste, resonance and imagination—these are the three prime characteristics of the new musical 'City of Angels.'" And for *USA Today* David Patrick Stearns, in a decidedly mixed review, wrote: "The show sounds like nothing Coleman or anybody else has written for Broadway."

Dissatisfaction among the reviewers ran deeper than Stearns's mixed notice. Howard Kissel, in the *Daily News*, admitted, "I want to be supportive about 'City of Angels.' Not because I enjoyed it. But because I know the American musical is in trouble." A second opinion in this paper came a few weeks later, and on December 22 Doug Watt's review ran under the headline "'Angels' is Heavenly." In it he praised everything from Gelbart's "dazzling book" to Coleman's "large and exceedingly versatile score." Watt also proclaimed that Zippel was "Coleman's smartest lyricist since his work with Dorothy Fields and Carolyn Leigh."

In many respects, some of the reviews confirmed the fears that Coleman had about the show before its opening. He knew that he was "going to do a jazz score with a completely different sound from even the Broadway jazz I've written. . . . I wanted to score this like a film and avoid conventional 32-bar songs." The composer simultaneously worried that "doing something different is often not recognized and my constant nightmare is that everyone will pick on it. . . . I don't wish them to begrudge us what we've done."[41]

Regardless of any of the negative reviews, the praise from the *New York Times* was all that was necessary to ensure the show's health at the box office. Ironically, it would also have meant that the show's cast recording would have been released by RCA.

While the show had prepared for its opening, the label sent a proposal to the producers and creative team. In it, Rosenfield recalled, "Everything was negotiable within the realm of reasonableness, except they put in one line saying, 'If the reviews aren't good (Frank Rich, *New York Times*), then we have the right not to record it.'"[42]

Having a clause that gave the record company the ability to reconsider after opening was not unusual, but citing one specific review as grounds for it was extremely rare. Rosenfield continued, "Word came back through David to me that Cy said, 'No. That's an insult to say that it all hinges on one man. You can't do that.' But also word came back from Cy saying, "Take that out and we've got a deal.'"[43]

The language was not taken out, and then came opening night and the *Times* review. The following day Rosenfield heard that RCA was trying to salvage the project, and late in the day he spoke to Zippel. "I said, 'So they think they're going to make this album.' And David said, 'It's going to Columbia.'"[44]

The cast album, like the show itself, broke with tradition: it was produced over the course of several weeks rather than in just one or two days. Harrell recalled, "I talked Cy into doing four days with the orchestra in session with no singers, and they played through I would say maybe seventeen of the show's twenty-two charts. There were a few that Cy said, 'You gotta really do this live. So don't track it.'" According to Harrell, what this meant was "the engineers had time to digest what the orchestra was supposed to be and get it all set. . . . It was really clean, and you can hear Billy Byers's every little nuance, which usually when you're trying to do a whole album of a show in one weekend, everything gets mishmoshed together."[45]

The care lavished on the album went well beyond the time allotted for its recording and mixing. Coleman, whom Zippel likened at one point to a "musical dramatist,"[46] created a new musical sequence for the beginning of the recording. "He set that album up so that no matter who you were, if you heard that opening part, then you know where you're headed," said Harrell, adding, "That's very sharp."[47]

As with his past cast recordings, the one for *City of Angels* allowed journalists to wax eloquent about Coleman and Zippel's achievements after having had the chance to digest the score after repeated listens (a luxury not afforded to a theater critic, who gets only one chance to experience a score before casting his or her opinion). In the May 6 edition of the *New York Times* Stephen Holden wrote, "Coleman's score, with lyrics by Mr. Zippel, is a spirited pastiche of 40's and 50's pop-jazz and film noir movie music. It casts knowing winks at everything from the 50's jazz trio Lambert, Hendricks and Ross to the score for the 1956 film 'The Man With the Golden Arm' and pumps into it all a healthy dollop of traditional Broadway brassiness."

And in a review in the *Washington Post* on June 15, Joe Brown said, "Thanks to some creative editing and production, Cy Coleman's period-evocative tunes and David Zippel's playful lyrics can stand alone when separated from Larry Gelbart's sly script and Robin Wagner's neato color-vs.-black-and-white setting."

The release of the album timed out so that it was available as the Tony voters considered the plethora of nominations that the musical had received—eleven in all, including one for best musical. The chief competition *City of Angels* faced was *Grand Hotel*, which had garnered one more nomination, in the choreography category—unsurprising since *Angels* had no traditional dance numbers. In fact, Coleman had eschewed them. Fred Barton recalled the composer mentioning this while they were prepping the Los Angeles production of the musical: "I told Walter Painter [who was responsible for musical staging of the show] from the get-go 'I don't want to see one pointed toe!'" Barton added, "That was typically demonstrative of how Cy knew what he wanted and told who it was what he wanted and done."[48]

When the Tonys were presented, *City of Angels* and *Grand Hotel* split the awards almost evenly, but it was *City of Angels* that triumphed in the major categories. It won for score and book and took home the prize for best musical. In addition, Naughton was named best actor in a musical, and Graff received the prize for featured actress in a musical.

After this, *City of Angels* settled in for a comfortable run that extended into early 1992. The show would go on to have a national tour featuring Barry Williams (best known as oldest son Greg on television's *The Brady Bunch*) as the detective, and in 1992 Blakemore would reprise his work as director on a production in London's West End. Before that would happen, though, Coleman was off to his next musical. In fact, it was a show that for a while looked as if it might give the composer two openings during the 1990–91 season.

28

The Will Rogers Follies

---

ity of Angels hadn't even finished a full week of previews when Mervyn Rothstein announced in the *New York Times* that a backers' audition for *Ziegfeld Presents Will Rogers* would be held at the renowned 21 Club before the end of the month. This report about the musical, which would have music by Coleman, lyrics by Betty Comden and Adolph Green, and a book by Peter Stone, also included the news that "the planned opening for the show, which has been in the works for three years, is early May."[1] Indeed, the show had been in development for a while, and unlike many of Coleman's other projects, where he had been part of the creative team from the outset, this one had started without him.

The piece was the brainchild of producer Pierre Cossette, who began his professional life as a booking agent in Las Vegas and transitioned to producing, becoming the man who brought the Grammy Awards ceremony to television in 1971. In the mid-1980s he was exploring the possibility of making a foray into the theatrical world. As he recalled in his memoir, "I had become convinced that the moment was right to break the British hold on the Broadway Musical Theater. My passion was to produce an Americana-style show that would counter all the British fare."[2]

Cossette had seen the one-man play *Will Rogers' USA*—which, starring James Whitmore, had had a one-week run on Broadway in 1974—and felt then that the story of the great American humorist deserved a grander treatment onstage. As he contemplated a show that might rival such imported fare as *Cats* and *Les Misérables*, Cossette remembered the solo show and decided that a musical biography of Rogers's life and exceptional career would be ideal for his purposes.

Born in 1879, in what was then known as Indian Territory and later became the state of Oklahoma, Rogers became one America's first media celebrities in the initial quarter of the twentieth century, with a career that encompassed vaudeville, Broadway, movies, radio, and even journalism, thanks to a nationally syndicated newspaper column. Part of Rogers's appeal was his ability to spin both ropes and a good phrase. Among some of his most famous adages were "I never met a man I didn't like" and "Be thankful we're not getting the government we're paying for." Rogers's life ended early and tragically: he was killed, along with aviator Wiley Post, in a plane crash in 1935.

After negotiating the rights for Rogers's life story, Cossette turned to James Lee Barrett, who had written the screenplays for *Shenandoah*, *The Green Berets*, and *Smokey and the Bandit*, among others, to do the script. For the score, the producer tapped "top country composer and songwriter John Durrell."[3] As for a star, Cossette engaged singer-songwriter John Denver, whose career was almost as extensive as Rogers's. Denver's hits included "Take Me Home, Country Roads" and "Thank God I'm a Country Boy," and as an actor he had starred in the popular movie *Oh, God!*

Unfortunately, Denver was not satisfied with Durrell's work. Furthermore, Cossette came to realize that what Barrett had written was not at all appropriate for the stage. "So, there I was, holding the rights to produce *The Will Rogers Follies* starring John Denver, forced to start from scratch with a new writer and a new composer."[4]

At this juncture Cossette went to Peter Stone, whose career as a writer for both stage and screen dated back to the early 1960s. His work in New York had garnered a Tony Award for the musical *1776*, and in Hollywood he had won an Academy Award for *Father Goose*, which Coleman had scored. Stone met with Cossette but didn't find the idea for the show all that appealing. He told Cossette, "Frankly, I know Will Rogers's life, and there's nothing in it except his career and the things he said."[5] Nor did the general idea of an onstage biography interest him: "You either have to lie and that doesn't serve history very well, or you end up with something strange but not very compelling."[6]

On reflection, however, Stone—much as Coleman had done with *On the Twentieth Century*—found a way into the material. He thought of Rogers's time in the *Ziegfeld Follies* in the 1920s and began to imagine having Rogers's life unfold onstage as if presented by the great showman. Armed with this conceit, Stone met with director-choreographer Tommy Tune, with whom he had worked on *My One and Only*. Tune, of course, burst onto the scene with his dances for—and Tony-winning performance in—Coleman's *Seesaw*. Since then his ascendancy among the creators of new musicals on Broadway had been steady, and he had directed and choreographed *A Day in Hollywood/A Night in the Ukraine*, *The Best Little Whorehouse in Texas*, and *Nine*, picking up an additional five Tony Awards.

Tune had the same initial reaction as Stone to the idea of putting a biography of Rogers onstage: "Rogers's life is not musical and he didn't have a highly conflicted life—he became a great man and died tragically."[7] But after listening to Stone's concept, Tune saw the possibilities and was immediately interested.

Tune's involvement meant that Cossette had rebounded. In addition to a book writer, director, and star, the producer had a composer, because Denver had signed on to write the show's songs. His busy schedule, however, began to cause delays in the project's evolution, and Stone came to realize that Denver might not want to write the music. He brought the issue up. "I said, 'Look John, maybe this is something you should star in but not write the score for.' He said, 'You're right.'"[8]

Cossette had already reached that conclusion, and to forestall further delays he had started talking about the piece with Coleman, who gravitated toward the idea and subject, suggesting that he write the score with Comden and Green. Since their time together on *On the Twentieth Century*, the trio had been hoping to find another show, and in absence of that they collaborated on the occasional song—for instance, they contributed a number to *Diamonds*, an Off-Broadway revue about baseball that Harold Prince directed in 1984, and they worked on a pair of songs for *Magic Me*, a special benefit concert.

After Denver's departure as composer, the quartet of writers started in on the show in earnest, and by March 1987 things were looking promising enough that word of the show's development could be shared with the press. "It's being slowly simmered," reported Enid Nemy in the *New York Times*, "and has already entailed many, many months of work. Even under the best of circumstances, it probably won't go into rehearsal until early next year." In addition to announcing the writers and directors, Nemy reported that the show would most likely be a vehicle for Denver. As Stone put it, "We're about midway through writing and organizing the material, and there are about half-a-dozen songs written."[9]

Denver's involvement with the show, however, would come to a complete end in short order. After the writers presented him with their songs, Stone recalled, "He wanted to change a lot of the lyrics and said, 'This is an old-fashioned show.' We said, 'No this is a new-fashioned idea that's never been tried before.' What he was talking about, I think was that the music was not rock. I sort of made a hard shove, because that seemed to be what he wanted, and he separated himself from it."[10]

But the star's departure did not kill the show, and the team continued to refine what they had even as Coleman continued working on the other musicals on his docket. By February 1989 the complete first draft included an array of sixteen numbers.

As 1989 progressed Coleman saw both *Welcome to the Club* and *City of Angels* reach Broadway. During the same time, Tune—with Stone's assistance as show doctor—shepherded the musical *Grand Hotel* to Broadway (which opened just as *Angels* was starting its preview period). As the two shows settled into their runs, Cossette began the process of raising money for *Ziegfeld Presents Will Rogers*.

Stone remembered, "Cossette had originally said to us, 'I don't know how to produce a show, but I can raise the money in twenty minutes.' The first backers' audition was at 21, very expensive, a hundred people invited, and I don't think we raised a dollar and a half."[11] Undaunted, Cossette scheduled two additional presentations, each, like the first, featuring Coleman, Comden, and Green as the performers of the musical material. Cossette's efforts were greeted with similarly disappointing results financially.

Alongside this lackluster fund-raising Cossette, Tune, and the team also began to consider who might be able to take the title role in the show. It was Cossette's wife, Mary, who suggested they consider Keith Carradine. "He'd be the perfect one," she said. Carradine had some Broadway experience. He had appeared in *Hair* during its original run at the Biltmore Theatre, and in 1982 he had starred alongside the great theatrical couple Hume Cronyn and Jessica Tandy in the play *Foxfire*. Carradine's primary credits, however, were on the screen, and his work there was significant. He had starred in films like *Welcome to L.A.*, *The Duellists*, and *McCabe and Mrs. Miller*, as well as Robert Altman's *Nashville*, in which he performed his original song, "I'm Easy," a tune that won him an Academy Award. When he was approached about auditioning for the role, Carradine agreed to come to New York; he later admitted, "I was quietly wishing for [the part]."[12]

The day of the audition arrived, and Carradine found himself on a Broadway stage with the entire creative team in the house. "I stood up on the stage and did what was required of me: sang a couple of songs and did a little bit of a monologue from the show. And then Pierre Cossette, who was producing and who had invited me in for the audition, asked me to go ahead and tell some stories, or tell a story that he had heard me tell before. It actually was a story about John Wayne on the set of *The Cowboys*."[13]

After that, he remembered, "I met everyone. I mean, I said, 'Hello' to everyone before the audition and then, after the audition, they were all really cordial and sweet and basically, I mean, I was sort of told right there and then that I had the role."[14] A slightly more dramatic account of the afternoon appeared in the *New York Times* just before the show opened. "'Halfway through the audition,' Mr. Cossette said, 'Tommy stands up and says, 'That's Will Rogers, and that's the end of it.'"[15]

Carradine's casting meant that there was now a star of significance to present at backers' auditions. To appear alongside him at such events playing Rogers's wife, Betty, Coleman turned to one of his leads from *City of Angels*, Dee Hoty, who recalled: "Cy said he wanted to talk to me about a show he was writing about Will Rogers. He played me the songs.

He didn't have anything written down." She liked what she heard, and eventually Coleman provided her a tape of the melodies and a lyric sheet. Hoty said that she spent her vacation in 1990 on the beach "trying to scan the words to the music" in preparation for a backers' audition that would be held at Tavern on the Green.[16]

Having Carradine and Hoty perform at this event was shrewd, but it did, according to Stone, ruffle feathers among the writers: "Betty and Adolph were upset. . . . They wanted to do their own songs. I went to them quite honestly and said, 'Look, one of our problems is that you're Comden and Green, you're performing artists, and when you get up to sing they're seeing you as Comden and Green, not as the characters in the play.'"[17]

Stone's instincts proved to be on target. Carradine's and Hoty's work was enough to secure the funding for the show, with people like longtime Coleman supporter Martin Richards, his partner Sam Crothers, and theater owner James M. Nederlander coming on board, as well as Japan Satellite Broadcasting, which invested nearly one-third of the show's $6.25 million budget. The deal was an historic one, and when the details of it were made public, it warranted coverage on the front page of *Variety*. In return for the investment, the company "won exclusive electronic rights for Japan and Southeast Asia, including limited broadcasts of a video of the show, a possible homevideo and dibs on first-class and touring rights for the region."[18]

With these investments it was now possible for a theater to be booked and an opening-night date to be set. The show would open on May 1, 1991, and, like Coleman's *Sweet Charity* twenty-five years earlier, it would play a newly refurbished Palace Theatre.

Tune, who had used a workshop-like rehearsal process in the development of *Grand Hotel*, decided to bring *Ziegfeld* to Broadway in a similar manner. A three-week workshop was scheduled in December 1990, during which the creators could determine the sort of structural and musical revisions they would like to make based on the casting and the show's needs. After this, a more traditional rehearsal period would begin with the revised material.

Beyond Carradine and Hoty, who landed the role she played at the backers' audition, the company included Dick Latessa, who had a line of Broadway credits that stretched back to the late 1960s, among them the original production of Stephen Sondheim's *Follies*, and would win a Tony Award in 2003 for *Hairspray*. He was on board to play Will's father, Clem. In addition, Cady Huffman, who had appeared in one incarnation of Coleman's *Let 'Em Rot*, was cast as "Ziegfeld's Favorite," the Follies chorine who was not so subtly having an affair with the impresario.

The show also featured a pair of specialty acts from beyond the realm of Broadway, including a whimsically named dog act, "The Mad Cap Mutts." And though Carradine learned and performed some rope tricks, Vince Bruce, who had been touring Europe since he was a child, was hired to offer a dazzling series of feats with a rope.

And there was one other central performer, although he was unseen. Screen icon Gregory Peck was hired to provide the voice of Florenz Ziegfeld, the man who would steer the musical—and thereby the arc of Rogers's life—to suit his own objectives as showman and artist.

The conceit of having Ziegfeld shape a seemingly amorphous evening from his office high above the theater gave book writer Stone the ability to have the details of Rogers's life unfold in a nonlinear manner, which countered one of his concerns about doing any sort of biography onstage. Ziegfeld's desire to have each segment be one of his signature production numbers also meant that Tune could give free rein to his inventiveness for stage pictures and choreography.

A quintessential moment in which audiences would see the men's sensibilities fused came early in the show: Just as a nineteen-year-old Will was about to head off to South America to begin his life as a cowboy, Ziegfeld interrupted the performance, announcing it was time for the romantic story line to be set in motion. When he learned of how Will and Betty met—at a post office in Ooologah, Oklahoma—he would have none of it. Such a place was far too ordinary for one of his shows. In short order, he decided that a more romantic and impressive locale would be the surface of the moon, and, thus Hoty, after arriving nestled in the arc of a crescent moon, delivered her first big ballad, "My Big Mistake," amid a sea of midnight blue.

Stone's conceit for the show also meant that Coleman had the latitude to create a broad spectrum of songs that would fit into the various archetypes of *Follies* performers. For Latessa this meant a ditty reminiscent of the broad comedy performed by the likes of Al Jolson and Eddie Cantor. Hoty got a couple of torch songs, and there were a pair of gentle country songs for Carradine. Coleman also wrote big production numbers that sounded like they might have been composed during the first decades of the twentieth century; but they were not mere pastiche, which, as Coleman remarked once, "is for kids."[19] Tune described Coleman's contribution: "There weren't a lot of dramatic events in Will Rogers's life, so we really depended on Cy to give us the contrasts of scenes and numbers. And he did."[20]

But even though the show's concept proved freeing for the writers, it placed incredible demands on Tune. "I didn't want to do a pastiche and I didn't want to do a period piece. I wanted it to be more vibrant than that," he told John Harris for a feature that ran in the May 13–19, 1991 issue of *Theater Week*. Tune described the show's mixture of production numbers, sketches, monologues, and vaudeville acts and added: "We've never used all of these things and fused them into telling about one man's life on this earth. We're really making it up as we go along, with nothing to fall back on. The rules that I've built up in my little warehouse of ammunition—information—on building a book show somehow did not apply." In 2013 Tune looked back on assembling this show, which was meant to appear as if it were being conceptualized on the spot, and said, "We had to keep effervescing it, because there wasn't a lot to hold on to."[21]

As a result, the musical was in a state of flux until just before the critics arrived to review it at the end of April; indeed, the song list in the opening-night program did not match what theatergoers saw onstage. Among the songs not listed in the program was one of Carradine's biggest numbers, the ecologically minded "Look Around."

Carradine recalled the last-minute addition: "They needed a song for me that would address the idea of humankind's relationship with nature and the subject of ecology. Will Rogers was quite dedicated to the preservation of our environment, and, having grown up on a ranch in Oklahoma, he was always very in tune with nature, the land, and the rhythms of nature."[22]

The day after the creators decided to include a number like this, Coleman, Comden, and Green called Carradine, Tune, and Hoty into a small space that they were using as a workroom at the Palace Theatre. Hoty said that it actually was "in a closet—it's where they sell merchandise now—into which an upright piano had been shoved." She continued, "And there's Betty and Adolph and they call out 'Keith, Keith, come here.' And they played the ecology song. Betty sang it, and I started to cry. And I said to Keith, 'There's your Tony.'"[23]

Carradine remembered being stunned that it appeared so easy for Coleman to write "a song for an actor to sit down and play on the guitar. That seemed to be out of his bailiwick, and yet what he came up with was something that was so playable. It was like perfectly designed for me to sit and do. What he knew was my strong suit, something with which I was very comfortable. And the song that he gave me to play, it's still something that I incorporate into my repertoire if I'm playing a gig somewhere."[24]

What Carradine didn't know was that Coleman had raided his trunk for the song. It was a melody he had started working on with Comden and Green for the *Magic Me* benefit about ten years before. As with anything that Coleman revisited, it had new flourishes and soon had a few more. According to Carradine, "I said to him after I had learned to play it, 'Cy, this is so beautiful; I just wish there was more.' He looked at me with this kind of twinkle in his eye, and he said, 'Really? You'd like more?' And I said, 'Yeah! It just feels as though it's two-thirds of the song that it could be. I would really love to have a full-on song.' And he said, 'Okay.' And he came back later that afternoon with what he referred to: 'Here. I've written an extension.' That was the word he used. Here's the 'extension.'"[25]

Other musical additions and embellishments that Coleman provided as the show rehearsed and previewed did not meet with similar levels of success. Hoty remembered one number Coleman had written that helped propel Will and Betty through their early years of marriage and the births of their children. "One day Cy wrote this vaudeville ditty for me. And while I was singing, I was supposed to catch the babies. There were four kids, and each baby was supposed to come at me from a different place. Well, I had trouble catching the babies, which kind of surprised me each time." The number lasted only a day or two, and, Hoty insisted, "It wasn't the music."[26] Rather, it was the ungainliness of having to field the prop children that were flying onto the stage.

While Hoty admitted that she didn't mind losing the number, she regretted the decision to cut a "beautiful verse" that Coleman wrote for "My Big Mistake." "I asked him, 'Did I not do it well enough? Is there something I can do?,' and Cy said, 'It doesn't match. It tips the song. We need something happy. It's too much of the same thing.'" When Hoty asked if he'd save the melody, she says his response was, "Yeah, I'll put it in my trunk for you, Dee."[27]

Beyond the new music, Coleman was also helping Tune shape the show through refinements to what had already been written. Originally the first act closed with two solos—Hoty delivered "Once in a While," and Carradine performed "Without You," the countermelody to Hoty's number. The two pieces converged, but as Tune said, "It was too late in the first act to have the whole song sung, then the whole counterpoint sung, and then put the two together. It was just too long, and I didn't know how to solve it because I loved it. But Cy figured it out. How to have both of them, where you didn't know we had chopped them. He made it happen. He always had a save. He saved me over and over."[28]

At times, though, it was the other way around. Just as Coleman was delivering "Look Around," Tune was attempting to tighten the show's opening number, which featured Carradine arriving on a rope from the flies after the company performed the production number "Will-a-Mania." After stepping onto the stage, he would begin his opening monologue. Tune recalled telling the songwriters, "I would like for him to start singing 'Never Met a Man I Didn't Like' and then let the music go under and have Keith start talking to the audience."[29]

Tune's idea was greeted with raised eyebrows, and he knew why: "That song was the finale of the show. The whole show led to him deciding that he never met a man he didn't like, and then visiting his whole life before he went up to heaven, and they were shocked about my idea."[30]

The director-choreographer strenuously pushed his collaborators and finally likened the tune to a theme song, such as Bob Hope's "Thanks for the Memory." "Then they got it, and it was just great. . . . It made the 'us' and 'them' evaporate, and we were just in a big room together. And it was a 'Follies' and not a theater piece. I think that was probably the best thing I did in the show."[31]

And though Coleman's facility with a melody was instrumental in the show's evolution, some of his work habits, which were by now deeply ingrained, made things difficult, particularly for music director and conductor Eric Stern, whom the composer had specifically invited to work on the show, from its workshop period forward.

Stern came to *Will Rogers* with considerable experience. He was a protégé of Jule Styne's for about twelve years. In addition, he had served in the capacity of music director for shows ranging from Charles Strouse and Stephen Schwartz's *Rags* to Peter Allen's *Legs Diamond*. Stern also had deep admiration for Coleman, whom he had known casually through theatrical circles and social events where the composer could often be found entertaining at the keyboard: "Amongst the composers that I've worked with (and I've worked with a lot of them and many of them very capable, gifted musicians), Cy was, hands down, the best pianist of any of them. Always was."[32]

As for the invitation to work on *Will Rogers*, Stern said, "I was so excited to do a Cy Coleman score." He also understood that it was different from the other Coleman show that was already on Broadway. "The kind of material that *The Will Rogers Follies* is, by its very concept, is not *City of Angels*. It is very pageant-oriented." As a result, Stern came to realize that "Cy was very—the word's not 'defensive'—protective of the score of *The Will Rogers Follies*, I think because he sensed its delicacy. It doesn't hit one over the head. It doesn't dazzle. It's a difficult style to excel in, and I think that he realized that he was walking a tightrope, and as a result he was very difficult in rehearsal."[33]

As an example, Stern pointed to the way in which Coleman developed some of the vocal arrangements. Rather than arriving with different parts notated, he would work with individual performers, creating them on the fly, in much the same way he might have quickly sketched out an arrangement with his jazz trio back in the 1950s. "He would get the four cowboys together in a group for like the top of act two or even a vocal background, and he would sit there and he would say, 'You sing that' and 'You sing that,' and it was all on his feet and he was never writing anything down. I was constantly scribbling with a pencil trying to keep up. . . . He'd be finished with the 'arrangement' at the end of the day, but unless someone went home and actually organized it and sewed the sections together and made sense of what he had done, there was no arrangement."[34]

Furthermore, Stern witnessed the kind of disaster that could happen given Coleman's disinclination to write music down and his predilection for improvisation as he worked. One afternoon, Stern said, the creative team gathered in Coleman's offices and "Cy sat down at the piano, and he and Tommy were talking about how to introduce the element of this Indian princess into the opening number of 'Will-a-Mania.' And Cy said, 'What about something like this?' And he sat down at the piano, and without any warning he improvised this incredibly silky, gorgeous, Debussy-meets-the-Wild-West [number], six or seven minutes of absolutely sublime, gorgeous music. And all of our jaws hit the floor."[35]

After Coleman finished, Stern recalled, "he whipped around and said, 'Does anybody have a tape recorder, because I'm not going to remember that.' And no one had known he was going to do it, and no one had turned on a tape recorder. No one caught it. And what he eventually wrote down on paper (or had written down) was a pale version of what he had improvised that day. I still wish to God that cell phones or smartphones had been invented then, just click the record button, because it was astounding. But what ended up in the show was pedestrian."[36]

Stern nevertheless found much to admire in Coleman's work and his attention to detail: "The elements of the steel pedal guitar and the harmonica, all of those elements in *The Will Rogers Follies* were at Cy's insistence. And they were wonderful flavors and he was right to insist on them. It really made the show worthwhile."[37]

Beyond the issues relating to content, there was one other hurdle for the creators: the title, which five months before opening was still up in the air. Originally announced as *Ziegfeld Presents Will Rogers*, the musical became known as *Ziegfeld Presents the Will Rogers Follies* in early 1991; then, a few months later, it was officially rechristened *The Will Rogers Follies*.

As Tune recalled, "Peter's original title just sounded so dry to me. I wanted to call it *At the Will Rogers Follies*, because I wanted it to be higher up in the ABCs [the theater listings in the *New York Times* that alphabetize based on the first letter of a show's title]. I also liked it because it gave the title movement. And then Betty said, in that dry way of hers, 'Why not *During the Will Rogers Follies*?' I laughed so hard I gave it up. Adolph wanted to call it *Will-a-Mania*, and I just thought he was pushing his song title, but that wouldn't have been a bad title for that show at all."[38]

Finally the show that had begun life in the mid-1980s opened on May 1, 1991. When the reviews started coming in, the reaction was decidedly mixed. In the *New York Times*, Frank Rich called it "the most disjointed musical of this or any other season," adding, "What the inspirational Rogers story and the blissfully campy Tune numbers are doing on the same stage is hard to explain and harder to justify, for they fight each other all evening." Jan Stuart in *Newsday* opined, "At its best, the fractured chronology generates some good-natured chuckles. At its worst, it feels stillborn."

Better notices could be found, particularly in the *New York Post*, where Clive Barnes stated simply and unequivocally, "It works," going so far as to say that Coleman had written "his best Broadway music in years. This is top-drawer Coleman with no apologies." Similarly, Howard Kissel in the *Daily News* concluded his review with "Gorgeous to look at, winningly performed, 'Will Rogers' is the homegrown musical Broadway has been awaiting a long, long time."

A couple of weeks after opening, Jack Kroll appeared to be giving the show another out-and-out rave when he said, "[The creators] have chosen a format so retro it's positively daring. They call it 'A Life in Revue,' which works out to be a kind of 'This Is Your Life' with songs and showgirls. These Broadway veterans, gambling that audiences are starved for simplicity, sweetness and sex, have supplied all that." But then, Kroll added, "It's not enough."

Theatergoers, however, were satisfied. *Will Rogers* settled into a run that would last for over two years.

A slew of Tony Award nominations did not hurt the musical, which picked up eleven, including best musical and one for Coleman, Comden, and Green for the score. The show won in both of these categories, making Coleman the only composer to win back-to-back Tony Awards for best score. Tune picked up a pair of prizes for his direction and choreography, and designers Willa Kim (costumes) and Jules Fisher (lighting) were also winners that year. Scenic designer Tony Walton failed to win for his sumptuous settings, including a grand staircase that spanned the stage and changed colors, syncing with Coleman's music and Tune's dances, but he didn't lose to John Napier, who put a helicopter onstage for *Miss Saigon*. Instead, the prize went to Heidi Landesman for her fanciful settings for the musical version of Frances Hodgson Burnett's children's tale, *The Secret Garden*.

When the cast recording came out, once again from Columbia Records, it bore the hallmarks of Coleman's fastidiousness as a producer, garnering new accolades for his work with Comden and Green. David Patrick Stearns wrote in *USA Today*, "It's some of the most effervescent fluff you'll ever hear," adding, "Most of this breezy score by Cy Coleman, Betty Comden and Adolph Green has an addictive combination of wit and uncloying cheerfulness."[39] The review from Gerald Nachman in the *San Francisco Chronicle* on December 5 had a similar glow: "It's clear to me that Cy Coleman has never written so many effortlessly catchy tunes, and while they're not the urbane Coleman of 'City of Angels,' they're not meant to be." He concluded by paraphrasing Rogers, saying, "I never met a song here I didn't like."

At Grammy Awards time in early 1992, the voters felt the same way. Coleman picked up an award for the cast album, recognized as both the composer and the disc's producer.

As *The Will Rogers Follies* continued on Broadway, celebrity casting helped to keep it in the public eye, starting with country singer Mac Davis, Carradine's replacement when he left to perform the show in Los Angeles. It was an ironic turn of events for producer Cossette. Davis had turned down the role when Cossette offered it to him in the show's earliest days. After Davis, the Broadway company boasted another country singing star, Larry Gatlin.

Big names weren't limited to the title role; they were also recruited to play the bombshell beauty Ziegfeld's Favorite. The first person to step into the role was Marla Maples, who was making headlines as Donald Trump's girlfriend and would eventually become his wife.

Casting the high-profile Maples was not, in Cossette's mind, merely a stunt. He believed that she had the talent necessary for the part. But he knew that casting Maples would be perceived as a publicity gimmick by the creators, so to ensure that she was well prepared for her audition for them, he had her work privately with both the show's assistant director and assistant choreographer.

Cossette remembered what followed after Maples, with six weeks of training, auditioned: "Cy Coleman was the first to speak. He said, 'Marla, would you be willing to work with me on the music for a couple of weeks and then come back and audition again?'"[40] She agreed, and after working with Coleman, Maples got the part. Another high-profile performer, actress-singer Susan Anton, eventually followed in the role.

The Will Rogers Follies continued at the Palace until just after Labor Day in 1993, playing 981 performances and becoming the longest-running show Coleman ever had on the Main Stem. The production's success led to the sixty-two-year-old assuming the role of Broadway elder statesman, but this didn't mean he was content to simply do what was expected of him . . . professionally or personally.

29

"If My Friends Could See Me Now"

The Tony and Grammy awards for *The Will Rogers Follies* put Coleman in a unique position: He became an artist who had been recognized for his music for five decades running, with nominations for the Tony dating back to 1962's *Little Me* and for the Grammy to 1958, when "Witchcraft" was nominated for both "Record of the Year" and "Song of the Year."

In 1992 Coleman's list of prizes became longer: he was inducted into the Theatre Hall of Fame, housed at Broadway's Gershwin Theatre (formerly the Uris, where *Seesaw* premiered). Among Coleman's fellow inductees were composer Harold Rome, acting teacher extraordinaire Stella Adler, and song-and-dance legend Gene Kelly. A similar honor came four years later from the Songwriters Hall of Fame (where Coleman was a 1980 inductee), which presented him with the Johnny Mercer Award in recognition of his body of work.

It was the beginning of a series of tributes and concerts that would continue through the next decade. Some would be small, private affairs, such as his induction into the famed Friars Club in 1996, while others, like a gala concert at Royal Albert Hall in London 1999 and a concert with Skitch Henderson at Carnegie Hall in 2002, were starry public events.

But Coleman wasn't simply basking in the spotlight. He was also using this time to toast the successes of his peers. For the first half of the 1990s Coleman took part in festivities honoring collaborators like Comden and Green and interpreters of his songs like Rosemary Clooney. He was among the artists who celebrated the twenty-fifth anniversary of the

John F. Kennedy Center for the Performing Arts in the first half of 1996, where, rather than performing his own hits, he joined with other pianists such as Peter Nero, Alicia Witt, and Christina Zacharias for renditions of Edvard Grieg's "In the Hall of the Mountain King" and John Philip Sousa's "The Stars and Stripes Forever."

Less than a month later, Coleman was back in the limelight at the Kennedy Center when he was its guest of honor during a one-night-only salute to Broadway, and his presence in the nation's capital wasn't going unnoticed. At the end of the year, when the arts journalists for the *Washington Post* drew up a short list of artists who they believed should be recognized with the annual Kennedy Center Honor, Coleman's name featured prominently.

Another retrospective—of sorts—on Coleman's career came when he created a gentle cartoon of his own biography, a brief musical that was part of a twentieth-anniversary special for PBS's *Great Performances*, a program comprised short films that the network commissioned from artists ranging from playwright Wendy Wasserstein to photographer Annie Leibovitz. In each, the artists created work that, as the show's narrator, Meryl Streep, explained, would reveal something "about their lives in art that show us the art in life." Coleman's contribution was *A Simple Melody*, which puts an intriguing spin on his life story as it follows Arnold, a piano prodigy during his preschool days, through adulthood. Along the way Arnold earns plaudits for his accomplishments first as a pianist and later as a composer.

The parallels—and differences—between Coleman's own life and Arnold's are simultaneously significant and amusing. Initially, the boy, unlike Coleman, has the full support of his parents, who start him on piano lessons. The family's finances fail while Arnold is in college, so he has to support himself. Once the movie starts to follow him on his path through a series of weddings, where he becomes the star of a small combo, Coleman (as well as screenwriter Alan Zweibel) has some fun with his earliest days as a performer, when he would hop between "classy affairs that require tux," as Coleman wrote in his scrapbook.

By the movie's end, Arnold, like Coleman, becomes a celebrity, not because of a wide body of work but because of the one "simple melody" that he's reimagined in a variety of ways. Coleman's also on hand in the film, playing the trombone and winking at Arnold during the final scene at the character's luxe mansion.

Coleman didn't just write the music for *A Simple Melody*; he also arranged and orchestrated it. As the movie's main tune goes through a seemingly endless array of variations—including different incarnations for the Jewish, Italian, and Greek weddings that Arnold plays, as well as a huge marching-band sequence straight out of *The Music Man*—Coleman's facility with diverse styles is astonishing.

A Simple Melody was directed and choreographed by Pat Birch, whose line of credits stretched back to the late 1950s, when she had appeared as a dancer in musicals like *Goldilocks* and a *Brigadoon* revival. In the early 1970s she began creating dances for shows like *You're a Good Man, Charlie Brown* and *Grease* and then went on to work with Harold Prince on such musicals as *A Little Night Music*, the 1974 revisal of *Candide*, and *Pacific Overtures*. Her credits also included film and television, notably the movie version of *Grease* and six seasons on NBC's *Saturday Night Live*.

Coleman and Birch first worked together when she did the musical staging for *Welcome to the Club* and became fast friends. She was the one who was initially approached by PBS about creating something for the special, and when she broached the idea of working together to Coleman, he agreed. After all, as she recalled, "He was always up for fun." Then, Birch said, "We sort of cooked it up."[1]

Screenwriter Zweibel, who, like Birch, had a long history with *Saturday Night Live* and had gotten to know her there, came in after she and Coleman had developed the scenario for the movie. As he recalled, "They needed a writer, but my contribution to it was minimal. They had the idea. And I loved the idea. I loved the idea of you taking one little, simple melody that would have seven notes or whatever it was and putting it in all of these different ways. . . . [I was] honored to be there, happy to help. I did whatever I could to put in beats of different visuals of the different kinds of ways that this simple melody could be played."[2]

Their work, along with that of Matthew Broderick, who played the adult incarnation of Arnold, and Jane Krakowski, who played Arnold's wife at the end of the film, prompted Associated Press reviewer Frazier Moore to extol the "frothy mini-musical."

Beyond having fun in this filmic manner, Coleman also found a way to express himself as a performer and have a good time by working with the Hole in the Wall Gang Camp in Connecticut. Paul Newman and A. E. Hotchner founded this organization for seriously ill young people and their families as a place where healing could take place on multiple levels each summer.

Each year, Coleman would take part in the organization's annual fund-raising events—sometimes as an actor, in shows like the one offered in 1994, "Snowy," a modernized and irreverent version of the *Snow White* fairy tale directed by Birch. Coleman, looked anything but his dapper celebrity self when he played one of the seven dwarfs, "Doc," with a cast that also featured Melanie Griffith and Ann Reinking, who shared the role of the Wicked Queen. Among the other dwarfs were Newman, Hotchner, James Naughton, Tony Randall, and Gene Shalit.

Coleman recruited other friends and colleagues to take part in special events for the camp, including Sally Mayes, who fondly remembered her time with Coleman and his coterie in a nontheatrical environment: "They were lovely. They're all pals, and they all hang out and they all drink scotch. . . . It was very boys club. You could just feel that. . . . It felt like *Mad Men*."[3]

Coleman's work with ASCAP also expanded during this time. In 1990 he went to Washington, D.C., to take part in the bicentennial celebration of U.S. Copyright and Patent Laws. His presence was both understandable and natural. After all, he had lobbied for the extension and expansion of copyright legislation in the late 1960s. He was also there to pay tribute to Peggy Lee, who was receiving the organization's Pied Piper Award in recognition of her work as both a singer and a songwriter. At Coleman's side for this event were Sammy Cahn, the songwriting team of Jerry Leiber and Mike Stoller, and Marilyn and Alan Bergman, with whom Coleman would be working much more closely over the course of the coming decade. His relationship with Marilyn Bergman, individually, grew deeper in 1994, when ASCAP went through a series of leadership changes after Morton Gould stepped down as the organization's president.

Bergman was elected to succeed him, leaving her post as writer vice president vacant. Coleman was chosen to succeed her, and with the new title came new responsibilities, both behind the scenes and in public. Just after assuming the title, he reflected on the reasons for devoting time to the organization: "It's a cause I believe in and spend a lot of time on, because composers deserve to get paid for their copyrighted work. People think they're having such a good time while listening to your music, they can't believe they need to pay for it."[4]

Marilyn Bergman, while talking about her work for ASCAP with Coleman, similarly said, "It's like the civil liberties union of songwriters and composers. Rights are rights, and when they're threatened hackles get raised, and just as Cy had good politics, he understood that some of this— forget the money—was just a question of that's just downright wrong. It's just thievery and disrespectful."[5]

Beyond the new title at ASCAP and the heightened recognition he was receiving, there was one other new facet to Coleman's life. There was a new woman at his side: Shelby Brown, whom he met on New Year's Eve 1992.

Coleman and Brown met when he visited an old friend, visual artist Ron Mallory, in his home in San Miguel de Allende, Mexico. By this time Mallory and Coleman had been friends for some thirty years. The men met in 1962, when Mallory was working as a model on a shoot in St. Thomas. One day, Mallory recalled, some friends said, "We have to go pick up this composer. Do you want to join us?"[6]

During their first few days together, the men discovered that they "got along beautifully"; furthermore, they realized that they were neighbors in Manhattan. "I lived on East Sixty-Eighth Street, and Cy lived on East 69th Street," Mallory remembered.[7]

Their acquaintance deepened and continued over the following decades, and the two men frequently traveled together: "Cy always invited me places." Mallory recalled a summer in the late 1960s when they shared a house in Monte Carlo. Coleman had inadvertently invited two women to visit at the same time: "So Cy comes into my room one day. He says, 'You've got to do me a favor.' And I said, 'What's up?' He said, 'I forgot I invited this other girl, and she's coming tomorrow. So can you pretend you're with the other girl? So she won't be angry?' I remember looking at Cy and saying, 'You've got to be kidding me.'"[8]

A similar situation unfolded in 1992. Coleman had traveled to Mexico with a girlfriend, and one night he invited Mallory to join them for dinner. Mallory brought along Brown as his guest for the evening, and as he remembered: "Shelby started talking to Cy, and I guess they fell madly in love. Cy dropped the woman he was with. And then Shelby and Cy, that's the whole story."[9]

She didn't recall it happening that quickly, but Coleman made an impression that evening. Sometime in 1992 Brown, who was in Mexico to work on a book, found herself traveling to Manhattan. While she was there she decided to call Coleman, not knowing if he would remember her. He did and invited her to lunch. The meal went well, and a few days later, while out again, he kissed her for the first time, and she said, "What took you so long?"[10]

Brown, who later admitted, "I don't like dating. Never have. Never will," moved in with Coleman not long after. "It was like being with the king of New York. I was living in Mexico in this crappy little house with my sister, and I moved to New York City. And it's like I'm in love with this guy, but from another planet. Betty and Adolph—I didn't know who they were. I didn't know musical theater. I'd been to a couple of shows in my life. It's not what they did, but who they were. I was in the room with the smartest, funniest, most amazing human beings I'd ever met. I was, like, blown away."[11]

Brown adapted to Coleman's world. "I stopped listening to my music, because he didn't care for it. Basically, he just listened to classical. He taught me a lot." As an example, she pointed to how, during a vacation in Spain, "we sat on the beach and he took me through every movement of [Beethoven's] first four symphonies."[12]

There were also differences in lifestyle. "I am a homebody; I like to be home all the time. Cy was used to being out all the time." This also meant,

not too surprisingly, that the couple had some varying ideas about food.
"When I met Cy, I knew how to cook the way I learned from my mom, sort
of Okie and real down-home stuff: fried chicken, mashed potatoes, etc. . . .
He did not care for my food. He liked restaurant food. That's what he was
used to, restaurant food. So I had to learn to cook Cy style, and that was
challenging and great. I really became more of a cook."[13]

Brown's abilities in the kitchen proved to be a boon to him after a
health scare in December 1995. "We were in Barbados with Hotch at
Christmas. And Cy had a tiny heart attack. It was fine, but they said 'You
have to change your diet.' And he said, 'Okay, I can do that.' And that's
when I became [a] health cook. And he really started liking my food. He
lost a ton of weight and got healthier."[14]

Less than two years later, on October 1, 1997, the couple married.
"[They] hit upon the idea of marrying next to Niagara Falls, a plan they
loved because it reminded them of old movies and musicals."[15]

By the time Colemans tied the knot, they had not only shared vacations, official trips to Washington, and the like; they had also weathered,
together, the financing, rehearsals, previews, and opening of a Broadway
show. It was a piece that had its genesis in the early 1980s and had been
on Coleman's docket ever since. In the space between *City of Angels* and
The Will Rogers Follies, he had found time to workshop it, and as the
1990s progressed, he did everything in his power to see that the tuner
finally reached Broadway.

30

The Life

The seeds for the musical *The Life* were planted in 1975 when Coleman, Betty Comden, and Adolph Green were all working on the songs for Phyllis Newman's *Straws in the Wind*. Another contributor to the show was lyricist Ira Gasman, who, with Galt MacDermot as composer, contributed two songs to the production, including the provocatively titled "It's Not Such a Brave New World, Mr. Huxley." Gasman also penned a lyric set to Stephen Sondheim's melody for "Broadway Baby" (from *Follies*), but his revision, "Test Tube Baby," went unperformed.

Coleman and Gasman met during the rehearsal process for *Straws*, and Gasman fondly recalled the banter of their first exchange: "I had been a fan of his ever since I'd heard *Sweet Charity*. Somehow I got up the nerve to introduce myself. 'I'm a lyricist.' 'Are you sure?' he joked, adding, 'What have you written, kid?' 'Well, I wrote a political revue, *What's a Nice Country Like You Doing in a State Like This?*' 'Catchy title. I hate catchy titles.'"[1]

Coleman asked if Gasman had any other projects in development, and Gasman mentioned a project he had begun. It centered on the seedy denizens of Times Square. Gasman would ultimately say that his inspiration came when "I was walking down 42nd Street one night, probably coming from Theatre Row, when suddenly a police car pulls over to the corner, two guys get arrested, a couple was arguing across the street. What theatre, I thought, right there in the street! It got me thinking about this show."[2]

As Gasman told Coleman, "'It's called *The Life*.' 'Well, that's certainly not a catchy title. What's it about?' 'It's about Forty-second Street, filled with prostitutes, pimps, and pickpockets.' 'How the hell am I supposed to write music for prostitutes, pimps, and pickpockets? Is that a musical?' 'It could be.'"[3] Despite the wisecracks, Gasman remembered that Coleman was intrigued and told him to set up an appointment so that he could hear Gasman read some of his lyrics and they could discuss *The Life* in greater detail.

As amusing and convenient as the anecdote is, it's contradicted by a note, dated August 3, attached to an early three-scene, fourteen-page draft of the musical that Gasman sent to Coleman. In the handwritten note, Gasman references his long friendship with the composer (indicating that it came several years after *Straws*) and says that the enclosed material is the first thing he has written that he believes warrants Coleman's consideration. The short script contains a scenario about a hooker named Queen; her pimp, Candy Man, and a teenage midwesterner, Mary, newly arrived in New York. It also contains lyrics for several songs, including one called "I'm Getting Too Old for the Oldest Profession." It was enough to attract Coleman's attention, and the two men began work on the show, seemingly at the beginning of the 1980s.

In many ways *The Life* would become the third in a triptych of Coleman shows about the darkness that crept into American culture during the 1970s. He began with *Home Again* and its look at what had happened to the nuclear family and American Dream over the course of five decades. Coleman's work in this vein continued with the unproduced *Atlantic City*, which explored how that once glamorous seaside resort fell into decay and disrepair. With *The Life*, Coleman moved to territory he had witnessed firsthand as New York teetered toward bankruptcy in the 1970s.

Yet *The Life* was set apart from the other two pieces by the fact that it was a musical drama in which the songs were integrated into the book rather than placed alongside an episodic narrative. It might have been *The Life* that Coleman, in part, was referencing in October 2004 when he told Jerry Tallmer of *The Villager*: "In a show I write for character and for the person. When it's not in a show, I just write for myself."

It's projects like these (either completed, still aborning, or about to begin) that help to explain a comment he made in 1981, when the crowd-pleasing *Barnum* was still playing: "Look, I have things to say. My own feelings, my own important statements. This is what I am, and this is what they are."[4] One would be hard-pressed to find the "statement" that *Barnum* made. However, with these other projects, as well as others, such as *Julian*, which had entered Coleman's consciousness in the 1970s, the man who was identified more often than not with frivolous entertainments was attempting to explore deeper and more meaningful subjects. In fact, he would eventually describe *The Life* as "the show we couldn't do in 'Sweet Charity,' which was a wonderful fairytale about hope. With 'The Life' you're into a new era."[5]

By late 1983 the collaboration had resulted in several additional songs for *The Life*. They had also worked on numbers for the short-lived revue *Shecago*, which boasted two Coleman-Gasman tunes, "I Start Sneezing" and "My Body," a song that ended up in *The Life*. Over the course of the next seven years, Coleman and Gasman would periodically work on the show. They had made enough progress on it by July 1986 that it was included alongside other shows like *Death Is for Suckers* and his Will Rogers project, which Coleman was writing with Comden and Green, to be included in a *New York Times* feature.

As the years progressed and *Welcome to the Club*, *City of Angels*, and *The Will Rogers Follies* all moved into production, Coleman didn't lose sight of *The Life*. By the spring of 1990, just before the Tony Award victories for *City of Angels*, it was in good enough shape for a showcase production that would be directed by Coleman's frequent collaborator Joe Layton.

One member of the company was Lillias White, who had been attached to the project since its earliest days and would be playing the role of Sonja, a hooker who was passing her prime as she moved toward thirty. White had gotten to know Layton and Coleman when she replaced Terri White in the role of Joyce Heth in *Barnum*. After that she worked with Layton on the short-lived revue *Rock and Roll! The First 5,000 Years*. Shortly after it closed, she remembered, "I got a call from Cy and Joe. They said they were doing this show. It was called *The Life*, and they wanted me to come in and sing some stuff. They also said I had the job. It wasn't an audition.

They just wanted to see how the music was feeling in my range and how it sounded."[6]

White was joined for the workshop by Pamela Isaacs, who played Queen, a woman trying to get out of "the life" with her boyfriend-pimp, Fleetwood, played by Edwin Louis Battle. Chuck Cooper was Memphis, a pimp who had a number of women working for him. The role of Mary, the young woman just arrived in the city, was taken by Lori Fischer.

Cooper, like so many actors of the period, remembered Coleman's significant presence during his audition: "I went in and did my up and my ballad or whatever, and he asked me if he could teach me a little something. He played a little bit of 'Don't Take Much' and taught it to me right there at the audition, and as I recall I don't even think I had a callback. When it's Cy, he knows when its right, and when it ain't, he also knows that. So I guess he heard something in my voice that he liked, and I got the job."[7]

Cooper remembered that during rehearsals—which took place not in Times Square, where the show was set, but rather at Westbeth Theatre, the downtown venue where the show was performed—Coleman's work with him was meticulous and caring. "Cy knew what our process was, and he knew how to merge that with what he desired musically and how to make the dramatic line match the musical line match the breath that you were taking. I can't remember where it was exactly in ['My Way or the Highway'], but he said to me, 'Just carry the note over the bar. Breathe before you attack this note, and carry the note over the bar, and that will lead you to the next level.'"[8]

Cooper found that Coleman's advice worked. What surprised him was how the composer "just kind of cavalierly threw this out there," and then, Cooper added, "I did it, and it busted the song open for me and helped me move through it in a place where I was stuck. He would do this all the time. He was very gentle, very patient, but he also expected you to do your work and come prepared, and as I said before, no slackers. He brooked no fools. You had to bring it because he was bringing it. That's how he rolled, and everybody knew that."[9]

During rehearsals and the two weeks of performances that *The Life* had at Westbeth, Coleman, Gasman, and Layton were able to explore and revise the piece, which Coleman had almost completely through-composed. Underscoring was heavily prevalent in the arrangements for the small combo, and the production featured extensive sections of recitative. In many regards *The Life* was sounding a lot like a latter-day incarnation of *Porgy and Bess*, and even the casting notices made reference to the Gershwin folk opera, describing Cooper's character as "a combination of Joe Williams and Charles Dutton, Crown in 'Porgy & Bess.'"[10]

The workshops demonstrated to the creators that they had "the nucleus of it,"[11] as White recalled, and that what had been accomplished in three weeks was enough to show them where work needed to be done before the show reached Broadway. But after the Westbeth engagement in August 1990, Coleman had to focus his energies on *The Will Rogers Follies*. It would be over two years before *The Life* resurfaced.

When it did, it wasn't in an announcement of upcoming Broadway plans but rather in casting notices in October 1992, which noted that the show would begin rehearsals on January 25, 1993, officially opening April 15. The casting notices also carried the names of the show's producers. *The Life* would come to Broadway under the auspices of Roger Berlind, along with Martin Richards and Sam Crothers (of the Producers Circle). Coleman and his old friend James Lipton were also backing the show.

Then, however, *The Life* went into a state of suspension, and just two weeks before the show was to have debuted, Bruce Weber mentioned it as he focused on what might open in the fall of 1993. In his April 2 *New York Times* "On Stage, and Off" column, he wrote, "Cy Coleman's 'The Life' is breathing out there somewhere."

What happened over the course of the following three years demonstrates how fiercely committed Coleman was to this specific show as well as the herculean efforts it was taking to secure financing for the production. Toward the end of the year lead producer Berlind, while discussing the troubles he was having in raising money for another project, a musical version of the film *Paper Moon*, mentioned *The Life*, calling it "a dangerous show." The report on his efforts also included the following: "Berlind came to Broadway from Wall Street. 'Ah yes,' he said, almost wistfully, the other day, 'the good old stock market. . . .'"[12]

Berlind, however, seemed to have to put the financing together for *The Life* in short order, because by the following January the Nederlander Organization had committed to having the production play at its eponymous Broadway theater late that year. This home for the show appeared to be even more of a sure thing a month later when the Nederlanders had to turn to the Shubert Organization to rent a theater—the Ambassador—for another production that might have used the venue, Bill Cartwright's *The Rise and Fall of Little Voice*.

The Life faced a new hurdle in May, however, when director Joe Layton passed away "after a long illness," as stated in his *New York Times* obituary on May 9. He hadn't kept the illness from Coleman, but the composer had attempted to keep it secret from potential investors. As Gordon Lowry Harrell, who became the show's musical director after the Westbeth performances, recalled, "Cy kept that very much under his hat. I remember them doing a backers' show, and they were somewhere over on the East Side. And Joe Layton wasn't there. And I said to Cy, 'Where's Joe Layton?' The truth of the matter was that Joe was at home dying. He was that sick. And Cy said, within earshot of several other people, 'Ah, you know Joe. You throw a nickel his way, and he jumps off the wagon.' Cy didn't want backers to know that Joe wasn't going to direct."[13]

Immediately following Layton's death there was an unexpected announcement about the show. David Newman, who cowrote the book for the musical *It's a Bird, It's a Plane, It's Superman* and later contributed to the screenplays for the first two *Superman* films starring Christopher Reeve, officially joined the creative team. In tandem with this news, the *New York Times* reported, "Among the shows that definitely aren't going to get to Broadway this fall, in spite of hopes, dreams or rumors is 'The Life,' the long-percolating Cy Coleman-Ira Gasman musical."[14]

Over the next six months Newman worked with Coleman and Gasman on revising the book, and by January 1995 a new version of the first act, with the billing of "Book by Ira Gasman, Cy Coleman and David Newman," had been completed. By the time the show opened, Newman would carry top billing.

The changes, though not radical, were significant. The role of a Times

Square bartender, Lacy, was built up so that the character could contextualize the history of the neighborhood and its denizens. In addition, the role of Sonja was altered. During the Westbeth staging she had been a drug addict. In the new version she no longer was relying on her pusher, which necessitated that "Reefer Man," one of the most interesting Coleman-Gasman tunes in the score, be cut; but even with this excision, the score for the first act boasted a healthy sixteen numbers.

As Coleman worked on the revisions, he also developed strategies to get the show and its music into the public's consciousness. From publisher Buddy Morris he had learned how important promotional versions of show tunes could be, and for *The Life* he decided to put a new spin on an old-school idea: he would record an album of cover versions of the musical's songs by artists ranging from Liza Minnelli to Lou Rawls to George Burns. "Cy's hoping this platter will be as lucky for the show as—the 14 sides that preceded the bow of 'Sweet Charity'!" *Variety* reported.[15]

When the album was announced in summer 1993, it was to have been an EMI recording, but eventually the label backed out, giving another clear indication of people's squeamishness with the property. Coleman then turned to RCA's Bill Rosenfield, who remembered, "Cy called me and said, 'In order for *The Life* to happen, we have to do this concept album. We have to get the music out there.'"[16]

Rosenfield, however, had severe reservations about the show. He had seen it at Westbeth and "hated [it]. I found it morally reprehensible. But I said to myself, 'You know something? I'm a pipsqueak in this world. I'm a speck of dust and he's Cy Coleman, and this company has fucked him over on *City of Angels* and *Will Rogers*, and even though I hate this show, I should say yes to this. We can bring it in for the right amount of money and such.'"[17]

Rosenfield said that he repeated this to Coleman and record producer Mike Berniker when they first met to discuss the album, and then added, "I also was doing a 'make good' for myself. And I said that to Cy. He and Mike came into the office and we were talking and I just laid it out. I said, 'I don't like this show. I really don't. But we owe you.'" Rosenfield also laid out the specifics for what Coleman and Berniker would have to deliver and then, he remembered, "They delivered a tape that was thirty-seven minutes long. I told Cy, 'I can't release this. . . . You have failed me here. It needs to be at least forty-four minutes long.'"[18]

Coleman made up the difference, recording "The Composer's Turn," a medley of three songs from the show. "He timed it out to be exactly what I had said. He did it the following week, and after that—and even though we were working on artwork and stuff like that—Cy was always a little frosty, because I had called him on that."[19]

Rosenfield continued, "I talked to Mike Berniker about it a few years later. And he said, 'It was just that you had said in the first meeting you were a speck of dust and he was Cy Coleman and who were you to question Cy Coleman? And the fact when we delivered it, you questioned Cy Coleman. And he felt kind of betrayed by that.' And I said, 'Well, you know I can't do anything about that.'"[20]

The album, *Music from "The Life": A New Musical*, was released in early 1996, and it did accomplish, at least on some levels, what Coleman had hoped: it brought twelve songs from the still-aborning show to the public. In one interview that appeared in tandem with the disc's release, Coleman described his intentions to Patricia O'Hare for the June 9 edition of the *Daily News*: "What I wanted here was to start with a song, then cast it to a particular singer's style. So we asked Billy Preston to do a gospel-style number; Joe Williams has a song that's like what he did with the old [Count] Basie band. Jack Jones has a lush sound and Liza does a traditional Liza number on the song called 'People Magazine.'"

Another artist featured on the album was comedian George Burns, who recorded his track, "Easy Money," at the age of one hundred. He died just as the disc was being released, which meant that it got an additional publicity push, as it was the last recording made by the legendary performer. Despite this, and despite the campaign that Coleman and RCA engaged in, "The album came out and didn't sell. Didn't do anything," Rosenfield said. "And we actually spent a fair amount of money trying to promote it, but there was nothing to promote. And we couldn't create artwork for the show because there was no show. There were a lot of different issues."[21]

Beyond recording the disc—which required flights back and forth between coasts to accommodate the schedules of the singers Coleman had
lined up—he was also actively involved in backers' auditions during these
three years. As Chuck Cooper recalled, "All I know is that we did so many
of those things that we lost count. I remember joking with Lillias and Pam
like, 'Oh, here we go again.'" Ennui wasn't settling in with him but rather
an odd contentment, as he realized, "Well, these are great songs, and if
they want to pay us to sing these songs in rich people's houses while we
eat up their food, that's fine."[22]

The process of securing funding was abetted by the announcement
in late 1996 of a new creative team for *The Life*. Michael Blakemore, who
had helmed *City of Angels*, was on board to direct, and Joey McKneely,
who had a long string of credits as a performer on Broadway and who had
just created the musical staging for the pop-hit tuner *Smokey Joe's Cafe*,
was on board as choreographer.

Blakemore actually became involved several months before his name
was officially attached to the production. "It really interested me, and not
just because of Cy, but also because I like shows that are about the life
under your nose. (Not that 'the life' is under everyone's nose.) But it was
about New York. It was a proper New York subject, but I wanted to do it."[23]

Along with his enthusiasm for the subject, Blakemore felt that "it had
absolutely brilliant lyrics by Ira Gasman." The director added, "I loved
the score when [Cy] sent me his sort of demonstration discs and some
arrangements of some of the songs." The director did have reservations
about the book, though, and over the course of the summer of 1996 he and
Newman worked together on revisions. "The book wasn't quite right. . . .
So I did a bit of work on the book myself, and I wrote the opening speech
for Jojo. I did a couple of scenes during the course of it and worked with
David over a long summer. We faxed each other back and forth."[24]

The result of the men's work was the most sweeping revision the script
had had in several years. Not only did Newman and Blakemore shift the
action from the mid-1970s to the early 1980s (in order to raise the specter
of AIDS), they also rethought the show's overall dramatic thrust. *The Life*
still centered on Queen and her boyfriend-pimp Fleetwood and the ways

in which his interest in a new woman affects their relationship. In the new version of the book, however, they were being manipulated in both subtle and direct ways by Jojo, once just a minor character but now both the audience's guide to the world (he delivered the opening monologue that Blakemore penned) and an Iagolike villain, a man willing to play people off one another in order to make a quick buck or further his own career in the worlds of the sex trade and adult entertainment. With this revision, *The Life* gained a significant dramatic, and even tragic, arc.

After the book revisions, which also brought a new song, a soaring eleven o'clock number for the two female leads, "My Friend," *The Life* got yet another staged reading in December—at the New Victory Theatre, which, symbolically, represented the reclamation of Times Square from the seedy squalor that the show was portraying. Blakemore remembered, "We had a desperate one week's rehearsal together, and that went pretty well, and a wonderful cast. Then Marty Richards was very much on our side and he wanted to go. I think Roger Berlind had another show going on, and he wasn't so keen on going at once. I was mad to get it on. So we sort of pushed it through, and then we started rehearsal."[25]

The reading came just after the first inklings of what the show's *actual* schedule might be had come to light. Audition notices in late September and early October noted that the musical would begin rehearsals in mid-January in anticipation of an April opening, but, unlike similar notices before, no specifics were given. For anyone watching the progress of *The Life*, the lack of specificity could have been seen as an ominous sign, particularly because the announcement coincided with what was described by *Back Stage* as "a logjam of musical productions waiting impatiently for Broadway houses."[26]

Coleman himself seemed to be among the musical's skeptics—he once quipped, "I started out as a young man on this project"[27]—but by January 1, 1997 *The Life* had an opening date of April 30, and once existing productions began shuttering during the usual winter-time slump on Broadway, the show found a home: the Barrymore Theatre, where *I Love My Wife* had enjoyed a two-year run in the late 1970s.

It was the end of a long journey for Coleman, as well as for three of his principals. White had been involved with the show for approximately fifteen years. Isaacs and Cooper had been working on it since being cast in the Westbeth workshop seven years earlier. As Cooper pointed out, however, "Cy was loyal to us beyond anything I've ever seen or heard of in show business. I've never heard of anyone sticking with actors over different directors over a period of years trying to get a piece together. It really is kind of a testament to the kind of guy he was."[28]

The company for *The Life* included more performers who had been with the show along the way, mixed with newcomers. Sharon Wilkins, for instance, who made her Broadway debut with the musical, was in the Westbeth staging. Others, like Vernel Bagneris, who played the sage bartender Lacy, came to the company during the show's last set of readings. But Sam Harris, who played the heavily revised character of Jojo, was cast just before rehearsals began.

Harris was the show's star attraction. Although he had only one other Broadway credit (Doody, in the early 1990s revival of *Grease*), he was a familiar face to general audiences because of his appearances on one of television's first reality series, *Star Search*, in which he had been the grand-prize winner.

The actor-singer vividly remembered his audition experience with the composer: "I decided to sing this coupling of 'There's Got to Be Something Better Than This' (from *Sweet Charity*) and 'Move On' (from *Sunday in the Park with George*) that I had [once] recorded with Peter Matz doing the brilliant orchestration. So I came in the room and I said, 'Cy, it's wonderful to meet you. I'm so excited to meet you. I should warn you that I have rewritten some of Dorothy Fields's lyrics in putting these songs together.' And he said, 'Well, did you change any of the music?' I said, 'Not really.' And he said, 'What the hell should I care for, then? She's dead.' And that was my introduction to Cy Coleman."[29]

Coleman worked closely with Harris after he was cast, particularly as he was the newest principal performer and the role had so recently been reconceived. "It was great for me, because then they could build it and the arrangements on me, and play with what I could do."[30]

Harris remembered, too, that their camaraderie had its ups and downs.

One particularly positive memory related to the show's opening number, "Use What You've Got." As he worked with Coleman, "Cy said, 'At the end, we're going to sit on this note.' He did the oddest thing, because, you know, typically in musical structure something is in increments of four bars or eight bars and there's the obvious button. We did it, and he kept playing, and I kept holding the note. It was this odd, endless, six-bar— they were slow bars—note that I had to hold and then not breathe after, to finish the song. Through every performance I did of that song, I secretly had to count on my fingers to know how many bars it was, because it was so odd. It made no sense to my musical head."[31]

It's the kind of musical choice that Harris said was emblematic of Cy in general. "He wanted to do things that were surprising or unpredictable. Just when you thought something would be happening, something else would happen."[32]

Harris also remembered a less cordial moment during rehearsals, when he was working on the number that opened the second act, "Mr. Greed." "[It] had a jazz vibe that allowed a lot of play, which Cy encouraged me to do." But the song wasn't just a solo for Harris. It was also a big dance number that Harris remembered McKneely re-choreographing "every day."[33]

Harris continued, "I was always trying to figure it out and be in it. . . . And I didn't learn it from Cy; I learned it sort of haphazardly, and then we were staging it. But I had never really solidified it with Cy. And the arrangement was ever-changing. So we were doing like the fourteen-thousandth version of this choreography, and I'm just sort of singing it but not really, because I'm doing choreography. And Cy comes in the back of the large rehearsal room and walks slowly and keeps walking and as he's continuing through he says to me, 'I hope you're not going to sing it like that in the show.' And exited."[34]

The rehearsal continued, but Harris said, "I was embarrassed. I was humiliated." During a break, Harris found Coleman and had a private conversation with him. "I said, 'You are Cy Coleman, and it is my great honor to be in this show performing your work, but until you have taught me the song, and until you have laid out what you want me to do so I can honor and respect your vision for this, please do not comment on my work publicly, in front of the company, ever, ever again." Harris's stand earned Coleman's respect. "From then on we were like the best of pals and collaborated on everything."[35]

White shared similar memories of Coleman during rehearsals: "Cy was a strict taskmaster. When he wanted to hear something, he wanted to hear it a certain way. I remember him givin' the business to Sam Harris. To Kevin Ramsey, because he wanted things a certain way. I remember Chuck working really hard to get the tones and the words out, and to be able to hold those notes and make them ferocious."[36]

Coleman's strictness during these rehearsals—markedly different from accounts of his work with performers on previous shows—may have had something to do with the problems that he was facing as he fulfilled duties as both creator and producer of the show. On the artistic side, he knew that there were doubts about the property altogether. As Blakemore recalled, "We were up against it because Cy had done a musical, *Welcome to the Club*, which was considered very male chauvinist, and it got terrible press." With this in mind, and remembering the conflicts they had had with their producers on *City of Angels*, Blakemore added, "So again, we went into rehearsals slightly ready for a battle."[37]

As the work on the musical continued, it still faced troubling financial issues. It hadn't been fully capitalized, and the process of raising backing continued. "[Cy] was wearing many hats," Harris said, "and we were in the middle of rehearsals, two weeks before we were onstage, stopping to do truncated backers' auditions for more money. So while we were staging this and putting it up and having final fittings and cutting songs and fixing things, they were raising money."[38]

The full backing was ultimately achieved, and with revisions (notably a new end to the first act) *The Life* finally reached its opening night on April 26 (a Saturday, and four days earlier than originally announced). When the reviews began appearing in the Monday papers, the critics were appreciative of the principals' performances, and White's specifically, but less enthusiastic about the show itself.

In his *New York Times* review Ben Brantley wrote that the book "reeks of bottom-drawer, movie melodrama" and complained that Coleman "provides some zesty jazz- and vaudeville-inflected tunes. But he often stretches them to the point of thinness." Still, Brantley found himself forced to admit that "'The Life' has at least one thing going for it, something that's been hard to locate in this season of big but bloodless musicals like 'Titanic' and 'Steel Pier': a definite human pulse."

In the *Daily News* Howard Kissel was sarcastic and rhetorical in the opening of his review: "Is anyone, by the way, nostalgic for 42d St. when it was a human sewer? Nostalgic enough, that is, to pay $75 to see the kind of sleaze you used to be able to get for free?" Michael Kuchwara echoed these sentiments and called the musical "an uneasy mixture of soap opera and sleaze."

Unlike his peers, however, Kuchwara did have good things to say about Coleman and the score: "He is a jazzy, adult composer, able to toss off with equal dexterity a smoky, sophisticated melody as well as a bouncy old-fashioned show tune. Gasman's lyrics are not on that level, but they will do."

The Life got one of its best reviews in a trade publication, the *Hollywood Reporter*, where on April 28 Frank Scheck's notice proclaimed, "[*The Life*] is a tawdry and at times distasteful affair that also happens to be the most exciting new musical of the Broadway season." He added, "Coleman's music and Gasman's lyrics offer a kind . . . of Broadway razzmatazz seldom heard anymore. The heavily rhythm-and-blues-inflected score offers one highlight after another, delivered by some of the most powerful voices currently heard on a New York stage."

The nominating committee for the Tony Awards sided with Scheck in its assessment of the show. When the nominations for the annual prizes were announced just over a week later, *The Life* scored an impressive twelve nods, the most of any show of the season. (Of the other nominated musicals, John Kander and Fred Ebb's *Steel Pier* garnered eleven; Maury Yeston and Peter Stone's *Titanic* received five; and *Juan Darien*, an offering directed by Julie Taymor for Lincoln Center Theater, nabbed six). Not only was *The Life* nominated for best musical, but performer Isaacs was recognized in the leading actress category, while Cooper, Harris, and

White all received nominations in supporting categories. Coleman and Gasman got a nod for best score, and they, along with Newman, were nominated for their book for the show.

The nominations gave the production a much-needed boost at the box office, and the day following the announcement, producer Martin Richards told Associated Press writer Kuchwara, "We got exactly what we needed. . . . There is a line right now at the box office."[39]

The Tony Award voters, however, were not impressed with the musical. They put all of their support behind *Titanic*, which won for each nomination it received. *The Life*, meanwhile, picked up only a pair of prizes, for performers Cooper and White.

The show fared well enough at the box office through the summer, but after Labor Day it began to experience some lean weeks. It was at this point that Vincent Canby filed a second review in the *New York Times*. As with Walter Kerr's follow-up on *Seesaw* in 1973, Canby's assessment was a love letter, headlined "Why Whisper About It? 'The Life' Is a Joy." Canby went on to praise almost every aspect of the show (he did admit the book was "serviceable" but even attempted to turn that description into a compliment). Most notably, he wrote, "Mr. Coleman has composed not only his most driving, big-beat score since 'Sweet Charity,' but also his most varied and melodic work since 'On the Twentieth Century.'"[40]

The timing of Canby's review could not have been better. Ticket sales rebounded and continued strong through the holidays. Then, however, as with many Broadway offerings, it began to struggle during the leaner winter months; by spring, it was playing at times to just over 50 percent capacity.

The decision to close came at the beginning of June, a little over a year after it opened, and when the curtain went down on *The Life* on June 7, it had played 466 performances. The show had consumed much of Coleman's attention for the past five years, meaning that for the first time in nearly a decade he watched one of his musicals shutter without knowing when his next one might be.

31

"It Needs Work"

When *The Life* played its final performance, Coleman was just one week away from his sixty-ninth birthday and still a newlywed. He had spent the bulk of the previous five years doing everything in his power to see that the musical reached Broadway, even as he embarked on his new relationship, and though he had juggled a quartet of projects (*The Life*, along with *City of Angels*, *Will Rogers*, and *Welcome to the Club*) along with personal matters just ten years before, he had not laid out a similar array of new shows for himself as the 1990s wound down.

True, there had been small projects (notably the mini–movie musical *A Simple Melody*), and Coleman had continued his philanthropic work. There had also been talk of shows that he might be working on, ranging from a musicalized version of the 1957 film *Sweet Smell of Success* to a stage version of the iconic film *A Star Is Born* for Andrew Lloyd Webber's Really Useful Company, but only one show had gone beyond the talking phase while Coleman was getting *The Life* into production.

The show was a revision of his 1989 flop, *Welcome to the Club*, and by the spring of 1998 it was in good enough shape to receive a developmental production at Goodspeed Musicals' Norma Terris Theatre in Chester, Connecticut. This new property was called *Exactly Like You*, and Coleman had devised it with his *Club* collaborator A. E. Hotchner and Pat Birch (who had done musical staging for the original). She recalled that after *Club* closed, "[Cy] wanted to play around with it, and I said, 'Let me take it and really do something totally different with it.' I came up with the idea of doing it in the courtroom. And getting rid of a lot of the macho stuff."[1]

Hotchner set about rewriting the show with Birch's thoughts in mind, and what emerged was a musical set in a courtroom where a man was on trial for assaulting his meddlesome and intrusive mother in-law. Friction understandably ran high between the defendant and his spouse, who still had deep feelings for one another, and as the trial proceeded, other romantic feuds developed. The female prosecutor and male defense attorney—once married—were still in love. Additionally, one of the jurors, a country singing star, came to the court wounded from her first four marriages and found a potential match in a man (her polar opposite) empaneled along with her.

The show also satirized America's thirst for televised trials (which had reach an apogee a few years earlier with the murder trial of O. J. Simpson), and the action was frequently interrupted by commentary from the anchors observing the events in the courtroom. Coleman and Hotchner also returned to a device used in *I Love My Wife*, and the production's four musicians doubled as performers, with the judge, for instance, serving as the keyboard player.

Coleman described the show as "a very sweet, zany and darling story. If you ask me what's it close to, I'd say it's closer to [the film] 'Adam's Rib' than 'Welcome to the Club.'" He had written over a dozen new songs for *Exactly Like You*, which were augmented by a handful of tunes from *Welcome to the Club* that had been repurposed and a couple that were performed as originally written, including "At My Side." As Coleman commented, "I'm not going to throw out a good ballad that works. What am I? a fool?"[2]

The staging in Connecticut gave the creators a clear sense of what revisions still needed to be made, and then, in early 1999, *Exactly Like You* got a second outing, in New York at Off-Broadway's York Theatre Company. The basic arc of the show remained, as did most of the score. The heaviest revisions involved its first moments, which gained a "Courtroom Cantata," and its finale, where a number was tweaked to turn it into a title song. Unlike the presentation in Connecticut, the York production was open to reviewers, and although the material had changed, the critics' response was not much different than that for *Welcome to the Club*. Charles McNulty, writing in *Variety* on April 19, described the show as a "new musical comedy that never manages to transcend the silliness of its book," adding that "not even the lushly varied rhythms of Coleman's score can salvage the shamelessly cliché-ridden antics."

Peter Marks's *New York Times* review on April 27 noted Coleman's determination to make a success out of the older musical and then said that the new one "suggests that fealty to one's failures in no way guarantees an eventual transfer to the win column." If there was one "win" to be had from the production, it had already come by the time Marks's piece ran: Coleman had scored a Drama Desk Award nomination for outstanding music.

After the engagement at the York, Coleman, Hotchner, and Birch continued to revise, rework, and retitle the show. A few years later it resurfaced, slightly modified, under the name *Lawyers, Lovers, and Lunatics*, playing at the Parker Playhouse in Fort Lauderdale, the Royal Poinciana Playhouse in Palm Beach, and the Forum Theatre in Metuchen, New Jersey. With all of these stagings, Coleman demonstrated how he had learned the ropes of developing new work through the American regional theater system. This musical was one of four that he would test out in this manner over the course of the next five years, while another would be produced outside the American model altogether.

The musical that took Coleman abroad was also the one that allowed him to work with a financial freedom he hadn't had on Broadway in many years: *Grace*, a show about Grace Kelly, the American film star who became princess of Monaco. The piece was the brainchild of Dutch businessman-turned-producer Bert Maas, who had a twofold agenda. He wanted to pay tribute to the actress who had fascinated him when he was a teenager, and in doing so he also hoped to establish a theatrical empire akin to that of Joop van den Ende, who since 1988 had been successfully carving out a niche for himself in Holland as a producer of popular musicals.

Before approaching Coleman about writing the score, Maas engaged a book writer–lyricist, Seth Gaaikema, who began his career in musical theater in 1956 translating English lyrics for Dutch productions. Among his earliest credits in the late 1950s and early 1960s were shows like *My Fair Lady* and *Oliver!* Gaaikema had also enjoyed a career as a popular television comedian.

His script centered on Kelly's life with Prince Rainier of Monaco, following her from just before her marriage through the early 1960s, when Alfred Hitchcock, who directed her in *Rear Window*, *Dial "M" for Murder*, and *To Catch a Thief*, was trying to lure her back to Hollywood to star in the film *Marnie*. Under pressure from the royal family, she ultimately turned down the role, and Gaaikema used this slice of her life to explore how Kelly had been consistently manipulated by men—first her father, then the director, and finally her husband.

While putting the show together Maas also hired a director, Frans Weisz, who had never worked in the theater but had a number of film credits, including the 1975 comedy *Red Sien* and a 1988 drama, *Havinck*, which was screened at Cannes. Together the two men cast the show's principals. Dutch musical theater luminaries Joke de Kruijf and Ernst Daniel Smid would play Kelly and Rainier, respectively, while Rob van de Meeberg was cast as Hitchcock.

It was at this juncture that Maas turned to Coleman. When they met in 2000, Maas described his plans for *Grace*, which was going to open in a theater that would be built especially for the production. Maas was sparing no expense in creating the venue, which would ultimately become a palace worthy of a princess, studded with crystal chandeliers, outfitted with huge murals, and surrounded by wrought iron gates bearing the initial "G."

Beyond his plans for the decor of the facility, Maas had also engaged a celebrated designer for the musical itself: Broadway's Eugene Lee (the scenic designer for Harold Prince's landmark stagings of *Candide* and *Sweeney Todd*). Maas was prepared to commission Coleman for the score, and in addition he was committed to paying for Coleman, his family, and his creative team to live in Amsterdam during rehearsals.

It was an offer Coleman couldn't refuse. After he accepted, he reached out to Birch. As Coleman's wife, Shelby, recalled, "He said, 'I'm not going to do this with someone who doesn't know how to stage a show.'"[3] Birch remembered, "Cy called me and told me that the producer had all the money in the world. And there was a great set, and they were building a new theater."[4]

At this juncture Coleman needed to figure out what sort of music the show required. He later reflected, "A lot of that was determined by the fact that they cast it before the show was written, which is amazing to me. They have to do that in Holland, they told me, because if you want some stars, there's a limited talent pool." After he heard the principals sing, he decided that the show would require "big music. . . . These are not small voices. Musically, I wanted to do a meld of European style and American style—the European feeling along with American pizzazz."[5]

Coleman's aims for the music were more than thoroughly realized. The show boasted over two dozen numbers—lushly romantic waltzes, buoyant ragtime, and seductive jazz. Furthermore, Coleman gave all of the music the sort of dramatic sweep that one associates with movies from the era of the studio system in Hollywood. More than any score he had written since *On the Twentieth Century, Grace* demonstrated the fusion of his classical, pop, and theater experience, and when played by a thirty-seven-piece orchestra using lush orchestrations by Don Sebesky, it had a grandeur unlike any score he had previously written for the stage.

But Coleman's accomplished music was part of a production that faced significant obstacles. As Birch described it, "The guy who was directing couldn't get control of a big musical. I had a huge job helping him out and choreographing at the same time. . . . And the rules are on their side. You cannot fire anybody. So was it easy? No. Was it fun? Sometimes. We had good times. We were living right next door to each other. Shelby cooked. We had wonderful dinners."[6]

Beyond Birch and his own family, Coleman also brought another American to Amsterdam: Mary-Mitchell Campbell, who served as musical coordinator on the show. Coleman and Campbell had come to know one another three years earlier when she served as rehearsal pianist for a concert presentation of *Sweet Charity* that was a starry benefit for Broadway Cares/Equity Fights AIDS. "The first time he ever spoke to me was coming over to the piano to ask me to transpose 'There's Got to Be Something Better Than This' for Chita Rivera," Campbell recalled.[7] Shortly after this, he phoned and asked her to come to Connecticut to assist with a Hole in the Wall Gang benefit. During her time there, she found herself sight-reading for renowned violinist Isaac Stern, in performance.

"I begged Cy to do it. I said something about him having played Carnegie Hall, and I said, 'You should go out and play for Isaac Stern and sight-read for him in concert.' My favorite part of that whole story was that he said, 'You're young. You're resilient.' But then he came out on the stage and helped me fix the music stand, which was broken, and I was like, 'You don't have to come out and do this.' And he was like, 'Well, I'm not going to *abandon* you.'"[8]

In retrospect, Campbell realized that the incident was "a bit of a litmus test,"[9] and when it came time to do *Grace*, he invited her to be part of the team. In addition to serving as the musical coordinator, she collaborated with Coleman on the arrangements.

Campbell described her time in Amsterdam as "a wild adventure" and shared several revelatory stories about the show's development. "[Eugene Lee] ended up leaving. I don't honestly remember why, and we had a different set designer come in to make [Lee's sets] work, and that was not the most successful marriage. It was very amusing, because all of these set pieces were showing up and nobody knew really what they were for."[10]

Beyond the problems with the physical production and extensive delays in the construction of the theater itself, there were difficulties because of the language barrier between the American and Dutch collaborators. Coleman and Gaaikema developed methods of communication while working on the songs. At times Gaaikema would describe the mood and the emotional through-line of a scene, and from this Coleman would write a melody to which Gaaikema would set a lyric. Or sometimes Gaaikema would provide Coleman with a lyric, which he also recited, so that the composer could hear the rhythms, and then a melody would be developed.

Campbell explained that Coleman had never been given exact translations of the lyrics, and this became an issue. During the opening of the second act, a scene set on Aristotle Onassis's boat, one song "wasn't getting a very good response when we were in previews. And we weren't sure what was going on with it. So Cy comes to me one day in the theater and says, 'I think we need to think about cutting it. I think it's just too long. I think people just get bored.'"[11]

Before trimming the song, however, Coleman asked Campbell, who had a working knowledge of Dutch, to translate a lyric. "I said, 'Well, the start is "Power makes me horny. Power, I really like it."' And he said, 'That can't be right.' And I was like 'Uh-huh.' And he's like, 'That can't be what it says.' And I said, 'I'm pretty confident on this one.' And so he called a couple of directors and asked them, 'Can you tell us what this means.' And they said the same thing. So he looked at me, 'Well. Maybe it's not the music.'"[12]

Eventually the troubled show reached its opening night in October 2001. Critical reception was tepid at best. In the city's morning daily, *Volkskrant*, critic Hein Janssen took the production to task on every level, including the ostentatiousness of the theater's decor.

For Coleman and his colleagues, the reviews were an end to what had been a difficult process, and so they decided to enjoy some time in Amsterdam before returning home. The night after the opening a group of them took a canal boat ride and at one point decided to take in a show in the city's famed red-light district. Coleman and Campbell were seated together, and as Campbell recalled, "The curtain went up, and it was a live sex show. So since we had this kind of fatherly/daughterly vibe to us, it was really kind of awkward. It was *really* awkward."[13]

After watching the proceedings onstage in silence, Campbell broke the ice "by saying something about them looking bored." She added, "He jumped on that and said, 'Yes. Yes. They look very bored. That's why I wrote 'Big Spender.'" Coleman continued talking about the genesis of the song from *Sweet Charity*, and then, Campbell said, "A woman came out—there were all of these vignettes—completely by coincidence doing her number to 'Big Spender.'"[14]

The performer's routine was the same as one seen in the movie *Priscilla, Queen of the Desert*. She danced "with things coming out of her body," as Campbell put it, before adding, "We started laughing, and we were on the third row. And I said, 'You play the best places.' And he said, 'Yes, but am I getting royalties?'"[15]

After Coleman left Amsterdam, *Grace* limped quietly into the New Year, sometimes playing to fewer than four hundred people in its specially built twelve-hundred-seat theater. Maas attempted to spur ticket sales but to little avail. Before the end of February 2002, the show closed at a complete loss, and Maas was facing lawsuits from creditors who had yet to be paid.

With *Grace* behind him, it was back to smaller-scale stagings for Coleman. One of these was for a tuner that had been on his plate for several years: a musical version of playwright Wendy Wasserstein's children's book *Pamela's First Musical*.

Wasserstein, who had won the Pulitzer Prize for her play *The Heidi Chronicles*, had hinted that she was collaborating with Coleman in 1998, but at the time she would not commit to what the show was about. Then, on January 20, 1999, the *Daily News* reported that *Will Rogers* producer Pierre Cossette would "develop a 'big-band musical' with Cy Coleman and Wendy Wasserstein to open next year."

Whether this show and the musical version of *Pamela* were one and the same is unclear, but by 2002 Coleman and Wasserstein, along with lyricist David Zippel, had been working on the project for a number of years. Zippel recalled its genesis. "When the book came out, I called [Wendy] and said, 'This would make a great TV musical. Let's write a TV musical about it.' She called me back about six months later and said, 'Okay. I have a producer. Let's do a TV musical. Let's pick a composer.' And I said, 'Who do you want?' And she said, 'I want Cy Coleman,' and I said, 'That's who I want,' and it was like a love match from the very beginning. The three of us were so happy and got along so well."[16]

Wasserstein's book tells of a young girl's fairy tale–like trip to Broadway, courtesy of her flamboyant Aunt Louise. For the musical Wasserstein expanded the story, providing the title character with a simple but effective conflict: attempting to reconcile her own extravagance and imagination, modeled on that of her aunt, with the more staid traditions of her widower father, her siblings, and her father's new girlfriend. In both the original illustrated book and the new script Wasserstein sent an unabashed valentine to the theater and the people who create it, and in writing the music for the show Coleman followed suit, creating a plethora of brassy, razzmatazz numbers that Zippel outfitted with insider jokes, puns, and references.

Once they had finished drafting their television musical, the creators began to think about casting. "When it came time to discuss who would play Aunt Louise, Cy, Wendy, and I thought that Meryl Streep [who had starred in one of Wasserstein's earliest plays, *Uncommon Women and Others*] would be an ideal choice," Zippel recalled, "so Wendy called Meryl, and Meryl read it and said, 'I'd love to do it.' But another script for a TV musical, *Geppetto*, starring Drew Carey, was further along in development, and Disney [which had been planning to produce *Pamela*] ended up making that movie instead. In an act of incredible kindness, they gave us the rights back when we asked if we could change *Pamela* into a stage musical, and that's how it became a stage musical."[17]

Shortly after Coleman's return from Amsterdam, he and his collaborators had the chance to explore how what they had written would work onstage through a series of workshops at Lincoln Center Theater, which had a long-standing relationship with the playwright, having produced *The Sisters Rosensweig* and *An American Daughter* on Broadway. Zippel remembered, "Andre Bishop [Lincoln Center Theater's artistic director] was kind enough to give us a workshop. He said, 'It isn't the kind of show we do, but we'd like to help you develop it.' So they gave us two workshops. It was a great experience, and we learned a lot from both of them."[18]

Beyond giving the authors an understanding of how the musical worked in performance, the workshops at Lincoln Center also helped propel the show to its next stage. Two developmental productions were scheduled. The first would be offered in late 2005 at Goodspeed Musicals' Norma Terris Theatre, where *Exactly Like You* started. The second was slated for 2006 at TheatreWorks in Palo Alto, another nonprofit dedicated to nurturing new musicals.

By this time Coleman's docket of shows in process had rebounded to the level of the late 1980s. One piece had actually been publicly presented during the course of the *Pamela* workshops and had started to look as if it might be a viable Broadway property. Another was inching toward its first public staging. Again, these two shows were developed under the auspices of nonprofit organizations, and both would help fill Coleman's schedule until *Pamela* was back in rehearsal.

Campbell, who, after *Grace,* was also part of the workshops for *Pamela,* noticed Coleman's penchant for working on multiple shows like this, and she asked him if he ever worried about working on too many shows at the same time. His response was: "'No. You need to have a lot of projects simultaneously, because they won't all happen, and they'll all get delayed. So you just have to keep plates spinning. But it's important that you do multiple things. If you just do one thing, you'll just be waiting and waiting and waiting. And I learned a long time ago that's not how you want to live your life.'"[19]

One of the "plates spinning" for Coleman was the song cycle *Portraits in Jazz*, which debuted at the Kennedy Center in Washington, D.C., in May 2002. He wrote it with lyricists Marilyn and Alan Bergman, the Oscar- and Grammy-winning team who had penned the lyrics for songs ranging from "The Way We Were" to "The Summer Knows." Alan Bergman recalled how the project began: "Billy Taylor called us one day from the Kennedy Center. He said, 'If we commission you to write a jazz song cycle, would you write it?' And we said, 'Yeah. But what is that?' He said, 'It's whatever you would like.' And then we said, 'With whom would you like us to write it?' He said, 'You pick the composer.' And we called Cy, because of his jazz roots."[20]

During their initial conversation about the project, after reiterating the Bergmans' original question about what a jazz song cycle might be, Coleman quickly joined them in creating it. He later said that the answer that he and the Bergmans had arrived at for their mutual query was to craft a series of songs "about the jazz world. . . . About the people who inhabit it. . . . About the people who play in it. About the lives of the musicians, the managers, the people who hang out in the bars." In doing this, he said, the song cycle "became about jazz."[21]

Beyond allowing them to explore new ground in the creation of a completely undefined piece, the collaboration with Coleman gave the Bergmans a chance to work in a new manner. "We prefer to write to music. That's our preference, but with Cy—and more often than with any other composer—we worked with him in a room," Alan Bergman said. Marilyn Bergman added, "I think it was because he had so much to contribute." Alan Bergman agreed and then gave an example: "We got an idea, and we wrote down four or five lines. And he looked at it and he said, 'Well, you know, how do you hear this?' Asking us which way he should go rather than putting it down on the piano."[22]

The team ultimately developed fifteen songs. Some were biographical, such as "The Double Life of Billy T.," which paid tribute to Dorothy Tipton, who dressed as a man in order to find work as a jazz pianist. Others were more atmospheric, such as the gentle, bluesy ballad "Music You Know by Heart" and the smooth, Latin-influenced "In Miami."

With the pieces written for the show that Kennedy Center materials described as "part concert, part theater, part series of 'jazz ruminations,'" a cast was assembled that included Broadway performer Lillias White in addition to jazz singers Carl Anderson, Patti Austin, Janis Siegel, and Steve Tyrell. *Portraits in Jazz* was offered for a single performance, and as Alan Bergman remembered, "It was a smash. . . . When it was over, they came to us saying, 'This is just the intermission, right?' And we'd only done fifteen songs. We didn't have any more."[23]

The audience's reaction that evening prompted Coleman to turn to his collaborators and say, "Well, we can't do this for just for one night. Let's make a theater piece out of it." So they set about trying to refashion the show into a traditional musical format. But this raised a question, as Marilyn Bergman observed: "It was a series of songs, . . . [and] each song was a kind of self-contained story. So, if each little song is a kind of self-contained story, how do you connect them?"[24]

Birch, who staged the concert, thought that Warren Leight, author of the Tony Award– and Pulitzer Prize–winning play *Side Man*, who had also contributed to the event, would be an ideal candidate for further developing the show. "But then Cy goes to Larry Gelbart," she said, "and Larry comes up with this idea of a sort of Everyman who's going to explain jazz."[25]

The idea stuck. The songs were packaged in a show named *Like Jazz* (echoing the phrase "like cool, man"), and it was put on the schedule for the 2003–4 season at the Mark Taper Forum in Los Angeles. The theater's artistic director, Gordon Davidson, would direct, and Birch would choreograph. The cast for the new incarnation of the show once again featured Austin and White, along with Harry Groener (a Tony nominee for his performances in *Cats*, *Crazy for You*, and the 1980 revival of *Oklahoma!*), who was cast in the new role developed by Gelbart. Along with a ten-person dance ensemble, the musical also had as headliners another Broadway veteran, Cleavant Derricks (a Tony winner for *Dreamgirls*), and vocalists Jennifer Chada and Jack Sheldon.

After a rehearsal period that Birch simply characterized as being "pretty funny,"[26] *Like Jazz* opened and received the sort of praise the creators might have expected after the initial Washington concert. In his review in the *Los Angeles Times* on December 5, Reed Johnson said that they had found "a way to translate this relentlessly shape-shifting art form into a warmly memorable entertainment." Johnson praised Gelbart's conceit for pulling the disparate songs together, calling it "a spare but effective narrative through-line," adding, "Yet in the main, the show's coherency derives from the practically seamless fit between the Bergmans' charming, sophisticated lyrics and Coleman's effortlessly urbane melodies." In the *Los Angeles Daily News* that day, Evan Henerson found more to praise in the cast than the material, but he did predict that the show's songs would "have some staying power."

A few days later, on December 9, Tony Gieske's *Hollywood Reporter* review began with "Almost everything works in this 'new kind of musical,'" and the piece had a "Bottom Line" summary that said, "Songs about something like substance in a revue that is something else—something like a hit."

Only Phil Gallo, in a *Variety* notice from December 4, dissented. In his assessment of the show, saying it provided little except "a cursory history lesson and a load of stream-of-conscious malarkey in the text and lyrics."

The reviews in the general press ensured that *Like Jazz* played to capacity houses into early 2004, and at that point it looked as if the show was set for a Broadway transfer courtesy of Transamerica, which had provided enhancement money for the Taper production and was poised to serve as the show's primary Broadway producer. Unfortunately, the company had invested and lost money on two other Broadway shows, *Brooklyn* and *Hot Feet*, and this prompted the withdrawal of Transamerica's planned support of *Like Jazz*.

"The Transamerica people came to us and said, 'We're going to get out of Broadway. Whatever you have of ours, you keep. Good luck to you.' . . . And that was the end of that," Alan Bergman recalled.[27] It was just another example of the kind of delay to which Coleman had become accustomed.

Unsurprisingly, even as *Like Jazz* opened, he was back on the East Coast preparing another musical, *The Great Ostrovsky*. Coleman had first started on this show in late 1998, the same year he had begun *Pamela*, as a vehicle for comedian and satirist Alan King, who in addition to his work in clubs and onscreen had Broadway credits as a performer and producer.

For this tuner, set in the halcyon days of the Yiddish Theater in New York, when companies dedicated to presenting work specifically for Jewish audiences abounded on the Lower East Side, Coleman was working with yet another new collaborator, but one who was an old acquaintance: Avery Corman. "I had originally met [Cy] in St. Thomas in the '60s when he was down there visiting a friend of his, Marty Clark, a songwriter who wrote with Bob Haymes," Corman recalled.[28] Since that time they had stayed in touch, primarily through their friend David Newman, who had written the book for *The Life*. In the intervening years Corman had written the screenplays for movies such as *Oh, God!* and *Kramer vs. Kramer*. When the idea of *Ostrovsky* first came up, Coleman approached Corman, sensing he would have an affinity for the material.

Corman drafted a script about a fictional impresario, David Ostrovsky, who, as the musical opens, is enjoying success with adaptations of classics ranging from a musical version of *The Dybbuk* to a version of *King Lear* with a happy ending. Unfortunately, changing times and the machinations of unscrupulous producers undermine the man, forcing him to retire, but only briefly. In the tradition of the character's own productions, Ostrovsky gets to enjoy a theatrical comeback and a happy ending.

Coleman returned to his earliest musical roots for this piece, writing a score filled with the klezmer music that his parents so enjoyed. He did not, however, work in mere pastiche. "[Coleman] says he liked the story and the challenge of incorporating the distinctive sound of klezmer music into a Broadway score" was the way that Douglas J. Keating described the composer's work in a March 17 *Philadelphia Inquirer* feature.

One thing Coleman didn't talk about with Keating was the provenance of one song in the score, "On Top," which had a melody that came from Coleman's trunk. He had written it in 1995 for Liza Minnelli when she replaced a vacationing Julie Andrews in *Victor/Victoria*. The song had gone unused, so when *Ostrovsky* came around he pulled it out and penned a new klezmer-sounding verse that segued into a driving Broadway-style showstopper.

Coleman might have been able to transform a quintessential Minnelli tune into a song for the company manager of a Yiddish theater troupe, but he was not able to reconcile his own hard-nosed business sense with King's. According to Corman, "there was never any legal work done between any of the parties" while the script and score were being drafted, and when it came time for contracts to be written, King made demands. Coleman told Corman that he found King's conditions "untenable," and then, Corman said, "Suddenly I got a phone call from Alan one day, 'I'm not going forward with this. The terms are not what I want.'"[29]

"What happened next, after Alan withdrew," Corman remembered, "is Cy knew Marjorie Samoff, who was running the Prince Music Theater in Philadelphia, and he got in touch with her, and then they offered us a production."[30] The staging, however, would be dependent on the nonprofit's securing the funding for it.

Eventually, the theater committed to the show, asking Douglas C. Wager, who, after a long tenure at Arena Stage in Washington, D.C., had just joined the Prince's staff as director in residence, to stage it. In addition to Wager, the show's creative team would include Birch, who would both choreograph and codirect.

A Broadway-worthy cast was assembled for the three-week Philadel-phia engagement. Bob Gunton (who earned a Tony nomination for his performance as Juan Perón in *Evita* when it debuted in America) was cast as Ostrovsky. The company also featured Louise Pitre (fresh off her success as Donna Sheridan in *Mamma Mia!*) and Jonathan Hadary (who received a Tony nomination for his performance as Herbie opposite Tyne Daly in *Gypsy*), along with such Broadway veterans as Nick Corley, Paul Kandel, Daniel Marcus, and Kirsten Wyatt.

Bringing the show to life was by all reports difficult. As the creators worked to refine it, artistic differences developed. Corley recalled it as "one of those shows where, if they wanted to talk about the piece itself, we were ushered into the hallway. We spent a lot of time there." He added, "The budget aspect of the show was stressful. . . . [It] kept getting slashed, but they were still trying to get the show on. So there was supposed to be an ensemble, and the ensemble got cut from the show right before we started rehearsal, so we had like, what, a two-person ensemble."[31]

Corman, too, remembered how the show's limited finances affected things, particularly the music: "I always thought for budget reasons we were short an instrument that would have given it a bigger lift, and the music would have more of a klezmer feel than it had."[32]

Regardless of these issues, Corley said, "It was a happy group, and I think a lot of that was Cy. I mean, we didn't really care because we were working with Cy, and he was building songs on us. He made us all feel good about what we were doing. And I have to say that that was the fun of it."[33]

For Corley, one particularly enjoyable number was a comic patter song that he shared with Daniel Marcus, who recalled, "About two weeks into rehearsal—there was a side room directly across the hall from where we were—Cy says, 'Come over here. Come in here.' And we go in and he just starts playing." It was there that Coleman built the arrangements and expanded on the tune, telling the actors, "Try this and you try this."[34] "It was," as Corley said, "classical musical comedy, like a scene from a movie."[35]

Once in Philadelphia the company continued to face changes. "The opening number did change every single day up until the moment we opened," Corley recalled, "and we were like, 'Can we pick a version to go out and do for the audience tonight?'"[36] And yet, Marcus pointed out, "[Cy] was all guns firing trying to come up with solutions. And he was so happy. That's the thing I take away most from that experience. You know the guy with the thing in Boston that's not working out and that pressure and that need to come up with something. . . . [Cy] liked that pressure."[37]

The Great Ostrovsky did finally face the critics, almost all of whom found ways to praise the music. "Coleman is known for his masterful melodies–and 'Ostrovsky' is loaded with them," wrote J. Cooper in a March 23 *Philadelphia Weekly* review. In the March 23 edition of the *Jewish Exponent* on the same day, Michael Elkin said that Coleman had written "show tunes that show a bravura and braggadocio underscoring the unctuous and the anxious who dominated Second Avenue."

The problem, both critics felt, was with Corman's book. "Corman doesn't take a page out of the life of Yiddish theater's titans; he shreds it, bissel by bissel," was Elkin's assessment, while Cooper used his praise of the songs to damn Corman's work, writing, "If only Corman's story were as full-bodied as the show's score."

Neither book nor score was praised in the *Variety* review that ran on April 4, after the show had concluded its limited engagement. With the notices in mind, Coleman and Corman began to consider their next steps with *The Great Ostrovsky.* As the year progressed, this project, along with *Grace*, *Pamela's First Musical*, and a few others in earlier stages of development, would occupy Coleman, as would his family life and a return to the realm of performing.

32

Finale

As Coleman was juggling these myriad projects, he was also taking on a new personal responsibility. His wife, Shelby, remembered how he was the first to raise the subject of having children. "He came home one day and said, 'I realize I never asked you . . . do you want to have kids?' And I said, 'Yeah, well you know. . . .' (I was 38 at the time.) 'Yeah, I'd like to have kids, but I think the time might have passed.' And he was like, 'No. No. I never thought about it, but if you want to have kids, we should have kids!' And I said something, and then he said, 'Yes. You should have a kid!' A friend had convinced him he was depriving me of motherhood.'"[1]

Coleman's sudden interest in the idea of children may have come from his friend journalist Malcolm MacPherson, a man he had known since the late 1960s, when they met at a house party in London. Coleman later became godfather to one of MacPherson's children. And as MacPherson's widow, Charlie, recounted, "Cy was so great with the kids. He would basically buy out F. A. O Schwartz, and these gifts would come in boxes the size of a refrigerator. He was just so generous."[2]

It was just one instance of the paternal instincts Coleman showed over the years. Houston Huddleston, son of one of Coleman's early collaborators, Floyd Huddleston, remembered how Coleman helped him out as he began his career, "Cy wrote my introductory letter when I was trying to get into the American Film Institute."[3]

Beyond such relationships, Coleman demonstrated a father's instinct with music director Mary-Mitchell Campbell ever since they first met:

"He was very mentorlike, and he also had a kind of fatherly overtone with me. It was a surrogate father kind of thing. . . . He really wanted to teach me, and it was obvious that he had taken a real interest in and made an investment in my career."[4]

At home he and Shelby continued talking about having children. Eventually, she said, "We both went through the humiliating, horrible process of fertility testing. His was the least of it. Mine was a lot more invasive. . . . He was given a clean bill. He came home one day, saying, 'It ain't me, baby. My fish are swimmin'.'"[5]

There was some question, however, about what would be necessary for her to conceive, and so rather than subjecting themselves to the rigors of proactive conception, the couple began to consider adoption and eventually embarked on that process.

There were some disappointments along the way, but eventually, in 2000, the couple brought home a baby girl, whom they named Lily Cye. She was born just as Coleman was finishing up his first full studio recording in nearly thirty years, *It Started with a Dream*. Shelby recalled that she flew to California on her own to be with Lily Cye's birth mother while Coleman stayed behind to finish up work on the CD. As soon as the child was born, though, he hopped a plane to California to be with his wife and new daughter.

According to both his wife and his friends, Coleman took to fatherhood quickly, and by the time Lily Cye was a toddler, Shelby remembered, "she had the run of the whole house. He had an open-door policy. It didn't matter who was there. Any collaborator he was working with at that time will tell you, she'd come in and he would stop everything to play with her, get down on the floor with her."[6] He even gave her a memento from his early career: the toy piano he had grudgingly played back in the 1950s.

Lily's presence was also felt at the theater while Coleman was working. She and her mother were present throughout the process of Coleman's work on *Grace* in Amsterdam (the toddler was even at the show's opening night), and Nick Corley remembered watching Coleman with his daughter during rehearsals for *The Great Ostrovsky* in Philadelphia: "When Shelby would come with his daughter, she would come running into the room, and he would pick her up and swirl her around and forty years just dropped away. It was great to watch that happen, to just see the years melt away. It always made me happy when they'd stop by rehearsal."[7]

The album he had been working on when Lily Cye was born hit stores in early 2002, and in tandem with its release, Coleman also made a rare cabaret appearance, offering two concerts at Joe's Pub at the Public Theater in March. They were his first cabaret appearances in nearly thirty years, and as Coleman indicated in an interview two years later, his absence from that world had not been intentional. Of performing, he said, "It's one of the things I have to do."[8] But with his work on Broadway, scheduling had always been an issue.

For a while in the 1970s, Coleman had been able to satisfy this need through his work with symphonies, where he could play just one night, but even this had proven to be problematic, and so he curtailed this side of his career. In October 1981, he described what had caused this for Barbara Delatiner and the *New York Times*: "'Here I was in Boston, trying to get things into shape [for *On the Twentieth Century*] . . . and I was expected to take off and go to Tulsa and Chattanooga and the last thing on my mind was playing a concert. Why, I had to find a piano shop that would let me use its Steinway, and I'd sneak away from rehearsal to go down into the shop's basement to practice. That was it. No more concerts and no more conflicts.'"

As Coleman was describing in 2004 how intrinsic performing was to his nature, he was preparing for a two-week stint at the uptown club Feinstein's at the Loews Regency Hotel, coincidentally just a few blocks away from the Sherry-Netherland Hotel, where he had had his first big success as an entertainer. "As soon as I heard 'Would you play these two weeks at Feinstein's?' I thought, 'Another opportunity. Let me get it ready.'"[9]

Coleman's stint at Feinstein's ran from October 12 to October 23, and in the show he offered up some of his hits, anecdotes about his career, and one interpretation of a jazz standard he had not written ("Green Dolphin Street"). It was an engagement that prompted Stephen Holden to write in the *New York Times* on October 22, "[Coleman] still commands the keyboard with the authority of a sharp-shooter."

After the Feinstein's gig, Coleman settled back into a routine of father and married man about town. There were meetings about his various musicals, including an upcoming revival of *Sweet Charity*, but, unusually, he was not in the throes of any rehearsal process. "I'm established now. I'm more secure and I'm not so hungry," he told Robin Finn for an October 8 *New York Times* feature. As for his social life, that also changed in the new century. Shelby recalled, "Our original deal when we were first together and got married was that we would stay home at least two nights a week. I made him promise me that. . . . So when Lily was born, before she came, I said, 'This has to change. We're going to flip it. We're going to have to be home five nights a week, and he did it.' He said, 'Okay.'"[10]

One evening out for the couple was November 18, 2004: the opening of Michael Frayn's play *Democracy*. It wasn't just an interest in one of Broadway's newest offerings that drew Coleman to the show; he was also there to support old friends. The production was staged by *City of Angels* and *The Life* director Michael Blakemore and featured James Naughton, who starred in Coleman's *I Love My Wife* and *Angels*.

After the performance the Colemans went to Tavern on the Green, where Cy had spent so many early mornings performing on the 1950s television show *Date in Manhattan*. During the course of the opening-night party, Coleman talked with A. R. Gurney about an English-language revision to the musical *Grace* and was waiting for Blakemore and Naughton to arrive when he complained that he was not feeling well. He and Shelby left the party and hurried to New York Presbyterian Hospital. As soon as they arrived at the emergency room, Coleman collapsed and died, a victim of heart failure. He was seventy-five years old.

In Coleman's November 20 obituary in the *New York Times*, Robert Berkvist quoted one of his final interviews. Just one month before he died, Coleman said, "Retirement? It won't work for me. I'm lucky to be in a profession where you can keep getting better. To put it in musician's terms, my chops are good."

The night before the obituary ran, the lights on Broadway were dimmed in tribute to a man who had had eleven musicals produced there, had written full scores for over a dozen others, and was at work on at least three more new musicals at the time of his death. It was a workload that well illustrated an anecdote his friend and colleague Campbell shared with Playbill.com the morning after her mentor's death: "We had talked a lot about doing a revue of his, of his work. . . . And he didn't want to do it because, he said, 'I'm not done.' . . ."

CODA

Coleman's sense of not being finished echoed well after his death, first with a revival of *Sweet Charity* starring Christina Applegate (best known for her work on television's *Married . . . with Children*) in the title role. Before he died, Coleman and director Walter Bobbie had begun examining songs originally intended for the show to see if they might be appropriate for the new staging. And although Coleman would not live to hear it performed on Broadway, "A Good Impression," one of his earliest collaborations with Dorothy Fields, was included in the production.

Beyond this, *Like Jazz* was rumored for the 2005–6 season for a while, but as of this writing it has not returned to the stage in any incarnation. However, another of Coleman's projects, *Pamela's First Musical*, has continued to evolve and receive stagings. In the spring of 2008 it was presented in a starry benefit concert at New York's Town Hall with two-time Tony winner Donna Murphy playing Aunt Louise. Later that year it was presented in an abbreviated form at an industry event in the hopes of attracting a producing team, and for a while it looked as if *Pamela* might make it to the stage. But as Coleman always knew, delays could and did happen. It wasn't until five years later that the musical resurfaced—with a new book writer attached, Tony Award–winning playwright Christopher Durang—and talk began that the show would be included on the schedule for Two River Theater in Red Bank, New Jersey, in 2016.

But even as these musicals struggled to come to the stage, some of the mainstays of Coleman's work continued to enjoy popularity among theater creators and audiences. In the United States, *On the Twentieth*

Century received a one-night-only concert production in 2005 as a benefit for the Actors' Fund, and in 2014 an often-discussed full-scale revival starring Tony and Emmy winner Kristin Chenoweth was officially slated for production in early 2015 by Roundabout Theater Company. The news of this production came just after another of Coleman's musicals, *Little Me*, had enjoyed an acclaimed presentation in New York as part of City Center's *Encores!* series.

In Great Britain a production of *Sweet Charity* that started at the Menier Chocolate Factory reached the West End for a run in 2010, and in 2013 a new production of *Barnum* starring American actor Christopher Fitzgerald and coproduced by hitmaker Cameron Mackintosh played at the Chichester Festival. A third British offering, a major revival of *City of Angels* at the Donmar Warehouse that opened in December 2014, was sold out for the entirety of its run months before its first performance.

Coleman's songbook has similarly lived on in a variety of ways. In 2009 New West Records released *The Best Is Yet to Come*. The album featured covers of songs like "Why Try to Change Me Now?" and "Too Many Tomorrows" by popular stars such as Fiona Apple and Patty Griffin. That year also saw a revue of Coleman's songs, also titled *The Best Is Yet to Come* and assembled by David Zippel, premiere in Los Angeles. The show provided audiences with a chance to look back on Coleman's well-known tunes while also premiering several numbers from one other show that he had been working on at the time of his death: a musical about Napoleon Bonaparte, with lyrics by Zippel and a book by Larry Gelbart.

As Zippel recalled, "It was Larry who had the idea of doing *Napoleon*. It was something that both Cy and I both thought, 'Really?' But when he talked about his point of view and the way to tell the story, it was really intriguing. And because it was Larry Gelbart and he was such a great wordsmith and had such great dramaturgical skills, we realized this could be something really special. . . . It was about these two people who were in love with one another but never at the same time."[1]

The conceit for the show was that it opened at Malmaison, one of the grandiose homes shared by Napoleon and Josephine, after it had fallen into disrepair. Audiences were to have been taken into their world and back into their heyday courtesy of the Marquis de Sade as he looked back on their love affair.

When the revue had its New York premiere two years later, the song list had been slightly revised but still included numbers from the Napoleon project. Erik Haagensen described one of them in a review for *Back Stage*, "Only the Rest of My Life," as being "a tantalizing mixture of passion and humor." He went on to write that the four selections in the revue "suggest [the Napoleon musical] has a score of rare quality."[2]

Sadly, Coleman's death, which was followed by Gelbart's passing in 2009, means that the show will remain unfinished. As Zippel said, "It was theatrical and really interesting. Only Larry could write it in this way, and that's one of the reasons why there was no point in moving forward after we lost Larry, but first we lost Cy."[3]

The revue's New York premiere coincided with what would have been Coleman's eightieth birthday—nearly sixty years after his debut as a songwriter. Though styles and tastes had changed in the intervening decades, critics were still praising the composer's facility with a melody. In his May 26 review in the *New York Times*, Charles Isherwood saluted the "coolly swinging, jazz-inflected compositions" and said the music had "style and flash of its own." In many respects, Isherwood's final description of Coleman's music could have been applied to the composer himself.

SELECTED BIBLIOGRAPHY

Listed below are the books consulted in the preparation of *You Fascinate Me So*. All newspaper and magazine articles and reviews referenced are indicated in the body of the text or in footnotes. For a discography of Coleman's recordings, cast albums, and other 45s, LPs, and CDs featuring his work, visit www.YouFascinateMeSo.com.

Libretti

Bennett, Michael, and Dorothy Fields. *Seesaw*. New York: Samuel French, 1975.

Bramble, Mark, and Michael Stewart. *Barnum*. Garden City, New York: Nelson Doubleday, 1980.

Comden, Betty, and Adolph Green. *On The Twentieth Century*. New York: Samuel French, 1980.

Gelbart, Larry, and David Zippel. *City of Angels*. New York: Applause Theatre, 1990.

Simon, Neil, and Carolyn Leigh. *Little Me*. In *The Collected Plays of Neil Simon, Volume 2*. New York: Plume, 1977.

Simon, Neil, and Dorothy Fields. *Sweet Charity*. New York: Random House, 1966.

Stewart, Michael. *I Love My Wife*. New York: Samuel French, 1980.

Source Material/Inspiration

Baker, Russell. *Growing Up*. New York: New American Library, 1982.

Dennis, Patrick. *Little Me*. New York: E. P. Dutton, 1961.

Gibson, William. *Two for the Seesaw*. New York: Samuel French, 1960.

Rice, Elmer. *Dream Girl*. New York: Dramatists Play Service, 1973.

Sneider, Vern. *The King from Ashtabula*. New York: G. P. Putnam's Sons, 1960.

History, Biography, and Reference

Aerosmith, with Stephen Davis. *Walk This Way: The Autobiography of Aerosmith*. New York: HarperEntertainment, 2003.

Ball, Lucille. *Love, Lucy*. New York: Berkley Boulevard Books, 1996.

Balliett, Whitney. *American Musicians II: Seventy-one Portraits in Jazz*. New York: Oxford University Press, 1996.

———. *American Singers: 27 Portraits in Song*. New York: Oxford University Press, 1988.

———. *Collected Works: A Journal of Jazz, 1954–2000*. New York: St. Martin's Press, 2000.

Beddow, Margery. *Bob Fosse's Broadway*. Portsmouth, NH: Heinemann, 1996.

Belafonte, Harry, with Michael Shnayerson. *My Song: A Memoir*. New York: Alfred A. Knopf, 2011.

Bell, Marty. *Broadway Stories: A Backstage Journey Through Musical Theatre*. New York: Limelight Editions, 1993.

Bennett, Tony, with Will Friedwald. *The Good Life*. New York: Pocket Books, 1998.

Blakemore, Michael. *Arguments with England: A Memoir*. London: Faber & Faber, 2004.

Bloom, Ken. *American Song: The Complete Companion to Tin Pan Alley Song*. New York: Schirmer Books, 2001.

Brady, Kathleen. *Lucille: The Life of Lucille Ball*. New York: Hyperion, 1994.

Bricktop, with James Haskins. *Bricktop*. New York: Atheneum, 1983.

Bryer, Jackson R., and Richard A. Davison, eds. *The Art of the American Musical: Conversations with the Creators*. New Brunswick, NJ: Rutgers University Press, 2005.

Caesar, Sid, with Bill Davidson. *Where Have I Been? An Autobiography.*
New York: Crown, 1982.

Caesar, Sid, with Eddy Friedfeld. *Caesar's Hours: My Life in Comedy,
with Love and Laughter.* New York: PublicAffairs, 2001.

Cossette, Pierre. *Another Day in Showbiz: One Producer's Journey.*
Toronto: ECW Press, 2003.

Crow, Bill. *From Birdland to Broadway: Scenes from a Jazz Life.* New
York: Oxford University Press, 1992.

De Barros, Paul. *Shall We Play That One Together: The Life and Art of
Jazz Piano Legend Marian McPartland.* New York: St. Martin's Press,
2012.

Drell, Adrienne, ed. *20th Century Chicago: 100 Years, 100 Voices.*
Chicago: Sun-Times, 1999.

Evanier, David. *All the Things You Are: The Life of Tony Bennett.* New
York: John Wiley, 2011.

Feuer, Cy, with Ken Gross. *I Got the Show Right Here: The Amazing,
True Story of How an Obscure Brooklyn Horn Player Became the Last
Great Broadway Showman.* New York: Applause Theatre & Cinema
Books, 2003.

Filichia, Peter. *Broadway Musical MVPs, 1960–2010: The Most Valuable
Players of the Past 50 Seasons.* New York: Applause Theatre & Cinema
Books, 2011.

———. *Broadway Musicals: The Biggest Hit & the Biggest Flop of the
Season, 1959–2009.* New York: Applause Theatre & Cinema Books,
2010.

Flinn, Caryl. *Brass Diva: The Life and Legends of Ethel Merman.*
Berkeley and Los Angeles: University of California Press, 2007.

Friedwald, Will. *A Biographical Guide to the Great Jazz and Pop Singers.*
New York: Pantheon Books, 2010.

———. *Sinatra! The Song Is You: A Singer's Art.* New York: Scribner,
1995.

Frommer, Myrna Katz, and Harvey Frommer. *It Happened on Broadway:
An Oral History of the Great White Way.* New York: Harcourt Brace,
1998.

Gavin, James. *Intimate Nights: The Golden Age of New York Cabaret*. New York: Grove Weidenfield, 1991.

Gelbart, Larry. *Laughing Matters: On Writing "M*A*S*H," "Tootsie," "Oh, God!" and a Few Other Funny Things*. New York: Random House, 1998.

Gottfried, Martin. *All His Jazz: The Life and Death of Bob Fosse*. New York: Bantam Books, 1990.

Green, Stanley. *The World of Musical Comedy*. 4th ed., revised and enlarged. New York: Da Capo Press, 1984.

Greenspan, Charlotte. *Pick Yourself Up: Dorothy Fields and the American Musical*. New York: Oxford University Press, 2010.

Grubb, Kevin Boyd. *Razzle Dazzle: The Life and Work of Bob Fosse*. New York: St. Martin's Press, 1989.

Guernsey, Otis L. Jr., ed. *Broadway Song & Story: Playwrights/Lyricists/Composers Discuss Their Hits*. New York: Dodd, Mead, 1985.

Hadleigh, Boze. *Broadway Babylon: Glamour, Glitz, and Gossip on the Great White Way*. New York: Back Stage Books, 2007.

Hamill, Pete. *Why Sinatra Matters*. New York: Back Bay Books, 2003.

Harper, Valerie. *I, Rhoda: A Memoir*. New York: Gallery Books, 2013.

Haskins, James. *Mabel Mercer: A Life*. New York: Atheneum, 1987.

Haygood, Wil. *In Black and White: The Life of Sammy Davis, Jr.* New York: Billboard Books, 2003.

Hirsch, Foster. *Harold Prince and the American Musical Theatre*. Cambridge and New York: Cambridge University Press, 1989.

Hischak, Thomas S. *Word Crazy: Broadway Lyricists from Cohan to Sondheim*. New York: Praeger, 1991.

Hotchner, A. E. *Everyone Comes to Elaine's: 40 Years of Movie Stars, All-Stars, Literary Lions, Financial Scions, Top Cops, Politicians, and Power Brokers at the Legendary Hot Spot*. New York: HarperEntertainment, 2004.

Ilson, Carol. *Harold Prince: The Director's Journey*. New York: Limelight Editions, 2000.

Kanfer, Stefan. *Ball of Fire: The Tumultuous Life and Comic Art of Lucille Ball*. New York: Alfred A. Knopf, 2003.

Kasha, Al, and Joel Hirschhorn. *Notes on Broadway: Conversations with the Great Songwriters*. Chicago: Contemporary Books, 1985.

Kelly, Kevin. *One Singular Sensation: The Michael Bennett Story*. New York: Kensington, 1990.

Kissel, Howard. *David Merrick: The Abominable Showman, an Unauthorized Biography*. New York: Applause Books, 1993.

Lahr, John. *Show and Tell: "New Yorker" Profiles*. New York: Overlook Hardcover, 2000.

Lee, Peggy. *Miss Peggy Lee: An Autobiography*. New York: Donald J. Fine, 1989.

Leonard, William Torbert. *Broadway Bound: A Guide to Shows That Died Aborning*. Metuchen, NJ: Scarecrow Press, 1983.

Levinson, Peter. *September in the Rain: The Life of Nelson Riddle*. New York: Billboard Books, 2001.

Lipton, James. *Inside Inside*. New York: Dutton, 2007.

Lobenthal, Joel. *Tallulah! The Life and Times of a Leading Lady*. New York: Harper Entertainment, 2008.

Long, Robert Emmet. *Broadway, the Golden Years: Jerome Robbins and the Great Choreographer-Directors, 1940 to the Present*. New York: Continuum, 2001.

Mandelbaum, Ken. *"A Chorus Line" and the Musicals of Michael Bennett*. New York: St. Martin's Press, 1989.

———. *Not Since "Carrie": 40 Years of Broadway Musical Flops*. New York: St. Martin's Press, 1991.

McPartland, Marion. *Marian McPartland's Jazz World: All in Good Time*. Urbana and Chicago: University of Illinois Press, 1987.

Mordden, Ethan. *Broadway Babies: The People Who Made the American Musical*. New York: Oxford University Press, 1983.

———. *Coming Up Roses: The Broadway Musical in the 1950s*. New York: Oxford University Press, 1998.

———. *The Happiest Corpse I've Ever Seen: The Last 25 Years of the Broadway Musical*. New York: Palgrave Macmillan, 2004.

———. *One More Kiss: The Broadway Musical in the 1970s*. New York: Palgrave Macmillan, 2003.

———. *Open a New Window: The Broadway Musical in the 1960s*. New York: Palgrave Macmillan, 2001.

Ostrow, Stuart. *A Producer's Broadway Journey*. Westport, CT: Praeger, 1999.

Peterson, Bernard L. Jr. *A Century of Musicals in Black and White: An Encyclopedia of Musical Stage Works By, About, or Involving African Americans*. Westport, CT: Greenwood, 1993.

Rich, Frank. *Hot Seat: Theater Criticism for "The New York Times." 1980–1993*. New York: Random House, 1998.

Richmond, Peter. *Fever: The Life and Music of Miss Peggy Lee*. New York: Henry Holt, 2006.

Sanders, Coyne Steven, and Tom Gilbert. *Desilu: The Story of Lucille Ball and Desi Arnaz*. New York: HarperEntertainment, 2011.

Sheed, Wilfrid. *The House That George Built: With a Little Help from Irving, Cole, and a Crew of About Fifty*. New York: Random House, 2008.

Simon, Neil. *Rewrites: A Memoir*. New York: Simon & Schuster, 1996.

Simonson, Robert. *The Gentleman Press Agent: Fifty Years in the Theatrical Trenches with Merle Debuskey*. New York: Applause Theatre & Cinema Books, 2010.

Steyn, Mark. *Broadway Babies Say Goodnight: Musicals Then & Now*. New York: Routledge, 1999.

Suskin, Steven. *More Opening Nights on Broadway: A Critical Quotebook of the Musical Theatre, 1965–1981*. New York: Schirmer Books, 1997

———. *Opening Night on Broadway: A Critical Quotebook of the Golden Era of the Musical Theatre, "Oklahoma!" (1943) to "Fiddler on the Roof" (1964)*. New York: Schirmer Books, 1990.

———. *Second Act Trouble: Behind the Scenes at Broadway's Big Musical Bombs*. New York: Applause Theatre & Cinema Books, 2006.

———. *The Sound of Broadway Musicals: A Book of Orchestrators & Orchestrations*. New York: Oxford University Press, 2009.

Tune, Tommy. *Footnotes: A Memoir*. New York, New York: Simon & Schuster, 1997.

Viagas, Robert, ed. *The Alchemy of Theatre—The Divine Science: Essays on Theatre & the Art of Collaboration*. New York: Playbill Books, 2006.

Wasson, Sam. *Fosse*. New York: Eamon Dolan/Houghton Mifflin Harcourt, 2013.

Whorf, Michael. *American Popular Song Lyricists: Oral Histories, 1920s–1960s*. Jefferson, NC: McFarland, 2012.

Wilson, Earl. *Sinatra: An Unauthorized Biography*. New York: Macmillan Publishing, 1976.

Winer, Deborah Grace. *On the Sunny Side of the Street: The Life and Lyrics of Dorothy Fields*. New York: Schirmer Books, 1997.

NOTES

Chapter One

1 Michael Elkin, "Cy Coleman's Musical Invite: 'Hey! Look Me Over,'" *Jewish Exponent*, August 9, 1985, 50.

2 Robert Kaufman, interview by the author, October 23, 2013.

3 Ibid.

4 Cy Coleman, ASCAP Foundation Living Archive Project interview, September 17, 2002.

5 Terrie Curran, interview by the author, October 26, 2012.

Chapter Two

1 Alan and Marilyn Bergman, interview by the author, May 7, 2013.

2 Michael Elkin, "Cy Coleman's Musical Invite: 'Hey! Look Me Over,'" *Jewish Exponent*, August 9, 1985, 50.

3 Cy Coleman, interview on *Marian McPartland's Piano Jazz*, October 25, 1990.

4 Mark Barron, "Doings on Broadway," *Leader-Republican* (Gloversville and Johnstown, NY), May 3, 1951, 5.

5 Cy Coleman, interview by David Kenney, *Everything Old Is New Again*, WBAI-FM, New York, NY, October 10, 2004.

6 "Clear Music Use with Us, 2 Pubs Say," *Billboard*, May 11, 1946, 17.

7 "Suddenly Seymour—The Life of Cy Coleman," TotalTheater.com, posted March 2004, accessed January 9, 2014, http://www.totaltheater.com/?q=node/323.

8 Ibid.

9   Steve Schwartz, "Classical Net Review - Classical Broadway," Classical.
    net, posted 2003, accessed June 22, 2014, http://www.classical.net/
    music/recs/reviews/b/bcd01038a.php.

Chapter Three

1   Cy Coleman, "Remembering Adele," *Piano & Keyboard*, November/
    December 1995, 24.

2   Ibid.

3   Ibid., 26.

4   Ibid.

5   Leonard Green, interview by the author, October 8, 2013.

6   Leonard Green, interview by the author, January 13, 2014.

7   "Goings On About Town," *New Yorker*, September 11, 1946, 4. "Goings
    On About Town," *New Yorker*, September 18, 1946, 4.

8   Cy Coleman, interview on *Marian McPartland's Piano Jazz*, April 4, 1982.

9   Ibid.

10 Balliett, *American Singers*, 201.

11 "New Acts," *Variety*, May 4, 1949, 47.

12 Cy Coleman, interview on *Marian McPartland's Piano Jazz*, April 4, 1982.

13 Ibid.

14 Ruth Allan, interview by the author, August 12, 2013.

15 "Goings On About Town," *New Yorker*, September 3, 1949, 4.

16 "Goings On About Town," *New Yorker*, July 9, 1949, 3.

17 Sheridan Morley, "Cy Coleman: Three or Four at a Time," *Times*
    (London), October 5, 1977, 13.

18 Leonard Lyons, "The Lyons Den," *Democrat and Leader* (Davenport, IA),
    August 21, 1949, 18.

19 Cy Coleman, interview on *Marian McPartland's Piano Jazz*, April 4, 1982.

20 Douglas Watt, "Tables for Two: Step Lively," *New Yorker*, November 19,
    1949, 150.

21 Ibid.

Chapter Four

1   "Night Club Reviews," *Variety*, January 18, 1950, 46.

2 "Night Club Reviews," *Variety*, April 19, 1950, 54.

3 "TV's Daytime Dilemma: Service Shows, Entertainment or Combo," *Variety*, March 8, 1950, 36.

4 Sam Chase, "Kathi Norris Brings Sunlight into WNBT Return to Day TV," *Billboard*, May 13, 1950, 9.

5 John Lester, "'Operation Petticoat' Launched over Video," *Long Island Star-Journal*, May 3, 1950, 30.

6 Cy Coleman, interview by David Kenney, *Everything Old Is New Again*, WBAI-FM, New York, NY, October 10, 2004.

7 Stuart Troup, "The Times of a Drummer," *Newsday*, August 5, 1983, B29.

8 Mundell Lowe, interview by the author, December 1, 2012.

9 "Concert Artist Finds Himself Playing Toy Piano for TV," *North Tonawanda Evening News* (NY), September 6, 1951, 5.

10 Ibid.

11 Rob Kendt, "Time for the Solo, Composer Cy Coleman Scores 'Jazz' at Taper," *Los Angeles Downtown News*, December 1, 2003, 21.

Chapter Five

1. Louis Calta, "'Stalag 17' Opens Today at 48th St.," *New York Times*, May 8, 1951, 38.

2 Ibid.

3 Dorothy Kilgallen, *Lowell Sun* (MA), January 17, 1952, 26.

4 Dorothy Kilgallen, *Lowell Sun* (MA), January 29, 1952, 12.

5 Betsy von Furstenberg, interview by the author, March 29, 2013.

6 Ibid.

7 Ibid.

8 Ibid.

Chapter Six

1 Mundell Lowe, interview by the author, December 1, 2012.

2 Bill Crow, interview by the author, February 12, 2013.

3 Ibid.

4 Ray Mosca, interview by the author, October 15, 2013.

5 Mundell Lowe, interview by the author, December 1, 2012.

6 A. W., "'Meet Danny Wilson,' Starring Frank Sinatra, Is Feature at Paramount Theatre," *New York Times*, March 27, 1952, 34.

7 Friedwald, *Sinatra!*, 198.

8 "Greenwich Village Gets Its Follies," *New York Times*, July 16, 1919, 14.

9 Belafonte with Shnayerson, *My Song*, 112.

10 Ken Urmston, interview by the author, June 4, 2013.

11 Ibid.

12 Cyrus Durgin, "'Anderson's Almanac,' New Revue at Shubert," *Boston Globe*, November 6, 1953, 17.

13 Ken Urmston, interview by the author, June 4, 2013.

Chapter Seven

1 Haskins, *Mabel Mercer*, 82.

2 Cy Coleman, interview by David Kenney, *Everything Old Is New Again*, WBAI-FM, New York, NY, October 10, 2004.

3 D. W., "Musical Events—Popular Recordings," *New Yorker*, February 27, 1954, 103.

4 Leonard Lyons, "Attractive Model Questioned," *Evening Standard* (Uniontown, PA), May 13, 1954, 21.

5 Irv Roth, "Cy Coleman," Since 1917 blog, October 3, 2007, accessed July 25, 2013, http://irvroth.wordpress.com/2007/10/03/cy-coleman/.

6 "Goings On About Town," *New Yorker*, December 11, 1954, 6.

7 Douglas Watt, "Tables for Two: Men of Jazz," *New Yorker*, June 11, 1955, 79.

8 Cy Coleman, interview on *Marian McPartland's Piano Jazz*, April 4, 1982.

9 "Top 30 Songs on TV," *Variety*, February 15, 1956, 59.

10 Mel Heimer, "My New York," *Titusville Herald* (PA), February 17, 1956, 11.

11 Julie Newmar, interview by the author, March 18, 2013.

12 "Tallu $29,800 (6), May Fold, Philly; 'Teahouse' $45,623," *Variety*, May 9, 1956, 59.

13 Cy Coleman, interview on *Marian McPartland's Piano Jazz*, April 4, 1982.

14 "Goings On About Town," *New Yorker*, December 1, 1956, 8. "Goings On About Town," *New Yorker*, March 9, 1957, 8.

15 Ray Mosca, interview by the author, October 15, 2013.

Chapter Eight

1 Whorf, *American Popular Song Lyricists*, 135.
2 Cy Coleman, interview on *Marian McPartland's Piano Jazz*, April 4, 1982.
3 Ibid.
4 Ray Mosca, interview by the author, October 15, 2013.
5 Cy Coleman, interview on *Marian McPartland's Piano Jazz*, April 4, 1982.
6 Whorf, *American Popular Song Lyricists*.
7 Friedwald, *Sinatra!*, 250.
8 Walter Winchell, *Syracuse Herald-Journal* (NY), July 3, 1957, 23.

Chapter Nine

1 Charles Cochrane, interview by the author, August 17, 2013.
2 Dorothy Kilgallen, "Voice of Broadway," *Anderson Daily Bulletin* (Greenville, PA), September 25, 1958, 4.
3 Jonathan Schwartz, "Just Around the Corner," *New York Magazine*, December 19–26, 1988, page 117.
4 William Glover, "Five Shows at a Time: Composer Coleman's Hot as a Stove," *Independent Press-Telegram* (Long Beach, CA), September 18, 1977, B-10.
5 "Art Ford to Do a Weekly TV Program on the Village," *Village Voice*, July 17, 1957, 3.
6 Barbara Carroll, interview by the author, September 9, 2013.
7 Dorothy Kilgallen, "Jottings in Pencil," *Schenectady Gazette* (NY), November 14, 1958, 22. Walter Winchell, "Walter Winchell's Notes on Broadway," *Charleston Daily Mail* (WV), June 15, 1959, 8.
8 Barbara Carroll, interview by the author, September 9, 2013.
9 "30 Records for Christmas," *Vogue Incorporating Vanity Fair*, December 1959, 186.
10 Cy Coleman, ASCAP Foundation Living Archive Project interview, September 17, 2002.
11 Carolyn Leigh to Bud Morris, March 7, 1960, Carolyn Leigh archive, New York Public Library.
12 Ibid.

13 Mel Heimer, "My New York," *Journal-Tribune* (Marysville, OH), February 16, 1960, 7.

Chapter Ten

1 Hedda Hopper, "Columnist Pensive on Golden Globes," *Los Angeles Times*, March 11, 1960, 25.

2 John Crosby, "Lucy Gives Advice to the Hayes," *Lowell Sun* (MA), March 28, 1960, 17.

3 N. Richard Nash, "Notes on the Eve of Rehearsal," *Wildcat* souvenir program, 4.

4 Richard Gelman, "Theatre Arts Gallery: Lucille Ball," *Theatre Arts*, December 1960, 19.

5 Bill Becker, "Return to Films for Lucille Ball," *New York Times*, June 17, 1960, 16.

6 Michael Elkin, "An American Musical Drought? A Broadway Turned Purely British? Here's a Cy of Relief," *Jewish Exponent*, August 28, 1987, 11X.

7 Viagas, *The Alchemy of Theatre*, 28.

8 Ibid.

9 Ibid.

10 Brady, *Lucille*, 264.

11 Clifford David, interview by the author, May 22, 2013.

12 Valerie Harper, interview by the author, April 10, 2013.

13 Ward Morehouse, "Demure Lucy to Debut in 'Wildcat,'" *Long Island Star-Journal*, September 7, 1960, 18.

14 "Lucy Takes Singing Lessons for Musical Comedy Debut," *Times Recorder* (Zanesville, OH), September 25, 1960, section 2B.

15 Brady, *Lucille*, 265.

16 Ball, *Love, Lucy*, 220.

17 Clifford David, interview by the author, May 22, 2013.

18 Harper, *I, Rhoda*, 49.

19 June Bundy, "Morris for Pre-Opening Exposure," *Billboard*, November 21, 1960, 6.

20 Ball, *Love, Lucy*, 220.

21 Sanders and Gilbert, *Desilu*, 244.

22 Kanfer, *Ball of Fire*, 225.

23 "Humor in Theatre Is Discussed At Meeting of the Drama Desk," *New York Times*, January 10, 1961, 28.

24 Brady, *Lucille*, 265.

25 "'Wildcat' Is Closed While Lucy's Sick," *Newsday*, February 7, 1961, 3C.

26 Dorothy Kilgallen, "The Voice of Broadway," *Coshocton Tribune* (OH), February 14, 1961, 4.

27 "Asides and Ad-Libs," *Variety*, April 5, 1961, 72.

28 "'Wildcat' Closing to Rest Miss Ball," *Cedar Rapids Gazette* (MI), May 30, 1961, 22.

Chapter Eleven

1 Ray Mosca, interview by the author, October 15, 2013.

2 Cy Coleman, interview on *Marian McPartland's Piano Jazz*, October 25, 1990.

3 Cy Coleman, ASCAP Foundation Living Archive Project interview, September 17, 2002.

4 Cy Coleman, interview on *Marian McPartland's Piano Jazz*, October 25, 1990.

5 Bennett with Friedwald, *The Good Life*, 172.

6 "Television Reviews," *Variety*, November 4, 1959, 42.

7 "Reviews and Ratings of New Albums," *Billboard*, September 5, 1960, 32.

8 Drell, *20th Century Chicago*, 133.

9 Sylvia Miles, interview by the author, July 31, 2013.

10 Hotchner, *Everyone Comes to Elaine's*, 43.

11 Earl Wilson, "Chess(ty) Sylvia Miles Fibbed," *Delaware County Daily Times* (PA), March 5, 1970, 39.

12 "To Cure Tension, Make Furniture, She Says," *Big Spring Herald* (TX), September 12, 1960, 5-A.

13 Earl Wilson, "Chess(ty) Sylvia Miles Fibbed," *Delaware County Daily Times* (PA), March 5, 1970, 39.

14 Lee Mortimer, "New York Confidential," *Pharos-Tribune* (IN), February 10, 1961, 4.

Chapter Twelve

1 Kasha and Hirschhorn, *Notes on Broadway*, 53.

2 L. K. Rose, "Investor's Report," *Back Stage*, May 19, 1961, 10.

3 Guernsey, *Broadway Song & Story*, 177.

4 Kasha and Hirschhorn, *Notes on Broadway*.

5 Feuer with Gross, *I Got the Show Right Here*, 235.

6 Whitney Bolton, "Glancing Sideways," *Evening Times* (Cumberland, MD), September 28, 1962, 6.

7 Earl Wilson, "Groucho Makes O'Brian's Broadway Debut Tonight," *Press-Telegram* (Long Beach, CA), December 28, 1961, B11.

8 Earl Wilson, "It Happened Last Night," *Newsday*, February 2, 1962, 6C.

9 Dorothy Kilgallen, "Joan Robertson Is Proving It's a Woman's World," *Lowell Sun* (MA), February 10, 1962, 8.

10 Howard Taubman, "Theatre: 'How to Succeed' a Success," *New York Times*, October 16, 1961, 34.

11 Simon, *Rewrites*, 111.

12 Emile Charlap, interview by the author, May 1, 2013.

13 Simon, *Rewrites*, 115.

14 Emile Charlap, interview by the author, May 1, 2013.

15 Feuer with Gross, *I Got the Show Right Here*, 236.

16 Fred Werner, interview by the author, April 23, 2013.

17 Barbara Sharma, interview by the author, August 7, 2013.

18 Feuer with Gross, *I Got the Show Right Here*, 236–237.

19 Viagas, *The Alchemy of Theatre*, 29.

20 Feuer with Gross, *I Got the Show Right Here*.

21 Fred Werner, interview by the author, April 23, 2013.

22 Ibid.

23 Emile Charlap, interview by the author, May 1, 2013.

24 Simon, *Rewrites*, 118.

25 Gottfried, *All His Jazz*, 154.

26 Earl Wilson, "It Happened Last Night," *Newsday*, March 4, 1963, 6C.

27 Dorothy Kilgallen, "Attorney General Robert Kennedy to Run in 1968," *Hamilton Journal* (OH), March 5, 1963, 4.

28 "Television Reviews," *Variety*, November 28, 1962, 29.

29 Rick Du Brow, "Caesar's Special Boring, Just Too Much Caesar," *Scottsdale Daily Progress* (AZ), November 26, 1962, 9.

30 Caesar with Davidson, *Where Have I Been?*, 180.

31 Ibid., 181.

32 Lawrence Van Gelder, "Judy Garland's Funeral Draws Her Colleagues," *New York Times*, June 28, 1969, 17.

Chapter Thirteen

1 Whitney Bolton, "Glancing Sideways," *Evening Times* (Cumberland, MD), September 28, 1962.

2 Earl Wilson, "That's Earl for Today," *Evening Standard* (Uniontown, PA), December 10, 1962, 2.

3 Earl Wilson, "It Happened Last Night," *Newsday*, January 8, 1962, 6C.

4 Cy Coleman, ASCAP Foundation Living Archive Project interview, September 17, 2002.

5 Kasha and Hirschhorn, *Notes on Broadway*, 53.

6 Cy Coleman, ASCAP Foundation Living Archive Project interview, September 17, 2002.

7 Jerry Parker, "A Revival of Harmony," *Newsday*, February 14, 1982, B7.

8 Ibid.

9 Jerry Tallmer, "That Broadway Feeling," *The Villager*, November 10–16, 2004, accessed June 28, 2014, http://thevillager.com/villager_80/thatbroadwayfeeling.html.

10 Ibid.

11 Cy Coleman, interview by David Kenney, *Everything Old Is New Again*, WBAI-FM, New York, NY, October 10, 2004.

12 Lee, *Miss Peggy Lee*, 226.

13 Leonard Lyons, "Laurence Harvey to Star in Guild's Stage Musical," *Salt Lake Tribune*, June 12, 1965, 12

14 Bricktop with Haskins, *Bricktop*, 285.

Chapter Fourteen

1 Cy Coleman, ASCAP Foundation Living Archive Project interview, September 17, 2002.

2 "Casting Bits," *Back Stage*, August 6, 1965, 11.

3 "Casting News," *Variety*, August 18, 1965, 58.

4 Viagas, *The Alchemy of Theatre*, 31.

5 Sharon Rosenthal, "A Day in the Life of Cy Coleman," *Daily News* (New York, NY), December 9, 1980, M6.

6 Simon, *Rewrites*, 215.

7 Ibid.

8 Sam Zolotow, "Builder to Stage 'Anya,' A Musical," *New York Times*, August 11, 1965, 42.

9 Thelma Oliver, interview by the author, February 15, 2013.

10 Ibid.

11 Simon, *Rewrites*, 226.

12 Thelma Oliver, interview by the author, February 15, 2013.

13 Lee Roy Reams, interview by the author, July 15, 2013.

14 James Henaghan, interview by the author, January 30, 2013.

15 Emile Charlap, interview by the author, May 1, 2013.

16 Lee Roy Reams, interview by the author, July 15, 2013.

17 Simon, *Rewrites*, 227.

18 James Henaghan, interview by the author, January 30, 2013.

19 Viagas, *The Alchemy of Theatre*, 53.

20 Ibid.

21 Milton Esterow, "Old Palace Theater Prepares for a Musical," *New York Times*, January 14, 1966, 36.

22 Vincent Canby, "Palace Returns: That's Showbiz," *New York Times*, January 30, 1966, 74.

23 Cy Coleman, ASCAP Foundation Living Archive Project interview, September 17, 2002.

24 Hobe Morrison, "B'way Slugged; Refunds a Factor; Gwen SRO $81,850, 'Dark' $33, 527 (7)," *Variety*, February 9, 1966, 58.

25 Cy Coleman, ASCAP Foundation Living Archive Project interview, September 17, 2002.

26 Mike Gross, "Record Labels Tasting the Sweet Smell of 'Sweet Charity' Success," *Billboard*, February 5, 1966, 8.

Chapter Fifteen

1 James Henaghan, interview by the author, January 30, 2013.

2 Joan Crosby, "Dorothy Fields of Broadway: Most Noted Unknown of Theatrical World," *Register* (Danville, VA), July 3, 1966, 7-D.

3 David Lahm, interview by the author, September 20, 2013.

4 Rex Reed, "Who Is Cy Coleman? Any Singer Can Tell You," *Independent Press-Telegram* (Long Beach, CA), May 15, 1977, L/S-2.

5 Mervyn Rothstein, "Cy Coleman Still Does It for Broadway," *New York Times*, April 9, 1989, H8.

6 Lewis Funke, "'Sweet Charity' Goes Abroad," *New York Times*, April 17, 1966, 119.

7 "Shevelove to Stage Comedy and Revue," *New York Times*, August 17, 1966, 37.

8 Cy Coleman, *Boozers and Losers* liner notes.

9 Jess Korman, interview by the author, February 26, 2013.

Chapter Sixteen

1 Earl Wilson, "Some 'Happy New Years' for Just About Everybody," *Galveston News* (FL), December 26, 1966, 10-B.

2 Lee Roy Reams, interview by the author, July 15, 2013.

3 "Equity O.K.s Gwen on 'Charity' Veto," *Variety*, June 14, 1967, 63.

4 Lee Roy Reams, interview by the author, July 15, 2013.

5 Joyce Haber, "No 'Sweet Charity' for Ross Hunter," *Los Angeles Times*, November 7, 1967, C15.

6 Charles Champlin, "Finest Hour for Bob Fosse and Feet in General," *Los Angeles Times*, May 11, 1969, O1.

7 Chita Rivera, interview by the author, May 22, 2013.

8 Cy Coleman, interview by David Kenney, *Everything Old Is New Again*, WBAI-FM, New York, NY, October 10, 2004.

9 Nancy Adams Huddleston, interview by the author, January 11, 2014.

10 Ibid.

11 Louise Quick, interview by the author, May 21, 2013.

12 Ibid.

13 Lee Roy Reams, interview by the author, July 15, 2013.

14 Dick Kleiner, "On the Set of 'Sweet Charity'," *Kokomo Tribune* (IN), March 24, 1968, 17.

15 Harry Neville, "'Charity' Took Composer a Year," *Boston Globe*, February 11, 1969, 30.

16 Phyllis Battelle, "Music Cycle May Turn to Higher Standard," *Cumberland Evening Times* (MD), March 18 1957, 4.

17 Jess Korman, interview by the author, February 26, 2013.

Chapter Seventeen

1 "Coleman Forms Record Co.," *Billboard*, July 12, 1969, 50.

2 "Armed Forces Dig '50 Stars,'" *Billboard*, August 23, 1969, 105.

3 Steve Leeds, interview by the author, June 18, 2013.

4 Ibid.

5 "Top 60 Pop Spotlight," *Billboard*, November 7, 1970, 62.

6 Steve Leeds, interview by the author, June 18, 2013.

7 Ibid.

8 Tony Bongiovi, interview by the author, December 26, 2012.

9 Ibid.

10 Ibid.

11 Jack O'Brian, "The Voice of Broadway," *Evening Observer* (Dunkirk-Fredonia, NY), March 28, 1967, 7.

12 "Coleman-Fields Writing 'Eleanor,' Roosevelt Tuner," *Variety*, December 10, 1969, 69.

13 Jerome Coopersmith, email to the author, May 13, 2013.

14 Ken Howard, interview by the author, September 15, 2013.

15 Kasha and Hirschhorn, *Notes on Broadway*, 61.

16 Hobe Morrison, "Never Mind Restaurateurs, How Do Play-Goers Like It?," *Herald Statesman* (Yonkers, NY), January 18, 1971, 13.

17 Houston Huddleston, interview by the author, January 11, 2014.

Chapter Eighteen

1 Jack O'Brian, "Liza May Ride on 'Seesaw,'" *Herald Statesman* (Yonkers, NY), November 16, 1971, 25.

2 Lewis Funke, "Gibson's Gittel," *New York Times*, April 9, 1967, 97.

3 Lewis Funke, "Sing Along with Gittel Mosca," *New York Times*, January 2, 1972, D1.

4 Lainie Kazan, interview by the author, October 26, 2013.

5 Don Pippin, author interview, November 23, 2013.

6 Ibid.

7 Ken Howard, interview by the author, September 15, 2013.

8 Lainie Kazan, interview by the author, October 26, 2013.

9 Ken Howard, interview by the author, September 15, 2013.

10 Ibid.

11 Ibid.

12 Ibid.

13 Don Pippin, interview by the author, November 23, 2013.

14 Ibid.

15 Tommy Tune, interview by the author, October 24, 2013.

16 Lainie Kazan, interview by the author, October 26, 2013.

17 Michele Lee, interview by the author, July 30, 2013.

18 Don Pippin, interview by the author, November 23, 2013.

19 Tommy Tune, interview by the author, October 24, 2013.

20 Ken Howard, interview by the author, September 15, 2013.

21 Bryer and Davison, *The Art of the American Musical*, 247.

22 Michon Peacock, interview by the author, May 28, 2013.

23 Ken Howard, interview by the author, September 15, 2013.

24 Ibid.

25 Leonard Lyons, "Lyons Den," *Times* (San Mateo, CA), April 12, 1973, 37.

26 Cy Coleman, interview by Paul Lazarus, *Anything Goes*, WBAI Radio (NY), September 7, 1980.

27 Michele Lee, interview by the author, July 30, 2013.

28 Robin Wagner, interview by the author, July 23, 2013.

29 "Lindsay Wows 'Em in Broadway Debut That's Simply Boffo," *New York Times*, March 24, 1973, 22.

30 Don Pippin, interview by the author, November 23, 2013.

31 Kasha and Hirschorn, *Notes on Broadway*, 56.

32 Tommy Tune, interview by the author, October 24, 2013.

Chapter Nineteen

1 Jack O'Brian, "By . . . ," *Schenectady Gazette* (NY), May 25, 1973, 28.
2 Jack O'Brian, "The Voice of Broadway," *Daily News* (Lebanon, PA), June 1, 1973, 14.
3 Earl Wilson, "Saloon Set Bored with Watergate," *Hartford Courant*, June 11, 1973, 18.
4 Terrie Curran, interview by the author, April 12, 2013.
5 Mandelbaum, *"A Chorus Line,"* 295.
6 Lewis Funke, "16—Count 'Em—16 'Pin-Ups,'" *New York Times*, June 3, 1973, 131.
7 Tommy Tune, interview by the author, October 24, 2013.
8 Terrie Curran, interview by the author, April 12, 2013.
9 Leonard Lyons, "Lyons Den," *Times* (San Mateo, CA), October 29, 1973, 11.
10 Phyllis Newman, interview by the author, October 3, 2013.
11 Ibid.
12 Ibid.
13 Ibid.
14 Ibid.

Chapter Twenty

1 Michael Stewart, *I Love My Wife* Backers' Audition, undated recording.
2 Ibid.
3 William A. Raidy, "Season's Big Musical Overcame Early Troubles," *Syracuse Herald-Journal* (NY), May 7, 1977, 8.
4 Robert Cushman, "After All, It's Not Gomorrah," *Observer* (London), October 9, 1977, 29A.
5 Viagas, *The Alchemy of Theatre*, 34.
6 Robert Cushman, "After All, It's Not Gomorrah," *Observer* (London), October 9, 1977.
7 Viagas, *The Alchemy of Theatre*.
8 Ibid.
9 John Miller, interview by the author, August 1, 2013.
10 Ibid.

11 John Corry, "Cronyn, Tandy and Nichols Gamble on 'The Gin Game,'" *New York Times*, May 6, 1977, 48.

12 Ilene Graff, interview by the author, June 11, 2013.

13 James Naughton, interview by the author, October 29, 2013.

14 "Director Gene Saks Delivers Triple with Broadway Triumph," *Lima News* (OH), May 8, 1977, B4.

15 James Naughton, interview by the author, October 29, 2013.

16 Joanna Gleason, interview by the author, July 20, 2013.

17 Ilene Graff, interview by the author, July 21, 2013.

18 Ibid.

19 John Miller, interview by the author, August 1, 2013.

20 Holly Hill, "Composer Coleman Keeping Busy," *Herald Statesman* (Yonkers, NY), August 24, 1977, 30.

21 James Naughton, interview by the author, October 29, 2013.

22 Radcliffe Joe, "'Wife' Witty and Charming," *Billboard*, April 30, 1977, 17.

23 Radcliffe Joe, "Soon-to-Open B'way Show Heralded by Known Ballad," *Billboard*, April 9, 77, 10.

24 Holly Hill, "Composer Coleman Keeping Busy," *Herald Statesman* (Yonkers, NY), August 24, 1977, 30.

25 Robert Cushman, "Happy Impotence," *Observer* (London), October 9, 1977, A28.

26 John Corry, "'Bojangles!' to Bring the Old Soft Shoe to New York Stage," *New York Times*, December 22, 1978, C2.

27 John Miller, interview by the author, August 1, 2013.

28 Ibid.

Chapter Twenty-one

1 Rex Reed, "Comden and Green Toss a Party for Themselves," *Independent Press-Telegram* (Long Beach, CA), February 12, 1977, L/S 2.

2 Viagas, *The Alchemy of Theatre*, 35.

3 Betty Comden and Adolph Green, "A New Head of Steam for the Old 'Twentieth Century,'" *New York Times*, February 19, 1978, section 2, 6.

4 Ibid.

5 Rex Reed, "Comden and Green Toss a Party for Themselves," Independent Press-Telegram (Long Beach, CA), February 12, 1977, L/S 2.

6 Cy Coleman, ASCAP Foundation Living Archive Project interview, September 17, 2002.

7 Ilson, *Harold Prince*, 251.

8 Harold Prince, interview by the author, September 12, 2013.

9 Ibid.

10 Ibid.

11 Ibid.

12 Larry Fuller, interview by the author, June 4, 2013.

13 Ibid.

14 Kevin Kelly, "'The Mel Brooks Lady' Gets Chance to Shed Image," *Boston Globe*, December 18, 1977, A8.

15 John Cullum, interview by the author, November 1, 2013.

16 Larry Fuller, interview by the author, June 4, 2013.

17 Ibid.

18 Ibid.

19 Harold Prince, interview by the author, September 12, 2013.

20 Ibid.

21 Judy Kaye, interview by the author, October 30, 2013.

22 Larry Fuller, interview by the author, June 4, 2013.

23 John Cullum, interview by the author, November 1, 2013.

24 Patrick Pacheco, "Kevin Kline Taken for Granit," *After Dark*, May 1978, 92.

25 John Cullum, interview by the author, November 1, 2013.

26 Kevin Kelly, "'The Mel Brooks Lady' Gets Chance to Shed Image," *Boston Globe*, December 18, 1977, A10.

27 Harold Prince, interview by the author, September 12, 2013.

28 John Cullum, interview by the author, November 1, 2013.

29 Larry Fuller, interview by the author, June 4, 2013.

30 Robin Wagner, interview by the author, July 23, 2013.

31 John Cullum, interview by the author, November 1, 2013.

32 Harold Prince, interview by the author, September 12, 2013.

33 Ibid.

34 Terrie Curran, interview by the author, August 27, 2013.

35 Larry Fuller, interview by the author, June 4, 2013.

36 Ibid.

37 "Madeline Kahn Leaves 'On the Twentieth Century,'" *New York Times*, April 25, 1978, 46.

38 Tony Bongiovi, interview by the author, December 26, 2012.

Chapter Twenty-two

1 "Composer Cy Coleman Has Habit of Teaming Up with Sundry Companions for Words to Fit Tunes," *Register* (Danville, VA), September 18, 1977, 11B.

2 Barbara Fried, interview by the author, April 24, 2013.

3 Mike Gross, "London Deal with Coleman," *Billboard*, January 22, 1972, 1.

4 "Top Singles of the Week," *Variety*, May 23, 1972, 52.

5 "Blind Date with Stone the Crows," *Melody Maker*, July 22, 1972, 39.

6 Barbara Fried, interview by the author, April 24, 2013.

7 Ibid.

8 Russell Baker, letter to author, April 9, 2013.

9 Ibid.

10 Ibid.

11 Leo Seligsohn, "Baker's Musical Is a Sign of the Times," *Newsday*, July 30, 1975, 11A.

12 Barbara Fried, interview by the author, April 24, 2013.

13 Russell Baker, letter to the author, April 9, 2013.

14 Jack O'Brian, "Continuing to Produce Plays for New Season," *Leader-Herald* (Gloversville-Johnston, NY), July 27, 1977, 4.

15 Russell Baker, letter to the author, April 9, 2013.

16 John Corry, "'King of Hearts' to Come Back Wearing a New Coat of Arms," *New York Times*, June 16, 1978, C2.

17 Barbara Fried, interview by the author, April 24, 2013.

18 Craig Jacobs, interview by the author, July 31, 2013.

19 Ibid.

20 Ibid.

21 D. Michael Heath, interview by the author, April 22, 2013.

22 Teri Ralston, interview by the author, May 17, 2013.

23 Craig Jacobs, interview by the author, July 31, 2013.

24 Russell Baker, letter to the author, April 9, 2013.

25 Baker, *Growing Up*, 151.

26 Barbara Fried, interview by the author, April 24, 2013.

27 Craig Jacobs, interview by the author, July 31, 2013.

28 Teri Ralston, interview by the author, May 17, 2013.

29 Craig Jacobs, interview by the author, July 31, 2013.

30 Barbara Fried, interview by the author, April 24, 2013.

31 Ibid.

32 Russell Baker, letter to the author, April 9, 2013.

33 Ibid.

34 Carol Lawson, "'Home Again, Home Again' Closing Out of Town," *New York Times*, April 14, 1979, 15.

35 Teri Ralston, interview by the author, May 17, 2013.

36 Ibid.

37 Russell Baker, letter to the author, April 9, 2013.

38 Barbara Fried, interview by the author, April 24, 2013.

39 Ibid.

40 Ibid.

41 Russell Baker, letter to the author, April 9, 2013.

42 Craig Jacobs, interview by the author, July 31, 2013.

43 Barbara Fried, interview by the author, April 24, 2013.

44 Teri Ralston, interview by the author, May 17, 2013.

45 "Meyer Friedman Pleads Guilty in Federal Tax Case," *Variety*, December 16, 1981, 65

46 "Again, Again, and Again," *Variety*, April 25, 1979, 106.

Chapter Twenty-three

1 Mark Bramble, interview by the author, September 9, 2013.

2 Ibid.

3 Ibid.

4 Ibid.

5 Ibid.

6 Michiko Katutani, "Jim Dale Is Toast of Broadway," *New York Times*, May 2, 1980, C3.

7 Mark Bramble, interview by the author, September 9, 2013.

8 Kasha and Hirschorn, *Notes on Broadway*, 57.

9 Mark Bramble, interview by the author, September 9, 2013.

10 Judy Gordon, author interview, August 20, 2013.

11 Ibid.

12 Ibid.

13 Ibid.

14 Harold Prince, interview by the author, September 12, 2013.

15 Mark Bramble, interview by the author, September 9, 2013.

16 "Chorus Calls," *Back Stage*, December 21, 1979, 64.

17 Andy Teirstein, email to the author, August 3, 2013.

18 Ibid.

19 Ibid.

20 Judy Gordon, interview by the author, August 20, 2013.

21 Tony Walton, interview by the author, December 12, 2012.

22 Ted Kociolek, interview by the author, August 22, 2013.

23 Jim Dale, email to the author, February 6, 2014.

24 Marianne Tatum, interview by the author, July 13, 2013.

25 Terri White, interview by the author, September 11, 2013.

26 Ibid.

27 Mark Bramble, interview by the author, September 9, 2013.

28 Ibid.

29 Bramble and Stewart, *Barnum*, 65.

30 Mark Bramble, interview by the author, September 9, 2013.

31 Ibid.

32 Ibid.

33 Judy Gordon, interview by the author, August 20, 2013.

34 Mark Bramble, interview by the author, September 9, 2013.

35 Ibid.

36 Ibid.

37 Ibid.

38 Judy Gordon, interview by the author, August 20, 2013.

39 Ibid.

40 Mark Bramble, interview by the author, September 9, 2013.

41 Judy Gordon, interview by the author, August 20, 2013.

42 Ibid.

43 Jay Sharbutt, "Cy Coleman Isn't Singing the Blues," *Alton Telegraph* (IL), May 3, 1980, C-4.

44 Phyllis Battelle, "Music Cycle May Turn to Higher Standard," *Cumberland Evening Times* (MD), March 18, 1957, 4.

45 Judy Gordon, interview by the author, August 20, 2013.

46 Mark Bramble, interview by the author, September 9, 2013.

Chapter Twenty-four

1 "Urges Show LPs Be Cast In New Light for Legit Investors," *Variety*, February 13, 1980, 197.

2 Sharon Churcher, "'Atlantic City''s Forgotten Man?," *New York Magazine*, March 22, 1982, 8.

3 Jack Heifner, interview by the author, February 21, 2014.

4 Ibid.

5 Ibid.

6 Ibid.

7 Ibid.

8 Phyllis Newman, interview by the author, October 3, 2013..

9 Carol Lawson, "Broadway," *New York Times*, November 14, 1980, C2.

10 Ibid.

11 Mike Burstyn, interview by the author, June 7, 2013.

12 Ibid.

13 Ibid.

14 Jay Sharbutt, "Cy Coleman Isn't Singing the Blues," *Alton Telegraph* (IL), May 3, 1980, C-4.

15 Sally Quinn, "Teddy and the Unreachable Star," *Washington Post*, August 15, 1980, C6.

16 Mark Bramble, interview by the author, September 9, 2013.

17 Mary Campbell, "Cy Coleman Sees Big Hit in 'Little Me,'" *Daily Herald* (Chicago), January 10, 1982, section 5, 7.

18 Sheldon Harnick, interview by the author, October 23, 2013.

19 Ibid.

20 Ibid.

21 Cy Coleman, ASCAP Foundation Living Archive Project interview, September 17, 2002.

22 Sheldon Harnick, interview by the author, October 23, 2013.

23 Ibid.

Chapter Twenty-five

1 Lee, *Miss Peggy Lee*, 245.

2 Larry Kart, "Look Out, Broadway! At 62, Peggy Lee Is Ready to Tell All," *Chicago Tribune*, February 13, 1983, D11.

3 Richmond, *Fever*, 358.

4 Larry Kart, "Look Out, Broadway! At 62, Peggy Lee Is Ready to Tell All," *Chicago Tribune*, February 13, 1983, D11.

5 Richmond, *Fever*, 362.

6 Ibid., 363.

7 Judy Gordon, interview by the author, August 20, 2013.

8 Tommy Tune, interview by the author, October 24, 2013.

9 Advertisement, *Back Stage*, November 18, 1983, 102.

10 Michael Sneed and Cheryl Lavin, "Sneed & Lavin Inc.," *Chicago Tribune*, November 25, 1983, 24.

11 Ted Kociolek, interview by the author, August 22, 2013.

12 Ibid.

13 Ted Kociolek, email to author, May 28, 2014.

14 Robin Wagner, interview by the author, July 23, 2013.

15 Barbara Fried, interview by the author, April 24, 2013.

16 Nan Robertson, "Broadway," *New York Times*, May 17, 1985, C2.

17 Robin Wagner, interview by the author, July 23, 2013.

18 Paul Rosenfield, "Fosse, Verdon and 'Charity': Together Again," *Los Angeles Times*, July 21, 1985, O3.

19 Craig Jacobs, interview by the author, July 31, 2013.

20 Enid Nemy, "Broadway," *New York Times*, January 24, 1986, C2.

21 Charles W. Hall, Douglas Stevenson, "Bob Fosse Dies After Collapsing on D.C. Street," *Washington Post*, September 24, 1987, A8.

22 Craig Jacobs, interview by the author, July 31, 2013.

23 Terrie Curran, interview by the author, October 26, 2012.

24 Ibid.

25 Mark Bramble, interview by the author, September 9, 2013.

Chapter Twenty-six

1 Dena Kleiman, "Cy Coleman, Composer with a Knack for Juggling," *New York Times*, July 13, 1986, H4.

2 Allan Knee, interview by the author, January 10, 2014.

3 Ibid.

4 Ibid.

5 David Zippel, interview by the author, May 21, 2013.

6 Ibid.

7 Allan Knee, interview by the author, January 10, 2014.

8 Ibid.

9 Ibid.

10 Ken Mandelbaum, "Million and a Half Dollar Baby," *Theater Week*, April 24–30, 1989, 23.

11 Ibid., 24.

12 Eleanor Charles, "Musical-Comedy Tryout," *New York Times*, July 26, 1987, CN22.

13 "Mixed-to-Pans Greet 'Let 'Em Rot' in Fla.," *Variety*, March 2, 1988, 103.

14 Nan Robertson, "On Stage," *New York Times*, July 29, 1988, C2.

15 Ken Mandelbaum, "Million and a Half Dollar Baby," *Theater Week*, April 24–30, 1989, 25.

16 Bill Rosenfield, interview by the author, November 16, 2013.

17 Edwin Wilson, "The Road to Broadway," *Wall Street Journal*, August 29, 1988, 7.

18 Ken Mandelbaum, "Million and a Half Dollar Baby," *Theater Week*, April 24–30, 1989, 25

19 Edwin Wilson, "The Road to Broadway," *Wall Street Journal*, August 29, 1988, 7.

20 Mervyn Rothstein, "Cy Coleman Still Does It for Broadway," *New York Times*, April 9, 1989, H5.

21 Terri White, interview by the author, September 11, 2013.

22 Mervyn Rothstein, "Cy Coleman Still Does It for Broadway," *New York Times*, April 9, 1989, H8.

23 Sally Mayes, interview by the author, September 3, 2013.

24 Ibid.

25 Craig Jacobs, interview by the author, July 31, 2013.

26 John Miller, interview by the author, August 1, 2013.

27 Mervyn Rothstein, "Cy Coleman Still Does It for Broadway," *New York Times*, April 9, 1989, H5.

28 Terri White, interview by the author, September 11, 2013.

29 Sally Mayes, interview by the author, September 3, 2013.

Chapter Twenty-seven

1 Gelbart, *Laughing Matters*, 238.

2 Cy Coleman, interview by Peter Filichia, 1989.

3 David Zippel, interview by the author, September 3, 2013.

4 Ibid.

5 Ibid.

6 Ibid.

7 Ibid.

8 Ibid.

9 Larry Gelbart, interview by Peter Filichia, 1989.

10 David Zippel, interview by the author, September 3, 2013.

11 Larry Gelbart, interview by Peter Filichia, 1989.

12 Kinky Friedman, "Gelbart Hard-Boiled: The Case of the Alter Ego," *New York Times*, December 10, 1989, H37.

13 David Zippel, interview by the author, September 3, 2013.

14 Michael Blakemore, interview by the author, August 27, 2013.

15 Ibid.

16 Ibid.

17 Ibid.

18 Ibid.

19 David Zippel, interview by the author, September 3, 2013.

20 Michael Blakemore, interview by the author, August 27, 2013.

21 Ibid.

22 Dee Hoty, interview by the author, August 24, 2013.

23 Ibid.

24 Randy Graff, interview by the author, July 21, 2013.

25 Gordon Lowry Harrell, interview by the author, May 31, 2013.

26 Kinky Friedman, "Gelbart Hard-Boiled: The Case of the Alter Ego," *New York Times*, December 10, 1989, H37.

27 Yaron Gershovsky, interview by the author, August 5, 2013.

28 Michael Blakemore, interview by the author, August 27, 2013.

29 Larry Gelbart, interview by Peter Filichia, 1989.

30 Randy Graff, interview by the author, July 21, 2013.

31 Ibid.

32 Ibid.

33 Gordon Lowry Harrell, interview by the author, May 31, 2013.

34 Michael Blakemore, interview by the author, August 27, 2013.

35 Gordon Lowry Harrell, interview by the author, May 31, 2013.

36 Ibid.

37 Michael Blakemore, interview by the author, August 27, 2013.

38 Ibid.

39 Bill Rosenfield, interview by the author, November 16, 2013.

40 Robin Wagner, interview by the author, July 23, 2013.

41 Peter Filichia, "Death Is for Suckers," *Theater Week*, December 18–24, 1989, 18.

42 Bill Rosenfield, interview by the author, November 16, 2013.

43 Ibid.

44 Ibid.

45 Gordon Lowry Harrell, interview by the author, May 31, 2013.

46 David Zippel, interview by the author, September 3, 2013.

47 Gordon Lowry Harrell, interview by the author, May 31, 2013.

48 Fred Barton, interview by the author, January 10, 2014.

Chapter Twenty-eight

1 Mervyn Rothstein, "On Stage," *New York Times*, November 17, 1989, C2.

2 Cossette, *Another Day in Showbiz*, 187.

3 Ibid., 188.

4 Ibid., 189.

5 Bell, *Broadway Stories*, 152.

6 John Harris, "The Making of *The Will Rogers Follies*," *Theater Week*, May 13–19, 1991, 17.

7 Ibid.

8 Bell, *Broadway Stories*, 153.

9 Enid Nemy, "Broadway," *New York Times*, March 13, 1987, C2.

10 Bell, *Broadway Stories*.

11 Ibid., 154.

12 Douglas Martin, "Can Keith Carradine Lasso the Essence of Will Rogers?," *New York Times*, April 28, 1991, H5.

13 Keith Carradine, interview by the author, August 16, 2013.

14 Ibid.

15 Douglas Martin, "Can Keith Carradine Lasso the Essence of Will Rogers?," *New York Times*, April 28, 1991.

16 Dee Hoty, interview by the author, August 24, 2013.

17 Bell, *Broadway Stories*.

18 Jeremy Gerard, "New Japanese Bird to Sing Broadway Tune," *Variety*, April 1, 1991, 74.

19 Sheed, *The House That George Built*, 296.

20 Tommy Tune, interview by the author, October 24, 2013.

21 Ibid.

22 Keith Carradine, interview by the author, August 16, 2013.

23 Dee Hoty, interview by the author, August 24, 2013.

24 Keith Carradine, interview by the author, August 16, 2013.

25 Ibid.

26 Dee Hoty, interview by the author, August 24, 2013.

27 Ibid.

28 Tommy Tune, interview by the author, October 24, 2013.

29 Ibid.

30 Ibid.

31 Ibid.

32 Eric Stern, interview by the author, September 4, 2013.

33 Ibid.

34 Ibid.

35 Ibid.

36 Ibid.

37 Ibid.

38 Tommy Tune, interview by the author, October 24, 2013.

39 David Patrick Stearns, "Broadway Recordings Transcend the Stage," *USA Today*, November 22, 1991, 6D.

40 Cossette, *Another Day in Showbiz*, 202.

Chapter Twenty-nine

1 Pat Birch, interview by the author, October 16, 2013.

2 Alan Zweibel, interview by the author, October 5, 2013.

3 Sally Mayes, interview by the author, September 3, 2013.

4 Terry Morris, "Cy Coleman Continues to Score," *Dayton Daily News* (OH), May 20, 1994, 13.

5 Alan and Marilyn Bergman, interview by the author, May 7, 2013.

6 Ron Mallory, interview by the author, June 12, 2013.

7 Ibid.

8 Ibid.

9 Ibid.

10 Lois Smith Brady, "Shelby Brown and Cy Coleman," *New York Times*, October 5, 1997, 49.

11 Shelby Coleman, interview by the author, October 1, 2013.

12 Ibid.

13 Ibid.

14 Ibid.

15 Lois Smith Brady, "Shelby Brown and Cy Coleman," *New York Times*, October 5, 1997, 49.

Chapter Thirty

1 Ira Gasman, interview by the author, June 12, 2013.

2 Harry Haun, "The Origins of Life," *Playbill.com*, June 23, 1997, accessed July 9, 2014, http://www.playbill.com/features/article/64521-The-Origins-of-Life,.

3 Ira Gasman, interview by the author, June 12, 2013.

4 Barbara Delatiner, "'Piano Hands' Seeking New Coda," *New York Times*, October 18, 1981, LI15.

5 Matt Wolf, "Giving His All to Charity," *Times* (London), May 13, 1998, 33.

6 Lillias White, interview by the author, October 24, 2013.

7 Chuck Cooper, interview by the author, October 22, 2013.

8 Ibid.

9 Ibid.

10 "Equity Stage," *Back Stage*, May 25, 1990, 14A.

11 Lillias White, interview by the author, October 24, 2013.

12 Jeremy Gerard, "Clash of the Titans," *Variety*, November 1, 1993, 51.

13 Gordon Lowry Harrell, interview by the author, May 31, 2013.

14 Bruce Weber, "On Stage, and Off," *New York Times*, June 24, 1994, C2.

15 Army Archerd, "Farrow a 'Widow' in Return to Pix," *Variety.com*, July 8, 1993, accessed January 12, 2014, http://www.variety.com/article/VR1117862213?refcatid=15.

16 Bill Rosenfield, interview by the author, November 16, 2013.

17 Ibid.

18 Ibid.

19 Ibid.

20 Ibid.

21 Ibid.

22 Chuck Cooper, interview by the author, October 22, 2013.

23 Michael Blakemore, interview by the author, August 27, 2013.

24 Ibid.

25 Ibid.

26 Robert Simonson, "'Big' Yields Shubert to 'Chicago,' as Shows Re-Shuffle," *Back Stage*, October 4, 1996, 3.

27 Peter Marks, "On Stage, and Off," *New York Times*, October 11, 1996, C2.

28 Chuck Cooper, interview by the author, October 22, 2013.

29 Sam Harris, interview by the author, July 19, 2013.

30 Ibid.

31 Ibid.

32 Ibid.

33 Ibid.

34 Ibid.

35 Ibid.

36 Lillias White, interview by the author, October 24, 2013.

37 Michael Blakemore, interview by the author, August 27, 2013.

38 Sam Harris, interview by the author, July 19, 2013.

39 Michael Kuchwara, "Buoyant Producers Hope for a Bounce from Tony Nominations," Associated Press, May 2, 1997.

40 Vincent Canby, "Why Whisper About It? 'The Life' Is a Joy," *New York Times*, October 5, 1997, AR5.

Chapter Thirty-one

1 Pat Birch, interview by the author, May 29, 2013.

2 Frank Rizzo, "The Endeavor To Make a Musical New Again," *Hartford Courant* (CT), May 16, 1998, F8.

3 Shelby Coleman, interview by the author, October 1, 2013.

4 Pat Birch, interview by the author, October 16, 2013.

5 Kenneth Jones, "Cy Coleman Discusses His Unique Dutch Musical, *Grace*," *Playbill.com*, January 10, 2002, accessed April 11, 2013, http://www.playbill.com/news/article/67083-Cy-Coleman-Discusses-His-Unique-Dutch-Musical-Grace.

6 Pat Birch, interview by the author, October 16, 2013.

7 Mary-Mitchell Campbell, interview by the author, November 12, 2013.

8 Ibid.

9 Ibid.

10 Ibid.

11 Ibid.

12 Ibid.

13 Ibid.

14 Ibid.

15 Ibid.

16 David Zippel, interview by the author, September 3, 2013.

17 David Zippel, email to the author, July 20, 2014.

18 David Zippel, interview by the author, September 3, 2013.

19 Mary-Mitchell Campbell, interview by the author, November 12, 2013.

20 Alan and Marilyn Bergman, interview by the author, May 7, 2013.

21 Kenneth Jones, "Will Cy Coleman and the Bergmans' *Like Jazz*, 'a New Kind of Musical,' Find a Broadway Home?," *Playbill.com*, March 15, 2004, accessed April 11, 2013. http://www.playbill.com/news/article/84967-Will-Cy-Coleman-and-the-Bergmans-Like-Jazz-a-New-Kind-of-Musical-Find-a-Broadway-Home.

22 Alan and Marilyn Bergman, interview by the author, May 7, 2013.

23 Ibid.

24 Ibid.

25 Pat Birch, interview by the author, May 29, 2013.

26 Ibid.

27 Alan and Marilyn Bergman, interview by the author, May 7, 2013.

28 Avery Corman, interview by the author, October 8, 2013.

29 Ibid.

30 Ibid.

31 Nick Corley, interview by the author, August 2, 2013.

32 Avery Corman, interview by the author, October 8, 2013.

33 Nick Corley, interview by the author, August 2, 2013.

34 Daniel Marcus, interview by the author, August 2, 2013.

35 Nick Corley, interview by the author, August 2, 2013.

36 Ibid.

37 Daniel Marcus, interview by the author, August 2, 2013.

Chapter Thirty-two

1 Shelby Coleman, interview by the author, October 1, 2013.

2 Charlie MacPherson, interview by the author, October 14, 2013.

3 Houston Huddleston, interview by the author, January 11, 2014.

4 Mary-Mitchell Campbell, interview by the author, November 12, 2013.

5   Shelby Coleman, interview by the author, October 1, 2013.

6   Ibid.

7   Nick Corley, interview by the author, August 2, 2013.

8   Cy Coleman, interview by David Kenney, *Everything Old Is New Again*, WBAI-FM, New York, NY, October 10, 2004.

9   Ibid.

10 Shelby Coleman, interview by the author, October 1, 2013.

Coda

1   David Zippel, interview by the author, September 3, 2013.

2   Erik Haagensen, "The Best Is Yet to Come: The Music of Cy Coleman," *BackStage.com*, posted May 25, 2011, accessed January 25, 2014, http://www.backstage.com/review/ny-theater/off-broadway/the-best-is-yet-to-come-the-music-of-cy-coleman_2/.

3   David Zippel, interview by the author, September 3, 2013.

INDEX

*Grateful acknowledgment is made to the following for permission
to use both published and unpublished materials:*

Phil Birsh: Excerpts from *The Alchemy of Theatre: The Divine Science.*
All rights reserved, Playbill Inc.

Peter Filichia: Excerpts from Peter Filichia's 1989 interviews of Cy
Coleman, Larry Gelbart, and Michael Blakemore regarding *City
of Angels.*

June's Tunes Ltd. Partnership: Material from Carolyn Leigh's files at
the New York Public Library.

David Kenney: Excerpts from the October 10, 2004 interview with Cy
Coleman on the WBAI-FM program *Everything Old Is New Again.*

Paul Lazarus: Excerpts from *Anything Goes*, WBAI-FM, New York.

Linda O'Bryon: Excerpts from the Cy Coleman interview with Marian
McPartland on *Piano Jazz* courtesy of South Carolina ETV Radio.

Brian E. Sheehan: Excerpts from *Variety* reviews, 1947–1965. © 2014
Variety Media, LLC, a subsidiary of Penske Business Media, LLC.

Jim Steinblatt: Excerpts from the ASCAP Foundation Living Archive
interview with Cy Coleman of September 17, 2002 courtesy of The
ASCAP Foundation Living Video Archive.

Lynn Summerall: Excerpts from interviews with Cy Coleman and
Tommy Tune for *The Musical Theater,* WBJC-FM, Baltimore.

Unless otherwise indicated, all photographs are used
courtesy of Notable Music Co. Inc.